021

HOW THE OLD WORLD ENDED

Also by Jonathan Scott

Algernon Sidney and the English Republic, 1623–1677 (1988)
Algernon Sidney and the Restoration Crisis, 1677–1683 (1991)
Harry's Absence: Looking for my Father on the Mountain (1997)
*England's Troubles: Seventeenth-Century English Political Instability in
European Context* (2000)
Commonwealth Principles: Republican Writing of the English Revolution (2004)
*When the Waves Ruled Britannia: Geography and Political Identities,
1500–1800* (2011)
Liberty, Authority, Formality: Political Ideas and Culture, 1600–1900
(edited with John Morrow, 2008)

HOW
THE
OLD
WORLD
ENDED

The Anglo-Dutch-American
Revolution, 1500–1800

Jonathan Scott

YALE UNIVERSITY PRESS
NEW HAVEN AND LONDON

Published with assistance from the foundation established in memory of Oliver Baty Cunningham of the Class of 1917, Yale College.

For information about this and other Yale University Press publications, please contact:
U.S. Office: sales.press@yale.edu yalebooks.com
Europe Office: sales@yaleup.co.uk yalebooks.co.uk

Set in Adobe Garamond Pro by IDSUK (DataConnection) Ltd
Printed in Great Britain by Gomer Press Ltd, Llandysul, Ceredigion, Wales

Library of Congress Control Number: 2019941076

ISBN 978-0-300-24359-8

A catalogue record for this book is available from the British Library.

10 9 8 7 6 5 4 3 2 1

In memory of Patrick Collinson and Mark Kishlansky

CONTENTS

CONTENTS

MAPS

INTRODUCTION

He that gives a Book to be publish'd . . . is sayd, and that truly, to lie downe and expose himselfe to Stroaks, and not seldome to deserve them.

John Evelyn[1]

In Alexandria, a certain Thompson from Sunderland has inscribed his name in letters six feet high on Pompey's Pillar. You can read it a quarter of a mile away. You can't see the pillar without seeing the name of Thompson, and consequently, without thinking of Thompson . . . All imbeciles are more or less Thompsons from Sunderland.

Gustave Flaubert in Egypt, 1851[2]

This book is concerned in the first place with how the old world ended, and only secondly with why. Thus its primary interest is in historical process.[3] In 1649 Gerrard Winstanley wrote: 'the present state of the old world . . . is running up like parchment in the fire, and wearing away'.[4] Did the old world erode gradually, or burn? The answer given here is both. Comparably, in the present day, incremental climate change is supercharging catastrophic events.

The present book has been, it is hoped, a gradual rather than catastrophic development. I first began lecturing on Anglo-Dutch themes in Cambridge in 1997. In Pittsburgh I taught a course called 'The Anglo-Dutch Achievement, 1550–1750' at both undergraduate and graduate level. In Auckland that became 'Anglo-Dutch Early Modernity'. Over the years these courses, focused on the analysis of primary documents, attracted brilliant students who contributed enormously to my thinking about the subject. Some of those documents, like William Temple's *Observations* (1673) and *An Account of Several Voyages* (1694) continue to play a role here as eyewitness testimony.

In 2000 my *England's Troubles* attempted to set what was still primarily told as a national political story within a comparative European context. This was more than an exercise in historiographical reframing. Since what destabilized and toppled the Stuart monarchy, and so made possible the English revolution, was fiscal-military failure on the European stage, the story in question could not be comprehended as merely national. The most important seventeenth-century transnational relationship was Anglo-Dutch.[5] When I elaborated upon this suggestion in an essay called 'What the Dutch Taught Us', I was asked to consider a book-length treatment of this theme but was then tied up by the project that became *Commonwealth Principles* (2004).[6] The last sentences of that book read: 'Yet concerning the importance of the Anglo-Dutch achievement there seems much less doubt. By the consequences of this the world would genuinely be transformed.'[7] One reviewer commented that assessment of the validity of this claim would need to await a subsequent book explaining what that achievement was held to be.

Seeking a different field and fresh material I subsequently embarked upon the aquatic turn that produced *When the Waves Ruled Britannia* (2011). An examination of the use of geographical language in British political writing, this was an attempt to approach the history of ideas in a new way. It furnished an opportunity to read three centuries of maritime voyage literature and maps on my front porch in Point Breeze, Pittsburgh – the furthest I had ever lived from the ocean – while flying annually to London to look for manuscripts in the British Library and National Maritime Museum. The book became an analysis of the role of water: riverine, estuarine, maritime and oceanic, in the life and thought of early modern Europe and its empires. Here too the Dutch loomed large, masters of the waters as they were. It will be evident that this research has informed my present approach to a question which has meanwhile enlarged itself like topsy: how are we to explain the Industrial Revolution that brought the early modern period to an end? Readers who suspect a damp fuse burning in the Low Countries, leading to subsequent fireworks across the North Sea and Atlantic, will not be on the wrong track.

My *TLS* essay had begun: 'The United Kingdom stands on the threshold of its future, apparently immobilized by an idea about its past. That idea is

Britain's separateness from the rest of Europe.'[8] This is not a theme the political currency of which has meanwhile faded. *England's Troubles* had challenged this idea as it might have been entertained by historians of the nation, New British Historians, Anglo-American Atlanticists, and/or J. G. A. Pocock, a field in his own right.[9] Since then much important work has explored European, Atlantic and global contexts for early modern British history, and the relationships between them.[10] The present book considers how by interaction both with the United Provinces of the Netherlands, and with its own unique colonies in temperate-climate North America, Britain became the site for a revolution that changed the world.

Thus whereas *England's Troubles* attempted to understand, as the first and third among its three subjects, the destruction and then reconstruction of the British military-fiscal state, the present study discusses the disappearance and subsequent replacement of an entire social, economic and political way of life.[11] While the context of the former study was European, that of the present one is global. This must be emphasized since this book concentrates upon the trans-Atlantic subsection of a global process of European empire building within which, for the Dutch, its East Asian component was prior, larger and wealthier. Similarly within the British Atlantic theatre I emphasize the key demographic, cultural and economic role of a northern and continental subsection, although its southern and Caribbean zones were as colonial posses-sions much more profitable. The reason for this is that my subject is not a place, but a process. Thus the explanatory focus is upon a connected sequence of social, economic, cultural and political developments which may be called Anglo-Dutch-American early modernity. This introduces us to another theme of the present study, as true of Dutch agriculture as of British empire: that what proves to be historically transformative sometimes derives, not from the first or traditional path of success, but from a harder road of struggle.

Although it uses some archival sources this book is not a research mono-graph. Nor does its author read Dutch. Like *England's Troubles* it is an extended, three-part analytical essay predominantly based on printed primary and secondary material. It is not a history of the Industrial Revolution, but an engagement with the early modern European life and world to which that revo-lution put paid. That engagement takes the form not of a survey but of an argu-ment directed to the question posed by my title. For the early modern Netherlands the historian is blessed by a rich and sometimes brilliant literature, much of it available in English. Dutch as much as English historiography has distinct and characteristic emphases. Neither is particularly strong on the history of the other country, which makes understanding this world-changing transnational relationship the first challenge. My modest encounter with American history here was doubtless stimulated by seven years in Pittsburgh, originating site of the Seven Years War. In addition my approach and choice of materials have been influenced by my involvement in Auckland since 2009 with the course History 103: Global History. For all this, the book remains discernibly, if not in explanatory focus then in its approach, expertise and limitations, a study of early modern England, and Britain, in European, Atlantic and global contexts.

As such it develops some established personal interests concerning the historical importance of the physical environment, in particular water; the interconnectedness of politics, culture and ideas; the Anglo-Dutch relationship in general and the transformational impact of the English republic of 1649–53 in particular. The book's second new challenge, to set these themes within the contexts of economic and social history, has taken the author out upon an ocean. But the attempt is important, not only because people in the past did not live their economic, social, religious, political and cultural lives separately.[12] Here that truth is encapsulated by the migrations, within nations, from countryside to cities, across Europe, the North Sea, Atlantic and Indian Oceans, by means of which ideas and historical practices were transmitted, modified and connected. One pleasure of the present study has been to engage with long-range social and economic analyses which are better than political histories at transcending chronological and geographic/national boundaries.[13] Yet within these broad comparative frameworks there remains a need for more emphasis upon the explanatory importance of particular developments, contrasts, connections and events.

This is, finally, a book about the republican prehistory of the Industrial Revolution. This may seem surprising, since relatively few recent British political historians have acknowledged either the profound importance or the specifically republican character of the mid-seventeenth-century English revolution. If the first industrial revolution occurred in Britain, and if Britain has never had a genuine experience of republican (post-monarchical, pre-Cromwellian) government, then republicanism can hardly be part of the explanation. Yet there was a republican revolution in England between 1649 and 1653 which constituted a turning point, not only in English but in world history. To see its transformational impact it is necessary to go beyond politics to the economy, culture, the history of ideas, and the acquisition of hard global power (provoking a European naval revolution). It is also necessary to go beyond England since the republicanism in question had an Italian and Dutch pre-history, and an American postscript. Anglo-Dutch republicanism, not only in theory but practice, established the foundations of the modern British state and empire, as well as of the modern world economy. This is also, therefore, a study of the long-term contexts, and consequences, of the English revolution; of a three-hundred-year-long Anglo-Dutch-American republican 'moment'.

Winstanley excoriated the worn-out 'old world' as a 'husk without the kernall ... the cloud without rain'.[14] In the wake of its immolation he expected 'the earth ... [to] become ... a common treasury again'.[15] In an analysis indebted to Winstanley and to the Leveller William Walwyn, *England's Troubles* argued that the English revolution was less a political event than an intensely creative radical cultural process.[16] This was both deeply grounded in European history and unique in its quality and duration. My attention here is upon another revolution and the Anglo-Dutch-American process that made it possible. There remains every reason, however, to see Winstanley's experience, and the year 1649 in particular, as standing at the centre of this wider upheaval, one which replaced the old world with another that might, had he lived to see it, have broken his heart.

In Auckland I owe much to friends, colleagues and former students including Maartje Abbenhuis, Catherine Balleriaux, Felicity Barnes, Lisa Bayley, Malcolm Campbell, Genevieve De Pont, Lindsay Diggelmann, Louis Gerdelan, Anna Gilderdale, Annalise Higgins, Ryan Jones, Di Morrow, Kim Phillips (who co-taught Anglo-Dutch Early Modernity with me in 2014), Jake Pollock, Barry Reay, David Thomson, Nicola Wright and Joe Zizek. I am grateful to the University of Auckland for two periods of Research and Study Leave, in 2014–15 and 2017, accompanied by funding for international travel. Special thanks are due to those regular lunch and dinner partners, my basket of digestibles: Tom Bishop, Matthew Trundle and especially Erin Griffey, who has saved my life more than once, and who knows a thing or two herself about the Dutch republic. Among the imbibables, reduced in number for the benefit of my health, John Morrow holds the fort and keeps me sane, if not always sensible. In Italy, Germany and Finland I have been grateful for my friendship with Martin Van Gelderen, Antoinette Saxer and Markku Peltonen. In the UK I am indebted to Mike Braddick, Glenn Burgess and Mandy Capern, Colin and Sandra Davis, Barry and Jane Everitt, Germaine Greer, John Morrill, Roger Paulin, and Richard and Peggy Smith. At Yale University Press, Julian Loose first approached me about writing this book eighteen years ago. When I found it to be under way his critical input and support, supplemented by two wonderful readers' reports, got the baby out of the bathwater. Then Rachael Lonsdale, Marika Lysandrou and, in particular, my copy-editor Richard Mason, got her dressed and ready for school.

How the Old World Ended is dedicated to the memory of two dear friends. I first met Patrick Collinson in 1988 when his departure from Sheffield for Cambridge created a vacancy for me, not only in his old department, but for a while in his old house. From there Pat and Liz introduced me to the Peak District, where I subsequently bought a cottage. They thought nothing of climbing a high peak above Edale and then stripping off completely on the way back down at a tea-coloured waterhole to soak, Pat removing his prosthesis last, and regaling me with the story about the two of them swimming out naked from Sounion at the southern tip of Attica to 'find all the tourists looking down at us in the crystal clear sea'.[17] I heard about Pat's first academic post in Khartoum; his and Liz's honeymoon travelling by donkey across the Ethiopian highlands, drinking donkey's milk from a gourd; and their subsequent removal to the scarcely less anthropologically exotic University of Sydney. Later I moved back to Cambridge where Pat's inclusiveness, open-mindedness, and generosity as Regius Professor of History set a tone for the Faculty, unless the Wallabies were playing the All Blacks in the rugby world cup, in which case he succumbed in short order to the cloven hoof of parochialism. After his retirement I was honoured, with my family (including daughter Sophia, to whom Pat referred as the Electress), to enjoy many visits to Hathersage, walking, listening to the clavichord, and to the no less melodious tinkling of gin and tonics in the garden.

Mark Kishlansky was a warm, wise and hilarious man who was also a bit naughty, which suited me down to the ground. We met accidentally in 1990 when he was visiting Chatsworth House in Derbyshire with Peter Lake and I was doing the same with Julian Hoppit. We repaired to lunch in my tiny seventeenth-century cottage in Ashford-in-the-Water, where Mark held forth on behalf of modern American plumbing against the yellow half or sitting-bath upstairs ('What do you do in it? How do you get out?'). This pose as a mere American, constantly confounded by British culture and behaviour, served him well, partly because he was in love with British culture (history and literature in particular). And, of course, it was not entirely a pose.

Ordering 'twice-fried' balls of goat cheese at a Cambridge pub, Mark asked the waitress, as Hercule Poirot might have queried a sofa full of suspects, if the balls could by any chance have been fried either once or three times, since he had heard there were counterfeit goat balls circulating in the area. In San Francisco's Chinatown he somehow extracted from a completely ordinary-looking café with no other customers the best Chinese meal I have ever had. At the University of Pittsburgh he oversaw my own extraction of the highest salary I had at that point in life ever received. In such emoluments he took an interest of almost poetic intensity, seeing in them an opportunity for Deans to apply the resources of a major educational institution to cliometric recognition of the value of his friends. When I became a father, a role for which I was woefully underprepared, Mark offered brilliant reassurance and support. Concerning reviews of one's books he counselled: 'Never respond unless they attack the dedication.' On one occasion Pat, introducing Simon Schama in Cambridge, recalled arriving in Boston, to visit Harvard, to be asked by a suspicious immigration officer: 'Do you know Schama?' To which he responded: 'I know Kishlansky.'

International migration is hard. Indeed it is possible for a newly arrived traveller to become so preoccupied by the challenges of their immediate situation that they lose sight of the bigger picture. I have gained enormously from twenty-five years living and working outside New Zealand, and just as much from having had the opportunity thereafter to return. I have appreciated reconnecting with New Zealand friends and relatives, in particular my sisters Rachel and Kate. But there is a price to be paid for these moves, by the whole travelling family. In the aftermath my beloved children, Sophia and Tom, born in Cambridge, raised (if that is the word) in Pittsburgh, Auckland and Seattle, and recently returned from visits to Africa, East Asia and Central America, inherit the world which history has created. In 2019 this is not a legacy for the faint-hearted.

Yet I am hopeful on their behalf. There is something impressive, and inspiring, about my children's generation. We don't find meaning in life by looking, but make it by living. I hope they can enjoy it, one day at a time.

PROLOGUE

Fewer than three hundred years ago there occurred the most fundamental reordering of human existence since the beginning of agriculture. How was this possible, involving as it did the disappearance of an entire and heavily defended way of life? The Industrial Revolution is a major field for economic and social historians. But explaining it requires us to understand a complex of developments across the early modern period connecting the sub-fields of environmental, economic, social, political, intellectual and cultural history, and to examine the unfolding of world-changing processes and events, including the large-scale migration of peoples.

To begin with, this transformation must be explained in regional and global terms. Between 1500 and 1800, as Europe established its first global colonies, the Anglo-Dutch North Sea region overtook the Mediterranean as the epicentre of material and cultural capital. Considering the emergence of industrialization within this context the present study goes beyond parallel histories of the Netherlands and England to offer the first systematic account of an Anglo-Dutch relationship that intertwined close alliance and fierce antagonism to intense creative effect between the Dutch Revolt and the Glorious Revolution (1566–1689).[1] Thereafter it attempts to explain why, following Anglo-Dutch industrialization (or proto-industrialization) during the sixteenth and seventeenth centuries, there occurred an exponential Industrial Revolution in Britain from about 1780.

Part of the answer to this question hinges upon the development in temperate-climate British North America of a unique type of European colony, one established for the settlement of people and culture, rather than for the extraction or cultivation of things. During the eighteenth century this sub-section of European

1

empire became demographically explosive because it was outside the zone of mosquito-borne tropical diseases. This was the most dynamic market driving the growth of British manufactures. It was an economic development rooted in environmental, social, cultural and political history: that of the migrational Protestantism which carried Scots, English, Dutch and eventually Swedish and German pilgrims across the Atlantic on their seventeenth-century errand into the wilderness.

In tying together these European and Atlantic themes, this book offers an account of England's republican revolution of 1649–53 as a – perhaps the – turning point in modern world history. It was a spectacular attempt to change not only English government but social and moral life in the direction pioneered by the Dutch Revolt and republic from the late sixteenth century. It enacted a revolution in the military-fiscal and especially naval resources of the state to confront and overcome Dutch competition. One result was the Plantation and Navigation system that nationalized and weaponized the Anglo-American economic relationship. It was only within the context of this navally protected trading monopoly that more than a century later the Industrial Revolution could be triggered by the alchemical power of American shopping.

Wrapped around this argument is a broader discussion ranging from ancient to modern periods, and from the Elizabethan Silk Road to the seventeenth-century Indian Ocean coast of Australia. This examines developments including exploration and colonization, agricultural and scientific revolution, and the emergence of the first world city. It addresses issues such as the relationship of geography to cultural change, and of urban/maritime to terrestrial/aristocratic power. It asks questions concerning the exact location of the Isle of Pines, whether human societies have ever controlled their destinies, and why European travellers to the South Pacific reported that oysters grew on trees. This book offers a wide-angled engagement with history as the study of human life at a time when the environmental, political and economic consequences of industrialization have given us a renewed awareness of the fragility of that condition.

CHAPTER ONE

THE ANGLO-DUTCH-AMERICAN ARCHIPELAGO

Full fadom five thy father lies,
Of his bones are Coral made:
Those are pearles that were his eies,
Nothing of him that doth fade,
But doth suffer a Sea-change
Into something rich, & strange.

William Shakespeare, The Tempest I, 2

AN EARLY MODERN WATER WORLD

During the period from 1500 to 1800 European societies were, as they had long been, and despite their economic, political and cultural diversity, predominantly agricultural. By the late eighteenth century, in the United Kingdom of Great Britain, an economic revolution had arrived which would sweep these societies away. Once its power had been demonstrated it was imitated elsewhere in Europe, then in America, Turkey, Japan, Russia and eventually China, and this is a process which is still under way. Before the Industrial Revolution living standards increased slowly, if at all. But in the two centuries since 1800 the average real income of the world's population has multiplied almost tenfold, and 'in the industrialized world . . . 15–20 times'.[1]

Historians have long studied the causes of this epochal development. This book is also interested in causes, but more in understanding how a long-standing, sophisticated and heavily defended way of life became vulnerable to extinction, an outcome in the interests of relatively few and perhaps planned by none. In fact the Industrial Revolution was the last stage of a process which had

3

been under way for some time: a sharp take-off made possible by acceleration down a long runway.[2] For some scholars the chronology of this longer process was primarily early modern.[3] For others it incorporated the medieval period.[4]

For most historians of industrialization a crucial role was played by the seventeenth-century Dutch republic, 'the first modern economy'. The arrival of that commercial and cultural wonder has been understood within either or both of two comparative frameworks. One describes a process of European urban economic and cultural development running from late medieval and Renaissance Italy through early modern Germany and the Netherlands via the Dutch republic to London.[5] The other observes an early modern displacement within Europe of Mediterranean by north-western economic and cultural predominance. The result of this 'little divergence' within Europe was a new leading sector within the global economy around the southern shores of the North Sea which turns out upon close inspection to have been Anglo-Dutch.

The present account focuses upon developments within what may be retrospectively designated an Anglo-Dutch-American archipelago. This was a geographical constellation, incorporating the Northern Netherlands, the British Isles and Atlantic North America, connected by people, their culture and ships. In more modern metaphorical terms it scrutinizes the Anglo-Dutch subsection of the runway, and the aviation fuel in question, which was importantly North American. It describes a series of economic, cultural, political and military changes which began in the region between the Baltic and North Sea before crossing the North Sea, and then the Atlantic. The result was the process here called Anglo-Dutch-American early modernity. This world-changing current of invention (oceanic to begin with, electric eventually) achieved a breakthrough in the Low Countries, gathered heft and momentum in seventeenth-century England, and by connection with North America made something new.[6]

To that extent this story has a Westerly direction of travel. In 1589 Richard Hakluyt's *Principall Navigations, Voiages and Discoveries of the English Nation* organized its voyages '*into three* severall parts, according to . . . the Regions whereunto they were directed'.[7] So also Max Weber ascribed the birth of capitalism to the Westward spiritual progress of a trans-Atlantic 'Calvinist diaspora . . . the English, Dutch and American Puritans'.[8] This was the trajectory of West European Atlantic empire in general, within which the Anglo-Dutch (and French) North American component constituted a post-Iberian second stage.

The English poet Andrew Marvell mocked Dutch religious heterodoxy as a mutant outcome of the broader Westward progress of Christianity:

> Sure when Religion did it self Imbark,
> And from the East would Westward steer its Ark;
> It struck, and splitting on this unknown Ground,
> Each one thence pillag'd the first piece he found:
> Hence *Amsterdam* Turk-Christian-Pagan-Jew,
> Staple of Sects, and Mint of Schism grew.[9]

But this end of a journey, upon the treacherous shoals of the Dutch coast, is where the present account begins. It begins specifically upon that shifty unpromising shore, in a Dutch water-world which posed unique challenges for a European agricultural society, before Protestantism, and partly because of those challenges. This suggests that if we ever see a portal into another world it may look, not like an oasis with palms, or a kaleidoscope of colours, but rather a liminal marsh. Marvell scoffed:

> Holland, that scarce deserves the name of Land,
> As but th'off-scowring of the *British* Sand;
> And so much Earth as was contributed
> By *English* Pilots; when they heav'd the Lead.[10]

In 1550 the Low Countries were a small, though precociously wealthy, component of the vast Habsburg Empire, Europe's global power. That north-western subsection which became the United Provinces was smaller still. Within this environment land and water were intertwined, making the Northern Netherlands an hydraulic society, 'defined by the ubiquity of water'.[11] It was as if, wrote the seventeenth-century English ambassador Sir William Temple, 'after a long contention between Land and Water, which It should belong to, It had at length been divided between them'.[12] Water was, wrote John Evelyn in 1674, the 'most impetuous, and unconstant element'.[13] Whether as rain, river, waves or tide, it never stood still. This made it a potential force for change (the modern, perhaps, in early modern) in a cultural context anchored in precedent and hostile to innovation.[14] Temple added: 'No man can tell the strange and mighty Changes that may have been made in the faces and bounds of Maritime Countreys . . . by furious Inundations . . . of Land-Floods, Winds and Tides.'[15] Shakespeare's *The Tempest*, a rumination upon this theme and element, deployed the term 'Sea-change'.

In Thucydides' *History of the Peloponnesian War* Athens, a maritime and naval city, was depicted as a culture constantly in motion (*kinesis*). The Corinthians lambasted the agrarian Spartans: 'An Athenian is always an innovator, quick to form a resolution and quick at carrying it out. You, on the other hand . . . never originate an idea, and your action tends to stop short of its aim . . . Your inactivity has done harm enough.'[16] The Dutch were also a people in motion, inventive, rule-breaking. By the sixteenth century some Southern Netherlandish cities – Brussels, Antwerp, Ghent – had achieved unprecedented wealth, developing economic and fiscal inventions pioneered in Italy.[17] Beyond this, Amsterdam and Holland developed a distinct economic and social culture on the basis of new trades (the Baltic grain trade) and maritime industries (the North Sea fishery). Meanwhile, relatedly, all along the Western Seaboard Dutch agriculture was being transformed.

In the early modern period water was the only efficient means of transport. In this connection: 'The commercial greatness of Holland was due not only to her shipping at sea, but also to the numerous tranquil water-ways which gave such cheap and easy access to her own interior and to that of Germany. This advantage of carriage by water over that by land was yet more marked in a period when roads were few and very bad, wars frequent and society unsettled.'[18]

Water also connected the United Provinces to England and Scotland, and both to Ireland and North America. Had this not been the case, ideas, technology and people would not have traversed the archipelago to such striking effect. 'The seventeenth century was a period of . . . upheaval . . . in England and the Dutch Republic, resulting in repeated, voluntary and forced, movements of peoples . . . Men and women moved with comparative lack of difficulty (travel by water was . . . easier and safer than travel overland) . . . the[ir] proximity . . . captured in the Dutch designation of the stretch of the North Sea between Holland and England as the "Narrow Sea".'[19]

For the same reasons trade and the cultural life of cities were shaped and limited by their relationship to rivers and the sea. Beyond them oceans (the Atlantic, Indian and Pacific) laid early modern Europe's path to discovery of the world.[20] Charles Darwin arrived at his understanding of natural selection, a process involving small but constant change over a very long time, after completing a five-year global circumnavigation. On the one hand this exposed him to oceanic scale. 'It is necessary to sail over this great ocean [the Pacific] to comprehend its immensity.'[21] On the other it subjected him to constant motion, resulting in seasickness. 'I hate every wave of the ocean with a fervour . . . I loathe, I abhor the sea and all ships which are on it.' The combination proved fruitful, as in his discussion of coral reef formation, the result of long-term interaction between living organisms and the sea.[22]

The formative importance of England's relationship to the United Provinces has long been recognized.[23] This book considers its most important consequence, in the first place by situating the relationship within this early modern water world. At its core were two estuarine deltas facing each other across the North Sea: that created by the Maas, Rhine and Scheldt rivers to the East, and the Thames on the Western side. As the Mediterranean had been, so between 1588 and 1688 this body of water became a dynamic axis of world history. One recent study evokes 'that lost world . . . around the North Sea in times when . . . the sea connected . . . peoples, beliefs and ideas, as well as pots and wine and coal'.[24] The historically unprecedented growth of early modern London, both symptom and catalyst of the economic transformations at the heart of this study, was partly enabled by its close maritime links first to Flanders and Brabant (Bruges, then Antwerp) and then to Zeeland and Holland (Amsterdam, Middelburg, Rotterdam).[25]

Although the lands and cultures on either side of this North Sea corridor were distinct, the facing coasts were similar. Daniel Defoe recorded that south Lincolnshire and north-west Norfolk were 'very properly call'd *Holland*, for 'tis a flat, Level, and often drowned Country, like *Holland* itself; here the very Ditches are navigable, and the People pass from Town to Town in Boats, as in *Holland*'.[26] Of south-eastern England William Camden wrote that the origin of its first settlers was suggested by the fact that 'the . . . names of our townes end in *Burrow, Berry, Ham, Steed, Ford, Thorp* and *Wich*, which carry a just and equall correspondence unto the terminations of the Dutch townes; *Burg, Berg, Heim, Stadt, Furdt, Dorp*, and *Wic*.'[27] Writing in 1676 to counter the view that England had once been 'joined to the Opposite Continent, by a narrow Isthmus', Aylett Sammes rebutted Camden, arguing that the country had in fact been settled by seagoing Phoenicians, and dismissing the observations of Verstegan concerning the great geographic similarities between French and English shores of the Channel: '*Dover* . . . as it is derived in great probability, by Mr. *Lambard*, it comes from the word DURYRRHA, which in the *British* Language betokeneth, a place *steep* and *upright*, an evident sign of the Antiquity of those Cliffs.'[28]

Economic historians describing an integrated North Sea region, despite striking Anglo-Dutch social and political differences, reference commonalities like high rates of literacy and late age of marriage (the European Marriage Pattern), which appear to have assisted family accumulation of social and material capital.[29] Yet within the region proto-modern GDP growth appeared in the Netherlands more than a century before it arrived in England. Dutch political historians complain that their English colleagues don't read the history of the United Provinces; neither group has made much of the idea of a supra-national (which is to say regional) locality.[30] But perhaps they should. In September 2014 campaigners for an independent Scotland complained of three centuries of government and neglect by 'London and the Southeast'. That was certainly the region which won the English Civil War, engineered the Anglo-Dutch revolution of 1649–1702, and created the modern British state, economy and empire, so that in 1707 Scotland decided to climb on board. Meanwhile Scotland had its own long-standing cultural and economic ties to the Netherlands, as close as England's own.[31]

Economic and cultural change in England was regionally uneven. By the early seventeenth century Dutch immigrants fleeing war with Spain accounted for a third of the population of south-east English towns. Of 9,302 resident aliens in London in 1567, 77 per cent were Dutch, leading one scholar to remark that 'by the turn of the seventeenth century, London might well have been characterised as Europe's little Netherlands'.[32] It was from the same south-eastern counties, as well as from Holland itself, that the majority of seventeenth-century American 'pilgrims' emigrated. The settlement of continental North America was an Anglo-Dutch process, not only because the United Provinces had its own colony in New Netherland (from 1609), but because Plymouth and Massachusetts Bay were in part the work of English separatists and congregationalists ('godly republicans') who had been living in Leiden and Rotterdam.[33] Accordingly one nineteenth-century Massachusetts congregationalist demanded to know:

Why are Cambridge and Oxford so different? . . . Cambridge . . . is right in the heart of these eastern counties . . . which in the fourteenth century were thickly planted with the Dutch weaver-heretics, and in the sixteenth century . . . by the republican and Bible-reading Protestants of the Netherlands . . . Oxford, in the midland counties, has always been royal, conservative, and reactionary; while Cambridge has been parliamentary, liberal and progressive . . . Oxford educated champions of episcopacy, and the ecclesiastics of the Established Church . . . Of seventeen most prominent New England clergymen . . . fourteen were trained at Cambridge.[34]

ARCHIPELAGIC HISTORY

Within this water world, what does it mean to speak of an Anglo-Dutch-American archipelago? Geographic language has played an important part in the recent reconceptualization of early modern British history. A generation ago national terminology prevailed. Within that framework local studies made the vital point that much early modern life was lived within the county, town or parish. Then came the historiography of the 'British problem', important because from 1603 there was a British multiple-monarchy and, thereafter, because of that under-resourced institution's collapse amid a 'war of three kingdoms' (1638–51).[35] Within this context J. G. A. Pocock spoke of the three Stuart kingdoms (and one principality) as an 'Atlantic Archipelago'.

Pocock's formulation was fruitful partly because it described not so much a geographical object, or set of objects, as a constantly evolving constellation of relationships. A history of this archipelago was therefore an account of the inhabitant cultures of the British Isles in their interaction, presuming no political or cultural hierarchies, and eschewing Anglocentricity. Subsequently Pocock extended this archipelagic construction to the entire British Empire.[36] Yet it is a stretch to describe the islands between the North and Irish Seas as Atlantic in scope (or character). Early modern Scotland, England, Wales and Ireland were all European as well as incipiently national cultures with their own complexities and histories. The real 'British problem' has been a privileging of early modern relationships between component parts of what later became the United Kingdom of Great Britain (from 1707) and Ireland (from

1801) at the expense of other European relationships of equal or greater historical importance.

The present study identifies an archipelago which became genuinely Atlantic in extent, and oceanic in its operations. This was only one outcome of a multidimensional historical process, the context of which was global. Approaching it I gratefully acknowledge Pocock's emphasis upon cultural multiplicity and relationship. There was, of course, no Anglo-Dutch-American state, nor were the component parts of this aggregation obviously or merely islands. But continents, archipelagos and islands are relational categories the cultural construction of which has always been dependent upon historical context.[37] William Temple described Holland as 'an Island made by the dividing-branches of the ancient *Rhyne*, and called formerly *Batavia*'.[38] A North American wrote during the eighteenth century: 'Is not the situation of the United States insular with respect to the power of the Old World: the quarter from which alone we are to apprehend danger? Have not the maritime states the greatest influence upon the affairs of the universe?'[39] In history England's claim to insularity (which has no Scots equivalent) has had a political rather than geographic foundation.[40] More broadly Greg Dening observed: 'The Europeans of the sixteenth century discovered that the world is an ocean and all of its continents are islands.'[41] Within this context, the Anglo-Dutch-American archipelago describes an area the terrestrial components of which were connected by culture, and drawn together by their relationship to water and the technology by which it was mastered for purposes of agriculture, travel, exploration, war and trade.

Exploring the Industrial Revolution in a global context some historians have compared the economies of north-eastern China and Japan, and north-western (Anglo-Dutch) Europe in the late eighteenth century.[42] Differences between these regions at opposite ends of Eurasia included technology, resources, empires, and maritime empires in particular. In 1800, Ken Pomeranz argued, each had reached a comparable stage of economic development, with commercialized agriculture, highly developed manufacturing and efficient water-borne communications. To explain why the Industrial Revolution occurred in Britain rather than China, Pomeranz focused on British America, particularly as a source of raw materials, including coal, timber, sugar and cotton.[43]

This thesis has subsequently been challenged, and the force of that challenge acknowledged by Pomeranz. While China was the world's richest and most sophisticated economy under the northern Song Dynasty, Chinese GDP per head had probably been overtaken by that of Renaissance central and northern Italy by the fifteenth century. It was certainly surpassed in Holland during the sixteenth century, and thereafter by seventeenth- and eighteenth-century Britain.[44] Thus British and Dutch economic historians discern a 'deep' two-stage preliminary to the Industrial Revolution, involving a great divergence between East Asia and Europe (1200–1800) followed by a little divergence between the Mediterranean and North Sea (1500–1800).[45] These were enabled by the transformation of Europe's global power and commerce, the arrival of printing and then of Protestantism, and the competitive and co-operative behaviours of city-states, cities and states.

Against this background we must distinguish between industrialization, which reached a new stage of development in the sixteenth-century Netherlands and then seventeenth-century England, and Britain's post-1750 Industrial Revolution, which had no Dutch or other precedent. One of the factors which made the latter possible, the present study argues, was indeed Britain's unique relationship to a group of North American colonies, though not for the reason that Pomeranz gave. Other European empires had extracted resources on a huge scale for centuries without triggering Industrial Revolution. It was the role of the thirteen colonies as consumers of manufactures, rather than a source of raw materials, which helps to explain the first outbreak anywhere in the world of 'exponential' industrial growth (see Chapter 15 below).

During the subsequent century James Belich has described 'the rise of the Anglo-World', product of a global 'settler revolution'.[46] Its demographic footsteps were visible in the super-cities of London, New York, Chicago and then Melbourne. If this westward march looks like a continuation of the Anglo-Dutch-American process, that is no coincidence. The 'migrational tsunami' of the settler revolution was one aspect of the exceptional demographic dynamism of the British-American-Australasian imperial diaspora relative to the Spanish, French and Russian. Part of the explanation for that lies in the exceptional demographic history of English-speaking North America. The larger explanation lies with the Industrial Revolution itself, and its impact on both demography and migration. The settler revolution spoke English partly because so did the first Industrial Revolution. During the nineteenth century 22.5 million migrants left Britain and Ireland for the overseas colonies and ex-colonies, a more than tenfold increase over the previous century.[47] The Anglo-world 'grew over sixteenfold in 1790–1930, from around 12 million to around 200 million – a far greater rate than Indian and Chinese growth, as well as Russian and Hispanic', though this included a North American component indebted to German, Italian and other non-English-speaking migration.[48]

Considering the Anglo-Dutch-American process we begin not with politics but local and regional geography, economy and society. Thus Jan de Vries and Ad van der Woude warned against the 'excess of attention given by historians to the nation state . . . here the unifying themes lie elsewhere. History here is not the result of commands from the political centre.'[49] Indeed, as we will see, of this history the making, or invention, of three new states was one result (see Chapter 13 below).

TIME, INVENTION AND HISTORICAL AGENCY

Early modern evokes not simply a period, but also a conception of time. The Industrial Revolution profoundly impacted our cultural relationship to time, and so our understanding of human historical agency. Here as elsewhere it established the foundations of modernity.[50] This was so although modernity became a global phenomenon encapsulating far more than economic history.[51] Most challengingly, exponential industrialization was perhaps the most decisive and irreversible rupture in the history of humankind. It is hard to get such a suggestion into proper historical perspective, partly because in the modern world change is taken for granted, and so present-day students write as if the Industrial Revolution was inevitable. To the contrary, particularly given the inelastic limits of pre-industrial agricultural economies, it should have been impossible.

Normally, at a certain point in demographic recovery within any agricultural society resources per capita began to diminish. Thus by the sixteenth century even central and Northern Italy (and Iberia) had entered a period of stagnation and then decline. This study argues that what changed this equation over the long term were two developments in particular. One was an agricultural revolution assisted, in the fifteenth and sixteenth centuries, by a new post-Italian type of trade (the Baltic grain trade), or rather an old type placed on a new technological and functional footing. The second was the foundation, in seventeenth- and eighteenth-century Ireland and English North

America, of a new kind of European colony, for the plantation of people and culture, rather than of things. One of these established the basis for the eventual displacement of agricultural by industrial economies by changing agriculture. The other laid a platform for a flood of migrants and their lifeways by displacing and sometimes eradicating indigenous Americans. An Anglo-Dutch revolution knit these two developments together and made the Industrial Revolution an Anglo-Dutch-American story.

In Donna Tartt's *The Goldfinch* the hero's mother remarked: 'I guess that anything we manage to save from history is a miracle.'[52] Deprived by the charnel-house of life of the people he most needs, Theo falls in love with a luminous Dutch Old Master.[53] Historians have long referred to the Dutch 'Golden Age' from which Carel Fabritius' *The Goldfinch* (1654) emerged as the product of an 'economic miracle'. The subsequent Industrial Revolution which began in Britain was more miraculous still: a genie of hyper-productivity and transformation initially released from an ordinary-looking lamp. But who or what was its creator? Europe's agricultural societies strove for seasonal, cyclical continuity rather than change. Alongside this revolving present, with its associated deference to tradition, 'few features of medieval scholarship are so distinctive as an utter indifference to the pastness of the past'.[54] If, later, some Enlightenment-era intellectuals in Europe and America came to congratulate themselves on living in the most advanced societies in history, even they were celebrating the present, not attempting to eradicate it.

Yet between the Renaissance and Enlightenment some Europeans rethought the relationship between present and past. Through its insistence upon the recovery of classical texts in their original languages, humanism underlined their distinction. Then discovery of a New World unknown to the ancients opened up the prospect of discovery, described in England as invention, more broadly. Writing in 1667 Thomas Sprat hoped that with its '*ships* spreading their Sails in all Seas' London would prove 'most properly seated, to bring home matter for *new Sciences,* and to make the same proportion of Discoveries . . . in the *Intellectual* Globe, as they have done in the *Material*'.[55] It was one function of the Royal Society's journal *Philosophical Transactions* to 'vindicate good inventions to their proper Authors'.[56]

Sprat's *History of the Royal Society* celebrated a culture of invention which he distinguished from 'the hazard of . . . *Novelty*', or '*Innovation*'.[57] 'If to be the

Author of *new* things, be a crime; how will the first Civilizers of *Men,* and makers of Laws, and founders of *Governments* escape? Whatever now delights us in the Works of *Nature,* that excels the rudeness of the first Creation, is *New.*'[58] For the morbid inclination to set the past above the present '*Experiments* are a sovereign cure. They give us a perfect sight of what is before us . . . they make us live in *England,* and not in *Athens* or *Sparta.*' Their overall result, however, was not to denigrate the past, or to displace it, but rather to build upon it.[59]

More than a century earlier Machiavelli had counselled that the best that could be achieved in the present was a properly textually informed 'imitation' of ancient Rome. What made Rome a superior political model to contemporary Venice was that it had been a republic for expansion.[60] In 1667 Sprat was able to redeploy this distinction in defence of the idea of an expansion of learning, resulting in a potentially universal empire of knowledge. The Royal Society's ambition of 'advancing its stock by a *sure* and *double increase*; by adding *new Discoveries,* and retaining *antient Truths*' exhibited

> [a] largeness, and generosity, which. . . . excels any *other Sect*; as the *Roman Commonwealth,* did that of *Venice.* The latter . . . has . . . been careful to preserve itself unmingled . . . on the defensive; making no great progress in the World: whereas the *Romans,* by a far more frank and honourable counsel, admitted all . . . gave the liberty of *Roman Citizens* to whole Towns, and Countreys . . . and so deservedly extended their Empire, as farr as the . . . *civil World* did reach.[61]

For Sprat, Restoration society would not be 'unmingled', but rather a meeting place for cultures and civilizations. Similarly, for another student of Machiavelli, Algernon Sidney, 'those who will admit of no change would . . . deprive . . . mankind of the benefits of wisdom, industry, experience, and the right use of reason'.[62] Sidney located these benefits within the history of those cultures – Greek, Roman, Italian, Dutch and English – which had been prosperous because they were free. Human flourishing (virtue) was incompatible with autocracy. On this point he contrasted seventeenth-century Anglo-Dutch improvement with Italian decline:[63]

Such as are bred under a good discipline, and see that all benefits procured to their country by virtuous actions, redound to the honour and advantage of themselves . . . contract from their infancy a love to the publick . . . On the other side, when . . . the best are despised, hated, or mark'd out for destruction; [and] all things calculated to the humor or advantage of one man, who is often the worst . . . all application to virtuous actions will cease . . . We need no other proof of this than what we have seen in our own country, where, in a few years good discipline, and a just encouragement to those who did well, produced more examples of pure, compleat, incorruptible, and invincible virtue than Rome or Greece could ever boast; or if more be wanting, they may easily be found among the Switzers, Hollanders and others; but 'tis not necessary to light a candle to the sun.[64]

This celebration of the English republican achievement of 1649–53 was deeply influential in Enlightenment Northern Europe (the Netherlands, France and Germany) and America. In thus speaking of and for the Anglo-Dutch-American experience Sidney was also describing what some historians have identified as the social and cultural preconditions of the Industrial Revolution, 'the product of specific interactions between incentives, economic structures, knowledge accumulation and human capital formation'.[65] Combined with 'improved institutions . . . new technologies (printing), Protestantism . . . and the growing demand for skilled labour in the rapidly growing cities', these help to explain the 'little divergence' between economic development in the North Sea region and that in the rest of early modern Europe.[66]

Historians have studied technological innovation within the competitive economic environment of Dutch cities.[67] They have noted awareness among English and Scots merchants of the economic importance of advancing knowledge, and attraction to the press and learned societies by which it was disseminated.[68] One study claims the emergence of a distinct English discourse of 'improvement . . . gradual, piecemeal, but cumulative betterment', epistemological as well as material.[69] This was a period when Europeans became accustomed to the idea of invention across a range of endeavour from agriculture and travel to politics and science. In particular we associate the Industrial Revolution with new technology. This was the case, in the felicitous formulation of one University of Auckland undergraduate examinee, 'from the spinning jenny to the flying

saucer'. But it was one thing, and a big one, to witness invention of the chronometer or the steam engine. It was another to live through an epoch of fast,
comprehensive and irreversible change of total reach and eventually global extent.
Keith Sinclair noted that the lateness of the European settlement of New Zealand

> meant that it occurred . . . after the Reform Bill – and . . . the 'industrial
> revolution'. Not only settlers but steam engines and investment capital came
> here . . . New Zealand was settled in an age of change. To us there seems
> nothing remarkable about change . . . But I suppose that only a tiny minority
> of the billions . . . who have lived saw in their lifetimes any significant alter-
> ations in their social structure or in their instruments of production or war.
> For many ages men could travel no faster than foot or hoof or sail.[70]

Global societies are currently experiencing uncomfortable social and political
turbulence as a result of accelerating economic and technological change. But
this was not the situation anywhere before 1750. It may also be a feature of the
present, confronted as we are by ominous global problems, to underline the
question of human historical agency.[71] The idea that the Industrial Revolution
might constitute an object lesson in the history of unintended consequences
derives from our awareness of consequences which are frightening. If it has
initiated a process of environmental change which remains out of control, this
also strikes at what were until recently dominant Western assumptions about
progress. Perhaps the penny dropped first in Naples:

> Naples was the great European metropolis where faith in technology, in
> science, in economic development, in the kindness of nature, in history
> that leads of necessity to improvement, in democracy, was revealed, most
> clearly and far in advance, to be completely without foundation. To be
> born in that city . . . is useful for only one thing: to have always known,
> almost instinctively, what today, with endless fine distinctions, everyone is
> beginning to claim: that the dream of unlimited progress is in reality a
> nightmare of savagery and death.[72]

Since the idea of progress was itself a product of Enlightenment there is no
reason to expect it to have persisted. The present-day revolt against elites in the

United States, Great Britain, France and elsewhere is certainly connected to a sense of loss of agency. In the words of a postcard: 'Where am I going, and why am I in this handbasket?'[73] Yet few pre-modern human societies assumed that the course of history was primarily a consequence of human effort. Europeans living without modern medicine or technology, in a partially tamed landscape, in close proximity to weather and the seasons, to infirmity, infant mortality and epidemic disease, understood themselves to be in the hands of God. Thus if the Industrial Revolution was not the product of a plan; if the processes which made it possible took shape over centuries; if they entailed unanticipated interactions between developments in different parts of the world; and if they ushered in changes beyond the imagination of contemporaries themselves – then perhaps we are being reminded of something our ancestors knew. We don't make history. It is the other way around.

A generation ago Charles Tilly, John Brewer and Geoffrey Parker analyzed different aspects of the early modern phenomenon of military-fiscal state building.[74] This was a modernization achieved in response to the escalating demands of warfare by political agents of the central state. During the Dutch Revolt these demands were the making of the new republic; and during the Anglo-Dutch revolution of the soon-to-be United Kingdom.[75] Subsequently Steve Hindle, Michael Braddick and others described the concurrent but distinct process of English social state formation.[76] This was the achievement of no single will or intelligence, but the aggregation over time of the disparate efforts of thousands of local office holders. What united these agents of a weak central authority were the problems they faced, and the cultural resources available to deal with them. Over the long term, as the social state was formed by a host of local micro-organisms, all drawing nutrients from the same wide sea, Cardinal Richelieu proved no match for the coral polyp. This 'bottom up' social historical analysis aligns with the historiography which sees industrialization emerging from 'a million mutinies': decisions made across centuries by individuals, families and communities concerning marriage, work, education and consumption.[77]

In his recent study of the First World War, Christopher Clark tells a 'story . . . saturated with agency. The key decision makers – kings, emperors, foreign ministers, ambassadors, military commanders . . . walked towards danger in watchful, calculated steps.'[78] Yet none of the dangers each had in mind remotely

17

equated to the catastrophe which eventually ensued. In that sense 'The protagonists of 1914 were sleepwalkers, watchful but unseeing, haunted by dreams, yet blind to the reality of the horror they were about to bring into the world.'[79] The war was a complex event, the product of many decisions rather than one, and in the event of a magnitude which could not have been predicted. Yet at least war was a known condition. These decisions, though inadequately informed, were taken in historically proximate real time. In the present study we are considering a different kind of process, resulting from developments in many places over centuries, which was not only unprecedented, but which had consequences that could not have been imagined; indeed which remain incompletely understood.

One earlier long-term complex process was the peopling of the globe by *homo sapiens* travelling out of Africa. Their route took them into Europe, through the Near East, South Asia, Australia, East and then Northern Asia, across the Bering Sea and then north to south through the Americas. This great migration seems to have been accomplished primarily by short coastal sea journeys undertaken in daylight within sight of land. The trail is marked by carbon-dateable shellfish middens lying undisturbed a mile or two off the coast, since ocean levels have since risen. This record is constantly being updated by archaeology and genetic science. According to data reported in August 2015, the Americas may have been populated by a single sequence of migrations originating in Siberia in about 23,000 BCE. According to new evidence published in 2017, Aboriginal peoples may have arrived in Australia's Far North 80,000 rather than 50,000 years ago.

None of these travellers had any consciousness of the Barrier Reef to which they were contributing: that of a worldwide species migration.[80] But it is only by reconstructing their experience as a whole that we can grasp a universal feature of history. Humans have always sent out migrants or colonists to explore, search for resources, escape, expel or punish. Those involved have had to adapt to new climates, ecologies, cultures and technologies. According to Darwin, adaptation is the key to species success. This is one context within which to understand the centrality of migration to the circumstances that made the Industrial Revolution possible. The Anglo-Dutch-American archipelago was not only populated, but to some extent constituted, by the largest international migration until that time in European history, which unfolded between 1560 and 1760 and came to be trans-Atlantic in scope.[81]

When early moderns discussed human agency they frequently did so in the moral language of industry versus idleness. An important theme among English writers was admiration and envy of Dutch industry and improvement. As Slingsby Bethel wrote on the eve of the third Anglo-Dutch war: 'I cannot think their Trade or Wealth . . . to be a[n] . . . honest foundation for a quarrel; for their commerce [is] . . . alone the effect of Industry, and Ingenuity.'[82] It was partly this language which encouraged Max Weber to ascribe the origins of capitalism to the impact of a particular mode of Protestantism. What caused it, he argued, was an emphasis upon industry which was spiritually rooted. Moreover, he was correct to notice that in praising the moral example of the Dutch, and advocating its imitation, some seventeenth-century English commentators attributed this industry to a theological imperative.[83]

Many historians have now accepted the idea of an 'industrious revolution' anchored in the secular realm of household decision-making and consumer choice.[84] But early modern English commentators also related Dutch industry to a necessity imposed upon Netherlanders by high population density, high prices, war, and/or a uniquely demanding physical 'situation'.[85] According to Paul Slack, whereas elsewhere 'there had for centuries been innovations which would now be called improvements', in seventeenth-century England 'the word and notion were extended to the country as a whole, so that improvement became a fundamental part of the national culture'.[86] Yet in 1667 Thomas Sprat reported:

> At first . . . [the *Hollanders*] were as lazy as the worst of ours . . . their Coasts lay desolate to the Sea, without Bancks, or Towns, or Ships, or harbors . . . But when by the number of their people they were forc'd to look abroad, to Trade, to Fish, to *labor* in *Mechanics*; they soon found the sweetness as well as toyl of their *diligence*: their successes and riches still added new heat to their minds; and thus they have continued *improving*, till they have not only disgrac'd but terrify'd their *Neighbours*, by their *Industry*.[87]

This book takes seriously the suggestion that the unique geography and location of the north-western Netherlands played a crucial role in creating the first post-agricultural society (see Chapters 2–3). The Dutch themselves located what was distinct about their society in a bluntness, directness, simplicity, candor and capacity for labour which they distinguished from the 'hypocrisy, cleverness, falseness and mannerism of more "civilized" nations'.[88]

Compared to the Netherlands, England was natural-resource rich.[89] By contrast with the seven northern Dutch provinces domestic supplies of coal, wool, grain, and metals were abundant, though depletion of timber was driving the greatly increased use of coal from the 1570s.[90] However, under pre-industrial circumstances these factors were not always advantageous. Elizabethan England was a traditional agricultural society under enormous pressure from rising population. The Dutch reliance upon imports of everything from grain and herring to textiles and spices released the economy from local constraints and invested it with greater flexibility.[91] That it needed and could attract a vast pool of imported labour – Jewish and Christian, Italian, Spanish and Portuguese, German, French and English – gave it many advantages within a competitive European market for knowledge and skills.[92] These policies were admired and copied. In the words of Sir John Wolley, MP, in 1592: 'The Riches and Renown of [London] comes by entertaining of Strangers and giving liberty unto them. Antwerp and Venice could never have been so rich and famous but by entertaining of Strangers, and by that means have gained all the intercourse of the World.'[93]

The most important difference between 'England and the Low Countries [was] . . . their socio-political institutions'.[94] In these terms, indeed 'it is difficult to think of two regions within Europe that were less similar'. England was a rural, aristocratic territorial monarchy. The sixteenth-century Netherlands was the most urbanized part of Europe. In Holland, as early as 1514 'only one quarter of the labour force was active in agriculture, another 15% in other primary activities (digging peat, fishing), 20–25% in services (trade and transport in particular), while a staggering 38% was occupied in industry'.[95] Relatedly, from the beginning of the sixteenth century the Netherlands began an unprecedented growth of real GDP per head, despite rising population, which constituted the leading edge of the North Sea regional 'little divergence'.[96] In England such growth began more gradually and almost a century and a half later, continuing through the eighteenth century until the Industrial Revolution.[97]

Some historians have treated this as a deferred catch-up within a single economically integrated region.[98] Yet in view of the two countries' socio-political dissimilarities the staggered chronology was important. This was so not least because English growth began during a century of extreme religious and political instability, involving crises, civil war and republican revolution.[99] Concerning 'the evolution of an improvement culture in the later seventeenth and early eighteenth centuries', Slack comments that 'it is striking . . . that the . . . circumstances which sustained it were both coming into existence in the 1650s, after a political revolution'.[100] It is hardly less important, then, that the Dutch republic was also the product of a revolution (though its economic 'miracle' had earlier foundations), one which directly inspired its English successor almost a century later.

Between these two events the most important Anglo-Dutch cultural link was predominantly Calvinist Protestantism. The struggle against Spain drew Elizabethan England and the Netherlands together as both found themselves on the front line of a militarized confessional divide within a European fiscal-military state system imposing its own implacable demands. 'Violence and war were the perpetual condition of Dutch early modernity.'[101] To win its war for independence the Dutch republic had to create not only a new globe-spanning economy, but a new, and new kind of, state. Nor could the militarily and fiscally unreformed, and perhaps unreformable, Elizabethan and early Stuart monarchies survive this era of European, imperial and global war. The result was a complex process of invention, embracing the economy, society, politics and the state, beginning in the Dutch water world, acquiring a new edge amid the blood and stench of the Anglo-Dutch naval wars, before crossing to North America. The effect was a Sea-change, exchanging bone and flesh for coral and pearl.

For a century or more British historians have effectively excused seventeenth-century English history from the sequence of four early modern republican revolutions among which it was, in fact, the most consequential participant (see Chapters 6 and 12 below). Following the last of them, in France, which caused an enduring British reaction, they have continued to send in a sick note.[102] But this has made it impossible to explain how the Industrial Revolution became possible, or why it first occurred in Britain. When this changes we may piece together the story of how the old world ended.

PART I

✳

ANGLO-DUTCH-AMERICAN EARLY MODERNITY

The rivers of Mi'kma'ki were not solitary currents of water but strands in a great net of liquid motion that defined the land and mingled with the sea in outward flow and inward rush of tide. Each tiny runnel, each roaring raceway, torrent and trickle, cascade and flood had its own habits and ways, and Mi'kmaq had to know those ways. This was the water world that Theotiste and Elphege began to learn.

Annie Proulx, *Barkskins*[1]

But if water created the world . . . [and] shaped and nourished it, water would also destroy it. Here one came to the aspect of Leonardo that is most frightening and perhaps least sympathetic . . . His imagination was . . . apocalyptic.

Robert Hughes, *Things I Didn't Know: A Memoir*[2]

Legend:
- Netherlands
- Spanish Netherlands
- Bishopric of Liège
- ---- Limit of Louis XIV's acquisitions

North Sea

Emden

GRONINGEN

FRIESLAND

DRENTHE

Kampen

OVERIJSSEL
Deventer

Haarlem
Amsterdam

UTRECHT
The Hague
Utrecht
Arnhem

GELDERLAND

Yarmouth
Lowestoft

Sole Bay

ENGLAND

Rotterdam

Nijmegen

ZEELAND

LANDS OF THE GENERALITY

Breda

Harwich

Bruges

Antwerp

Chatham

Ghent
Schelde

BRABANT
Brussels

Liège

LIMBURG

Dover

Dunkirk

FLANDERS

Calais

Lys
Lille

Namur

Dungeness

ARTOIS

HAINAULT

Rhine

Arras

CAMBRESIS

Meuse

LUXEMBOURG

FRANCE

Luxembourg

0   50 miles
0   80 km

1. England and the Netherlands, *c.* 1648.

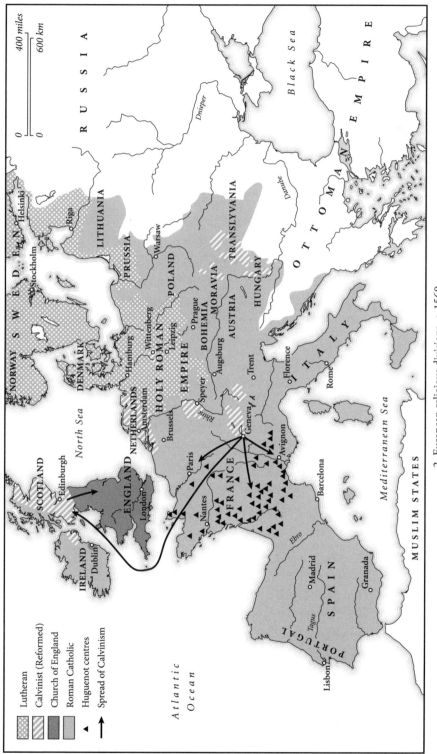

2. European religious divisions, c. 1560.

CHAPTER TWO

THE FIRST INDUSTRIAL REVOLUTION

'This is the land of Narnia,' said the Faun, 'where we are now; all
that lies between the lamp-post and the great castle of Cair Paravel
on the eastern sea. And you – you have come from the wild woods
of the west?'

'I – I got in through the wardrobe in the spare room,' said Lucy.

C. S. Lewis, *The Lion, The Witch and the Wardrobe*[1]

WHAT DIFFERENCE DID IT MAKE?

The Industrial Revolution involved the transformation of organic economies
by means of a 'complex of changes which gave birth to the modern world'.[2] In
Europe, East Asia and elsewhere those economies were agricultural. Thus we
are discussing the replacement of an economy 80 per cent of the output of
which might have been agricultural (with 10 per cent manufacturing, predominantly textiles, and 10 per cent services including trade) by another in which
manufacturing became the dominant sector. This involved a transition in the
scale of manufacturing from artisanal to large-scale workshop and then factory
production. In Britain that entailed technological innovation, but it would not
have been possible in the first place without prior sustained changes in the rest
of the economy and society.

As Tony Wrigley observes, Britain 'in 1800 was the most heavily urbanised
country in Europe other than Holland, even though in the mid-sixteenth
century . . . [it] had been among the least urbanised'.[3] That urban sector,
containing now 60 per cent of the population, could not have developed
without a revolution in agricultural productivity over the previous two hundred

years enabling the labour of the remaining 40 per cent to feed a national population which had itself doubled from 4.2 million in 1600 to 8.7 million in 1800.[4] But grain-growing agricultural economies were extraordinarily difficult to change. This is the most important reason the Industrial Revolution was not only improbable, but almost miraculous, since so many factors had to combine to make it possible. Not only were industrialization and the Industrial Revolution (in Britain consecutive stages in a long-term process) not inevitable. By the rules of pre-modern economies they should never have occurred, which may be one reason humanity is still struggling with the demographic, geopolitical and environmental consequences.

The result was much more than an economic transition. There was no aspect of human life that the Industrial Revolution did not transform. It is the ubiquity as much as the profundity of the transformation which make it the most important historical development since agriculture itself. The result entailed a departure from what Peter Laslett called 'the world we have lost'.[5] Folk memories of this long remained, and still do. It was partly in their pursuit (of uncrowded rural life, relative self-sufficiency, the cycle of the seasons) that millions of nineteenth-century migrants travelled to Europe's colonies and ex-colonies.[6] It was into this cultural memory bank that a professor of medieval and early modern literature tapped when he had a group of children climb into an item of bedroom furniture and find their way through it backwards into a snowy forest.[7] Unlike Edmund, Lucy and the others, we cannot go back, or thereafter return from that past when we are ready, and so the second characteristic of industrialization as a transformative process was and is its irrevocability.

The Industrial Revolution replaced small-scale local economies and societies where resources were limited and inflexible with much larger ones where they were moved around the world and within which they could, in theory, be accumulated limitlessly. Industrial economies were much richer than agricultural ones, though wealth remained unevenly spread. The principal repositories of value became, not food, but material culture, in particular money.

Industrialization transformed demography, and so (among other things) the social experience of space. In 1500 England and Wales had 2.5 million people; between 1650 and 1700 that figure paused below 5 million, dipping and then recovering. From 1750 the shape of the population graph changed completely, climbing steeply through 9 million (1800) to 20 million (1900), massive emigration notwithstanding. In the Netherlands a similar graph shape (increase, pause but in this case no dip, increase) took off exponentially, the trademark of the Industrial Revolution, fifty years later in 1800. The population of English-speaking North America went from 1.5 million in 1750 to 8 million in 1815, 15 million in 1835, and 35 million in 1865. The present population of the British Isles is almost 70 million, and of the world seven and a half billion, predicted to be nine billion by 2050.

For most people industrialization replaced rural with urban life. In 1550 the Netherlands was the most urbanized region in Europe; the Northern seven provinces, where agricultural land was poorer, the most urbanized part of that; and England and Wales conspicuously rural.[8] By the late seventeenth century London was the largest city in Europe and the second largest in the world (after Peking); and by the early nineteenth century Britain was the most urbanized country in the world. Thereafter came James Belich's booms, bangs and busts, New York, Chicago, Melbourne and points in between, a whole westward-moving urban percussion section drawing upon global migration.

Industrialization replaced the economic unit of the family farm (involving both genders and all ages) with that of the employer and wage labourer. This was part of a more general social atomization, replacing societies within which people had primarily identified as members of a group and which had communicated orally in shared social spaces, with ones where people also read privately and silently. Within the new phenomenon of urbanization emerged the individual. Societies which had bonded vertically, connecting persons of unlike social status in mutual relationships of service and protection, gave way to others connected horizontally, into associations of comparable economic interest and class.

This was a social reflection of the political and spatial arrangement of the mill or factory floor (hundreds or thousands of workers working and acting together). Informing factory production were the principles, first, of economy of scale (which required a mass market) and division of labour. Whereas previously a textile worker might have made a whole shirt, now many collaborated, each repeatedly completing one contributing task. This might be exceptionally boring. But it hugely sped up, and cheapened, production. Individuals alienated from the products of their own labour, which were the property of their employer, lost the ability to make a shirt. But they acquired the capacity to buy several. Previously farmers had planted at one time of the year, made tools at another, repaired clothing, put up a fence, harvested, cooked, haggled and sold. Now all of these tasks and many others became specialized and related within a larger, market-driven economic and social complex.

The Industrial Revolution profoundly altered the human relationship to nature, and to time. Communities that had united for self-protection against the night and the natural world were replaced by others by which the disappearing wilderness was valorized. Industrialization replaced the seasonal cycle and calendar with the factory clock. A working year which had had busy periods (harvest) and slower ones (winter) became more uniform and continuous. Experiences of time which had been cyclical became linear. Like all living things humans have a biological (circadian) clock synchronized to the rising and setting of the sun as the relationship of night to day changes across the seasons. In a pre-industrial rural world with limited technology (including artificial light) these cues packaged the most crucial information concerning optimal times for every type of leisure and work.[9] Now we function in an urban world of continuous activity, light and stimulation, including twenty-four-hour screen and phone time, and jet travel which can move people immediately from one season, climate and time zone to another.

Within the cultural space called Enlightenment adherence to tradition was replaced by acceptance of change accompanied, eventually, by belief in progress. Innovation became expected and ongoing. Enlightenment preceded industrial revolution. But like humanism before it, upon which it drew, it was a cultural product of European cities which registered these changes first, and which responded to other contemporaneous developments like the discovery of the New World and the development of science (natural philosophy) as well as of specific and related technology. In London in the early 1660s Thomas Sprat found 'the Genius of *Experimenting* is so much dispers'd, that . . . all places and corners are now busie, and warm about this Work; and we find many Noble Rarities to be every day given in, not onely by the hands of Learned and profess'd Philosophers; but from the shops of *Mechanicks*; from the Voyages of *Merchants*; from the Ploughs of *Husbandmen*; from the Fishponds, the Parks, the Gardens of *Gentlemen*'.[10] During and after industrialization this new urban world became the site for a series of experiments in (among other things) public health, medicine, transport and town planning.[11]

Industrialization replaced self-sufficiency with exchange, and pre-money or partly commercialized economies with ones where money was the medium of exchange. It replaced one primary economic resource, land, with another, labour. It altered the relationship of genders and families as well as of public political communities. It made geographically rooted communities into more mobile families and individuals. It homogenized (because it commercialized) culture and consumption.

In retrospect it is the longer-term consequences of the Industrial Revolution that are the most striking. Positively these include a huge increase in material wealth, as measured by GDP, and improvement in health, as marked by life expectancy. These have been accompanied by numerous beneficial developments in science, medicine and technology. Although it has been uneven this progress has been global, and has to date reduced disparities of wealth and health between countries and regions.[12]

On the other side of the ledger sit the dangerous and potentially catastrophic consequences of human population growth, industrialized agriculture, technological (including weapon) development and fossil fuel use. Attracting most attention is the warming climate; in the front line are the oceans:

Earth is poorly named. The ocean covers almost three quarters of the planet . . . Climate and weather systems depend on the temperature patterns of the ocean and its interactions with the atmosphere . . . The ocean stores more than nine-tenths of the heat trapped on Earth by greenhouse gas emissions . . . Greater concentrations of carbon dioxide in the water are making it more acidic . . . scientists expect almost all corals to be gone by 2050. By the middle of the century the ocean could contain more plastic than fish by weight.[13]

Like the benefits, these contemporary problems manifest on a global scale and include resource depletion, loss of biodiversity and species extinction, insecure and proliferating weapons of mass destruction, the absence of effective mechanisms of global government, increasing economic inequality within nations (and perhaps between generations), ageing populations and declining tax bases.

These are some features of the world we have gained and with them a new stratigraphic era: the Anthropocene.[14] Since all are products of human history, it has recently been argued that historians have a particular capacity and responsibility to inform public policy responses to them.[15] At the least these are developments which we might wish urgently to understand.

THE LIMITS OF PRE-INDUSTRIAL ECONOMIES

Why was the Industrial Revolution so unlikely? The most advanced early modern agricultural economies, in Europe, as in China, were dominated by grain. That meant wheat, barley, rye and oats in Europe and wheat or rice in China, alongside animal husbandry. In both places, particularly where served by waterborne transport (sea, rivers and canals), agriculture was becoming more specialized and market-oriented. Because grain yields were much higher in China, and its cultivation labour-intensive, China's population was greater, and its cities larger (until the eighteenth century). Nevertheless, in China, Europe and elsewhere, and whether or not agriculture was accompanied by trade in luxury goods, all such societies were strictly limited in what they could produce. They were limited by the available land area; by grain yields; by the impact of grain production upon soil fertility; by the (usually) annual cycle of the harvest; by the weather at harvest time; and by the perishability of agricultural produce.

Most early modern European economies north of the Mediterranean and south of the Arctic Circle grew grain. The annual yield of a grain of wheat varied between 3:1 and 10:1 – on average 6:1 or 7:1. This meagre product reflected the fact that grain depleted the soil of nutrients, in particular nitrogen. Fertility could be restored by leaving fields fallow, so that in much of Europe one field of every three was left unplanted each year, reinforcing the second inflexible limitation of this system: available land area. Another way of restoring or increasing fertility was manure. But in Europe manure required animals (Chinese and later European farmers used human waste); animals needed pasture, and land under pasture could not be used for growing grain.[16] In addition most animals could not be kept alive over the winter.

All agricultural economies were bound by such closed and interlocking circles of finite resources. The most important was the harvest. In a good year enough was harvested to set aside seed for the following year's planting, and to feed people through the year. But there was limited surplus beyond that, and little that could have been done with it even had there been. Ninety per cent of what an agricultural economy produced was food which, especially before refrigeration, was perishable. This was one reason the rhythms of agricultural economies were cyclical, devoted to maintaining continuity from year to year; not linear and cumulative, as industrial societies became able to be. Moreover, not all years were good, the annual outcome being at the mercy of climate and weather which lay outside human control. Thus one recent historian has asked whether the development of grain-based agriculture might not have been an evolutionary wrong turn, or form of imprisonment, assisting the predictable resourcing of an overseeing class while consigning the majority to toil, monotony and poverty.[17]

The limits of agricultural economies determined their population densities, long-term rises and falls of population occurring within strict boundaries imposed by relatively inelastic food resources. Likewise their limited urbanization, with 10.8 per cent of the European population living in towns of 5,000 people or more in 1600, and still only 13 per cent in 1800.[18] If there had been no surplus at all beyond the immediate needs of peasant farmers there would have been no European aristocracy, clergy, traders, manufacturers, lawyers or soldiers. Although such groups did exist in limited numbers, even the largest early modern towns and cities were small by modern standards. In 1550 the largest (Constantinople, Naples) had 100,000 people; by 1650 Paris and London each had four times that number, though the overall European urban population as a proportion of the total had barely changed.[19]

THE FIRST POST-AGRICULTURAL ECONOMY

Within such societies one way of adding to the prosperity of cities, as long as those cities could be fed, was to bring in 'rich trade' goods: precious metals, luxury products and foods, as also to develop manufactures and services. This happened in northern Italy – Venice, Florence, Genoa, Milan – and in southern Germany and the Netherlands. It could not in itself alter population levels: Spain and Italy, the primary regional recipients of New World silver, both suffered population declines in the seventeenth century, and everywhere in Europe outside the North Sea region (the Netherlands from the sixteenth century and Britain from the seventeenth) post-Black Death population recoveries had a ceiling.[20] The only way to raise the ceiling was to break through the resource limits of the grain-growing economy.

This meant increasing agricultural production, getting food from elsewhere, or finding some other way to breach those limits. None of these developments involved industrialization, but they do seem to have been indispensable preconditions for it. In addition they do seem to have occurred for the first time in the fifteenth- and sixteenth-century Netherlands. Following this process we need to bear in mind the overall relationship between agriculture, manufactures and trade. Manufactures and trade could not grow as sectors of the economy unless those engaged in these activities were fed. That usually involved urbanization, although an additional feature of economic development in the early modern western Netherlands was the growth of non-agricultural occupations and services in the countryside. Vibrant cities exerted a crucial economic influence as markets as well as pools of non-agricultural labour.[21] By 1500 the Netherlands had overtaken central and northern Italy as the most densely urbanized part of Europe. The largest cities (Antwerp, Bruges, Ghent) were in the south, but the highest proportion of urban dwellers as a percentage of the whole was in Holland. This epicentre of manufactures (especially textiles), rich trades and finance became the richest in the world. Moreover, the size of these cities, and of the Dutch population in general, more than doubled between 1500 and 1650, and maintained that population over the next hundred years.

So how were these towns and cities fed? Jan de Vries and Ad van der Woude commented: 'Dutch historical writing long placed agriculture in a subordinate position. This reflected the belief that the urban, trading economy of the Dutch Republic functioned independently from the agriculture of its hinterland and, hence, was unconstrained by the limitations of the rural economy. This is not our view.'[22] Just as 'in most pre-industrial economies agriculture dominated economic life', so in the early modern Netherlands also it must be understood first 'because of the integral part it played through interaction with commercial and industrial activity in creating the dynamic qualities of the seventeenth-century economy'.[23]

By the seventeenth century the city-centred subordination of Dutch rural life had been achieved. The countryside was

> . . . largely shaped from the city and in accordance with urban needs . . . the economic activities in rural areas (agriculture, forestry, truck farming, peat cutting . . .) . . . ownership structures . . . communication and transportation

(roads and canals), and water management in all its forms, including the supervision of dikes and dunes, transformed the Dutch countryside at a very early point into an integrated man-made landscape.[24]

This apparent inversion of the usual urban-rural relationship of dependence was one of many unique features of the Dutch Golden Age. But the 'man-made landscape' was a product of this uniqueness, not its cause. For its cause, De Vries is right to stress, we need to look to the dynamic quality of the landscape itself, beginning with its impact upon social structure. That, exceptionally, most peasants in late medieval Holland were free, and widely involved in decision-making, owed much to the challenges posed by the physical environment:

> In the sandy regions such as Drenthe and the Campine, the Frisian areas on the North Sea, and the newly reclaimed coastal areas, such as Holland and coastal Flanders . . . territorial lords . . . had to lure people from outside by granting them . . . freedom . . . in many of the coastal areas . . . the self-organisation of the rural population was . . . expressed in the context of water management . . . Here . . . free confederations were responsible . . . under the constant threat of flooding, necessitating co-operation and communal organisation.[25]

More broadly, in a pre-industrial agricultural economy the unique challenges facing agriculture in the northern and coastal provinces drove economic and social innovation. Throughout the medieval period these had inspired land reclamation, by which painstaking, expensive activity, at which technology the Dutch became the world's leaders, the amount of land available for agriculture was increased. Beyond this, however,

> [a] deterioration of the hydrographic situation in the peat zones of Holland . . . imposed a certain flight from agriculture in the fifteenth century, while the growth of towns had expanded the range of non-agricultural employments for rural dwellers throughout the region . . . The demographic expansion and new commercial possibilities that grew . . . from the end of the fifteenth century into the sixteenth triggered a forceful response in this rural society of 'petty commodity producers'.[26]

The most important of these new commercial possibilities was the bulk trade in grain. Alternative to the southern rich trades, which were Italian in origin, this became the basis of a new maritime and merchant culture centred in Amsterdam.[27] During the fifteenth century shortfalls in local grain production had been made up by one-off importations from Brabant and northern France.[28] By 1500, however, Amsterdam had turned to the Baltic to put this trade on a new footing. Soon 'not only the towns, but also the majority of the Dutch countryside were . . . dependent on grain imports'.[29] Holland was equipped to seize this opportunity by the extent of its shipping and other maritime infrastructure, a consequence in part of the North Sea fishery.[30] By the mid-sixteenth century the grain trade (now 'the mother trade') supplied not only domestic needs, but had become a lifeline for the cities of Iberia and Italy.

Thus if Dutch towns became 'unconstrained by the limits of the rural economy', that was made possible by the fishery and the grain trade. To this extent the basis for Dutch industrialization was laid, not by attempting to defeat the closed circle of low grain productivity, but by purchasing the grain elsewhere, from Polish nobles exploiting serfs working with an annual grain yield lower than that in Holland. Yet more importantly for the Anglo-Dutch-American process the grain trade made possible the spread and completion of an agricultural revolution informed by techniques pioneered in Flanders and Brabant as early as the fifteenth century involving 'cash crops or cattle breeding . . . [and] intensive horticulture which pointed to the virtues of deep digging, heavy fertilizing, culture and continuous weeding'.[31] Liberated from the rigidities of monocrop grain production (low fertility, need for fallow, limited and unpredictable yields), Dutch farmers could now produce whatever would fetch the best prices in rich urban markets.

One result was diversification, with huge increases in livestock, vegetables and market-garden produce, and dyestuffs for textiles. Another was development, by experimentation, of winter fodder crops which could not only keep animals alive over the winter, but also restore nitrogen to the soil. With these, increased manure from livestock, and the distribution upon fields and gardens of 'nightsoil' from towns and cities, the old limits of agricultural yield were breached. Although many of these techniques originated in the south of the country, it was in the coastal Northern Netherlands, especially Holland, that agricultural specialization spread fastest. This occurred in the context of a more general reorganization of the economy, rural as well as urban, in the direction of market-oriented and often maritime goods, skills and services.

It was this broader development of its hinterland which equipped Amsterdam to capitalize on the economic fall of Antwerp during the Revolt to become the seventeenth-century entrepot of all world trade, rich and bulk.[32] Both the grain trade and fishery, striking inventions in terms of their scale, and their impact across both rural and urban economies, entailed innovations in ship design (of the flyboat or *fluit*, and herring *busse*, respectively). In 1500 the Dutch had still been dependent upon Breton and Hanse shipbuilding. By 1610 their ship-building sector was the largest and most technically advanced in Europe.[33] These developments were unprecedented, partly because they were responses to a uniquely agriculturally challenged environment, drawing upon the equally unique maritime potential of that situation, between the Baltic and the Mediterranean, and at the intersection of rivers, canals and the sea.[34]

Thus if we ask why only the sixteenth-century Netherlands avoided the Malthusian trap of finite resources and so population stagnation into which Italy was once again falling, our answer begins in the countryside. The drivers of economic prosperity in the large cities of the Southern Netherlands were not new. Nor was industrial or mercantile development within cities. What permitted the sixteenth-century Dutch economy to grow and diversify on a state-wide scale was its liberation from the production and demographic limits of pre-industrial agriculture. Thus there are two reasons for beginning this account of Anglo-Dutch-American early modernity in the Dutch water world. One is that it was from this that there emerged, in the Northern Netherlands, the first post-agricultural, which is to say industrialized, economy. The other is that in all pre-industrial economies, in the Netherlands, Britain and else-where, the dominance of agriculture made it impossible to fundamentally change the economy without changing agriculture itself.

For 'the first modern economy', or industrialized state, the Baltic grain trade was crucial. For the subsequent Industrial Revolution, agricultural revo-lution would be indispensable. The sixteenth-century Netherlands supported its growing population in cities and countryside by the two together, in inter-action. This was paid for by the world's richest economy, trading with and supplying manufactures and services to Europe and the world.

WHY DID THE INDUSTRIAL REVOLUTION
FIRST OCCUR IN BRITAIN?

By the 1670s, 40 per cent of Dutch people worked in agriculture, 32 per cent in manufacturing and 28 per cent in services, including trade and shipping.[35] But this modernizing process stopped short of what Tony Wrigley called exponential growth – of the kind which later occurred in Britain, and which rewrote the rules of industrialization as understood by Adam Smith as comprehensively as the agricultural revolution did those of traditional farming. One of those rules was demographic. By 1800 Britain was on a path of unprecedented population growth. It had become the epicentre of European urbanization and there had been a transformation in the size of the largest cities. Across England and Scotland the changing economy had acquired an ability to feed millions of people not engaged directly in agriculture.

This was a result, first, of industrialization and its contexts, including empire, financial and mercantile infrastructure, and the military fiscal state. With roots in the late sixteenth and early seventeenth centuries, this had taken particular hold since the revolution of 1649. It was partly anchored, as in the Netherlands, in a developing social world of domestic consumption.[36] The subsequent Industrial Revolution, involving a transformation in the scale of manufacturing, began in about 1780. Like the Dutch grain trade and fishery, and the transformation of Dutch agriculture, it occurred in response to market opportunities. Like them it called forth technological innovation as the spinning jenny transformed textile manufacturing, and the steam engine steelmaking. As in the Dutch case it required an elaborate infrastructure of water transport, in this case to link energy and raw materials to factories and to move finished goods to market. By the nineteenth century Britain was the dominant maritime economy and empire; its rivers were connected by canals, and its cities by the ocean, to each other and the world.

Yet why did the first Industrial Revolution occur in Britain? To put it differently, why did 'the Netherlands ... not lead Europe into an Industrial Revolution?'[37] In fact they did lead Europe towards that outcome. Without the example of Dutch modernizations in agriculture, manufactures, trade and shipping, politics, culture and political economy, the first Industrial Revolution would not have occurred. But it occurred in Britain, rather than elsewhere, because it was the culmination of an Anglo-Dutch-American process.

It was not until after 1750 that large British cities developed outside London. Before then what was crucial was the market demand, and global empire, created by one super-city. The growth of early modern London was without pre-modern precedent: from 50,000 people in 1550 to 125,000 in 1603, 550,000 in 1700 and one million by 1800. By 1700 one of Europe's small to medium-sized kingdoms hosted its largest city. Fernand Braudel exclaimed:

> How can one begin to describe the role played by London in making Britain great? The capital city created and directed England from start to finish. London's outsize dimensions meant that other cities hardly began to exist as regional capitals . . . In no other western country, as Arnold Toynbee remarked, did one city so completely eclipse the rest.[38]

Within the British Isles, London was twenty times the size of the next largest town.[39] It was also, like the economies of Antwerp and Amsterdam, supranational in scope. Particularly after 1660 it became a magnet for the 'huge streams of skilled people that were on the road in west and central Europe between c.1570 and 1715'.[40] By 1700 London was an Atlantic and global phenomenon, drawing on the economic resources, markets and migrants of France, the Netherlands, Asia, the Caribbean and North America.[41] When its only contemporary rival for size, Paris, got to 450,000, it stopped growing: it had reached the limits of the pre-industrial urban possible. How did London go beyond these cities?

The answer is partly because it was fed.[42] During the sixteenth century London's consumption of grain tripled and then during the seventeenth century it tripled again. In times of dearth grain was imported, mainly from the Baltic, supplied by Hanseatic merchants in 1549 and by Dutch ones in the early seventeenth century. But, overwhelmingly, London's grain supply was domestic and, after 1660, when the nation's population increase stopped for half a century, there emerged a large-scale export trade in grain for the first time.[43]

London was fed because throughout the seventeenth century England (first the South-East, then the South, West Country and Midlands) had been transforming its agriculture, mainly by introducing Dutch techniques: fodder crops, systems of rotation eliminating fallow, market gardening, intensive animal husbandry, water meadows, and land reclamation in the Fens.[44] In 1699 John Evelyn reported triumphantly to the Royal Society that there were now enough English-grown ingredients to make a salad.[45] During the same decade Londoners consumed 88,400 beef cattle and 600,000 sheep each year (and, in 1725, 187,000 swine, 52,000 sucking pigs, 14,750,000 mackerel and 16,366,000 pounds of cheese).[46] Without the Dutch agricultural revolution there would have been no English agricultural revolution, or certainly not the one which occurred. Without the English agricultural revolution the spectacular growth of London could not have been sustained. Without supersize London there might have been no revolutionary modernization of the English state, economy and empire.

However, apart from the market demand, investment wealth, financial expertise, non-agricultural labour resources and international mercantile infrastructure created by London three other factors contributed to the Industrial Revolution in Britain. Had this not been the case it should have occurred in the Netherlands first, where the major cities collectively had all of these things to a similar degree. One was natural resources, especially of energy. The primary Dutch energy resources, aside from human and animal power, were peat, wind and water. Moreover, almost all the materials for its manufactures were imported. Britain, by contrast, had metal (tin, lead, iron ore) wood, coal (which burned hotter than peat), grain and wool. Explaining why the Industrial Revolution occurred in Britain, Tony Wrigley emphasized this energy gap, with Ken Pomeranz adding that when its own coal and timber became depleted Britain was able to import them (along with fish, sugar and cotton) from colonial America. Thus although English economic development started later than Dutch, Britain had resources, including of land and people, on a different scale.[47] Algernon Sidney made this prediction as early as 1665:

[If] Holland, of all Europe the most unwholesome, unpleasant, unprovided, of all things requisite to the life of man; yet through good government and liberty of traffic so rich, powerful and prosperous that no state in Europe dares singly contest with it . . . England, if so governed, may promise itself incomparably more, abounding in all they want . . . apprehending no opposition but that of the Stuart family.[48]

The second precondition of the Industrial Revolution, following completion of the Anglo-Dutch Revolution of 1649–1702, was a centralized military-fiscal and imperial power on a scale with which the United Provinces (and eventually France) could not compete. During the eighteenth century 'the expansion of long-distance trade required . . . a strong, highly centralized and militarized state, and the minimum size – in area, population and wealth . . . grew larger with each passing century'.[49]

Yet the most important factor was the third. This was a demand for manufactured products even more demographically dynamic than the Dutch urban market which had created the Baltic grain trade, protected by that 'militarised power' from European competition. Pomeranz pointed out that Britain's tropical plantation colonies furnished a captive market for British exports, including as they did a slave population of half a million.[50] Yet such plantation agriculture was not unique to Britain. However, alongside European empires for the extraction of mineral and agricultural resources, for trade, and for the disposal of convicts, only Britain established colonies, in Ireland and North America, for the settlement of people and culture. By the eighteenth century only in British North America – not the Dutch East Indies, or Spanish America, or the Caribbean – had there emerged a rapidly expanding European settler population.

This owed less to design than to a climate free of tropical mosquito-borne diseases. In 1700 the population of British America was 300,000. By the time of their Declaration of Independence in 1776 the thirteen colonies had two and a half million people, an almost tenfold increase. By 1798, despite independence, Britain's American colonies and former colonies were buying 57 per cent of its manufactured output (furniture, ships, textiles, tools and machinery, guns, luxury goods, household stuff, books, food and drink). The same colonies were supplying 32 per cent of its imports (timber, fish, sugar, tobacco, skins and furs, coal and iron ore, cotton).[51] The thirteen colonies shared with the mother country a language, history, culture and tastes which could not be satisfied by any other supplier. But more importantly this demographically explosive captive market had been created a century and a half earlier by a militarily protected mercantilist system anchored in the Navigation Acts, the product of an English republican revolution shaped by emulation of the Dutch.[52]

Thus there is a twofold answer to the question: why did the first Industrial Revolution occur in Britain? To a considerable extent England acquired its agricultural revolution, and its initial London-based manufacturing and commercial economy, by importing and adapting Dutch techniques. This was assisted by the arrival of economic migrants and Protestant refugees. These developments did not occur in China or France because they did not share this economically dynamic and culturally cohesive North Sea space, particularly after the Revocation of the Edict of Nantes (1685).

Secondly, unlike both France and the United Provinces, Britain created a mass colonial market for its manufactures. This was a consequence not only of the distinct evolution of one part of its empire, but also of the seventeenth-century Anglo-Dutch revolution. It was in North America that there emerged the socially egalitarian, religiously tolerant, Protestant republic which Dutch-inspired English republicans had attempted to found in their own country in 1649. Protected by trade legislation developed in response to Dutch competition, this colonial market helped to create a second maritime geography of invention, now spanning the Atlantic rather than just the Baltic and North Sea.

Crucial to both of these developments was not only geographic proximity, or archipelagic contiguity achieved by mastery of maritime transport and trade. As important was the shared religion of Calvinist-dominated Protestantism in an age of Counter-Reformation. This furnished the basis for Anglo-Dutch military co-operation against Spain in 1585 and against France from 1689. It underpinned a series of migrations between 1560 and 1780 across both the North Sea (in both directions) and the Atlantic. It was because Anglo-Dutch-American early modernity was a cultural process that what turned out to be crucial about European global empires for the Industrial Revolution was less the resources they yielded than their cultural behaviour, in this case their capacity to consume.

Writing in 1584 Richard Hakluyt had argued that North American plantations would serve 'for utterance of . . . great quantitie of the commodities of our Realme'. In this he had in mind the opportunity to employ any English poor 'such as by any kinde of infirmitie cannot pass the seas thither . . . in making of a thousand trifling thinges . . . [for] the savages', as well as 'woollen clothe, their Contrie being colde'.[53] But he used far more space describing (largely imaginary) colonial resources awaiting exploitation. He gave no sign of imagining a demographic revolution in English-speaking North America sufficient to change the very nature of the economy and society whose indefatigable servant he was.

⟞⊷⊶⊷⟝

CHAPTER THREE

A GEOGRAPHY OF INVENTION, 1500–1600

If we trace commerce in its progress through TYRE, SYRACUSE, CARTHAGE, VENICE, FLORENCE, GENOA, ANTWERP, HOLLAND, ENGLAND etc, we shall always find it to have fixed its seat in free governments. The three greatest trading towns now in the world are LONDON, AMSTERDAM, and HAMBURGH; all free cities, and protestant cities; that is, enjoying a double liberty.

David Hume, 'Of Civil Liberty'[1]

'The sea is something the land can never be, Madame,' Otto says. 'No patch stays the same.'

Jessie Burton, *The Miniaturist*

THE ATLANTIC NORTH-WEST

If early modern England and the Netherlands shared a North Sea regional space, over this period its role and importance were transformed. In 1500 the locus of European economic and political power, and culture, was the Mediterranean. By the eighteenth century, David Hume, who grew up near Berwick-upon-Tweed, looking out over 'the German ocean', could associate London with Amsterdam and Hamburg at the apex of a progressive history of commerce and liberty.[2] In 1550 London was small and economically backward. An English society of villages and aristocratic country houses contrasted sharply with a precociously urbanized Netherlands replete with merchants (including resident English merchants), manufacturers and mariners. Yet as Amsterdam became rich by connecting the maritime trading practices of the Hanse towns with the urban culture of Flanders, so over the following century and a half London too would be transformed by a comparable and connected regional dynamic.[3] By 1700 it was a world city, 'home to thousands of Protestant immigrants from Western Europe, Scots and Irish, Jews and Turks, Africans both slave and free, Americans and Asians'.[4]

How much of the transformational force of Anglo-Dutch-American early modernity derived from the rise of Europe's north-west? Hume's history described two broader reorientations of wealth and power. The first was from south to north (from 'VENICE [to] . . . HOLLAND') and the second from east to west (from 'TYRE, SYRACUSE [to] . . . ENGLAND').[5] Contextualizing both was a larger transformation of Europe's place in the world. Before the early modern period, among world civilizations Western Europe was unremarkable. In population, wealth, culture and technology it was inferior to China and in some respects to the Islamic world of the Near East. Comprising a complex of peninsulas and their surrounding islands at the western edge of Eurasia, it was smaller than the Ottoman, Chinese and perhaps Incan Empires, and unlike them all it was politically divided.

Two and a half centuries later Europeans bestrode the globe.[6] They held huge swathes of territory in Latin America, North America, the East and West 'Indies', North-East Asia, India, Africa and the Pacific. The greatest expansions were east by Russia (beginning with the conquest of Sibir in 1580), and west by the Atlantic powers Portugal, Spain, France, the United Provinces, Britain and Denmark. With the exception of Russia, this was an achievement of European seafaring, and when it reached the Pacific, Russia also became a maritime power. This was not, initially at least, because of superior European maritime know-how.

Much of the technology underpinning the rise of early modern Europe, including printing, navigation and gunpowder, developed in China first. Yet in China long-range voyaging was suppressed, as was printing in Constantinople. These were successful political attempts to control the movement of people and of ideas. In Europe there was no central power capable of exercising such control, even had the will existed to do so. On the contrary, despite strenuous attempts to shield valuable information from rivals, in Europe new developments and discoveries tended to unleash a field of competitive response. As a result, not only was the early modern acquisition of global empire the work of many powers, rather than one. Political and (from 1517) religious competition were primary motors of the process, driving it faster and further than would otherwise have been the case.

This was the European political geography of invention, upon which the Anglo-Dutch-American process would draw. Historians of the economic divergence of early modern Europe from East Asia have emphasized the importance of the competitive, non-centralized institutional structures of European cities and states. Competition to attract merchants and trade gave European cities an edge over those of the Middle East and China.[7] In Renaissance Italy some city-states were equipped with the advanced legal, political and moral claims of republican civic humanism. Both contributed to what Jan Luiten van Zanden has called a constitutionalized, ' "bottom-up" process of institution building'.[8] With that addition of Protestantism which Hume saw as conferring a second layer of freedom, these were developments upon which the cities of the North Sea region, and therefore the Dutch, English and American republics in turn, were able to build.[9]

Helping to drive the Iberian phase of European global discovery had been the Ottoman conquest of Constantinople and then the Balkans. Central European cities like Venice and Vienna found themselves on the Eastern frontier. This blocked (in particular Venetian) access to Eastern luxury goods via the Levant and Silk Road.[10] In 1488 Bartolomeu Dias rounded the Cape of Good Hope and between 1497 and 1499 made a return voyage between Lisbon and India. This was a navigational revolution to which Portugal's Iberian rival Spain had to respond. It began with conquest of the Canary Islands, followed by the extraordinary first voyage west from there by Christopher Columbus in 1492, seeking a shorter route to East Asia. Spain's first response to Ottoman contestation of the Mediterranean had been the Reconquista of Islamic southern Spain, including Granada. This established the pattern of military expansion, economic exploitation and conversion to Christianity carried into the New World by the conquistadors. Hernán Cortés, who seized the Aztec Empire governed by Montezuma in 1519 with a few hundred men, was a veteran of the Reconquista who referred to Aztec temples as 'mosques'.[11]

Another factor informing Europe's global expansion from 1500 may have been the demographic impact of the mid-fifteenth-century Black Death. One consequence of the catastrophic 50 per cent population loss was an improvement for the survivors in the level of available food resources and an increased demand for consumer goods. 'This demand may very well . . . have contributed to the increasing number of European trading voyages across the world's oceans in the fifteenth, sixteenth and seventeenth centuries.'[12] Thereafter Europe's transformed understanding of the world ushered in a new era in the history of ideas. Columbus, Amerigo Vespucci and others demonstrated that practical experience could yield new knowledge. According to one historian, this 'discovery of discovery . . . the assumption that there are discoveries to be made . . . transformed the world, for it . . . made modern science and technology possible'.[13]

The same developments laid the basis for a loss of European economic leadership by the Mediterranean cities. As the Atlantic became a gateway to both the East and West Indies, during the second half of the sixteenth century a second stage of empire building began in the United Provinces, England/ Britain and France. This contributed to early modern Europe's 'little divergence', entailing a transfer of economic primacy from Venice and Florence to Antwerp and then Amsterdam, followed by London. In 1500 the largest cities in Europe (Constantinople, Naples, Venice, Milan, Córdoba, Seville) had all been Mediterranean. By 1700 these had been eclipsed by London and Paris, with populations of 550,000 and 450,000 respectively. In the next rank, at about 200,000 inhabitants, Constantinople and Naples were joined by Amsterdam.

Within Atlantic Europe, some historians have ascribed the shift in power and wealth from south to north to political factors:

Given that the Genoese, Portuguese and Spanish had pioneered these overseas ventures, it might be expected that they would derive the greatest benefits from them . . . Nevertheless, it was the ports of the southern North Sea – Antwerp, Amsterdam and London . . . that eventually drove the greater trade . . . In Holland and Britain, political checks on rulers were sufficient to ensure that they were unable to appropriate the bulk of the gains from trade, with the result that mercantile capitalism thrived . . . [whereas] In Spain and Portugal . . . rulers were . . . sufficiently strong to exploit these opportunities themselves and prevent a strong merchant class from constraining their powers to appropriate.[14]

This was one factor which made the Dutch Revolt of 1566 to 1648 a hinge upon which early modern European history turned. The other was religion. Max Weber wondered whether the rise of the early modern North Atlantic, and so of capitalism, could be understood as an effect of Protestant theology and manners. Certainly at the heart of what became a protracted military struggle between Northern Dutch merchants and the Spanish Crown was a contest between Counter-Reformation and Calvinism. Spain could not accept the spread of heresy within the Netherlands but could not eradicate it there either. One reason for this was that Spain's global empire had become so enormous that with early modern technology and communications it was almost impossible to govern and defend. It was partly the strategic position of the Netherlands on the northern border of its traditional rival France which meant that Spain could not let it go. But that also made it difficult to supply with troops – either overland or by sea. Above all Spain could never give the Netherlands its undivided military attention because it had to defend its Mediterranean heartland against Ottoman power.[15]

Even so the Revolt had almost been crushed, in 1585, when England entered the war, prompting the (for Spain) calamitous descent of the Armada. This, given the extent of the Elizabethan government's unpreparedness, could have turned out very differently. As Daniel Defoe wrote later:

> I have heard that when the *Spanish Armada* in 1588 was . . . by the meer hand of Providence . . . *More than our* Opposition dispers'd [and] scatter'd . . . Q. *Elizabeth* was often heard to say, that *had they enter'd the mouth of the Thames*, with 32,000 Men of the best Troops the World ever saw *England must have submitted*, and she had been undone.[16]

These are all reasons for seeing the rise of the North Sea economies as having been contingent rather than inevitable. As it turned out, pressed by the Ottomans and goaded by Portugal, Spain conquered the Americas but could not handle North European Protestantism as well. Put another way, the Reconquista succeeded within Iberia and spawned a powerful follow-up on the other side of the Atlantic, but it did not succeed in the Netherlands. While that demonstrated that even Spanish power had its limits, it also had something to do with the nature of the adversary Spain here faced.

48

One challenge was the complex of rivers, islands and canals which separated the Northern Netherlands from the South and gave the rebels sanctuary in and access to the ocean. The regional water world which connected Holland and Zeeland to England also sheltered them from Spain. Another problem was the exceptional economic prosperity of the Netherlands, even before the Revolt. That these cities were the richest in the empire fed both the Revolt and its savage repression. Both activated the resistance of a Calvinist international connecting France, southern Germany, the Netherlands, England and Scotland. A final difficulty for Spain was the impact of the military struggle in multiplying the rebel republic's prosperity and ingenuity. The emergency circumstances of wartime accelerated a process of invention already set in train by the agricultural challenges of the landscape.

THE DUTCH WATER WORLD

In the Netherlands three great rivers, the Scheldt, Maas and Rhine, converged into a single delta. To their south, Antwerp, Ghent and Brussels were emporia of commerce, and of manufactures, surrounded by intensively cultivated farmland. North of the rivers the economy of Amsterdam was dominated by the bulk trades (timber and grain) and the fisheries, with the rural population involved, alongside agriculture, in peat cutting, freight shipping, the digging of canals and building of dykes.[17] While Venice in 1450 had about 300 ships, 'by the 1560s, Holland . . . is estimated to have had some 1,800 seagoing ships, around 500 of which were based in Amsterdam . . . the great majority used for voyages to the Baltic, Norway, or Western France or Portugal'.[18]

The seven provinces north of the rivers had always been more independent of the south-centred government, and were also freer of seigneurial rule. Jan de Vries and Ad van der Woude describe 'a tangle of small rivers and a profusion of sea arms and lakes, giving the region an amphibious character'.[19] Andrew Marvell joked about 'these *Half-anders*, half wet, and half dry', 'their *Mermaids*, with their tails of fish', and he linked this hybridity to a related confusion in religious and economic affairs: 'That *Bank of Conscience*, where not one so strange/Opinion, but finds Credit and Exchange.'[20]

Sir William Temple wondered whether the Low Countries had been 'level'd to what we see, by the Sea's breaking in and continuing long upon the Land;

since recovered by its recess, and with the help of Industry.'[21] This not only made the land 'flat like the Sea in a calm', but

> ... to consider the great Rivers, and the strange number of Canals that are found in this Province [Holland], and do not only lead to every great Town, but almost to every Village, and every Farm-House in the Countrey; and the infinity of Sails that are seen every where coursing up and down upon them; One would imagine the Water to have shar'd with the Land; and the people that live in Boats, to hold some proportion with those that live in Houses.[22]

The country was so flat, and the canals were so ubiquitous, that looking across it produced the illusion of sails moving up and down the land. '[T]his is one great advantage towards Trade, which is natural to the Scituation . . . the . . . level and softness of the Soil, which makes the cutting of Canals so easie work as to be attempted almost by every private man.'[23] Elsewhere in Temple's account water appeared as 'Frosts', 'Waves' ('the violent Rage of the Waters breaking in that way'), rain, flood ('the whole Countrey at that season seems to lye under water, which in Spring is driven out . . . by Mills'), 'Fog and Mist'.[24] 'The extream moisture of the Air . . . [making] all Metals apt to rust, and Wood to mould' set the Dutch, 'by continual pains of rubbing and scouring, to seek a prevention or cure', resulting in 'the brightness and cleanness . . . in their Houses'.[25] The Dutch scraped and swabbed their cities as sailors did a ship.

Defence of this environment against the ocean involved dykes ('They have lately found the common Sea-weed to be the best Material for these Digues'), watermills and windmills.[26] Thomas Scott, an English Protestant living in Utrecht explained:

> The Sea lyes continually raging upon their Coasts in such a manner, as if it would hourly eate them up . . . yet they keepe out this strong enemie at the armes end by art and industrie . . . it is incredible what paines they take, setting a kind of long grasse upon the . . . barren sands, as curiously and carefully, as wee set flowers and hearbes in our gardens: which grasse once getting root, bindes the earth together, that the winde cannot readily come

to blow it away, and teacheth them by the like combination to turne their weaknesse into . . . strength.[27]

From idleness the sea extracted diligence; from the vice of 'privacie', interdependence and community. Dutch historians still locate 'the cooperation essential to water management, at the heart of a particular kind of egalitarian and cooperative society'.[28] Indeed the Dutch made these elements their allies:

> But see what profit they make of this Adversarie . . . these waters worke for them continually as faithfull servants, conveying their carriages . . . to and fro, in a cheape, easie, and safe manner . . . Nay not only the water, but the winde also is their journeyman, and labours continually for them by Mils and other Engines; some pumping and forcing the waters out of their surrounded pastures; some pressing oyles, others bearing flaxe, hempe, copper; some grinding corn, others spice; some making paper, others sawing timber; and briefly, neither man, woman, or child, neither sea nor land, neither water nor winde suffered to be idle.[29]

The struggle with water had equipped the country to withstand the subsequent inundation of the Spanish Inquisition. 'Thus wee see how this people maintaine their owne, both against the King of *Spaine* and the Ocean.'[30] The Revolt was punctuated by storms, floods and the collapsing of sea defences, resulting in hundreds or thousands of casualties.[31]

Thus in the north water set the Dutch in motion, imposing an unending cycle of management and response.[32] After drainage, then subsidence, and then improved drainage, requiring innovation, there would come a 'point [where] . . . residents faced the choice of [more] innovation or emigration'. Technological results included dykes, polders, pumps, and windmills which could be rotated to face any wind.[33] This landscape had 'a structure of unusual plasticity . . . The physical features of the northern Netherlands . . . exhibited a dynamism that is both unusual and fascinating.'[34] Such ingenuity and effort notwithstanding, 'on the subsiding soil of Holland, arable cultivation became steadily more problematic . . . Much of this land . . . supported fowlers and fishermen more readily than farmers.'[35] Fertility was constantly threatened by salinity. Thus the Northern provinces were distinguished within the Low Countries by the relative poverty, and decline, of their agricultural resources.

Yet in the same element lay opportunity, most obviously in the form of transport, inland and maritime. As Sir William Temple observed, 'one Horse shall draw in a Boat more than fifty can do by Cart'. Dutch rivers offered trade access deep into German-speaking Europe. Canals connected villages, towns, rivers and the sea. By the seventeenth century the republic had an internal system of transport including horse-drawn-barge canals carrying 30,000 passengers a month between Haarlem and Amsterdam.[36] The location of the North Sea between the Baltic, Atlantic and Mediterranean gave the Dutch an advantage over both Hanse traders to the north and French and Portuguese ones to the south.[37] This was key to development both of the bulk trades and the fishery. Waterborne (including river) transport was also essential to the southern rich trades connecting Germany, England and the Mediterranean, although 54 per cent of the exports of Antwerp, which on the eve of the Revolt accounted for 75 per cent of the total exports of the Low Countries by value, departed overland.[38]

A NEW TYPE OF EUROPEAN ECONOMY

Arising from these circumstances, the Baltic grain trade was the crucial innovation. In addition to easing demographic constraints in both countryside and cities it enabled the development of specialized, market-oriented agriculture. In the process it underpinned the rise of Amsterdam. Without the bulk trades the Dutch economy might have remained merely a second northern Italy, a pocket of rich trade and manufacturing cities surrounded by productive agriculture. Even with the conquest of the Dutch East Indies, Amsterdam might only have combined the achievement of Venice with that of Portugal. But neither Italy nor Portugal inhabited the Dutch water world. Creating the bulk trades required new types of ship, shipbuilding and materials mostly from the Baltic, a deep well of maritime manpower, waterborne transport networks and mercantile networking, and strong municipal communities free of central government interference. English observers ascribed Dutch success to 'The Hollanders undermasting and sailing . . . with so few men . . . such of their Shipping as carry cheap and gross Goods . . . whose sale doth not depend much upon

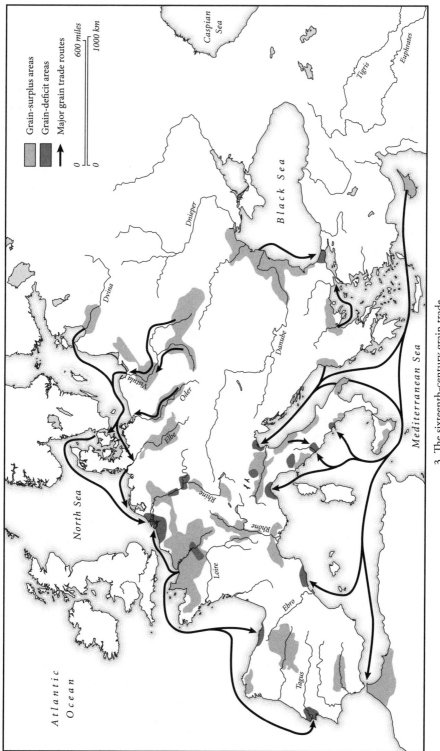

3. The sixteenth-century grain trade.

Season.'[39] All of this drew upon centuries of interaction with the north-western seaboard.

Specifically the bulk trades developed by adaptation of the practices of the Hanse towns. Grain and fish were staples of the medieval Hanseatic trade connecting the Baltic and North Sea.[40] Dutch traders first broke into the Hanseatic monopoly by offering merchants in the Hanse cities herring, salt and woollen cloth on a scale and at a price made possible by the economy of scale of the herring *busses*. In exchange, from 1450, cheap grain was available from the German and Polish lands east of the Elbe. Over time this proved capable of replacing existing imports from northern France 'provided transport costs were pared to a minimum . . . As the western demand for Baltic grain grew, exporters in the several Hanse cities found themselves depending increasingly on the Hollanders to provide low-cost shipping capacity. Consequently, these merchants evaded and ignored the official policies of the Hanse and of its leading center, Lubeck.'[41]

It was on the basis of its success in this commercial struggle that Amsterdam emerged by the mid-sixteenth century as the leading commercial centre of the Northern Netherlands.[42] In the process the *fluitschip* – a lightly crewed, unarmed, grain-carrying barge which adapted the *hulk* to the needs of the Baltic trade – emerged from 'a long chain of minor refinements carried out by shipbuilders relatively free of guild restrictions or government intervention'.[43] Once established the trade grew extraordinarily: grain imports from the Baltic in 1460 totalled 6 million kilograms; in 1500, 20 million kilograms; and in 1560, 110 million kilograms.[44] Driving this in the first place was the market furnished by the prosperous, growing and exceptionally urbanized Netherlands. Then merchants began carrying grain to Iberian and Italian cities in exchange for rich trade commodities. Historians have contrasted Amsterdam's management of this trade 'with . . . Bruges and Antwerp, cities which . . . had little shipping of their own, and whose fame as trading emporia rested not so much on the active trade of their citizens as on their function as staples and markets for foreign merchants'.[45]

In several ways the grain trade leveraged the North Sea fishery. By the early seventeenth century this had a comparable annual value to the English textile trade. It deployed 250 herring *busses* (manned by 3,000 men) in 1470; and 500 by 1560.[46] Supporting what the English naval commander William

Monson called this 'Golden mine', building upon 'their long travels, their excessive paines . . . their ingenious inventions . . . [and] our ffish' was a medieval migration of the richest herring ground from the Hanse-dominated Baltic to the North Sea.[47] The fishery combined the technology of salting the catch on ship ('pickling') with the annual location by 'well nigh 20000 [sic] ffishing vessels' of 'ye scull of the Herrings like a Hound that pursues the Head of a Dear in hunting', to their sale 'esteemed as a precious food, in all parts of Europe and that the return thereof giveth them means . . . in maintaining their inestimate war against so great and potent an Enemie as the King of Spaine'.[48]

By liberating the Netherlands from the limits of low-yield grain production the grain trade facilitated an agricultural revolution entailing an increase in livestock which (in addition to meat, butter, cheese and hides) had a dramatic impact on soil fertility. Dutch farmers grew market-garden produce, including vegetables, fruit and flowers; flax, dyestuffs and hops for the textile and brewing industries; and fodder crops – turnips, clover, pulses and legumes – which both kept animals alive over the winter and returned nitrogen to the soil, eliminating the need for fallow.[49] Vibrant agriculture supported the growth of urban staples such as textile processing, brewing, porcelain making, the production and finishing of luxury goods, and the 'rich trades' in fruit, wine, silver, silk, sugar and spices from the Levant, Iberia, Italy and East Asia. The cities of the southern Netherlands became European leaders in mercantile processing and international and local financial services. By 1560 Antwerp anchored the most developed fiscal and trading economy in Europe, providing services to and drawing resources – raw materials, labour, skills and money – from a far wider area.[50]

By comparison to the big cities of Flanders and Brabant the towns of Holland were smaller and, importantly, of similar size. Although in the north, Holland was unarguably dominant, within it no one town had pre-eminence. Thus Temple remarked that the 'Lake of fresh water . . . by the name of *Harlem Maer*' might easily be drained for agriculture but never would be, with Leiden depending on it for fresh water, and Amsterdam being determined that Leiden should remain cut off from the Rhine, and so from 'Maritime Trade'.[51] On the eve of the Revolt the Northern Netherlands, and Holland in particular, were distinguished both by their high overall urbanization and their cohesiveness, since no one town controlled the grain trade or the fisheries.[52]

THE DUTCH REVOLT

As the precocious economy of the Netherlands made it a political prize, so this did not make it easy to rule. 'Anyone hoping to govern the Low Countries successfully . . . had to win the confidence of the urban patriciate and persuade them to open their purse strings.'[53] Revolts in 1477 and in the early 1490s had produced demands for recognition of the constitutional rights of the States-General and of the provincial States.[54] However, with the absorption of the Low Countries into the Habsburg Empire came their fiscal exploitation in the Habsburg struggle against France. The Crown's exactions developed dramatically during the 1540s and 1550s, drawing upon those advanced mechanisms of taxation and public credit (including excise and 'renten', or government bonds) guaranteed by these representative institutions and later to inform England's own seventeenth-century financial revolution.[55]

Until the accession of Philip II in 1555 this situation was being managed by a ruler, his father Charles V, born in Ghent, who understood Netherlandish culture and spoke the language. Thereafter, however, and even following the peace of Cateau-Cambresis with France in 1558, an unheard-of demand for three million guilders was made by an absentee, acting through a regent, Philip's sister the Duchess of Parma. Sir William Temple recorded:

> Philip, a Spaniard born, retaining . . . the Severeness and Gravity of the Nation, which the *Flemings* call'd Reservedness and Pride; conferring the Offices of his House . . . upon *Spaniards*, and thereby introducing their Customs, Habit and Language into the Court of *Flanders*; continuing after the Peace . . . the Demand of Supplies from the States which the War had made necessary . . . He soon left off being lov'd, and began to be fear'd.[56]

Into this powder keg fell a religious spark: 'the Wars of Religion, breaking out in *France*, drew great numbers of *Calvinists* into all those parts of the *Low-Countries* that confine upon *France* . . . and the Admiration of their Zeal . . . and . . . Compassion of their Sufferings . . . gain'd them every Day many Proselytes . . . This made work for the *Inquisition*.'[57] In April 1566 two hundred noblemen petitioned against the Inquisition as an assault upon 'all freedom' and an instrument of 'slavery'.[58] This was followed – as later would be the comparable Scots National Covenant (1638) – by the mass gathering of signatures, so-called hedge-preaching, and popular iconoclasm. This uprising was confronted head on by the Duke of Alva, whose Council of Troubles apprehended and sentenced 9,000 people between 1567 and 1568, executing over a thousand, and whose troops slaughtered the rebel army in July 1568. Thereafter occupying Spanish troops 'treated all Netherlanders as heretics'.[59] Imposition in the same year of sweeping new taxes, including the hated 'tenth penny', consolidated the motives informing the Revolt.[60]

The Duke of Alva's crackdown sounded like a gunshot across Protestant Europe. It produced 60,000 refugees, part of an ongoing displacement of people from France and Germany to the Netherlands, from the southern Netherlands to the north, and from the Netherlands to England and Scotland. There followed a regional war for the freedom of the Netherlands, a global war for the integrity of the Spanish Empire, and a European civil war between Reformation and Counter-Reformation. The most important military response to Alva's recovery of Flanders came in 1572, the year also of the Massacre of Protestants on St Bartholomew's Eve in Paris and elsewhere in France. This, with significant English support, was the landing of the Sea Beggars, who captured Brill and then Flushing in Zeeland, emboldening other towns to the north in Holland (Haarlem, Leiden, Dordrecht) to rebel.

Now the war re-centred within the Anglo-Dutch water world. With Amsterdam and Utrecht in loyalist hands, Alva responded with massacres in Mechelen, Zutphen and Naarden, where after the city was stormed the population was put to death.[61] In 1576, however, Spanish finances collapsed and troops sacked Antwerp (the 'Spanish fury'). Spanish power in the south imploded, while the rebels signed the Treaty of Utrecht in 1579, until a recovery led by the Duke of Parma culminated in the recapture of Antwerp in 1585. The leader of the Revolt, the Prince of Orange, retreated from Brabant to Delft in Holland in 1583, and the following year he was assassinated.

In the face of a resurgent Spain, leadership of the Revolt fell to Holland and began to acquire a distinctively republican character. The years 1584–9 saw a desperate struggle for survival by the rebel federation against Parma in the south and east. In 1584 the rebels asked Elizabeth I to become sovereign, and although she refused, England entered the war in 1585. Then, from 1590, the military situation began to change. Between 1590 and 1604 the whole of the eastern and southern border of what would become the United Provinces was recaptured. This partly reflected the refocus of Spanish military effort elsewhere, first towards England, and then to intervene in war-torn France (1590). The political leadership of the Revolt was consolidated by Holland and its leader Johan van Oldenbarneveldt. Most important was the Dutch military revolution under Prince Maurits, transforming effectiveness and discipline, and turning a force of 20,000 troops in 1588 into one of 51,000 in 1607.[62]

The 1590s also saw a spectacular expansion of economic activity. This was made possible partly by recovery of control of the rivers and estuaries. In addition the fall of Antwerp, followed by blockade of the Scheldt, first by Parma and then by the rebels, began its decline. One hundred and fifty thousand refugees, many bearing capital, technology and skills, fled to the Northern provinces. Between 1582 and 1609 the population of Leiden tripled, while Flemish migrants introduced there, as they would in England, the lighter, brighter 'new draperies'.[63] Refugees could be absorbed because the grain trade and fishery supported the food supply. The relocation of South Netherlanders, Portuguese Jews and others, combined with Amsterdam's 'willingness to adapt institutional arrangements first to increase its share of the Baltic grain trade, and then, after the fall of Antwerp . . . to become the principal gateway of Northwestern Europe', helped turn the city by 1650 into 'the undisputed center of world trade'.[64]

The same period consolidated such distinctive features of the republic as city-centred political authority, localized religious toleration, and a rich scientific, artistic and intellectual life.[65] One result, as in Switzerland, was a territorial republic governed by a matrix of cities rather than by or as a city-state. Another was a social and political culture which was more egalitarian and less aristocratic than that of, for instance, Venice or Florence.[66] There followed a resurgence of the rich trades, given a further boost by a lifting of the Spanish embargo on Dutch ships in the Iberian Peninsula in 1590. Linking both trades (rich and bulk), the republic now enjoyed a near-monopoly of the supply of Mediterranean spices, silver, sugar and wine to Northern Europe – commodities purchased in the Mediterranean with grain, fish and manufactures, especially linens and 'new draperies'. When in 1598 Philip III reimposed the embargo this threatened the whole construction.[67] The Dutch response was the most dramatic component yet of the still-unfolding economic 'miracle'.

It took the form of immediate and heavy investment in the long-range voyaging necessary to secure the commodities of these rich trades directly. The first long-distance company was established by a consortium of nine merchants in 1594. The first voyage left Texel for the East Indies in April 1595, consisting of 4 ships and 249 men armed with 100 cannon provided by the States of Holland. The last detail is crucial. Upon the viability of the economy depended the outcome of the war, and therefore the existence of the state. This explains some elements of speed, scale and risk-taking: what became the VOC (Vereenigde Oostindische Compagnie, or Dutch East India Company) was the maritime arm of a state at war. 'These companies . . . were allowed to conclude treaties . . . wage defensive wars, and to build strongholds in their regions . . . [they] constituted in fact extra-territorial states within the Dutch republic.'[68]

In 1597 three of the four ships returned with no profits and only eighty-nine survivors, but with the possibility of direct access to a militarily vulnerable Portuguese East Indies verified. In 1598 frenetic investment in Holland and Zealand produced three more fleets, owned by three new companies. Fourteen months later one returned with four richly laden vessels and a profit of 400 per cent. By 1601 fourteen fleets, and sixty-five ships, had sailed to the Indies; in 1602 the States-General regulated the trade by the charter of the VOC. The first territorial conquests were made in 1605.

***

The Dutch republic emerged amid major changes within Europe, and in Europe's place in the world. It had one basis in the uniquely dynamic and demanding northern physical environment and another in the no less exceptionally wealthy urban economy of the south. The Revolt added other ingredients, including Protestantism, wartime solidarity and further innovation, and the transnational movement of refugees. To some the result, in the United Provinces of the Netherlands, looked like more than a new economy. It was a new kind of society: a 'New World' not across the Atlantic, but within Europe itself. Visitors

were . . . struck by the innumerable 'novelties' and innovations . . . in virtually every field of activity . . . the prodigious extent of Dutch shipping and commerce, the technical sophistication of industry and finance, the beauty and orderliness, as well as cleanliness, of the cities, the degree of religious and intellectual toleration . . . the excellence of the orphanages and hospitals, the limited character of ecclesiastical power, the subordination of military to civilian authority, and the remarkable achievements of Dutch art, philosophy, and science.[69]

Thus Sir William Temple described the singularity, not only of the republic's 'situation', but of its political institutions, wealth, technology, relative equality, liberty and social security. One study took Temple's 'wonder' as a starting point for asking: 'Did the Dutch Republic really strike out into "uncharted waters"?'[70] Its experience certainly had singular components, including 'a radical and enduring transformation of the rural sector in the seaward provinces of the Northern Netherlands' responding to 'trading opportunities with a burgeoning urban sector'.[71] But the Dutch also built upon a process of European urban development (a 'blue banana' on the map) radiating north-west from Venice, Genoa and Florence to Nuremberg, Bruges and Antwerp. To these earlier experiments in trade and industry, literacy, religious tolerance, art and technology, and civic self-government, the Dutch republic added, among other things, Protestantism, natural philosophy, print culture and news.[72] Thereafter in England 'after the Interregnum, and especially after 1688', similar factors informed a culture of 'improvement . . . when information about land and trade, population, wealth, and well-being . . . circulated through parliamentary debate and a popular press, as well as in correspondence between friends and conversations in coffee-houses. That was what enabled improvement to become a morality of collective cooperation in a national purpose.'[73]

This comparative context is essential. But to explain how pre-industrial history ended it is not enough. Sixteenth-century England was, unlike the Netherlands, but like eighteenth-century North America, a predominantly rural society. Bananas were not a local crop. To answer our larger question involves understanding, first, how the economic and demographic limits applying to agricultural societies, in Europe or China, were breached. Even within the Netherlands this question cannot be answered by reference only, or primarily, to the history of cities. The economy of the Dutch republic, as a federated state of seven provinces, resulted from centuries of rural–urban interaction in a unique regional location:

The notion that the United Provinces was, in any sense . . . the city-state of Amsterdam, implying that Amsterdam ruled the rest as Venice and Genoa ruled their subject territories, is a total misconception. Nowhere else in the early modern world was the close economic collaboration of a network of maritime towns, fishing ports, and inland specialized agriculture anything like so intricately organised and federated as in the Dutch republic during the seventeenth century.[74]

Beyond this we must explain why the prodigious Dutch industrial development which peaked and then plateaued during the late seventeenth and early eighteenth centuries was itself subsequently transcended by a game-changing Industrial Revolution.[75]

To that explanation the economic and political growth of London was central. But to understand how the old world ended, we need not only to trace the broader impact of the Netherlands upon its very different North Sea neighbour: upon its agriculture, wider economy, Protestant political and print culture, seventeenth-century revolution and eighteenth-century empire. We need to see how on the west coast of the North Sea many of these developments were taken in different directions. 'Compared to their Dutch counterparts', for instance, 'English statesmen were . . . . driven to give equal attention to the protection of manufacturing, agricultural and commercial interests. For the Dutch . . . the last-mentioned remained . . . paramount.'[76] It is partly because without any of its three components Anglo-Dutch-American early modernity would not have unfolded as it did that we may suspect there was nothing inevitable about the Industrial Revolution.

—◆—

CHAPTER FOUR

THE WEST COAST OF THE NORTH SEA

[F]or the season it was winter, and . . . the winters of that country . . . be sharp and violent and subject to cruel and fierce storms, dangerous to travel to known places, much more to search an unknown coast. Besides, what could they see but a hideous and desolate wilderness, full of wild beasts and wild men . . . the whole country . . . full of woods and thickets, represented a wild and savage hue . . . [and] If they looked behind them, there was the mighty ocean which they had passed, and was now as a main bar and gulf to separate them from all the civil parts of the world.

William Bradford at Plymouth, Massachusetts, 1620[1]

During winter . . . Mr Malakite's fields slept . . . with a cover crop of mustard with yellow flowers to build up organic material in the soil . . . By the time I returned the fields were . . . filling with vegetables and fruit . . . We gathered green beans in five-gallon buckets and chard in a wheelbarrow . . . The Stupice tomatoes that grew near the sea had an intense taste. I was back in the seasonal subculture of market gardeners and the endless discussions across the trestle tables about blights or the failure of spring rains.

Michael Ondaatje, *Warlight*, set in post-WW2 Suffolk[2]

Compared to the northern Netherlands, English geography, particularly in the south, was agriculturally benign. Partly for this reason English society was predominantly rural rather than urban, aristocratic rather than mercantile, terrestrial rather than maritime, and monarchical rather than republican. When the naval commander William Monson described the Dutch pursuing 'ye scull of the Herrings like a Hound that pursues the Head of a Dear in hunting', he was translating the fishery into a language his English readership would understand. Later the abundance of English natural resources would help it to industrialize. In the sixteenth century they helped it to remain traditional. Yet Tudor society was far from static. It had a rich and connected Renaissance intellectual culture. The regional neighbourhood was transforming, both internally and in its relationship to the world. Moreover, in explaining how the Industrial Revolution became possible, that the English economy in 1600 remained dominated by agriculture was as important as the fact that so many Hollanders were mariners. In particular this underlay a mode of colonial settlement, in North America and around the world, without which that revolution might not have occurred.

As a well-watered agricultural economy in a mild climate sixteenth-century England was mostly self-sufficient.[3] It grew its own wheat, barley and oats, occasionally exporting to the Netherlands in times of abundance – from King's Lynn or Great Yarmouth in Dutch ships – or importing in times of dearth.[4] English agriculture was notable for the extent of animal husbandry (and therefore pasture), livestock production contributing between 30 and 50 per cent of output across the early modern period.[5] A long strain of 'dietary nationalism' celebrated relatively widespread access to meat. 'Oh,' wrote the Elizabethan John Aylmer, 'if thou knewest thou Englishe man in what welth thou livest, and in how plentifull a Countrye: Thou wouldest . . . fall flat on thy face before God, and geue him thanks, that thou wart born an English man, and not a French pezant, nor an Italyan, nor Almane.'[6] A growing sixteenth-century pastoral economy produced woollen broadcloth for export. In 1565 cloth constituted almost 80 per cent of English exports, accompanied to Antwerp by (for instance) tin and lead.

There was no English North Sea fishery, although Dutch fishermen landed at Scots ports and at Yarmouth.[7] But Elizabethan fishermen from the West Country worked the Newfoundland Banks alongside French, Spanish and Portuguese, attempting to create a settlement on the island.[8] Elizabethan manufacturing was limited: broadcloth was finished in Antwerp, until the outbreak of the rebellion in 1566; then, after a spell in Hamburg, in Middelburg in Zeeland. Most manufactures came from Italy, Germany and the Netherlands, including luxury textiles (velvet, silk), nails, needles, pins, soap, glass and mirrors as well as sugar, dried fruit and Asian spices.[9] Most of these goods were acquired through Antwerp, until the disruption by the Revolt helped to stimulate strenuous efforts by merchants and newly established trading companies to locate alternative markets and sources of supply.[10] At the same time Elizabeth I's chief minister William Cecil oversaw attempts to exploit the influx of Dutch Protestant refugees from the 1560s and 1570s to develop textile manufacturing in England.[11]

In 1560 English shipping was 'far behind . . . the Dutch . . . Spain and Portugal . . . Hamburg and . . . Lubeck . . . France . . . Venice or even Ragusa and Genoa . . . In 1562 the Dutch ships entering the Baltic to fetch timber and corn and hemp numbered 1192, the English fifty-one.'[12] The Newcastle colliery was the largest source of English coastal trade, and so of maritime expertise (in 1771 James Cook's *Resolution* was a converted collier). In the export of cloth most ships were operated by foreigners, Hanse, Flemish and Dutch. The later observation by Samuel Pepys that 'The trade of England till Henry 8th was drove by the Easterlings and strangers; consequently our coasts [were] known to them at that time better than by ourselves' applied until the early seventeenth century.[13] However, during the Dutch Revolt English merchants re-established footholds in the Baltic and the Mediterranean. By 1600–10 imports were arriving in quantity, not only via Antwerp and Amsterdam, but directly from Leghorn, Naples, the Greek Islands, Turkey and Egypt.[14]

At the trade's peak during the 1630s three hundred fishing vessels a year left Portsmouth, Falmouth, and Bristol for Newfoundland, returning their salted cod directly to the Mediterranean where it was exchanged for rich trade goods. Between 1588 and 1642 the tonnage of English merchant shipping doubled, albeit from a low base.[15] Yet the merchant fleet remained modest by European standards, and the Royal Navy (founded by Henry VIII) smaller. By 1624 one hundred English ships a year sailed to the Baltic; the Dutch sent twenty or thirty times that number.[16] Vessels of the Royal Navy over one hundred tons numbered twenty-eight in 1548, twenty-five in 1558, and thirty-one in 1603. The military actions of the Elizabethan state centred upon land campaigns in the Low Countries, and in Ireland.[17] When Charles I became involved in a naval war in 1626, the result in Cadiz was a fiasco. Long-distance voyaging in the sixteenth century was dominated by the West Country. By the seventeenth century it was led by London, which pioneered the East Indies, Mediterranean

(Turkey) and American trades; they used larger (and heavily armed) ships and became the mainstay of the mercantile economy.[18]

Sixteenth-century England was less urbanized, not only than the Netherlands but also France, the Holy Roman Empire and Mediterranean Europe. Outside the south-east this was partly a function of low population density. However, rurality was not only demographic but cultural. It is partly because for its elite Spain was a culture of cities (*civitas*) but England one of rural great houses and villages that these were the patterns of settlement reproduced in their respective American colonies.[19] As Peter Heylyn observed, essential to a city was

> continual confluence of Nobles, Gentry, Merchants, and all sorts of Trades: And by this means, *Madrid*, not long since a poor beggarly Village, is grown the most populous City in all *Spain* . . . [moreover] the Residence of the Nobility, beautifieth a City with stately and magnificent Buildings; which makes the Cities of *Italy* so much excel ours in *England*; their Nobles dwelling in the Cities, and ours for the most part in their Country houses.[20]

Thomas Sprat claimed that other Europeans 'have one great assistance, to the growth of Oratory, which to us is wanting: that is, that their Nobility live commonly close together in their Cities, and ours for the most part scattered in their Country houses . . . They prefer the Pleasures of the Town; we, those of the Field: whereas it is from the frequent conversations in Cities, that the Humor, and Wit, and Variety, and Elegance of Language, are chiefly to be fetch'd.'[21] Yet a doubling of the English and Welsh population between 1520 and 1650 made towns bigger. Over the same period the number of English people living in towns of over 10,000 inhabitants increased from 80,000 (3.1 per cent) to 495,000 (8.8 per cent).[22] However, these figures were dominated by the exceptional, almost tenfold growth of one city. By 1687 William Petty was boasting not only that '*the People of* London *are quadruple to those of* Amsterdam'. 'We . . . conclude, that *London* hath more *People, Housing, Shipping and Wealth*, than Paris and Rouen put together, and for ought yet appears, is more considerable than any other City in the *Universe*.'[23] In fact, until 1800, London remained smaller than Edo, in Japan, and Peking.[24] But not thereafter.

This insurgent metropolis was a product not simply of national but European regional history. Not only a court capital, like Paris, but a port, London was the product of a transforming North Atlantic economy and culture which eventually wrought its own (Anglo-Dutch and then British) political institutions.[25] As such it was a bomb ticking under the early Stuart monarchy, 'unruly . . . mutinous . . . the sink of all the ill humour of the kingdom', something of which both James I and Charles I were uncomfortably aware.[26] Figures concerning GDP per head show that the English economy began to grow at exactly the time that the Stuart monarchy began to falter (from the 1620s, and more firmly from 1650). The most important reasons for this lay in London.[27] Small wonder that between 1625 and 1649 English parliamentarians and republicans took inspiration from the Dutch Revolt, a prior and successful military defence of Protestantism, property and representative institutions against the pretensions of a centralizing ('arbitrary') monarch.

A TRADITIONAL SOCIETY UNDER PRESSURE

The themes of sixteenth-century English rural life were visible in its nucleated villages and woodlands; its vernacular and Latin literature; its most controversial economic issue (enclosure of arable land for pasture) and its most pressing social problem: a growth of population which stimulated a widespread perception of increasing poverty, crime and vagrancy. That England's economy and society were traditional did not mean that they were unchanging. Agricultural economies were also dynamic, though the processes involved were usually cyclical rather than transformative. In sixteenth-century Languedoc, as in England, population numbers were recovering following the Black Death. What began slowly was inclined to accelerate until the limit of agricultural productivity was reached. When population growth and static resources collided, the pain could reach into every aspect of social and political life.[28] In late Tudor and early Stuart England such population growth not only strained resources but drove wider changes within the economy as a whole.

Between 1520 and 1650 the English and Welsh population roughly doubled, to 5.5 million. One result was tremendous pressure to increase grain production. This informed a grievance, enclosure, which would simmer for three hundred years. The population growth which made grain production imperative simultaneously made wool more profitable.[29] In the famous words of Thomas More's *Utopia*:

Your sheep . . . that commonly are so meek . . . have become so greedy . . .
that they devour men themselves . . . For in whatever parts of the land
sheep yield the finest and thus the most expensive wool, there the nobility
and gentry . . . leave no land free for the plough: they enclose every acre for
pasture; they destroy houses and abolish towns.[30]

This population pressure drove the first phase of what would be a long-term
transformation of agricultural productivity:

From the mid-sixteenth century rising demand from a fast-growing population stimulated a sustained re-expansion of agricultural output, with
arable . . . growth initially outpacing that of the livestock sector. From the
mid-seventeenth century, however, population pressure eased, livestock
output growth accelerated and, significantly, remained ahead of that of
the arable sector throughout the eighteenth century notwithstanding the
resumption of population growth. What made this possible were the new
integrated mixed farming systems of the agricultural revolution in which
fodder cropping with roots, legumes and rotational grass, higher stocking
densities and increased on-the-farm recycling of nutrients played a crucial
role. Gains in arable productivity, in fact, became contingent upon expansion of the livestock sector.[31]

These new systems and crops originated in the Netherlands. The widest-
ranging impact of population increase between 1540 and 1640 was a fivefold
increase in prices, for food and everything else. It is because this inflation had
a tumultuous effect, not only upon society, but upon the military-fiscal state,
that the early Stuart monarchy became destabilized. The same inflation was
accompanied by a sharp decline in the real value of wages, and a rise in unemployment. These contributed to a process whereby subsistence farmers, without
goods to offer the market, and unable to supplement their income by off-
season work, were driven to sell their land. One result was a rise in poverty
accompanied by an increase in vagrancy:

One way or another, these wretched people – men, women . . . orphans,
widows, parents with little children and entire families . . . are forced to

move out. They leave the only homes familiar to them, and can find no place to go. Since they must leave at once without waiting for a proper buyer, they sell for a pittance . . . When that little money is gone (and it's soon spent in wandering from place to place), what remains for them but to steal, and so be hanged?[32]

In a world of limited surplus and rudimentary charity these developments tapped into a well of fear. The overall result was polarization of landowning and wealth distribution. Middling farm dwellers had more mouths to feed on the same amount of land, with their labour declining in value. More prosperous ('yeomen') farmers producing beyond their subsistence needs in a world of buoyant prices oriented themselves towards the market, not only for pastoral but arable produce. As poverty grew, so did prosperity and consolidation of larger landholdings. The increase in arable production was stimulated by experimentation with new techniques and crops by 'gentlemen with intellectual curiousity and above-average financial resources', assisted by contacts between 'the nobility and gentry of England and the continent'. In addition, 'A sense of obligation to one's fellow men to strengthen the economy, promote the commonweal, and provide work for the poor was part of an accepted philosophy, inspired by religious and political conviction.'[33]

Such belief informed the genre of 'commonwealth literature', of which *Utopia* was an early example, and Thomas Scott's *Belgicke Pismire* a later one. This called attention to the intertwined afflictions of poverty and polarization of wealth, which suggested that something was catastrophically out of order.[34] The predominant diagnosis was moral, and by implication religious (in More's analysis, pride; in Scott's, sloth; in Gerrard Winstanley's, covetousness; in all cases, selfishness, the antithesis of community).[35] Another response to poverty, theft and vagrancy was increased recourse to the criminal law. Holinshed claimed (implausibly) that in Henry VIII's reign 72,000 thieves were hanged. Thomas More described this policy as one of terror.[36] Steve Hindle estimates that at least 2,928 people were sentenced to death in England during the reigns of Elizabeth and James I. Among Richard Hakluyt's reasons for commending to the queen a design for 'Western Planting' in North America in 1584 was as a means 'for the manifold ymployment of nombers of idle men':

Truth it is that . . . wee are growen more populous than ever heretofore: So that . . . many thousands of idle persons are wthin this Realme, wch having no way to be sett on work . . . often fall to pilfering and thevinge and other lewdness, whereby all the prisons of the lande are daily pestred and stuffed full of them, where either they pitifully pyne awaye, or els at lengthe are miserably hanged, even xxii at a clappe oute of one Jayle.[37]

Another result was the greatest raft of social legislation of the period: the Elizabethan Poor Laws of 1572. These regulated grain prices, outlawed hoarding, and systematized local charity, empowering local office holders to keep order and establish houses to set the poor on work. Other, subsequent attempts to address poverty and its consequences stood at the heart of the radical thought and legislation of the English revolution.[38]

THE WESTERN DESIGN

Alongside these challenges England was deeply and immediately affected by the Dutch Revolt, which produced, among other things, an influx of refugees. One result was the conviction, which would last for two centuries, that Protestants on both sides of the North Sea faced a common existential danger. The resulting anxiety helped to inform English entreaties – whether contemplating Flemish agriculture, the Dutch fishery, Holland's trade, or the decayed state of England's Channel harbours or havens – for English effort, expenditure and ingenuity comparable to that of the Dutch. In the view of John Leake, in 1577: 'We ought to favour the strangers from whom we have learned so great benefits . . . because we are not so good devisers as followers of others.'[39] What English Protestants especially wished to emulate – chafing at the reluctance of their queen – was the Dutch preparedness to take up arms. Meanwhile they developed a more ambitious, trans-Atlantic response.

Constructing a history for his proposed 'Western Design', Richard Hakluyt recounted expeditions across the Atlantic to North America by English and Welsh adventurers from the medieval period to the mid-sixteenth century.[40] English navigators responded to the arrival of the Duke of Alva in the Low Countries as the Portuguese and Spanish had to that of the Ottomans in the

Mediterranean: by looking west. Seeking a polar equivalent of the discovery by Bartolomeu Dias of the route around the Cape of Good Hope, Elizabethan explorers searched for a North–West passage above Canada to 'Cipangu' and 'Cathay' (Japan and China): 'a straight and short way open into the West even unto Cathay'.[41] Voyages to North America's eastern seaboard were undertaken by courtiers, soldiers and merchants such as Martin Frobisher, Sir Humphrey Gilbert and Sir Walter Ralegh. Here royal patronage and private commercial investment enabled dreams of gain and glory which sometimes ended in disaster. Englishmen landed in Newfoundland and Hudson's Bay, kidnapping natives and collecting quantities of fool's gold. Hakluyt acknowledged that the North Atlantic was tempestuous and cold but emphasized the navigational advantages of the short summer nights. He added that North America was 'nearer unto her Majesties Dominions, then to any other part of Europe'.

In 1585 Ralegh made the first English attempt at North American settlement at Roanoke, on the east coast of North Carolina. The following year the colony was abandoned, its governor, Captain Ralph Lane, giving his view that 'the discovery of a good mine by the goodnesse of God, or a passage to the Southsea, or someway to it, and nothing els can bring this country in request to be inhabited by our nation'.[42] It was the arrival of a Spanish army in the Low Countries which elevated the Western Design from speculative venture to strategic necessity. Spain derived from its mines in the 'Indies' much of its ability to sustain troops in the field. Now England would have to compete or perish. The Dutch conflict was part of a world war in which there could be no safety from the Spanish menace without a counterweight to the imperial resources upon which it drew. This was also the context for establishment of a Dutch global empire, including a West Indies Company formed after the Twelve Years Truce (1609–21) with the purpose of preying upon Spanish and Portuguese shipping.

'I can assure you,' added Hakluyt, 'that Abraham Ortelius the great Geographer told me at his last being in England in 1577 that if the warres of fflaunders had not bene, they of the Lowe Contries had meant to have discovered those partes of America, and the northwest straite before this tyme.'[43] In his 'Discourse of Western Planting' Hakluyt united the imperatives of royal religious duty, danger from Spain, and the advantage of an outlet for England's surplus population, with a highly creative account of North American resources, including gold, silver, pearls, silkworms, dyestuffs, spices, timber, furs, wine and olive oil. These comprised an alternative source for 'all the commodities of Europe, Affrica, and Asia, as far as wee were wonted to travel, and supply the wants of all our decayed trades'.[44]

By the term 'Planting' Hakluyt was pointing the way towards a distinctively English (and Scots) Protestant colony involving the settlement of people and culture rather than merely the extraction of things. The method to be deployed, which was the work of farmers, religious settlers and soldiers, not merchants, was already being trialled in Ireland. The subjugation of Ireland, held to be a necessity for the safety of Protestantism, was driven by ideologies wielding the distinction between Reformation and Counter-Reformation, and civility and barbarism. Humphrey Gilbert, the West Country hero who drowned returning from Newfoundland in 1583, had starred in an Irish adventure directed by Quentin Tarantino, slaughtering entire villages and marking his progress with displays of parallel rows of severed heads.[45] When 'barbarous Indians' resisted English settlement, similar conduct reappeared in seventeenth-century New England.

When permanent English American colonies evolved, in Virginia and New England, they were terrestrial and agrarian. Dutch New Netherland, by contrast, had a 'seaward orientation' with its capital New Amsterdam on the island of Manhattan. There the merchants and seamen employed by the West Indies Company were transient, living 'with the movement of the seas and rivers, tides and currents . . . trained to read the turning pages of the seas, to be restless . . . altering course suddenly, moving ahead by seeking familiar coastal markings or new sightings . . . separate . . . from the native people'.[46] On the other hand, the relationship of English settlers to native peoples, whose land they were appropriating for agriculture, descended into bloodshed.

When from Leiden in 1620 the English congregation of William Bradford pondered their removal to some new place, 'The place they had thoughts on was some of those vast and unpeopled countries of America, which are fruitful and fit for habitation, being devoid of all civil inhabitants, where there are only savage and brutish men which range up and down, little otherwise than . . . wild beasts.'[47] Comparing Dutch and English movements in Connecticut, Donna Merwick commented:

> Among other things, they are using space differently; as linear in the case of the Netherlanders, as planal in that of the English. The Dutch are voyagers,

71

travellers enacting their transience . . . for the English . . . Saybrook is a foothold to inland places, to broad and (allegedly) unsettled valleys suitable for the beginning of rural communities.[48]

According to Native Americans the Dutch were 'something on water, but no account on land'.[49] This contrasting mode of settlement, and relationship to the land and its people, laid the basis for the eventual conquest of New Netherland by England in 1664 and English domination of North America. Elizabethan maritime boosters such as John Dee urged the queen to make England 'something on water' also. This would require 'many Thousands of Soldyers . . . not only hardened well to broke all rage and disturbance at Sea, and endure healthfully all hardnes of lodging and dyet there, but also . . . practiced . . . to great perfection of understanding all maner of fight at Sea'.[50] Ralegh cited the example of Athens, which had established its power with the naval defeat of Persia at Salamis in 480 BCE. On the eve of battle the oracle had advised Themistocles: look to your wooden walls. 'This was Themistocles' opinion long since . . . that he that commands the sea, commands the trade, and he that is Lord of the Trade of the world is lord of the wealthe of the worlde.'[51]

In the short term this advice went unheeded. The Elizabethan war with Spain depended upon privateering. In 1577 it did produce the most famous English voyage before Captain Cook, John Evelyn noting that 'our Drake' was 'the First of any Mortal, to whom God vouchsafed the stupendous Atchievement of Encompassing, not this *New*-World alone, but *New* and *Old* together'.[52] Sir Francis returned in 1580 laden with Peruvian booty, and with the protests of the Spanish ambassador ringing in Elizabeth's ears.[53] However, 'Behind . . . Elizabethan legend and nationalist propaganda lay a long and painful series of failures and disasters, only occasionally relieved by some brilliant feat such as Drake's voyage.'[54]

Leading that propaganda was Hakluyt's *Principall Navigations, Voiages and Discoveries of the English Nation* (1589). This treated, first, voyages to the South-East: to the Holy Land, the Near East and South Asia, and around the Cape of Good Hope; and, third, to the Americas, including passage through the Straits of Magellan into the Pacific, in particular by Drake. In between came journeys 'North and Northeast by Sea' around Norway, Lapland and northern Russia. One was by Anthony Jenkinson, the factor of the Muscovy

Company, who left Gravesend on 12 May 1557 seeking a 'vent' on the Silk Road for English 'carsies', a type of woollen not obviously designed for the desert and steppe of Central Asia. On 27 June, off Lapland, Jenkinson reported a 'raine bowe, like a semicircle, with both ends upward', and the 'whirle pool, called Malestrande . . . if there commeth any Whale within the current of the same, they make a pitiful cry'.[55] On 20 September Jenkinson made port at Vologhda, subsequently departing by sled for the ten-day trip south to Moscow.

After presenting his credentials to the 'Emperor', followed by months of arduous feasting, Jenkinson travelled by river south and crossed the Caspian Sea. He then continued south across the desert by caravan, engaging in desperate combat with 'rovers' – mounted muslim 'Tartars'. '[D]ivers men, horses and camels being wounded and slaine on both partes . . . had it not bene for 4. Handgunnes which I and my companie had . . . we had bene . . . destroyed.'[56] On 23 December he arrived 'at the citie of Boghar in the land of Bactria' on the old Silk Road. There he observed merchants from India, Persia, the Balkans and Russia, though contact with China was impeded by war. The Indians brought white cotton cloth, 'which the Tartars doe roll about their heads', and purchased 'silks, redde hides, slaves and horses'. Jenkinson offered them 'carseis for their commodities' without success.[57] Prevented by war with the Ottomans from proceeding further south, Jenkinson returned the way he came. His return journey, taking from 8 March 1559 until May 1560, was more hazardous still.

MIGRATION AND ECONOMIC DEVELOPMENT TO 1650

Thus in this agricultural society population pressure drove economic change. The average size of landholdings grew, as did markets, particularly London. So did the market for woollen textiles, at least until a severe Jacobean slump. Agricultural improvement accelerated, first in the south-east, the part of England most affected by Dutch immigration. 'By the seventeenth century sown clover was replacing grass, and turnips and carrots were being grown for fodder . . . In the eastern counties turnip husbandry as recommended by Weston was already practised . . . under the influence of immigrants from the Netherlands.'[58] Sir Richard Weston's *Discours of Husbandrie Used in Brabant and Flanders* was published by the republican agricultural improver Samuel Hartlib in 1650, with new editions in 1651, 1652 and 1655. The importance of clover and other fodder crops – Lucerne, sanfoin, spurry, all 'became the subject of lively debate and publicity in the Hartlib circle in the 1650s'.[59]

Partly through the influence of such publications, other informational circles, and personal fact-finding missions to the Netherlands, 'Dutch agriculture was the principal model for English improvers in this period . . . the successes were conspicuous in southern, eastern and Midland England by the end of the 1650s. They are most readily identified in the spread of crops like clover, coleseed, woad, fruit, and vegetables.'[60] The direct impact of Dutch immigration was equally important, and occurred earlier. As a result, 'London in 1640 had market gardens on all sides':

> Among the many Dutch and French Protestant refugees who fled to England in the sixteenth century were some, mainly Dutch, who were market gardeners . . . These men quickly . . . set up market gardens at Sandwich, Colchester, Norwich, Canterbury, Maidstone and London . . . Coming from that part of Europe where market gardening and intensive arable husbandry were most highly developed, they brought with them a great deal of practical and commercial expertise . . . It was the Dutch who first grew turnips and other roots for sale in England; they were probably the first commercial florists . . . [and] the first to raise seeds for the market.[61]

In helping to carry the agricultural revolution across the North Sea these migrants performed an economic role comparable in its long-term impact to that of the Protestant merchants and financiers who fled Antwerp for Amsterdam. Of England's second city, Thomas Scott reported in 1622:

> . . . looke upon the City of *Norwich* . . . The order and good government of the Magistrates, the diligence of the Citizens . . . is principally occasioned by . . . the *Dutch*, as also by a kinde of virtuous emulation, to which the *English* are excited by their diligence . . . they have beene the Inventers of many profitable Engines both for peace and warre: Travellers by Sea and Land are beholden to their labors; and for the belly, they have taught us by roots, fruite, and the Garden crop, to spare much flesh and Corne, if wee
> * were as wise and willing to use them as they doe.[62]

In England, as in the Netherlands, the key to agrarian improvement was an enhanced combination of animal and arable husbandry, along with the introduction of new crops.[63] During the second quarter of the seventeenth century Dutch engineers, led by Cornelis Vermuyden and funded by Dutch investors, reclaimed part of the Cambridgeshire Fens for agriculture, with impacts on the landscape that remain today.[64] As in the Netherlands these changes required not only expertise and technology, but the stimulus of a market. This was supplied by a population increase manifested most pressingly in London.

The overall economic impact of Protestant immigration was much broader. Most of the refugees who fled to England from the 1570s, from Flanders, Brabant, northern France and the northern Netherlands, were not farmers. 'They included salt-makers, copper and lead miners, manufacturers of glass and iron (gunsmiths from the Low Countries settled in Southwark in 1571) printers and engravers and – most numerous of all – clothworkers.'[65] By 1590 immigrant artisans comprised perhaps one-third of the population of Norwich, Colchester, Canterbury, Rye, Sandwich and the London suburbs. Some had been settled by a government project to 'plant' immigrant textile workers to establish 'new draperies' to compete with Dutch rivals such as Leiden.[66] In Norwich by 1582 there were 4,600 Dutch and Walloons. Between 1567 and 1586 the number of cloths produced by aliens there increased from 1,200 to 38,700 per year. These Norwich 'stuffs' used linen, silk and cotton as well as wool, and comprised forty different types of cloth, including bays, says, ollyet, damasks, values, carells, grograins and fustians.[67]

Other Dutch artisans settled in England and Scotland, including brewers, paper makers, sugar refiners, porcelain manufacturers, drainage engineers, rope, ship and sailmakers. In the later seventeenth century there was a major influx of French Huguenots. Italian-origin industries involving silk, glass, sugar refining and tin-glazed ceramic arrived in England during the 1560s and 1570s via Antwerp.[68] The brewing of beer, as opposed to ale, which revolutionized its keeping properties by adding hops, had originated in Germany and also arrived in London from the 1570s from the Netherlands.[69] In an age when literacy and formal education were limited, and practical experience acquired under apprenticeship was frequently essential, the movement of people was a key conduit for the acquisition of skills. It was no accident that

The most dynamic economies in the late sixteenth and early seventeenth centuries were those countries with high rates of immigration, principally . . . in the United Provinces, and to a lesser extent London. Many Dutch cities contained a staggering proportion of immigrants from the southern Netherlands, which in 1622 ranged from 18 per cent in Delft, 33 per cent in Amsterdam, 51 per cent in Haarlem to 67 per cent in Leiden.[70]

In 1608 a contemporary reported the English 'people mightily increased both in number . . . and in . . . skill . . . skilful of all kind and manner of trades'.[71] The same period saw English expeditions to learn about the construction, provisioning and sailing of Dutch and Baltic shipping.[72] Among skills imported from Antwerp and Amsterdam we must add printing and architecture.[73] All of these developments informed a long-term transformation of the occupational makeup of English society.[74] In 1520, 76 per cent of the population were farmers; in 1801 the figure would be to 36 per cent.[75] 'While the agrarian sector in England in 1600 was still dominant, at least one in every three male workers was in the secondary and tertiary sectors and by c. 1650 nearly one in two. In the early seventeenth-century there was no area of Europe other than Holland which could have bettered that sectoral distribution as an indicator of economic development.'[76]

The most famous feature of the Dutch economy was trade. 'The Dutch must be understood as they really are, the carryers of the world.'[77] 'The prodigious increase of the Netherlands in their domestic and foreign trade, riches and multitude of shipping, is the envy of the present and may be the wonder of future generations.'[78] It was here that from the 1590s the economic fortunes of the two countries appeared most painfully to diverge. Its trade to Antwerp disrupted, England remained barred from access to the Iberian ports, which enabled the Dutch recovery in textiles and the rich trades. During the war with Spain, England and Scotland suffered severe economic hardship. After the Dutch-Spanish truce of 1609 there was a resurgence of Dutch shipping.[79] England could not compete with low-cost Dutch carrying, and looked with envy at the industrial harvest of the fishery. Just over half of 714 ships visiting London over nine months between 1601 and 1602 came from the northern Netherlands.[80] By 1614 there was a fishery near Iceland operated by vessels from East Anglia.[81] Anglo-Dutch competition in the whaling grounds around the arctic island of Spitsbergen led to naval conflict in 1618.[82] Attempting to tax Dutch fishing and whaling, James I expostulated to Dutch representatives in 1621: 'Surely you are like leeches, bloodsuckers of my realm . . . I would not endure it either from France or Spain, do you think I . . . will bear it from you?'[83] The answer turned out to be yes.

Although the foundation of the English East India Company in 1599 preceded that of the Dutch East India Company (the VOC), it was under-capitalized and sent out twelve ships in its first nine years compared with the Dutch fifty-five ships in the first seven years.[84] Of the first eighty-one English ships that sailed, only thirty-five returned.[85] Attempts to contest Dutch control of Java, Sumatra and the Moluccas were sharply repelled, resulting in the execution of ten English factors in the 'massacre of Amboina'.[86] There was more success on the Indian subcontinent, with settlements at Surat (1607), Madras (1639) and Bombay (1622), and diversification away from the initial focus on pepper to the eventually more valuable import of silk and cotton fabric.[87]

National population increase drove the growth of London despite major visitations of plague and of other causes of catastrophic pre-modern urban mortality. This situation continued into the eighteenth century, by which time plague had given way to smallpox. Migrants surplus to the requirements of rural villages and landholdings seeking their fortunes in the capital may have numbered two million between 1550 and 1750.[88] In London they created a dynamic hinge between the traditional and modernizing economy, state and empire, linking town and country, especially in the south-east, partly by driving agricultural improvement. At the same time, from about 1620, and peaking during the 1630s, an enormous outflow of migrants across the North Sea, Irish Sea and Atlantic 'dramatically expanded . . . the population of all the English settlements of the wider Atlantic world'.[89] The largest initial outflow was to Ireland and there was also substantial emigration to mainland Protestant Europe. The same human tide secured the new colonies in the Chesapeake, the Caribbean and New England. 'In 1630 the colonial population was an esti-mated 9,500. Ten years later, despite the high mortality rates endemic to England's new colonial ventures, the population had grown more than five times, to 53,700.'[90]

During the eighteenth century England's North American colonies would witness an endogenous demographic explosion. Across the seventeenth century, however, the settlement process was wholly sustained by migration motivated by a complex mixture of economic hardship, religious zeal and social need. John Winthrop, future governor of Massachusetts Bay, included in 1629 'among his reasons for migrating, the reflection that England was overpopulated and growing weary of her inhabitants, along with the plea that the move would perfect the Reformation'.[91] The ships were disproportionately filled with young adults, males and persons in service (which, in this society, was a marker of generational, not simply of socio-economic, status).

***

The previous two chapters have visited both sides of the North Sea at a time when the region's place in European and global history was changing. Some of those changes were long-range economic and geopolitical developments. Others merged into a single war, the outcome of which would have fundamental implications for the future of Europe and of the world. Between the Dutch republic and Tudor /early Stuart England we have noted many environmental, economic, social, political and commercial contrasts. But in both places these wider regional challenges and changes – social, economic, religious and political – were equally sharply felt.

One result, initially at least, was to bring the two societies together. This was a consequence of proximity, even contiguity, within a water world connecting the North Sea, Baltic and Atlantic. It was equally a product of culture: the shared, predominantly Calvinist Protestantism which made England, Scotland and the United Provinces allies against Spain and then France. Both underpinned the Elizabethan and early Stuart flows of migrants and refugees, which were a force for regional economic development and integration.

As the Dutch and English economies converged, co-operation and co-option would give way to the competition and military conflict which were no less important aspects of the Anglo-Dutch-American process. Before coming to these, however, we need to turn to the wider European cultural and religious situation, and so to the 'Reformation' of which we have heard Winthrop speak.

CHAPTER FIVE

——✦——

SEA OF THOUGHT

The Lord hath brought us hither through the swelling seas, through perils of Pyrats, tempests, leakes, fyres, Rocks, sands, diseases, starvings: and hath here preserved us these many yeares from the displeasure of Princes, the envy and Rage of Prelats, the malignant Plotts of Jesuits, the mutinous contentions of discontented persons, the open and secret Attempts of barbarous Indians, the seditious and undermineing practises of hereticall false brethren.

John Winthrop, Massachusetts Bay Colony, 1643[1]

And when I came, in the Lord's mighty power, with the word of life into the world, the world swelled and made a noise like the great raging waves of the sea. Priests and professors, magistrates and people, were all like a sea, when I came to proclaim the day of the Lord amongst them, and to preach repentance to them.

George Fox, *Journal* (1652)[2]

THE NORTH-WEST EUROPEAN–AMERICAN CULTURAL SPACE

Anglo-Dutch-American early modernity, which made the Industrial Revolution possible, was partly driven by ideas. These included the idea of modernity itself, which grew from the thought that contemporary Europe was distinct from, and had in some ways outperformed, the cultures of the ancient world. In early seventeenth-century England Peter Heylyn quoted Sir Francis Bacon to the effect that 'we of these Ages have very good cause . . . to congratulate the present times, in that the World in these our days have *through-lights* made in it, after a wonderful manner; whereby we clearly see those things, which either were unknown, or blindly guessed at by the Ancients'.[3] 'Is it not evident,' asked John Dryden after the Restoration, 'in these last hundred years . . . that almost a new Nature has been revealed to us? . . . more noble secrets in optics, medicine, anatomy, astronomy, discovered, than in all those credulous . . . ages from Aristotle to us?'[4] This new way of looking at time, deriving from fresh experience in space, took time to mature. 'We might think that gunpowder, the printing press and the discovery of America in 1492 should have obliged the Renaissance to acquire a sense of the past as lost and gone forever, but the educated only slowly became aware of the irreversible consequences that flowed from these crucial innovations.'[5] Far from being lost, indeed, the past was a thing upon which it was now possible more confidently to build. Nor were the '*New* things' discovered by experimental philosophers '*Innovations*', so much as carefully wrought revelations of the workmanship of God.

Ideas motivated the movement of people across early modern Europe, the North Sea and Atlantic. Some of these migrants were refugees, others political and religious exiles, and others adventurers and pilgrims. This study identifies three transnational migrations of constitutive importance to the Anglo-Dutch-American process. The first involved Protestants fleeing from sixteenth-century Germany and France into the Netherlands, and then in some cases from the Netherlands into England. The second saw early seventeenth-century Scots and English Protestants sheltering in the Netherlands and then crossing the Atlantic alongside other Scots and English migrants to Ireland and the American colonies. Finally, after 1660, English dissenters seeking liberty of conscience in the Netherlands and the American colonies overlapped with French Huguenots fleeing to the Netherlands and England, feeding, after the Glorious Revolution, into a more general migration of European Protestant people, culture and capital into a world city.[6] At that point London, having anchored an Anglo-Dutch-American history since at least 1620, became capable of embedding it within a European enlightenment culture and a global commercial and military system.

Finally ideas drove the Dutch, Anglo-Dutch and American revolutions. Although early modern Europe's mass movements of people were not simply ideologically driven, they were products of a protracted trans-Atlantic cultural upheaval which had crucial religious and political as well as economic consequences. This impacted not only individuals and local communities, including colonies, but states.[7] England had been divided by the Reformation, especially between the Protestantizing south-east and the rural and conservative north-west. Protestantism sowed the seeds of critical thinking about both traditional Church government and monarchy.[8] The British civil wars were caused, not by Charles I, but by the impact upon a fragile state of a series of destabilizing problems – military-fiscal dysfunction, religious polarization, and social and economic stress. As in the Netherlands all had regional causes beyond the scope of any one ruler's control. Under these circumstances, unlike his father James VI and I, Charles elected the path of confrontation. In the words of the political theorist James Harrington:

> Nor was there anything now wanting unto the destruction of the throne but that the people, not apt to see their own strength, should be put to feel it, when a prince, as stiff in disputes as the nerve in the monarchy was grown slack, received that unhappy encouragement from his clergy which became his utter ruin.[9]

Like those earlier of Philip II, these policies had regional effects. Archbishop Laud complained about 'such an universal running to New England, and God knows whither, but such it is, when men think nothing is their advantage, but to run from government'.[10] Where events ultimately ran was into the revolution of 1649, a confessional cataclysm with world-changing consequences, including an Anglo-Dutch reconstruction of the English and British imperial state which would make the Industrial Revolution possible.

Of late seventeenth-century Radical Enlightenment, Jonathan Israel remarked that it 'was not inspired by any single nation, be it France, England or the Netherlands, but rather had its centre of gravity in north-western Europe and particularly in the inner circuit linking Amsterdam, the other main Dutch cities, Paris, London, Hamburg and Berlin'.[11] Thus it emerged from the same north-western region identified by Hume's account of religious and political freedom and commerce. Across this the units of movement and exchange were individuals, families, guilds, cities, universities, libraries, publishing houses, coffee houses, political and religious assemblies, books and newspapers. It is by reference to such associations that J. Luiten van Zanden recounted Europe's accumulation since the medieval period of a cultural basis for world-leading economic prosperity. This was 'relatively democratic, literate, with a dense socio-political infrastructure (including high levels of social capital), where people (often) obeyed the (written) law, and possessed relatively efficient methods for developing and adapting new and old institutions (such as guilds, universities, communes, citizenship, law courts, councils, meetings and parliaments, charters and privileges, markets and fairs)'.[12]

This 'bottom-up' accretion of skills, power and knowledge began in the civic communities of Mediterranean Italy and continued, after 1500, in the new leading economic and cultural zone around the North Sea. It was not identical to the Renaissance and then Enlightenment, having deeper social application, including to women as well as men. However, these phenomena overlapped, particularly after the arrival of Protestantism, as evidenced by the growth of literacy and book production. Average annual book production in Europe between 1522 and 1644 was twenty times that of China.[13] Literacy increased strongly between 1500 and 1800 in the North Sea zone and in Sweden, led by the Dutch republic in the late sixteenth century and then England by the late seventeenth. Each became a centre of vernacular language printed news and print culture. In this part of Europe literacy bridged the gap 'between propositional . . . and prescriptive knowledge – between common workmen and *savants*'.[14]

The remainder of this chapter reviews the acquisition by this North Sea area of a distinct cultural identity which became a mover of people and events. Our subject is a creative transnational and trans-Atlantic process which helped to break the power of two would-be hegemonic states and monarchies (Habsburg Spain and then Bourbon France, each of which tried to ally with the Stuart British Crown) producing in the process, on both sides of the Atlantic, three new states, and types of state.

NORTHERN HUMANISM AND NATURAL PHILOSOPHY

During the sixteenth century there emerged a north-western European variant upon Renaissance humanism. Humanists were preoccupied with recovery of the textually and linguistically authentic literature and culture of classical antiquity.[15] There was much variety, with focus upon Greeks or Romans, philosophers or politicians, military strategy or oratory. Yet most humanists shared a belief that the culture of the ancient world was not only precious, but essential for addressing the challenges faced by Europeans now. At the beginning of his *Discourses Upon the First Ten Books of Titus Livy* Niccolò Machiavelli wrote of his 'astonishment and grief' to see antiquity everywhere admired rather than imitated.[16] Such semi-detached inattention to the matter at hand was not only slack but disastrous. Humanists wanted urgency, engagement and utility.

Ancient culture had been pagan. This does not mean that humanists were against the Roman Catholic Church. It did, however, mean that Christians preoccupied by the problem of sin were re-engaging with pre-Christian cultures which had been more interested in the potential for moral achievement, which they called virtue. This made humanism the most powerful intellectual force informing republicanism, in Italy, and later the Netherlands and England. Civic self-government was extolled by the Florentine Leonardo Bruni as the only political path to virtue, and the only government appropriate to man.[17] Machiavelli, who agreed, added that the peacemongering, turn-the-other-cheek, other-worldliness of Christianity was directly responsible for the military ruin of Italy. Religion was too important, Machiavelli suggested, for the Church to be left in charge of it. Italy needed a religion appropriate to the military and political challenges it faced, one like that of ancient Rome.

Northern humanism became visible as a distinct cultural phenomenon in the sixteenth-century universities of Paris, the Netherlands, England and Germany. Its Anglo-Dutch leading lights included Erasmus and Thomas More. As Erasmus visited More and others in England, so More set the discussion published as *Utopia* in Bruges, in a text written in Latin. Northern humanism was characterized by a focus on Greek rather than Roman sources.[18] In addition it looked to classical culture as a way to rejuvenate and reform Christianity, an objective which led it to anticipate some of the subsequent stances of Protestantism. The resulting attempt to reorient Christianity away from ritual, and towards conduct, is also called Christian humanism. More's satire was one result and Erasmus' Greek New Testament another. Later, during the Revolt, Dutch humanists including Justus Lipsius and Hugo Grotius absorbed and responded to the intellectual impacts of Europe's religious wars, including Neostoicism and scepticism.[19]

Northern humanists like More, Jean Bodin and Michel de Montaigne took a close interest in what had been reported about non-European peoples. In the process two distinctions came clearly into focus: between the Americas and Europe, and between the present and the past. The acquisition by Europeans of knowledge of a wider world which had been unknown to the ancients underlined that the two societies were not only distinct – as humanists had emphasized – but different. Textually recovered classical models could not simply be imitated, as Machiavelli had counselled. Rather, their essence had to be extracted, and then applied to the circumstances of a different time and place. It is possible to see this acquisition of comparative perspective, involving a recognition of cultural diversity in time as well as space, as the most important intellectual impact of the discoveries. 'The almost miraculous sequence of events which led to the discovery, conquest and conversion of the New World did much to reinforce the linear and progressive, as against the cyclical, interpretation of the historical process in sixteenth-century thought.'[20]

Up to a point the result need have been no more than recovery of that cultural relativism by virtue of which Herodotus had once delighted to explain that 'some Indians, of the tribe called Callatiae' who ate their deceased parents, were horrified by the Athenian custom of cremating them.[21] In *Six Books of a Commonwealth* (1572) Bodin embarked upon a spectacular attempt to explain cultural diversity in terms of variations in geography and climate.[22] But in addition to underlining the difference between present and past, the discoveries also introduced the possibility that the future might astound. Thus the Elizabethan Edmund Spenser:

Who ever heard of th' Indian *Peru*?
Or who in venturous vessel measured
The *Amazons* huge river now found trew?
Or fruitfullest *Virginia* who did ever vew?

Yet all these were when no man did them know,
Yet have from wisest ages hidden beene
And later times thinges more unknowne shall show.
Why then should witlesse man so much misweene
That nothing is but that which he hath seene?[23]

Above all, the discoveries opened the way to the universal ambitions and empirical methods of natural philosophy. As the philosopher and clergyman Joseph Glanvill put it in 1661, 'There is an *America* of secrets, and unknown *Peru* of Nature . . . And I doubt not but posterity will find many things, that are now but *Rumors* . . . [to be] *practical Realities*.'[24] Natural philosophy built upon a quest for practical knowledge by travel, observation and experiment, with the results communicated between scholars, merchants and ingenious gentlemen (*virtuosi*) by personal and professional interaction, including in print. Thomas Sprat recounted the formation of '*Academies* . . . in many parts of *Europe* . . . first . . . in *Italy*'; then 'the *French Academy at Paris*'; and finally the '*Royal-Society of London*'.[25] The latter, he emphasized, was no narrowly national enterprise, freely admitting 'Men of different Religions, Countries, and Professions of Life . . . For they openly profess, not to lay the Foundation of an *English, Scotch, Irish, Popish,* or *Protestant* Philosophy; but a Philosophy of *Mankind*.'[26]

Experimental philosophy powerfully informed late Dutch and English humanism. In the United Provinces,

> in the absence of a royal court and a landed nobility, civic urban culture developed and throve . . . as a result of the Dutch overseas trading empire, exotic plants and animals began to make their appearance in the cabinets of curiosities of the rich Dutch patricians and merchants, feeding the public's imagination and interest in science. Anatomical dissections and scientific experiments became civic spectacles as well as academic pursuits . . . captured in such paintings as *The Anatomy Lesson of Dr Tulp* by Rembrandt and Vermeer's *Geographer*.[27]

Leading the seventeenth-century craze for plant collection, the Dutch East and West Indies Companies set up botanic gardens in Cape Town, Malabar, Java, Ceylon and Brazil, which exchanged plants with Amsterdam and Leiden.[28] In England private landowners had been collecting and growing exotic flora since the later sixteenth century. 'Infinite are the plants which we have,' commented Samuel Hartlib in 1651, and 'which the ancients knew not, as well apparent by their small and our large Herballs, and dayly new Plants are discovered'.[29] More than a century later Dutch 'natural history' and anatomical medicine opened up long-closed Japan to 'Dutch studies' (*Rangaku*) and Western science in general.[30] In England the experimental science championed by Francis Bacon informed both the anatomical discoveries of David Harvey and the republican political theory of James Harrington. For Harrington, as 'Art is the observation or imitation of nature', so 'parliament is the heart which, consisting of two ventricles . . . sucketh in and gusheth forth the life blood of *Oceana* by a perpetual circulation'.[31]

Natural philosophy had adherents across the English political spectrum, informing the republic's plans for conquered Ireland, the improvement culture of the Hartlib circle, and the interregnum meetings at Wadham College, Oxford, which preceded the Royal Society.[32] 'In Britain, within a few years of the passage of the Navigation Acts, the new Royal Society harnessed national commerce to the chariot of natural history. Robert Boyle in the first volume of the *Transactions of the Royal Society* (1666) gave detailed instructions on the collection of specimens "for the use of travellers and navigators".'[33] This undertaking reached beyond botanical collecting:

> It being the Design of the *Royal Society* . . . to study *Nature* rather than *Books,* and from the Observations, made of the *Phenomena* and Effects she presents, to compose such a History of Her, as may hereafter serve to build a Solid and Useful Philosophy upon; They have from time to time given order to several of their Members to . . . set down some Directions for *Sea-men* going into the *East* and *West*-Indies, the better to capacitate them for making such Observations abroad, as may be pertinent and suitable for their purpose.[34]

In 1694 *An Account of Several Late Voyages & Discoveries* complained that not enough was being done. '*Tis to be lamented, that the* English Nation *have not sent along with their* Navigators *some skilful* Painters, Naturalists, *and* Mechanists, *under publick* Stipends *and* Encouragement, *as the* Dutch *and* French *have done, and still practise daily, much to their Honour, as well as Advantage.*'[35] However, the following century collaboration between the Admiralty, Royal Society and Royal Academy would culminate in the spectacular voyages of Captain Cook (see Chapter 12 below), while natural philosophy, first in the Netherlands and then in Britain, contributed to the wider advances in technology, knowledge and communication which informed the Industrial Revolution (see Chapters 14–16).[36]

Yet if cultural variety was greater than had been understood, and human discovery actually in its infancy, could there really only be one way of understanding God, that of the notoriously worldly and corrupt papacy?

PROTESTANTISM

It was certainly striking that, just as Machiavelli was blaming Italy's woes upon Christianity, in Germany Martin Luther was making the exact opposite diagnosis. The problem, Luther announced in 1517, was not a surfeit of God's truth, but a radical deficit. Humanist biblical scholarship had undermined the textual foundation of much Roman Catholic discipline and doctrine. This disconnect from the Bible, and the broader corruption of the Church, had deprived Europeans of the word of God. Historically the papacy had long defined its authority against such challenges.[37] Holland had produced the Flagellants, and England the Lollards, while Christian humanism had identified an urgent need for spiritual reform.[38] Erasmianism overlapped with Lutheranism in its reaction against pride, its elevation of conduct (or manners) against ceremony, and its emphasis upon the Bible. But Erasmus refused to support Luther's break with Rome, and More was executed in 1536 for opposing Henry VIII's own.

Reformation became a social as well as cultural process, far from complete two centuries later.[39] But while its progress was contested, Protestantism came to unite the Atlantic North-West more deeply than anything else. While sundering nations it connected the region. Sir William Temple recalled the period when 'the Reformed Profession' was introduced into '*England, Scotland, Sweden, Denmark, Holland,* and many parts of *Germany*'.[40] In England this was partially enabled by the Henrician break with Rome and subsequent looting of the Church; but more enduringly by translation of the Bible. The vernacular Bible was the engine room of Protestantism, spread by printing, so that this cultural revolution sailed forth on a sea of ink (and speech), its sails filled by preaching.[41] Twenty-five million vernacular bibles were created in Luther's lifetime.

In central Europe establishment of the first Lutheran congregations was followed by a peasant uprising in support of a far more radical interpretation of the Protestant message.[42] Though savagely repressed, the appeal of Thomas Muntzer and others for Christian social equality and community would have a potent afterlife, in the Low Countries and England.[43] In England, Edwardian Protestantization was followed by Marian reaction. Heretics were burned and English and Scots exiles fled to the Netherlands, Germany and Switzerland to imbibe the example of 'the best reformed churches'.[44] According to Temple, by 1560 German Protestants 'were generally *Lutherans*, yet there was a great mixture both of *Calvinists* and *Anabaptists* among them'.[45] Under pressure from Charles V many fled 'down into the Seventeen Provinces, especially *Holland* and *Brabant*, where the Privileges of the Cities were greater, and the Emperor's Government less severe'.[46] This was the hornets' nest prodded by Philip II, as in 1566 the leaders of the Revolt resolved that the 'publique Profession of their Party should be . . . *Lutheran* . . . though with liberty and indulgence to those of different Opinions'.[47]

ANGLO-DUTCH-FRENCH-SCOTS-AMERICAN CALVINISM

Within Protestantism, as within humanism, there developed a second-generation Anglo-Dutch-French-subsection. Calvinism appeared during the 1550s in France, the western Empire, Switzerland, the Netherlands, England and Scotland. Calvinists were animated by the predestinarian theology of Jean Calvin, as well as (to widely varying degrees) the reformed clerical and lay Church government developed by him in Geneva. The 'Calvinist international' was a recognizable outgrowth of border-crossing Protestantism more generally.

By 1562 the arrival of Calvinism in France had provoked a civil war.[48] Two years earlier a Calvinist uprising in Scotland presaged a popular and enduring cultural revolution. Elizabeth's accession to the English throne in 1558 created a hybrid Protestant Church: episcopal in discipline, increasingly Calvinist in doctrine. In the Netherlands during the Revolt, Calvinism became dominant, something attributed by William Temple to the impact of refugees from France, and Calvinist influence from England, especially during the 1570s and 1580s. By 1600 there was a Calvinist doctrinal centre ground in England, Scotland and the United Provinces, despite radically dissimilar forms of church, as of political government. In the republic towns and provinces locally controlled and tolerated various degrees of diversity. The English Church, by contrast, was national, episcopal and compulsory.[49]

Elizabeth was not – to say the least – a zealous agent of Reformation. But her senior political servants became so, partly in response to the evolving confessional dramas in France and the Low Countries. Early in the reign England intervened in Scotland on the Protestant side to close the door against France.[50] That did not mean that Scots Presbyterianism was welcome in England, and Archbishop Richard Bancroft was not the only Episcopalian who regarded 'puritanism' and 'popery' as equally dangerous.[51] Scots Calvinists established a relationship with Dutch religious and humanist culture which bypassed England and remained important into the eighteenth century.[52] The struggle within Anglo-Scots Protestantism would be fatally reignited by Charles I and Archbishop Laud.[53] Their anti-puritan, anti-Calvinist policies, understood by their opponents to be 'popery', helped to radicalize Protestantism, Calvinist and otherwise, and drive it first across the North Sea to the Netherlands, and then across the Atlantic to America.

Popery was the word used by English and Scots Protestants to describe the militant Roman Catholic response to Protestantism promulgated from 1558 by the Council of Trent. Counter-Reformation became global: the Society of Jesus sent missionaries across Europe, including England and Ireland, but also to Spanish, Portuguese and French America, and to China and Tibet (they were expelled from Japan).[54] In the English view, popery was a 'design, by fire and sword, so perfectly to reduce all his majesty's dominions to the Roman Catholic religion, that [all] protestant[s] . . . should have been extirpated, both root and branch'.[55]

In response Protestantism too extended its range. The exodus of English and Scots puritans to the Netherlands began under Elizabeth and intensified under James and Charles.[56] Then it turned west. Between 1618 and 1621 immigrants to Virginia included three English separatist congregations relocated from the United Provinces.[57] The voyage that founded Plymouth colony in 1620 initiated not in the West Country town of that name (which was a port of call) but Delftshaven, where it was commissioned by members of the Nottinghamshire separatist congregation led by John Robinson in Leiden.[58] It, too, was heading for Virginia and its arrival in Massachusetts Bay may have been an accident.[59]

The congregation's departure from Leiden had been prompted in part by the approaching expiry of the Twelve Year Dutch-Spanish Truce (1609–21). Contemplating the future, William Bradford (Plymouth's first Governor) was not tempted by the prospect of a return from 'liberty in Holland' to 'the prisons in England'. He was troubled by reports of the Native Americans, 'who are cruel, barbarous, and most treacherous, being . . . furious in their rage and merciless where they overcome; not being content only to kill . . . but delight to torment men in the most bloody manner that may be'.[60] Yet 'They lived here but as men in exile, and in poor condition; and as great miseries might possibly befall them in this place, for the . . . truce were now out, and there was nothing but beating of drums . . . for war . . . The Spaniard might prove as cruel as the savages of America, and the famine and pestilence as sore here as there.'[61]

The Massachusetts Bay plantation founded at Salem in 1627 was an important destination for 'puritans' relocating both from England and the Netherlands. By 1636 the congregation of Hugh Peter, who had moved from Rotterdam, was said to number a thousand. Thus a nineteenth-century Boston Congregationalist described the intellectual formation of 'the Pilgrims' as decisively Dutch. In the United Provinces:

> men were trying the experiment of self-government . . . while from the presses of Leyden and other Dutch cities were issuing books that . . . analysed . . . methods of government, in the one republic of Northern Europe, in which at that time were living most of the political and military leaders . . . who settled Massachusetts, Rhode Island, Connecticut, New York, and Pennsylvannia . . . [alongside] the greatest university of Europe, that matriculated over two thousand English students in the seventeenth century.[62]

Leiden, a sixteenth-century foundation (1575), took many foreign students and was a major instrument of Scots as well as English and American education. 'Of all students from the British Isles and North America in the Netherlands in the seventeenth and eighteenth century, nearly three quarters took a degree in Leiden. Between 1680 and 1730, more than 860 Scottish students alone matriculated there.'[63]

EUROPE'S WARS OF RELIGION, 1562–1651

The political and military consequences of Europe's religious schism were devastating. The death toll following the German revolution of 1525 ran into hundreds of thousands. During four decades of civil war the population of France decreased while that of the rest of Europe was rising. Fatalities from the Thirty Years War (1618–48) are estimated at 5.75 million.[64] The wars of three Stuart kingdoms (1638–51) produced English casualties of 190,000 (3.7 per cent of the population), Scots of 60,000 (6 per cent of the population), and Irish of 660,000 (41 per cent of the population).[65] The Calvinist rebellion in Bohemia 'seen in the year 1618, was a warning . . . [to] all Christendome, whereupon followed . . . those horrible wars, lamentable wastings, barbarous destructions of countreys and cities . . . in Germanie . . . Catalonia . . . Portugal . . . Scotland, Ireland, England . . . from the papists . . . the King of Spaine . . . the Jesuits'.[66] 'Has there ever been an age,' asked one Dutch pamphleteer in 1650,

> in which there were born greater alterations, peturbations, changes, ascendancies, downfalls than in ours? . . . All foundations have been dissolved, that which seemed impossible has become possible . . . what was below has come out on top . . . sickness exists without cure, wounds without healing.[67]

The religious dimensions of these conflicts spread them. Protestantism advanced like a tide (the high tide was 1590), connecting political territories and crossing borders, carried by movements of people and the technology of print, including printed news, creating a military storm system. No ruler could contain a supranational religious conflict. The challenge might appear to have been particularly daunting for the ruler of a global empire like Charles V, or Philip II. But successive Kings of France were no more successful in the short term; and if, after 1618, Ferdinand II was as King of Austria, Bohemia and Hungary, that was not before he had called in large-scale and brutal international help. As ruler of another religiously fragmented multiple monarchy Charles I failed to emulate his success, partly because, as a suspected Catholic sympathizer, he was opposed by almost all of his own subjects outside Ireland.[68]

In France, Scotland, the Low Countries, Bohemia and England, Calvinists found themselves facing governments which appeared to have become murderous instruments of popery. Both Luther and Calvin emphasized the subject's obligation to political obedience. Reformation reinforced the authority both of princes and fathers, by removing competing claims to authority, and by emphasizing the condition of human sinfulness which made government imperative. Although the first fully political articulations of a right to resistance were published by Calvinists, these had been largely constructed from the earlier arguments of Roman Catholics like Robert Bellarmine and Francisco Suarez, as James VI and I and Sir Robert Filmer pointed out.[69] Thus, that most religious rebellions in Western Europe were Calvinist was a result, not of Calvinist doctrine, but of the fact that it was the second generation of Protestants who found themselves facing the Counter-Reformation.[70]

Confronting what Christopher Goodman called 'the horrible slaughter of thousands of martyrs', Protestants in France, the Netherlands, Bohemia and Britain all found ways to explain why the cause of God must now be defended by every means that lay to hand. 'Not to withstand such rages of Princes . . . is to . . . subvert all Lawes of God and man, to let will rule for reason, and thereby to inflame Gods wrathe against you.'[71] Later John Locke described such a desperate recourse to arms as 'an Appeal to Heaven' and argued that a prince seeking to make himself 'Arbitrary disposer of the Lives, Liberties or Fortunes of the People' dissolved the basis of his own authority. This gave his subjects a 'Right of War' against him, as the Dutch republican Hugo Grotius' *De Jure Belli ac Pacis Libri Tres* (Paris, 1625) had explained.[72]

In the face of such resistance, rulers like Philip II, Ferdinand II and Charles I came to consider Calvinism incompatible with obedience to princes. Elizabeth had supported a Calvinist uprising in Scotland with deep misgivings and resisted intervention in the Netherlands until the pressure became intolerable. Her successor James, though a Calvinist himself, had personal experience of the unruly Scots Kirk. When he came under parliamentary pressure to intervene in Bohemia he responded with instructions to his churchmen in 1622 to suppress unlicensed lay Calvinist preaching. Charles I appears to have begun to move against English and Scots Calvinism from the first year of his reign.[73] To his perception of a Crown 'besieged by . . . puritan republicans' revisionist historians have opposed an insistence that in fact early Stuart subjects were united in their loyalty to monarchy.[74] There was indeed a strong preference for this system in theory, provided that the monarch used his power in line with the religious and political wishes of his elite. Otherwise what was available, Charles I discovered and explained, was loyalty in practice, and in wartime, only upon 'conditions incompatible with monarchy'.[75]

THE CONFESSIONALIZATION, AND THEN GLOBALIZATION, OF ENGLISH POLITICS

Thus when Dutch Protestants took up arms against the Spanish Inquisition they were not the first to defend their faith against their own sovereign. Coming to the throne eight years earlier, Elizabeth inherited a religiously fractured kingdom. Her strategy was to stake and rigidly defend a conservative Protestant middle ground, while requiring formal conformity only. However, in Europe as a whole religious polarization and militarization were eating the middle ground away. By the end of Elizabeth's reign the allegiance of her subjects, including that of her entire political elite, had become religiously conditional, which is to say confessional. It was loyalty to a Protestant and Calvinist state first, and to the Tudor (and subsequently Stuart) dynasty only subject to that. This was the opposite of the outcome the queen had desired, and across the seventeenth century her successors struggled with the consequences. However in 1689, with the support of a Dutch army, this arrangement was given permanent legislative expression.

Like James, Elizabeth tried hard not to get sucked into a European religious war. But many of her subjects, including Cecil and Bancroft, believed that the wars in progress across the North Sea were ones in which England had a vital stake. This opinion was informed by news spread by word of mouth by travellers, soldiers and refugees. It was also sustained by a stream of publications in England covering the whole duration of the Dutch Revolt. These publications included pamphlets, analyses, histories and news reports. Among them Dutch publications were translated, English visitors to the Netherlands reported back, and printers in both countries evolved their wares to supply a lucrative English market fed by anxiety about the common threat from Spain.[76] Dutch Protestant readers also showed 'remarkably great interest' in news of England's religious and political troubles, from the Gunpowder Plot of 1605 to the wars of the three kingdoms (1638–51).[77]

The supranational nature of Protestantism, the military conflicts which it provoked, and the migrational and print culture by which it was sustained, all helped to push England into war in 1585. Thereafter the passions provoked by a struggle for the survival of European Protestantism played a decisive role in English and Scots politics until 1714 and beyond. The fiscal and ideological consequences of the demand for European military involvement underlay the fall of the early Stuart monarchy (which had been British, not simply Scots or English) and its replacement by a modernized economic, military and fiscal superpower. This state product of the Anglo-Dutch revolution of 1649–1702 was supranational and outward looking: Anglo-Dutch, Anglo-Scots, Anglo-German and Anglo-American.

The power of the United Kingdom was not only military-fiscal but cultural: that of a confessional state tethered to the international fate of Protestantism. After 1689 this hinged upon the outcome of a global 'second Hundred Years War' against France. Nor was the culture in question simply confessional, acquiring distinct political, social, literary, scientific and commercial components. All were grafted onto the stock of an English nationalism visible since Richard Hakluyt's *Principall Navigations* or earlier, defined in particular against Spain, France and Ireland. By 1707 this was tethered to a global confessional, economic and political role which was British rather than merely English.[78]

The case for Elizabethan intervention in Holland was strengthened by the Duke of Alva's brutality. It was one thing to live across the water from the Spanish Netherlands; another to see it become the surgeon's dissection table for Counter-Reformation terror. In 1570 the pope excommunicated Elizabeth, encouraging her subjects to rise against her; in 1572 thousands of French Protestants died in the massacres of St Bartholomew's Eve (Sir Philip Sidney, who would die fighting the Spanish at Zutphen, had to shelter in the English embassy in Paris). In the same year the landing of the Sea Beggars in Zeeland was triggered by an order by Elizabeth for them to leave English ports.[79] The landing attracted the active connivance of senior royal counsellors, William Cecil reporting: 'Here is all covert means used to let them of the Low Countries pass home to the help of the liberty of the[ir] country.'[80]

Meanwhile English nerves were frayed by a succession crisis which had been festering since 1563.[81] In the absence of a royal marriage and heir, or designated successor, the next in line to the throne was Catholic Mary, Queen of Scots. Only Elizabeth's life stood between the English Church and this potential triumph for European (and French) Catholicism. In 1584 William the Silent was assassinated. In 1585 Parliament produced its Bond of Association, promising that in the event of the queen's murder this would be avenged by all of her subjects before the succession was determined by a parliament (in fact Convention) summoned by the Privy Council.[82] In the event of her death, that is to say, there would follow an interregnum during which the confessional rather than dynastic integrity of the succession would be secured.

In the same year Elizabeth was persuaded by the same counsellors who had supported the Bond – William Cecil, the Earl of Leicester, Francis Walsingham – to take the plunge against Spain. Under the terms of the Treaty of Nonsuch (August 1585), signed in the same month as the fall of Antwerp to Parma, an English expeditionary force was dispatched under Leicester. The *Declaration of the Causes moving the Queen of England to give aid*, possibly written by Walsingham, described 'this our realm of England' as the 'most ancient allies and familiar neighbours' of the Dutch, 'and that in such manner, as this our realm . . . and those countries have been by common language resembled and termed as man and wife'.[83] Elizabeth's ministers 'knew that the frontiers of the British Isles lay in northern France, in the Low Countries, and in Normandy and Brittany. In the dozen years after 1585, fifty thousand English troops were sent overseas to advance English interests in northern Europe and to support the enemies of Spain.'[84]

Leicester's intervention was not a success. It provoked conflict over leadership of the Revolt between the Calvinist, aristocratic and monarchical Leicester and his Dutch allies, and the religiously tolerant, republican and mercantile States of Holland under Johan van Oldenbarneveldt.[85] English troops (inexperienced, badly organized and underpaid) performed poorly. Then, between 1587 and 1590, the situation changed. Facing the Armada, England abandoned the attempt to compete with the States of Holland. In the improbable words of the queen to the Dutch ambassador: 'your state is not a monarchy and we must take everything together and weigh its faults against its many perfections . . . we kings require, all of us, to go to school to the States-General'.[86] This was the first stage of a larger conflict with Spain which drew in Ireland and England's fledgling plantations in North America. Within this confessional geography the Netherlands were the fortified 'outworks' which had first to be taken before any popish design could be made good within the British Isles themselves. This made the United Provinces England's eastern military frontier.

The Treaty of Nonsuch marked the first of three key moments of Anglo-Dutch political proximity.[87] The others occurred in 1651 (the proposed union between English and Dutch republics, reoffered in 1654) and 1689 (the revolution settlement which inaugurated an Anglo-Dutch government with a Dutch king). Over the same period there were three Anglo-Dutch wars, in 1652–4, 1665–7 and 1672–3. These episodes of coalescence and conflict were closely intertwined. They were all manifestations of an intense, sustained and creative relationship which would produce not only newly wrought states on both sides of the Atlantic, but alongside them a dazzling array of economic, political and cultural innovations.

——◆——

CHAPTER SIX

THE STORM, 1618–49

[A] dreadfull storm and hideous began to blow . . . [and] beate all light from heaven; which like an hell of darknesse turned blacke upon us . . . our clamours dround in the windes, and the windes in thunder . . . For surely . . . as death comes not so sodaine nor apparent, so he comes not so elvish and painfull . . . as at Sea . . . It could not be said to raine, the waters like whole Rivers did flood in the ayre . . . What shall I say? Windes and Seas were as mad, as fury and rage could make them . . . there was not a moment in which the sodaine splitting, or instant over-setting of the Shippe was not expected.

Sir Thomas Gates, account of a voyage to Virginia in 1611[1]

In 1648–9 the Stuart ship of state, following a long and unprecedented tempest, was driven onto rocks and destroyed. The previous chapter surveyed the confessional weather prevailing from about 1560. Reflecting upon the origins of the troubles by which the government of Charles I would be over-whelmed, John Rushworth wrote in 1659: 'To learn the true causes, the rises and growths of our late miseries . . . had I not gone back as far as I do, I had not reached the Fundamentals . . . finding those proceedings to have their rise in the year 1618.'[2] The wars of the three Stuart kingdoms, from 1638 to 1651, were theatres within the wider European conflict called the Thirty Years War, and therefore also of the Wars of Religion in respect of which they furnished an infamous finale.[3]

Within this context the rebellions against Charles I constituted the Anglo-Scots chapter of the experience described in the Dutch pamphlet *The beginning and cause of the late troubles and calamities* (1571) – the Protestant taking up of arms against one's sovereign. Elizabethans had been electrified by the military struggle against Spain, which they had turned, mentally, into an Anglo-Dutch affair. Later the republican Marchamont Nedham claimed:

> When the *Spaniard* was likely to have swallowed up the People of the *United Provinces*, their Libertie and Exercise of the Protestant Religion in the days of Queen *Elizabeth* . . . so dear were their Liberties and the profession of the Protestant Religion with them to us, that it seem'd to be but one Nation, one Cause and quarrel; being entertained by us with the affections of Brethren, the love of Friends, and the respects of Neighbours and Allyes; nor have we envied at, but rejoiced in their welfare and prosperity.[4]

Defeat of the Armada and the war in Ireland contributed to a sense of Holy War. But to continue this to a satisfactory conclusion was beyond the capacity of English fiscal and military resources. As Conrad Russell commented: 'In the middle of the Thirty Years War, it must be an open question how long a monarchy which was unable to fight was able to survive.'[5] Here, too, the context for the collapse of the Stuart monarchy was regional and trans-Atlantic, rather than national. In this weather the vessel was not seaworthy.

This reflected the failure of the Tudor and early Stuart monarchy to keep pace with the consequences of price inflation and the European military revolution. While Elizabethan landowners might have begun to increase grain yields, and ministers and merchants inaugurated measures to diversify the economy, the reform of taxes proved beyond the capacity of the sovereign. 'In an age of inflation, rulers had to increase revenues . . . simply to stand still. A fivefold increase in revenues in the sixteenth century would still barely keep up with rising living costs.'[6] In addition to evading her first dynastic duty, the production of children, Queen Elizabeth resisted this need. Revenue at the end of her reign (1603) was 40 per cent less in real terms than it had been in 1509. To fund the Spanish war during the last five years of her reign £37,000 of Crown land was sold.[7] In the words of Robert Cecil: 'She selleth her land to defend us.'

The Earl of Clarendon later described 'the popular axiom of Queen Elizabeth, that as her greatest treasure was in the hearts of her people, so she had rather her money should be in their purses than in her own Exchequer'.[8] This was one of the 'perpetual love tricks with her people' by means of which, in the analysis of James Harrington, Elizabeth continued the theatre of monarchy while its substance (which he called dominion) was draining away. *'Wherefore the dissolution of this government caused the war, not the war the dissolution of this government.'*[9] In the Netherlands war had served as a catalyst for military revolution, expansion of the economy, and the creation of a new, formidable, but locally self-governing republican state. From it, by contrast, in 1604 the English monarchy emerged not only unreformed but depleted. Consequently the Stuarts inherited a political context which was popular, and an Exchequer that was empty.

Partly because of the impact of literacy and news, religious and political events had become the subject of animated public commentary. This was one aspect of the cultural impact of Protestantism on an increasingly dangerous European stage. Another was the transnational Calvinism which became a political driving force in an age of Counter-Reformation. For the Stuarts from 1603 these challenges had to be addressed across three religiously and politically disparate kingdoms.[10] Thus a popular determination to defend the Reformation by all means encountered the pacific, ecumenical and pro-Spanish foreign policy of James VI and I. James ended the war with Spain partly through financial necessity, though the new king also preferred peace, distrusted the Dutch as rebels, and wanted a cordial relationship with Europe's great power. By the time of the Bohemian crisis his subjects had become deeply concerned about the preparedness of their sovereign to defend the true religion. This was followed, under his more vigorous successor, by the alienation of an entire political elite, in Scotland as well as England, from a monarch in thrall to 'popery'.

The Dutch Revolt had pitted a representative assembly 'of the opinion that important political decisions such as those concerning successions, financial policy, legal issues and foreign affairs should not be taken without their consent' against a centralizing monarch who had, by 1559 'decided that the States-General formed a grave threat to royal power and . . . should not be summoned again'.[11] In England a 'crisis of parliaments' between 1625 and 1629 gave way to a decade of personal rule with 'all men inhibited . . . by proclamation . . . upon penalty of censure so much as to speak of a Parliament'.[12] When Scots and then English Protestants took up arms between 1638 and 1642 they followed the Dutch in committing to the defence of their Reformation by force. This was the first in a series of conflicts which did not secure Protestantism in England until 1689, or Calvinism in Scotland until 1707. These struggles on both sides of the North Sea were intertwined, beginning with a Scots rebellion supported by soldiers returning from the Netherlands and elsewhere, and ultimately hinging upon a Dutch invasion of England in 1688–9. In the long term Reformation could only be defended in North-Western Europe by a multinational (and cross-confessional) military alliance against Louis XIV and James II. This came to be led by an Anglo-Dutch government which completed the revolution of 1649–1702, securing in the process a British parliamentary monarchy, modernized war finance, a vibrant commercial economy and Protestant liberty of conscience.

THE COMING OF THE THIRTY YEARS WAR

Following peace with Spain in 1604, England retained control of two Dutch 'cautionary towns' and one fortress, until Dutch debts were paid in 1616. James undertook to mediate between the United Provinces and Spain. The republic recruited English and Scots soldiers to serve in foreign regiments under their own commanders. 'A minority of the Republic's troops spoke Dutch, while most were of French, Walloon, German, Swiss, Danish, Irish, English or Scottish origin.'[13] After the truce of 1609 the Dutch army was reduced to 30,000 men, of whom 5,000 were English or Scots.[14] When the Virginia Company made a renewed attempt to settle Jamestown between 1609 and 1611 the group included 150 'old soldiers trained up in the Nether-lands'.[15] It was led by two English veterans with Dutch service, Sir Thomas Gates and Sir Thomas Dale, released by the States-General in the (as it turned out, well-founded) belief that they would help the republic 'establish a firm market there for the benefit and increase of trade'.[16] Then between 1611 and 1616 many English residents of the Dutch cautionary towns chose to emigrate in Zeelandish ships to the Amazon and Wild Coast regions of Brazil and Guyana rather than to return home.

After attempts to grow and purchase tobacco in those regions and in Venezuela, tobacco production became established in Virginia during the 1620s and 1630s.[17] Its most important market was Dutch, both because 'the Virginia Company had begun to send tobacco to Flushing and Middelburg to circumvent James I's efforts to limit England's tobacco imports' and because 'in the Chesapeake . . . Dutch merchants both brought scarce European goods and offered better prices for their tobacco than planters could secure in England'.[18] When the Navigation Act of 1651 forbade this direct trade the price of Virginian tobacco rose sharply in England and varieties which had been developed for the Dutch market proved impossible to sell.[19] More than a century later the United Provinces remained by far the biggest market for British re-exports of colonial tobacco.[20]

Over the same period the political and religious life of the republic was riven between the mercantile leadership of the States of Holland (the so-called 'States Party') under Johan van Oldenbarneveldt, and the court of the Stadtholder, Maurice Prince of Orange, at The Hague. The House of Orange was associated with Calvinism and the States with Arminianism, a Protestant doctrine challenging predestination, and more favourable to religious toleration. Between 1617 and 1619 Dutch Calvinists, known as Counter-Remonstrants, engaged in a struggle with the States or Louvesteiners over the religious government of the republic. Maurice sought help from James, who sent English envoys to the Synod of Dort which drew delegates from across central and Western Europe as well as the Netherlands. In January 1619 the Remonstrants were expelled and their teachings condemned.[21]

Oldenbarneveldt was arrested and beheaded at The Hague in May 1619. This contest between Amsterdam and The Hague remained the fulcrum upon which Dutch politics turned, particularly at moments of crisis like 1650 and 1687–8. The Stuarts addressed it in dynastic terms, Charles I overseeing the marriage of his daughter Mary to Maurice's grandson William in 1641, as would Charles II that of his niece Mary to William's son (the future William III) in 1677.[22] However, when the English monarchy was abolished in 1649, and even after its restoration in 1660, during the Dutch stadtholderless period 1651–72, the opportunity arose to radically reconfigure the Anglo-Dutch relationship.

In 1618 European confessional polarization exposed the dangers of Jacobean pacifism. When Bohemia rebelled against Ferdinand II it offered the crown to James' Calvinist son-in-law Frederick Elector Palatine, and Elizabeth his queen. After pleas for military assistance were refused by James (but not by the Dutch republic), the rebellion was crushed by a Spanish-Austrian-Bavarian force at White Mountain on 8 November 1620. Frederick and Elizabeth were driven out, not only from Prague but the Palatinate (capital, Heidelberg) and both territories were Catholicized by force. 'We are those,' recorded one English pamphleteer, 'upon whom the end of the world has fallen.'[23] Later Caroline envoy Balthazar Gerbier remembered: 'As the preservation of the true Religion . . . was the mayne object wheron the People had fixed theire hearts, so were theire Eyes and Eares, Scouts to discover what past abroad . . . the reformed Churches abroad they held as contrescarps and outworkes of the Church of England.' Therefore:

> The apprehension of the People that the reformed Religion would not bee well defended seemes to be the original cause of som mistakes against king James and king Charles. The losse of Wesel proves the [first] Cause . . . The Losse of the Palatinat the second cause . . . [These] proved not only the cause of the prejudiciall opinion of the People, but of the Cooling of theire affections towards theire Souveraigne.[24]

Abetted by Jacobean military inaction, these events appeared to pose an existential threat to European Protestantism. [25] Animating this perception was a storm of news. English Protestants had been accustomed to European news circulated by manuscript, print, preaching and word of mouth. But from 1620 there arrived a new kind of regular periodical: those 'Pamphlets and weekly Intelligences . . . [which] have been multiplied and to[o] greedily received by the People' . The first corantos were published in Amsterdam and imported to London from there. This was a Dutch cultural intervention amid an English military and political crisis as deliberate as that by England into the Dutch Revolt in 1585. Its purpose, beyond the commercial exploitation of a lucrative market, was to inform and inflame English Protestant opinion.

The first news-sheet called *Corante uyt Italien, Duytslandt, &c* had appeared in Amsterdam in early 1618. The first corantos translated into English arrived in London on 2 December 1620 immediately after the battle of White Mountain, followed by further issues on 23 December and 4 January 1621.[26] Regular issues followed drawing upon Dutch, German and other publications, and connecting the city to a wider Protestant archipelago – Amsterdam, Leiden, Middelburg, Frankfurt, Cologne, Hamburg, Copenhagen.[27] Between all of these places the reuse of available material established another kind of Protestant international: 'from 1622 onwards . . . sixty to seventy percent of

English newsbook contents originated in the Netherlands'.[28] 'What newes?' asked one diary entry. 'Every man askes what newes? Every man's religion is knowne by his newes.'[29] As a result, Robert Burton asked, in 1624: 'Who is not sicke, or ill disposed . . . in whom doth not passion, anger . . . fear and sorrow raigne?':

> I heare new newes every day . . . [of what] these tempestuous times afford
> . . . of warre, plagues, fires, inundations, massacres, meteors . . . of townes
> taken, cities besieged in France, Germany, Turkey, Persia, Poland . . . dayly
> musters and preparations . . . so many men slain . . . shipwrackes, Piracies
> and Seafights . . . new books every day, pamphlets, currantoes, stories, new
> paradoxes, schisms, controversies.[30]

Approximately 600,000 corantos were published between 1622 and 1632.[31] The 'Jealous distrust that [James] would not easily bee moved to arme himself for the Protestants neither in Germanye, nor France' was the cause of 'those dayly Scandalls which both att home and abroade are most Injuriously heapened upon him'.[32] Dutch renewal of the war against Spain in 1621 further drew attention to the anomaly of Jacobean military abstention:

> I can come into no meetinges, but I find the predominant humor to be
> talking of the wars of Christendome and honour of their country . . . they
> spare not your Majesties sacred person . . . [but] wish Queen Elizabeth
> were alive again, who (they say) would never have suffered the enemies of
> her religion to have unballanced Christendome, as they have done within
> these few yeares . . . In your Majesties own tavernes, for one healthe that
> is begun to your selfe, there are ten drunke to the Princes your forraygn
> children.[33]

This public pressure crystallized royal anxieties about the obedience of Calvinist subjects to monarchy. James had excoriated local justices of the peace who 'in every cause that concerns prerogative, give a snatch against monarchy, through their puritanical itching after popularity'.[34] But there was an element of panic in his complaint about the parliament that begged him in 1621 to 'speedily and effectually take your Sword into your hand' that

103

[they left nothing] unattempted in the highest points of sovereignty . . .
except the striking of coin . . . [this was] an usurpation that the majesty of
a King can by no means endure . . . we cannot with patience endure our
subjects to use such anti-monarchical words to us.[35]

Such words were certainly available from Thomas Scott, writing from exile in
Utrecht. *The Belgicke Pismire* (London, 1622) counselled the English to '*Goe to
the* [Dutch] *Pismire, O Sluggard, Behold her ways, and be wise*' (Proverbs 6:6):

[C]onsider the wisedome of our *Prince*, which is so renowned . . . Let this
. . . assure us, that God hath not given Him so much light for nothing,
much lesse for evill. Let us thinke, that since He was intertained with . . .
so great signes of joy into this Kingdome, and hath been served since with
so much obedience . . . that Hee will [not] so much seeme to neglect his
own honour and safety, or our lives and liberties, as to leave us in the hands
of our enemies, or abase us in the eyes of other Nations, to leade us, or
suffer us to bee led into temporall or spiritual captivity.[36]

Scott enumerated the 'good Customes and Orders . . . established and practised amongst this diligent and happy people [which] . . . I could wish translated into our Commonwealth'.[37] They had rather chosen 'a safe Warre . . .
then an unsafe peace'. Where England was selfish and corrupt the United
Provinces was a commonwealth in fact, not only name.[38] There:

I observe a general freedome permitted and used, where generall actions
which concerne all, and are maintained by all, are . . . debated, argued,
sifted and censured by all men without contradiction . . . And this is
enough to make all wisemen . . . wish . . . that . . . our association might be
firme, our imitation safe . . . Let us . . . flocke thither where all things
abound, which wisemen and good men seeke: *Fidelity in bargaines and
contracts, wisdome in counsel, strength in warre, brotherly love and assurance,
modesty,* and *frugalitie . . .* in a word, *Pietie,* and *Religion.*[39]

Later, in 1629, Charles' minister Sir Francis Cottington ascribed the parliamentary refusal to pay tunnage and poundage after the dissolution of Parliament

to an 'infection' from the United Provinces 'whos kind of government pleaseth us much, and we would fayne be at it'.[40]

This perception of an assault on royal power permeated Charles I's complaints against his parliaments. For both James and Charles (and Elizabeth too) it was intolerable that subjects should attempt to determine royal marriage alliances or military policy. But a turning point was reached early in Charles' reign when, having responded to the public demand for war, the king suffered humiliation first on land (Mansfeld's expedition, 1625) and then at sea (Cadiz, 1626). For Charles the cause of these failures was clearly not royal inaction but the wilful disobedience of his subjects. Having pleaded for war, 'puritans' in Parliament now supplied it inadequately, and impertinently, upon conditions 'incompatible with monarchy'.[41] In Charles' first parliament Sir Robert Phelips reminded his collegues of a happier time when:

[t]hat glorious Q[ueen], with less supplyes defended herself, consumed Spayne, assisted the Low Cuntryes, relieved Fraunce, preserved Ireland . . . In Q Eliz tyme ther was never meetinge [of Parliament] but to reform greivances . . . We have given three subsidyes and three fifteenes to the Q of Bohemia, for which shee is nothing the better. Nothinge hath bene done.[42]

Three subsidies and three fifteenths were now worth a fraction of what they once had been. European armies were now much bigger and more expensive, their equipment and organization had changed, there was a desperate shortage of English military experience and logistical support, and Bohemia was strategically inaccessible. Elizabeth had been lucky, a quality which proved not to be hereditary. What were needed were new arms, armies, leaders, administrative methods and taxes. One way forward might have been to copy successful Dutch methods both of revenue collection and of military provision. During the 1620s a manuscript policy paper was prepared arguing for this solution. What it proposed was a reformation, not only of government but manners, in a merchant-friendly direction:

The best waie a State can . . . provide for a Warr is by Imitations of Those that have had the longest experience both of the provision + expense; and are nearest our owne times, if the Land bee capable of the same meanes.

The united Provinces, through their Policy of Govnm.t have subsisted long against One of the most potent Kings of the World . . . notwithstanding they are but a small people.[43]

As Scott had observed, this was made possible by their 'Frugality . . . the Foundation of a wise state . . . [and] Mother of all other Industries of Profitt'. In the contrary presence of 'Prodigality . . . [parliamentary] Subsidies make a great Noise but little Warr; the subject thinking they will doe miracles (how insufficient soever) by cause they are exhausted by sumes which they Feele; and for which they did not provide.' Second, the Dutch prioritized 'Traffique [trade] . . . As Frugality is a Wealth raised att home, soe Traffique is a Wealth brought home.' English Crown lands were no adequate fiscal basis for a state at war:

The Revenue of a Kings Land, is but as the Domaines of a Lordship, not to bee trusted unto but for a Mans private [income] Wheras a war being a publique worke must have a publique meanes . . . which nothing can better performe then Traffique: The meanes to inrich both king and Subject.

The Dutch understood that 'Traffique' was 'restrained by Impositions; and exceedingly hindred', but promoted by inviting in 'all Strangers and Strangers of all Religions by Freedome and Good Usage'. Their final master-stroke was:

Excise; a Revenewe drawne from Things belonging to Victuall and Cloaths, and to bee imposed generally upon the Subject; When the Prince is to make a greate and necessary Warre . . . This may bee spoken in the Approbation of Excise . . . That itt is more generall and continuall: and in the Collection of Subsidies many of the people are of necessitie omitted . . . That itt is a more easy way of Imposition to the Subject to pay by little and little in such a manner as if itt were in use hee would hardly . . . feele . . . itt.[44]

The document addressed 'those afraid of entertaining a Course for which wee have noe Precedent of our owne'. In fact 'wee have a Guide; which wee account safe even in a strange Country.' It added, in a striking defence of innovation: 'to thinke that all times either have or ought to have followed Presidents only, is an Errour; for then nothing had beene either helped or amended, and then had beene noe President at all.'[45]

Nothing was less likely than royal enthusiasm for this Dutch-style recipe for reform. The king's own wartime innovations in revenue raising, beginning with the Personal Loan of 1626–8, were associated by contemporaries with France.[46] Yet from 1649 the English military-fiscal state would indeed be entirely reformed along Dutch lines, building upon the first excise tax introduced by Parliament in 1643.[47] In the longer term Excise became foundational, not only to the modern and eventually globally dominant British military-fiscal state constructed between 1649 and 1760. Excise levied upon domestic manufactures combined with tariffs against imports financed the comprehensive system of state protection and regulation crucial to the eighteenth-century development of British industries such as silk, linen, cotton, iron, potteries, malt, beer, spirits, leather, soap, candles, paper and glass.[48]

Among parliamentarians there arose an alternative explanation of royal military failure which was predominantly confessional. Servants of the Crown laboured 'to put a jelosy betwixt the King and his well affected subjects by saying ther is a potent prevailing faction in the Kingdome ... calle[d] Puritanes'.[49] 'Never King,' explained one parliamentarian, in a not-subtle attack on the Duke of Buckingham, 'found a state so out of order.' 'Q Eliz ... governed by a grave and wise counsell, and never rewarded any man but for desert; and that so sparinglye.'[50] A key claim of the subsequent republican government of 1649–53 would be that it had replaced dynastic corruption with Dutch-style meritocracy: civic self-government resulting in virtue.[51]

In particular, 'As religion is decayed, so the honour and strength [of] this nation is decayed.' 'God has punished us because we have not spoken plainly ... and until we do so God will not bless us, nor go out with our armies.'[52] The state was infected by popery. When a Commons subcommittee reported in February 1629 'that if our religion is suppressed and destroyed abroad, disturbed in Scotland, lost in Ireland, undermined and almost outdared in England, it is manifest that our danger is very imminent', it listed among the causes of that 'danger here':

The suspension or negligence in execution of the laws against Popery ...
Divers letters sent by Sir Robert Heath, His Majesty's Attorney ... for stay

of proceedings against Recusants . . . The publishing and defending points of Popery in sermons and books, without punishment.[53]

In 1628 the Venetian ambassador reported the king's opinion that Members of Parliament were spearheading a 'popular assault on the very foundation of monarchy'. After dissolving his third parliament in 1629, Charles explained that the design of these individuals had been to use the necessities grown by that war to effect 'innovations (which we will never permit again) . . . to break through all ligaments of government, and to erect an universal over-swaying power to themselves'.[54] When nine years later the Scots rebelled he claimed that their design was 'not Religion, as they falsely pretend and publish, but it is to shake all Monarchical Government, and to vilify our Regal power'.[55] British historians have ascribed these utterances to paranoia. But they emerged from a ruler who was indeed experiencing in practice the fall of 'Monarchical Government' in his kingdoms; a fall which would inaugurate permanent change.

ANGLO-DUTCH-AMERICAN RESISTANCE

During the Personal Rule (1629–40) there followed an attempt to reform the culture of English Protestantism along anti-Calvinist, high clerical lines. These policies provoked the accusation of Arminianism, although 'Carolinism' was anti-doctrinal and had nothing in common with Dutch Arminianism other than opposition to Calvinism.[56] In fact, what Charles said about his opponents was true of his own policies: they were politically motivated. That opposition to them was spearheaded by Calvinists conditioned the makeup, not only of that resistance in England and Scotland, but also of the diaspora which fled abroad. This included another strand of Anglo-Dutch Protestantism: radical reformation. This had arrived in England via the Netherlands in the late sixteenth century. During the period 1618–48, as the storm became an Atlantic system, it established an Anglo-Dutch-American presence. Although most anti-Laudianism on both sides of the Atlantic was orthodoxly 'puritan' or (in England and Scotland) 'Presbyterian', there were radical Calvinists as well as anti-Calvinists (sometimes called Arminians). A hundred years later 'In America the dominant religion was [still] Calvinism . . . Congregationalists and Presbyterians, members of the German and Dutch Reformed Churches, most Separatists and Baptists concurred upon the Calvinist essentials.'[57]

Before the Revolt the Netherlands had taken in Anabaptists, who found a place to shelter alongside Lutherans and then Calvinists. Over the following century the openness of the United Provinces to heterodoxy became its most famous social feature. In 1673 William Temple reported that:

> [T]he *Jews* have their allowed Synagogues in *Amsterdam* and *Rotterdam*; and in the first, almost all Sects that are known among Christians, have their publique Meeting-places . . . The *Arminians*, though they make a great Name among them, by being rather the distinction of a Part in the State, than a Sect in the Church; Yet are . . . but few in number, Though considerable by the persons, who are . . . the more learned and intelligent men, and many of them in the Government. The *Anabaptists* are . . . very numerous, but in the lower ranks of people, Mechanicks and Sea-men, and abound chiefly in *North-Holland*.[58]

Since the early seventeenth century English and Scots congregations had formed in Amsterdam, Rotterdam and Leiden, the Dutch thereby reciprocating for the earlier English hosting of thousands of Dutch refugees.[59] Bishop Wren of Norwich reported on 'puritans' in his diocese and their passage to and from the United Provinces. He was said to have made 3,000 flee: Rotterdam had a particularly close relationship with dissent in Norfolk.[60] It also became the focal point for Anglo-Dutch mercantile relations:

> It was through their historic links with Rotterdam that the English and Scots were able to play a prominent and decisive role in the commercial life of Holland and the conduct of the North Sea trade in general. Soon after the transfer of the English staple from Delft to Rotterdam in 1635, the latter established its enduring position as the central conduit for Anglo-Dutch trade.[61]

From Dutch presses poured publications in which English 'bishops are dragged forth as thieves and murderers, vermin . . . spiritual wolves, prelatical dogs, crocodiles, asses, dunghill worms, locusts, venomous snakes and Amalekites to be put to the sword'.[62] During the 1620s and 1630s this Anglo-Scots-Dutch diaspora took its place within the American migration. Virginia, Plymouth and Massachusetts Bay were all settled from the Netherlands as well as England and they enjoyed cordial relations with nearby New Netherland. In 1627 Governor Bradford wrote from Plymouth to New Amsterdam wishing for 'love and good neighbourhood, in all our dealings; yet are many of us tied by the good and courteous entreaty which we . . . found in your country, having lived there many years . . . and shall never forget the same'.[63] The following year Bradford recorded that 'the Dutch sent again . . . from their plantation both kind letters, and also divers commodities, as sugar, linen cloth, Holland finer and coarser stuffs, etc.'[64]

From Massachusetts Bay in 1634 John Winthrop reported: 'Our neighbours of Plymouth and we had oft trade with the Dutch . . . at New Netherlands. We had from them about 40 sheep, and beaver, and brass pans, and sugar, etc.'[65] During the 1630s and especially the 1640s, when English shipping was disrupted by the civil war, merchants trading directly from Holland were also vital supports to these fledgling English colonies, appearing in greater numbers than English ships, offering better prices for colonial produce and lower rates of freight, and supplying:

> manufactures, brewed beer, linen cloth, brandies, or other distilled liquors, duffels, coarse cloth, and other articles suitable for food and raiment for the people inhabiting those places, in return for which are imported all sorts of . . . commodities, as . . . sugars, tobacco, indigo, ginger, cotton, and divers sorts of valuable wood.[66]

In 1634 Bradford recorded that a Plymouth vessel loaded with supplies in New Amsterdam had been stolen by a drunken Englishman resident in Virginia. 'But divers of the Dutch seamen, which had been often at Plymouth, and kindly entertained there, said one to another, "Shall we suffer our friends to be thus abused, and have their goods carried away" . . . They vowed they would never suffer it . . . and so got a vessel or two and pursued him, and brought him in again; and delivered them their bark and goods again.'[67]

During the 1630s migration to all of the American colonies intensified. The London port register for 1635 analyzed by Alison Games recorded the departure of 4,738 people in that year. They included Henry Vane jnr, between 1636 and 1637 the Governor of the Bay colony, and future architect of the English republic's navy.[68] Within America the predominant destinations were Virginia (2,009), New England (1,169) and Barbados (983). But in the same year, in addition to soldiers, another 1,034 migrants left for the European continent, the overwhelming majority for the Netherlands.[69]

In 1637–8, when active resistance to Caroline policies began in Edinburgh, Scots serving as soldiers in the Netherlands, Denmark and Sweden brought their military experience home. Now it was applied to defence of Scotland's Reformation, a purer and completer version, Scots agreed, than any other. Between 1637 and 1642 English-language pamphlets supporting the Scots cause were printed in Amsterdam and Leiden and smuggled into the Stuart kingdoms. Covenanters steeled themselves by reading Dutch histories and supportive political theorists like Althusius and Grotius. Most importantly from the Netherlands the Covenanters acquired arms, ammunition and men.[70] One historian has seen these developments as initiating the creation of an 'Anglo-Scoto-Dutch public sphere', a shared world of argument, translation and readership aspiring to establish a united military front for the defence of Calvinism/Protestantism.[71]

In the presence of the covenanting army Charles I's own military campaign fell apart. In 1640 a Scots invasion of England forced the king to summon Parliament and by 1642 he faced an English rebellion too. By the terms of the Solemn League and Covenant (1643) Scots and English parliamentarians committed to a reformed Church made safe from popery by the abolition of episcopacy 'and all of its dependencies, both root and branch'. In September 1642 Walter Strickland travelled as parliamentary envoy to The Hague to propose an Anglo-Scots-Dutch Protestant alliance. In the same year in Amsterdam parliamentary chaplain Hugh Peter, returned from Salem, 'preached three times last week to the English congregation ... some seditious things of very dangerous effect'.[72] During the war of 1642–6 English parliamentarians took comfort from Dutch precedent, in particular:

that passage of Grotius *De Jure Belli* where he saith, That if several Persons have a part in the *Summa Potestas* (of which he maketh Legislation a chief Act), each part hath naturally the power of defending its own Interest in the

Soveraignty against the other part if they invade it. And he addeth over boldly, That if in such a War they conquer, the conquered party loseth to them his share.[73]

Of the Dutch Revolt the royalist James Howell opined that no other conflict had 'produced such deplorable effects directly or collaterally all Christendom over'.[74] Now that the Reformation was being defended in England as well as Scotland, many opponents of Caroline policies in the Dutch or American diaspora returned. In addition to Peter and Vane they included John Lilburne, Richard Overton, John Goodwin, Henry Robinson and Philip Nye. 'The Civil War exacted a heavy toll among the top ranks of New England's leaders. Colony assistants, deputies, ministers, church elders – all found their role in God's service redirected by the Civil War.'[75] News of the war was eagerly sought in the colonies, where strong opinions on both sides were accompanied by strenuous attempts to avoid direct involvement.[76]

The predominantly parliamentarian posture of New England was not replicated everywhere. In May 1644 John Winthrop recorded in his journal news 'from Virginia . . . of a great massacre lately committed by the natives on the English there, to the number of 300 at least . . . because they saw the English took up all their lands from them, and would drive them out of the country'. But Winthrop preferred his own explanation, which was that the 'massacre occurred soon after' royalist Anglican Governor Sir Charles Berkeley 'had driven out the godly ministers we had sent to them . . . [so] that this evil was sent upon them from God for their reviling the gospel'.[77]

In 1643 English parliamentarians began Dutch-style fiscal reform, scrapping parliamentary subsidies and other customary taxes and replacing them with new ones including monthly assessment and excise.[78] In 1644–5 the legislation surrounding the creation of the New Model Army, most importantly the Self-Denying Ordinance, opened the way for meritocratic rather than aristocratic command of both the army and navy.[79]

FROM CIVIL WAR TO REVOLUTION, 1646–9

Between 1646 and 1649 an Anglo-Scots rebellion, inspired by the Dutch Revolt, and incubated within the Anglo-Dutch-American archipelago, gave way to revolution. Escaping the control of king and parliamentarians alike, developments in England transcended the familiar categories of crisis, invasion and war to culminate in an act so remarkable that it made the whole of Europe pause in stunned disbelief. This was the first public trial and beheading, by his own subjects, of an anointed king.[80]

This associated upheaval – a revolutionary iceberg of which the regicide was merely the tip – was driven by English radicalism. This was the deepest intellectual and moral consequence of England's troubles. Demanding fundamental religious, political, legal and social change, it had one context in the radical, anti-magisterial Reformation, with the earlier visitations of which in southern and central Germany, Austria, Switzerland and the Netherlands it had much in common. Its social focus was upon that practical Christianity which united Levellers, Diggers, so-called Ranters and Quakers.[81] To this, from 1649, would be added English classical republicanism, with contexts in the Italian and Northern Renaissance, drawing upon 'Aristotle . . . Plato, Plutarch, Thucydides, Xenophon, Polybius, and all of the ancient Grecians, Italians and others who asserted the natural freedom of mankind'.[82]

The literary and intellectual legacy of English radicalism survives within the avalanche of publications which followed the breakdown of press licensing between 1640 and 1660. Like the Dutch troubles, this last of Europe's wars of religion occurred within the London-centric context of a highly developed culture of the vernacular printed word.[83] As a result, alongside seventeenth-century England's extreme political instability it is impossible not to be struck by its astonishing intellectual fertility. This embraced science, literature, religion, philosophy and political thought. This was the century not only of Shakespeare, Jonson, Donne and Dryden, but Bacon, Newton, Hobbes and Locke; Walwyn, Winstanley, Lilburne and Coppe; Milton, Marvell, Harrington and Sidney. In the carefully chosen words of Sprat:

> The late times of *Civil War*, and *confusion*, to make recompense for their infinite calamities, brought this advantage with them, that they stirr'd up mens minds from *long ease,* and *lazy rest,* and made them *active, industrious* and *inquisitive:* it being the usual benefit that follows upon *Tempests,* and *Thunders* in the *State,* as well as in the *Skie,* that they purifie, and cleer the *Air,* which they disturb.

From 1640 radical Protestantism gained a foothold in London, and subsequently within the army. In 1647 the militarily victorious leadership of the House of Commons was swept aside by a New Model Army committed to ending religious compulsion and arbitrary power. The Leveller Richard Overton exulted:

> [U]pon this *Principle* the *Netherlanders* made a . . . defence and resistance against the King of *Spaine* . . . for the recovery of their just rights and freedoms; and upon the same *point* rose the *Scotch* up in Armes, and entred this Kingdome . . . and were justified for that very act by this present Parliament. Yea, and even this Parliament upon the same principle, took up Armes against the King. And now (*right worthy patriots of the Army*) you your selves upon the *same principle*, for *recovery of common right* and *freedome*, have entered upon this your present honourable and *Solemne Engagement*, against the oppressing party at *Westminster*.[84]

Now liberty of conscience, a demand of the Dutch Revolt since 1566, became a focal English requirement. What had been the result of 'this devilish spirit of binding the conscience' but rebellion, massacre and war?[85] That freedom from compulsion was no impediment to unity of religious substance was central to the religious culture of the New Model Army. As Oliver Cromwell wrote following the capture of Bristol in September 1645: 'Presbyterians, Independents, all had the same spirit of faith and prayer . . . they agree here, know no names of difference; pity it should be otherwise anywhere.'[86] This belief also derived:

> from London and other substantial towns, where independent, 'gathered' churches had proliferated since the early 1640s . . . [and] from the wars of the Low Countries . . . The many parliamentary soldiers who had served with the States' army knew from experience that diversity of belief among officers and men was no hindrance, indeed was a help, to good discipline and the successful pursuit of a common cause.[87]

Parliamentary commanders who acquired their military experience in the Netherlands included Sir Thomas Fairfax, the Earl of Essex, George Monk, the Earl of Warwick, the Earl of Bedford and Philip Skippon.[88] This exposed them to more than a military system. It gave them experience of an alternative Protestant society: one which was wealthy, modernized, successful, civilized and free. Partly as a result the Stuart monarchy was annihilated in the field.

On 30 January 1649, after seven years of war, Charles I was led to a scaffold in front of his Banqueting House and beheaded. The monarchy, House of Lords and Church were all abolished. Here the army departed from any official Dutch script to act as the instrument of a divine providence which demanded an accounting from 'Charles Stuart, that man of blood'. The king contributed to this outcome, depriving his opponents of room for manoeuvre by refusing to accept political as well as military humiliation. Later, revolutionaries in Paris showed that such events could be copied, now on the secular grounds of 'liberty, equality, and fraternity'. But before 1649 they had been unimaginable, and to that extent not only English but European history moved into uncharted waters.

In England in 1648–9, unlike in Germany in 1525, a radical Reformation army became the government. What English radicalism opposed was the 'outward bondage' not only of religious compulsion, but of economic, social, legal and political oppression. What radical Protestantism sought was Christianity in social practice, rather than merely worship. Subsequently this programme took the form of an attempted reformation of manners emphasizing, among other things, equality, community, charity, industry and sobriety.[89] All of this drew upon deep contemporary enthusiasm for godly and practical reform which, from 1649, began to reorganize English society and government in a partly Dutch direction, not only institutionally but morally.

When we ask why the later Industrial Revolution happened in Britain, rather than in the United Provinces, it is useful to remember that it was a revolution. It was not merely an incremental continuation of social and economic changes which had begun centuries earlier on the other side of the North Sea. Before 1650 the English economy had begun to grow and diversify, in agriculture, manufactures and shipping. The subsequent acceleration of these changes resulted in a proto-industrialization and commercialization the terms and dimensions of which, however, the Industrial Revolution transcended. The basis of industrialization in the Netherlands had been the development of 'services, especially finance, commerce and shipping'.[90] The Industrial Revolution in Britain was a product of manufacturing. The late eighteenth-century revolution in British manufacturing was enabled by the hyper-growth of a type of English colony and colonial culture of which there was no Dutch or French equivalent. What was necessary to this impact was the weaponization of England's relationship to its American colonies by the creation of an exclusive and militarily protected Atlantic trading system between 1649 and 1653.

By the early to mid-eighteenth century the United Provinces, for so long unique, were beginning to look quaint.[91] Between 1650 and 1750, and especially after 1713, the republic 'lost first its lead in manufactures, then in trade, and finally in finance, as well as its position as a European great power'.[92] The Industrial Revolution was, among other things, the long-term outgrowth of a radical political and military event: one that sent shock waves across Europe, and that created a new eighteenth-century superpower with which neither the United Provinces nor France could compete.

PART II

THE ANGLO-DUTCH REVOLUTION

> . . . though Holland seem to get the start of us, yet we may so follow as to stand at length upon their shoulders, and so see further.
>
> Hugh Peter, *Good Work* (1651)[1]

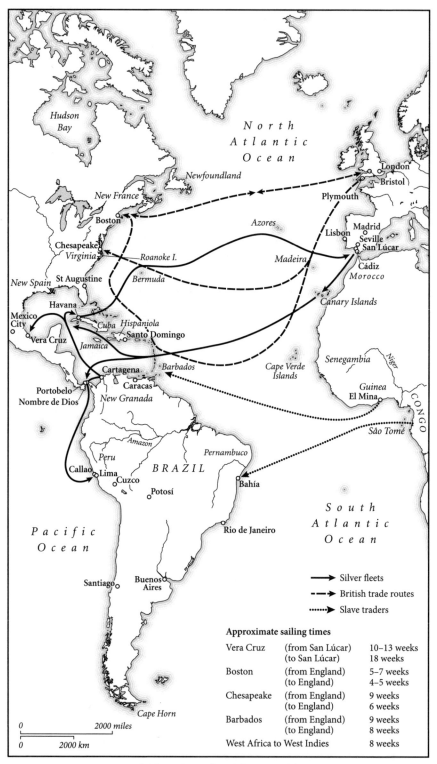

Hudson Bay

North Atlantic Ocean

Newfoundland

London
Bristol

New France

Plymouth

Boston

Azores

Lisbon   Madrid
Seville
San Lúcar

Chesapeake
Virginia

Roanoke I.

Madeira

Cádiz
Morocco

New Spain   St Augustine

Bermuda

Mexico
City

Havana

Cuba   *Hispaniola*

Canary Islands

Vera Cruz

Santo Domingo

Jamaica

Senegambia   *Niger*

Cartagena   *Barbados*

Cape Verde Islands

Portobelo
Nombre de Dios

Caracas

New Granada

Guinea
El Mina

CONGO

Amazon

Peru

Pernambuco

São Tomé

Callao   Lima
Cuzco

BRAZIL

Bahía

Potosí

South Atlantic Ocean

Rio de Janeiro

Pacific Ocean

Santiago   Buenos
Aires

→ Silver fleets

--→ British trade routes

·····→ Slave traders

Approximate sailing times

Vera Cruz	(from San Lúcar)	10–13 weeks
	(to San Lúcar)	18 weeks
Boston	(from England)	5–7 weeks
	(to England)	4–5 weeks
Chesapeake	(from England)	9 weeks
	(to England)	6 weeks
Barbados	(from England)	9 weeks
	(to England)	8 weeks
West Africa to West Indies		8 weeks

Cape Horn

0 ————— 2000 miles
0 ————— 2000 km

4. The early modern Atlantic world.

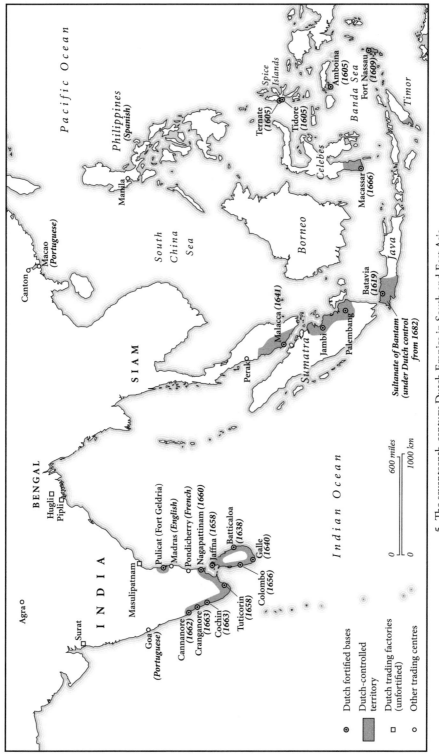

5. The seventeenth-century Dutch Empire in South and East Asia.

Pacific Ocean

Philippines (Spanish)

Manila

Macao *(Portuguese)*

Canton

South China Sea

Borneo

S I A M

BENGAL

Hugli
Pipli

Agra

I N D I A

Surat

Goa *(Portuguese)*

Masulipatnam

Pulicat (Fort Geldria)
Madras *(English)*
Pondicherry *(French)*
Nagapattinam *(1660)*
Jaffna *(1658)*
Batticaloa *(1638)*
Galle *(1640)*
Colombo *(1656)*
Tuticorin *(1658)*
Cochin *(1663)*
Cranganore *(1663)*
Cannanore *(1662)*

Indian Ocean

Perak

Malacca *(1641)*

Sumatra

Jambi

Palembang

Sultanate of Bantam (under Dutch control from 1682)

Batavia *(1619)*

Java

Timor

Celebes

Macassar *(1666)*

Ternate *(1605)*
Tidore *(1605)*

Spice Islands

Amboina *(1605)*
Fort Nassau *(1609)*

Banda Sea

0   600 miles
0   1000 km

Dutch fortified bases

Dutch-controlled territory

Dutch trading factories (unfortified)

Other trading centres

CHAPTER SEVEN

THE ANGLO-DUTCH REPUBLIC, 1649–53

> Do you not remember . . . that the Romans had a most flourishing
> and glorious republic after the banishment of the kings? Could it
> happen that you forgot the Dutch? Their republic, after the expul-
> sion of the king of Spain, after wars that were lengthy but success-
> fully waged, bravely and gloriously obtained its liberty.
>
> John Milton, *A Defence of the English People* (1651)[2]

> I doubt not, but many men, have been contented to see the late
> troubles in *England*, out of an imitation of the Low Countries;
> supposing there needed no more to grow rich than to change, as
> they had done, the forme of their Government.
>
> Thomas Hobbes, *Leviathan* (1651)[3]

THE ANGLO-DUTCH REVOLUTION

The year 1649 inaugurated a revolution in England – the real 'first modern
revolution' – with profound and permanent consequences. This would involve a
jarring process of change, over two generations, in the course of which the institutions, administration, power-structures and policies of English government were
remade to be capable of competing with their Dutch model.[4] That model was not
only political, military and economic but also religious, cultural and moral.

Although the focus of this chapter and the next is upon political and military developments, these had history-changing economic consequences. The
post-agricultural preconditions for the Industrial Revolution – commercial,
cultural, institutional and military – were all established at this time:

Britain was not among Europe's economic elite for most of the early modern period. It was only the long spell of unremitting growth beginning around 1650 that allowed it to catch up and ultimately surpass first Italy and then the Low Countries. This had already been accomplished before the sharp acceleration of growth *circa* 1830, highlighting the importance of sustained, rather than extraordinary rapid, growth.[5]

This was not simply a result of government policy. It reflected consumer demand anchored in growing private prosperity, as well as in an increasingly confident engagement with the world. But from 1650 it was powerfully enabled by a transformation of trade policy, of the military-fiscal state, and of financial and administrative sophistication. Comparative international evidence clearly links these changes to economic transformation.[6] The revolution of 1649 changed English government forever, under the leadership of a London-centred republican-mercantile alliance:

> The execution of Charles I in 1649 and the establishment of a republic had many causes . . . not . . . least . . . the feeling of many powerful interests . . . that hereditary monarchy could not reliably provide good governance . . . the establishment of a republic . . . showed a revolutionary willingness to change . . . That the monarchy was restored in 1660 should not hide the fact that the republic left important legacies; it had been part of a wider revolution of ideas about the human and natural worlds which were used to develop proposals to reform society and grow the economy.[7]

Chapters 5 and 14 discuss that 'wider revolution of ideas' as it affected both Dutch and English culture by the early seventeenth century.[8] From 1649 the Hartlib circle championed 'the simultaneous pursuit of economic betterment and a Baconian advancement of learning' promoting 'improvements in agriculture, commerce, and navigation'.[9] Specifically the English republic of 1649–53 was inspired by a Dutch republic which, 'bereft of mines, natural harbours and secure frontiers, but because of their institutions and habits . . . had defied the sea to build dykes and docks and successfully competed for the fisheries, commerce and finance of other nations. To many, the Dutch Golden Age showed what godliness and good government could achieve.'[10] Accordingly, during the revolution 'the impact of the Dutch went way beyond finance, accounting and trade . . . also informing manufacturing, printing, agriculture and natural philosophy . . . it was the Anglo-Dutch connection which created the modern British state.'[11]

For all of these reasons 'it has been persuasively argued that . . . [England's] second revolution, in and after 1688, did not introduce the institutional foundations for economic growth . . . but protected and built upon what had already been largely achieved'.[12] One result of the Anglo-Dutch revolution initiated in 1649 and secured from 1689 was 'a system of parliamentary and judicial constraints upon the crown' with economic as well as political consequences. 'Without well-defined and secure property rights resources may not be allocated to their most productive uses, and investment is inhibited.'[13] This was not a perspective invented by modern historians. In 1673 William Temple wrote concerning 'the Original of Trade' that the

> places where it has most flourished in the World, as *Tyre, Carthage, Athens, Syracuse . . . Rhodes, Venice, Holland . . .* are all Commonwealths . . . *Bruges* and *Antwerp . . .* show it may [also] thrive under . . . legal Monarchies . . . [but] Under Arbitrary and Tyrannical Power, it must of necessity decay and dissolve, Because this empties a Countrey of people, wheras the others fill it; This extinguishes Industry, whilst men are in doubt of enjoying themselves what they get, or leaving it to their children; The others encourage it, by securing men of both.[14]

Another admirer of Dutch government, William Penn, wrote similarly:

> 'tis the great interest of a Prince, that the People should have a Share in the making of their own Laws . . . [because] it makes men Diligent, and increaseth Trade, which advances the Revenue: for where Men are not Free, they will never seek to improve, because they are not sure of what they have, and less of what they get.[15]

We have seen that David Hume associated the history of commerce with free states and cities; Slingsby Bethel, a member of this republic's Council of Trade, added: 'nothing makes countries rich but Trade, and nothing increaseth trade but freedom'.[16] All of these commentators could have been, and Bethel certainly was, echoing the ideologist of Dutch 'true liberty', Pieter de la Court. 'All Republicks thrive and flourish more in Arts, Manufacture, Traffick, Populousness and Strength, than the Dominions and Cities of Monarchs, for where there is Liberty, there will be riches and People.'[17]

In his *Leviathan* Thomas Hobbes ascribed the English revolution to an attempted 'imitation of the Low Countries', seeking to replicate Dutch prosperity by copying the 'form of their government'. By 1651 – the year of the Navigation Act – Hobbes' retrospective (and mischievous) imputation of a commercial motive to the revolution looks understandable. In its early stages, however, the English republic emerged from a religious, political and military crisis which could not be settled on terms acceptable to the victors in any other way. This created a problem. How could this new order without any precedent in the country's history – the 'settling of the government . . . in way of a Republic, without King or House of Lords' – be normalized and embraced, especially by those at the helm?

Some historians have answered, in my view unconvincingly, that the parliamentarians of 1649–53 never managed the imaginative leap into post-monarchical government.[18] Others have found that bold public defences of the new government from 1649 as a 'republic' and a 'free-state' were in fact widespread.[19] Although it was installed by military power, participants in the regime regarded it as a new kind of state. This was elective and representative rather than monarchical and dynastic, and meritocratic rather than aristocratic. In March 1649 the government defended its decision 'to change the *Government* of this *Nation* from the former *Monarchy* . . . into a *Republique*'. In the 'Times of our *Monarchs* . . . *Injustice, Oppression* and *Slavery* were the [lot of] the *Common people*'. In '*Commonwealths*' by contrast 'they find *Justice* duly administered . . . the seeds of *Civil War* and Dissention, by particular *Ambition*, Claims of *Succession*, and the like . . . wholly removed . . . a just *Freedom* of their *Consciences*, Persons and Estates'.[20]

Accordingly the new governors looked for republican precedents upon which to model their experiment. The same *Declaration* asked:

> How much do the Commons in *Switzerland*, and other *Free States*, exceed those who are not so, in *Riches, Freedom, Peace*, and all *Happiness?* Our

Neighbours in the *United Provinces*, since their *change* of Government, have wonderfully increased in *Wealth, Freedom, Trade,* and *Strength*, both by sea and land.[21]

In 1650 Thomas Paget, a minister from Shrewsbury, agreed: 'There are manifold commodious advantages to people in Free-States: Manifold oppressions and damages . . . under Monarchy.'[22] In September 1651 a German envoy was advised by Master of Ceremonies Sir Oliver Fleming that the form of diplomatic address 'about a year ago unanimously decided in Parliament once and for all time' was '*Parlamento Reipublicae Angliae*', to which the boast was added: 'No republic since the beginning of the world ever rose up in so short a time without outside help by its own might except this one.'[23]

In December 1652 an overture from the French ambassador was rejected as lacking the word 'Reipublicae', and addressed merely to the 'Parlamento Populi Angliae'.[24] Meanwhile the government's newspaper *Mercurius Politicus*, 'which flew every week to all parts of the Kingdom . . . tis incredible what influence it had', intruded weekly doses of republican ideology. Thus issue 104, of 27 May 1652, began with the lesson 'That Children should bee educated and instructed in the Principles of Freedom', illustrated from ancient and early modern philosophy and history, and succeeded by news from Paris, Provence, Bordeaux, Brussels, Dunkirk, Edinburgh, Copenhagen, Norway, Lorraine, Warsaw, Alsace, Ireland, Sweden and the United Provinces.[25]

The Dutch was by far the most powerful neighbouring republic. It was Protestant and historically an ally. It had furnished an heroic demonstration that Counter-Reformation tyranny could be resisted. However, it was also new, details surrounding the peace agreed at Munster on 30 January 1648 remaining under negotiation. Moreover, it was 'a federation of cities, which, united in provinces, claim rights of sovereignty as small city-states'; or alternatively, in the words of the Zeeland delegation to the Great Assembly at The Hague in January 1651, 'a government which . . . is composed of *seven free and sovereign provinces*, each in turn consisting of diverse members and cities'.[26] Its political culture, 'corporate, provincial, collective, was based on the corporate structure of old Netherlandic society – families, neighbourhoods, cities, guilds, water management boards, polder administrations'.[27] It was profoundly different from centralized, London-dominated England. Therefore, beyond the fact of its republicanism it could not be a constitutional model. Moreover, the regicide on 30 January 1649 caused revulsion, not least because Orange and Stuart were dynastically related, and The Hague was a haven for royalist exiles.[28]

Yet the Dutch republic was a political and cultural prodigy, and a commercial and trading wonder. It constituted a religious, social and moral experiment of which many English parliamentarians and republicans had had beneficial personal experience. Accordingly the English republic set about remodelling government in the light of Dutch success, something which would not have been possible under monarchy. This was vigorously opposed, by the Dutch in particular. But such opposition had to contend with a highly centralized military government brought into being by two brutal civil wars. This government was also aggressive, revolutionary and imperial. From the Dutch the English republic would take the post-dynastic policies, and the fiscal and administrative practices, of a modern, mercantile and Protestant free state. These would be applied to the construction of a state and empire which were or became distinct, by measures directed in the first place against the competing economic pretensions of the Dutch themselves.

THE MORAL COMMONWEALTH

The English revolution aspired to a radical reformation of manners.[29] In this the Dutch republic was by far the most important inspiration. The Dutch could be mocked as worshippers of Mammon. However, their moral and social achievement was widely admired, and even their prosperity was understood to have its basis in industry. Max Weber noticed 'the keen observations on Dutch economic power . . . by the . . . Englishman Sir William Petty'. He traced its growth back to the especially numerous 'Dissenters' (Calvinists and Baptists) in Holland, who viewed '*work and the industrious pursuit of a trade as their duty to God*'.[30]

Thomas Scott's *The Belgicke Pismire* was full of observations concerning the organization, decision-making and policy of the exemplary Batavian ant colony. Underpinning everything was industry. As a disposition of soul this brought the community together. The ant was a 'common-wealth's man' rather than a 'common-woes' man', driven by the vice of 'privacie'. In the United Provinces the efforts of individuals benefited the whole, and provident work in the present built security for the future. This was a state organized to care for its needy and vulnerable; for everyone. 'Lett us observe the Lowe Countries in that Respect also . . . who out of the same Revenewe . . . provide not only for their owne poore, but for the poor of all Nations borne there; as a Man shall very seldome meet a beggar among them.'[31] This reflected 'a society in which the horizontal ties of power sharing were more important than vertical ties leading to monopolization of power'.[32] The result was an amelioration of the savage inequality which was the norm within Europe's aristocratic societies and dynastic states.

These were not aristocratic virtues; extravagance was a feature of courts. Nor were they simply mercantile. Venice, though like the United Provinces a mercantile republic, was governed by a nobility who valued magnificence and display. The elite of Amsterdam, by contrast, were commoners and Protestants, for whom frugality was an ideal.[33] From 1649 the English republic 'looked to Dutch precedents . . . in seeking to reform the administration of justice . . . and in trying to improve the provision of public welfare for the poor'.[34] Now that England was a 'true commonwealth' like Holland, wrote John Cook, it could aspire to a comparable level of social justice, where no one was 'exceeding rich, nor any beggars permitted'.[35] The larger force at work here was radical reformation, demanding greater equality, community and attention to poverty. On this Levellers, Diggers, republicans and Quakers agreed.[36] In the summary of George Fox:

> I was to bring people off from all the worlds' religions, which are vain, that they might know the pure religion, might visit the fatherless, the widows and the strangers . . . Then there would not be so many beggars, the sight of whom often grieved my heart, as it denoted so much hard-heartedness amongst them that professed the name of Christ.[37]

The Poor Man's Friend (1649) directed readers to Matthew 25:41, reminding them about 'God to whom an account must one day be given whether we have fed the hungry, cloathed the naked, visited the sick and imprisoned etc'.[38] The same concerns found expression in the republic's Act for the Relief and Employment of the Poor (1649).[39] They fed into the broader contemporary ferment on behalf of improvement, material and moral, inspiring the Protestant, transnational, ecumenical Hartlib circle which was closely connected to the new government. Hartlib's correspondents had ideas for every species of reform from welfare provision to Church government, agriculture, education and technology.[40]

William Temple remarked upon 'the simplicity and modesty of . . . [Dutch] Magistrates in their way of living . . . I never saw . . . Vice-Admiral *De Ruiter* . . . in Clothes better than the commonest Sea-Captain . . . Pensioner *De Wit* . . . was seen usually in the streets on foot and alone, like the commonest Burger of the Town.'[41] In 1651 Master of Ceremonies Oliver Fleming told the German visitor Herman Mylius that in England now 'no attention was paid to outward display; that men in Parliament with incomes of 60, 70 or more thousand pounds sterling who maintain whole manors nowadays often go on foot, without servants, let themselves be served a wretched dinner (*those were his words*) and so go on'.[42] For republican purser Richard Gibson, English naval power was transformed by a Dutch-inspired reformation of manners. 'It was by Seamen under Count Van der Marke that ye Briell was taken from ye Spaniard. And afterwards the siege of Leiden raised by Prince Wm of Orange. And by securing their Navigation the states of Holland got out of ye Spanish Tyrany and arrived at what they are.'[43] During the Civil War, Parliament had not been 'safe from the Treachery, Negligence Ignorance Cowardize + Covetousness of their Officers by Sea and Land until they came to ye Selfe denying Ordnance'.[44] After it ships were manned 'By Seamen well chosen not only to Comand but to mennage every place of charge in a ship, and not courtiers, Gentle[me]n, Decayed Cittizens or Pages'.[45] The qualifications of a seaman were industry, sobriety, 'Experience, diligence + Honesty'. The Anglo-Dutch war of 1652 was won by 'Courage and Conduct' in place of 'Bribery' and birth. According to Algernon Sidney, 'such was the . . . wisdom and integrity in those that sat at the helm, and their diligence in chusing men only for their merit was blessed with such success, that in two years our fleets grew to be as famous as our land armies'.[46]

Meritocracy as an English revolutionary ideology, in opposition to dynastic and aristocratic government, awaits its historian. 'Where the government is a Free State, there men are encouraged to the study of wisdom, truth, justice, &c. because not titles there, but good parts make men capable of honor, authority, and place.'[47] John Milton elaborated upon the moral superiority of republics a decade later:

a free Commonwealth . . . the noblest, the manliest, the equallest, the justest government . . . civil, and Christian, most cherishing to virtue and true religion . . . wherin they who are greatest, are perpetual servants and drudges to the public at thir own cost and charges . . . yet are not elevated above thir brethren; live soberly in thir families, walk the streets as other men, may be spoken to freely, familiarly . . . without adoration. Wheras a king must be ador'd like a Demigod, with a dissolute and haughtie court about him, of vast expence and luxurie, masks and revels, to the debauching of our prime gentry both male and female . . . to the multiplying of a servile crew, not of servants only, but of nobility and gentry, bred up then to the hopes not of public, but of court offices; to be stewards, chamberlains, ushers, grooms, even of the close-stool.[48]

Contemplating the collapse of the English cause, Milton added that this failure

must needs redound the more to our shame, if we but look on our neighbours the United Provinces, to us inferior in all outward advantages; who notwithstanding, in the midst of greater difficulties, courageously, wisely, constantly went through with the same work, and are setl'd in all the happie enjoyments of a potent and flourishing Republic to this day.[49]

POLITICAL ECONOMY AND ADMINISTRATION

As Lord Macaulay noted, the revolution of 1649 created a new military superpower.[50] Although English republicans understood this development in political and moral terms, it was more importantly the result of a step change in the material resources available to the state. This began during the Civil War with abolition of the old parliamentary taxes (subsidies; first fifteenths and tenths) and their replacement by excise (a tax on consumption) and assessment (a land tax) – customs duties remained. In addition the republic funded its military ventures by the proceeds of delinquency compositions and the sale of royal and episcopal lands. Between 1642 and 1660, it has been estimated, government income from these and other sources totalled 95 million pounds, an annual income more than five times that available to Charles I in the heyday of Ship Money.[51]

Beyond the windfall of confiscations this was the beginning of a permanent Anglo-Dutch revolution in political economy and civil and political administration. Like all successful early modern military-fiscal statebuilding it was an achievement of wartime (in 1642–56, 1665–7 and 1689–97).[52] It was also a product of parliamentary and/or republican government. One consequence was a new 'tax state'.[53] There was no attempt in 1660 to revive the fiscal infrastructure of the old regime: royal lands, knighthood fines, purveyance and wardship. 'Despite a . . . futile attempt by royalists to blank out the republican era and restore things to how they had been . . . the subsequent fiscal basis of the Crown retained . . . key innovations made during the last two decades . . . excise being the most controversial.'[54] These changes were accompanied by a broader makeover of political, fiscal and military administration. County committees, parliamentary committees, and for a period an Anglo-Scots Committee of Both Kingdoms oversaw every department of state, including the army and navy. Those services were 'new modelled' with an emphasis upon discipline, meritocratic appointment and more efficient delivery of victuals, equipment and pay.

The result was a sharp increase in the human as well as material resources devoted to the business of the state. Of the republican Admiralty, Michael Oppenheim remarked: 'In this period their daily duties, a personal eagerness to ensure perfection, and a broad sense of their ethical relation towards the seamen and workmen . . . was met with a success the Admiralty never attained before and has never equalled since.'[55] The fiscal settlements of 1660–5 and of 1689 were also parliamentary. The details were determined and then developed by committees pooling the necessary expertise. Following defeat in the second Anglo-Dutch war (1665–7), the Treasury was reformed along the same lines, not only its government, put into commission, but also its management and record-keeping:

Charles and his brother had been pondering the merits of Cromwellian administration, which they knew had been, characteristically, government by committee, and had decided that they preferred this republican style of managerial control to the courtly deference of some superannuated peer.[56]

The third and most powerful component of the modernization of the fiscal-military state would be the permanent provision of public credit.[57] Although decisively effected from 1694, this began in 1665, when Charles II, against vociferous advice to the contrary, surrendered his independent control of the order of repayment of Treasury loans to the House of Commons. This was the idea of ex-republican ambassador to the United Provinces, Sir George Downing. Its effect was to create the kind of legislative security for lenders which had underpinned the success of Flemish *renten* since the sixteenth century, and so to turn 'the exchequer into a kind of bank'.[58] The result, 'long before the post-Glorious Revolution period', was a crucial shift in the basis of public credit from the king to Parliament. 'This was not born of enlightened thinking but commercial aggression . . . [and] was, in all but name, a republican usurpation of royal authority.'[59]

SHIPPING NEWS: ENGLISH REPUBLICANISM WAS MERCANTILE AND MARITIME

The republic's most important Dutch import consisted in those mercantile and maritime policies which would change the course of British and world history. These created some essential preconditions for the Industrial Revolution, and more immediately they established the context for the first Anglo-Dutch war. The sudden prioritization of trade and naval power was the most revolutionary development of these years. Returning from two years in Amsterdam to become Secretary to the newly established Council of Trade in 1649, Benjamin Worsley advised the government to make 'Merchandise and Trading and the incouragement of it the Great Interest of the State, as many Commonwealths (I say not Kingdoms) have lately done. As of Venice Florence (when it was a *Common Wealth*) Genoa and Holland.'[60]

Henry Stubbe recalled in 1673: 'Those Subtle men who ruled in the Council of State . . . esteemed nothing more beneficial, just and generous . . . than to assert the Dominion of the Seas . . . and to vindicate the English commerce through all parts of the world. They did rightly apprehend that the strength of this nation consisted in Naval forces; and the life thereof was commerce.'[61] 'The tendency to trade,' Alfred Thayer Mahan wrote later, 'involving of necessity the production of something to trade with, is the national characteristic most important to the development of sea power.'[62]

The Dutch had placed the symbiotic relationship of commercial and naval power at the centre of state policy. Between 1649 and 1653 this strategy was copied by an English republican-mercantile political leadership. Charles I's government of the navy had stoutly resisted mercantile-maritime and non-aristocratic policy and influence. Sir Francis Bacon had written: 'To be master of the sea is an abridgement of a monarchy.'[63] The Lord Chancellor might have been referring to tension between the aristocratic imperatives of monarchical and the meritocratic requirements of naval and shipboard government.[64] The king's insistence on officers of social quality not only divided the navy, but divided its command structure from that of the private merchant vessels upon which it depended and which it was supposed to protect. In January 1642 the 'loathing, yearly growing in intensity, the seamen . . . had for their courtier captains' helped to drive the fleet to offer its service to Parliament. 'Charles's concern for the navy had always focused on his ships, not on feeding, clothing or paying the men who sailed them, and resentments ran deep.'[65] After the revolution these priorities were reversed.

Now Dutch mercantile strategy was translated to a different institutional environment. As a 'federated brokerage state' the United Provinces commissioned key aspects of its military requirements from privately funded and governed bodies like the VOC. 'In the Dutch republic the independent involvement of entrepreneurs in the organisation of warfare reached extraordinary proportions.'[66] More broadly, Dutch government 'combin[ed] . . . extensive local and provincial autonomy with structures that favoured the close involvement of capitalist elites in the execution of state tasks'.[67] The foundation of the English republic saw the close involvement in government decision-making of mercantile elites. But the associated administrative reordering, and radical augmentation of naval power, was funded and managed by a state which, already highly centralized, had been further liberated from customary legal and resource constraints by revolution. Between 1649 and 1653 there was a four-fold increase in the size of the navy. This enabled the writ of the new government to run not simply in British or European waters, but across the Atlantic.

On 3 October 1650 the Plantation Act promised to 'reduce all . . . parts and places [in America] belonging to the Commonwealth of England', an undertaking in which Worsley and his allies were closely involved.[68] This and the Navigation Act of 1651, long demanded by English merchants, laid the basis for ejection of the Dutch, not only from the English import trade which they dominated, but from that with England's North American and Caribbean colonies, to the supply of which they had been crucial.[69] The purpose of the legislation, and of its successor Acts during the 1660s, was to encourage not only trade but shipbuilding and the other maritime skills – sail-making, rope-making, map-making and navigation – which had underpinned Dutch success.[70] It was, that is to say, to establish within the English imperial world, and the world at large, a new maritime infrastructure and culture.

Although it arose in response to the need to secure the revolution in the face of rebellion in six American colonies, this was a strategy of revolutionary ambition and long-term effect, to include the creation of the world's greatest naval power.[71] However, the legislation could only be as effective as the naval ability to enforce it, and it was Dutch determination to test this which triggered the conflict of 1652–4. Thus John Streater celebrated 'that Act of Trade, that never to be forgotten Act . . . the Glory and Top of their great Advice . . . which occaisoneth a Chargeable and Dangerous War with *Holland*'.[72]

When Oliver Cromwell dissolved the republic in April 1653 he suggested that this was because its members had accomplished nothing. To the contrary, in fact, they were presiding over a successful war against Europe's leading naval power, in defence of mercantile policies which meant nothing to the army, at a cost of more than a million pounds a year. In the process they were creating a locus of prestige and authority alternative to that of the Lord General. During the dissolution Cromwell directed his invective specifically against the managers of the navy and war. '[A]nd at the going out . . . the Generall sayd to young Sir Henry Vane . . . that he might have prevented this extraordinary course, but he was a Juggler, and had not so much as common honesty.'[73] The witness was Vane's colleague Algernon Sidney, who remarked later of the war, 'they [the Dutch] were endangered and we destroyed by it'.[74]

Slingsby Bethel recalled:

When this late Tyrant . . . turned out the Long Parliament, the Kingdome was arrived at the highest pitch of Trade, Wealth, and Honour, that it, in any Age, ever yet knew . . . Our Honour, was made known to all the world, by a Conqueringe Navie, which had brought the proud *Hollanders*, upon their knees, to beg peace of us, upon our own Conditions, keeping all other Nations in awe.[75]

Bethel excoriated Cromwell as an ignoramus and imbecile on the subject of commercial policy, whose dissolution of the republic was a tragedy and the subsequent war against Spain even worse. The antithetical relationship between English republicanism, as manifested in government between 1649 and 1653, and Oliver Cromwell, is still not understood. The journalist Julie Burchill's description of Princess Diana Spencer as 'the best thing to happen to English republicanism since Oliver Cromwell' is a good example.[76] Sir John Seeley described the Navigation Act as the high-point of 'Cromwell's foreign policy'; Thayer Mahan repeated that 'the English navy sprang rapidly into a new life and vigor under his stern rule' and spoke of 'Cromwell's celebrated Navigation Act'.[77] Bernard Capp called his study of the republic's naval revolution *Cromwell's Navy*.[78] Dutch historians are no better: Maarten Prak called the Navigation Act Cromwell's proclamation and both he and Pepijn Brandon describe the Anglo-Dutch Union proposal of the same year as Cromwell's proposal.[79] All of these historians agree concerning the importance of this maritime and mercantile revolution, without realizing that it was achieved in spite of Cromwell, in his absence (in Ireland and Scotland), and that its success almost certainly provoked his destruction of the regime.

Similarly, Jonathan Israel has contrasted Dutch and English republicanism, the former being urban, mercantile and anti-aristocratic, and the latter rural and aristocratic. But the latter describes only James Harrington's entirely untypical *The Commonwealth of Oceana* (1656).[80] If one looks for other such English republicans there are none. Indeed Harrington's thought was not straightforwardly republican, being a hybrid of republicanism, royalism, natural philosophy and gentry-oriented Presbyterianism characteristic of the ruling class reconstituting itself around the Protectorate between 1656 and 1658.[81] *Oceana* was a pro-Cromwellian attack upon the republic and an attempt to woo the Lord Protector with anti-mercantile, terrestrial and pro-army policies.[82] Its fictional model commonwealth had no navy. For almost all English republicans, as we have seen, republics were typically mercantile and maritime.

In 1650 Henry Parker wrote: ' 'Tis ... apparent ... at this day, that the people of *Venice*, the *German* Hans-Towns, *Switzerland*, the *United Provinces* etc do more flourish ... then the *French*, *Turkish*, or any Royalists Whatsoever. 'Tis further as visible by the publike banks of Treasure kept in Democracies, and the strange splendour which Traffick brings them beyond Monarchies.'[83] John Streater added in 1654: '*Societies* or *Cities* were not only ordained for government and defence; but also for Trade and Commerce: the which I shall treat upon ... with Rules for increasing of Trade more effectually than yet hath been written by any'.[84] Later Algernon Sidney had his English courtier say of

the United Provinces ... we ... look on their power and riches ... security, happiness, and prosperity ... as a most pernicious example to England ... Holland, of all Europe the most ... unprovided, of all things requisite to the life of man; yet through good government and liberty of traffic so rich, powerful and prosperous ... [By] this example ... all our arguments for the splendour of a court and glory of a king ... are destroyed.[85]

The arrival of maritime and mercantile policy at the heart of English government was a republican achievement: post-monarchical, pre-Cromwellian, and inspired by Dutch example. The English republic of 1649–53 has been largely written out of seventeenth-century English political history. For too long the historiography of the century has been rendered inert by a charred crater at its heart, called 'Interregnum', signifying something absent, not present.[86] In fact the British Empire, Britain's century and a half of pre-eminent global power, and the Industrial Revolution, all had republican foundations.

RELIGION

The Dutch, Scots and English revolts were all attempts to defend Protestantism. Whereas from the beginning the Dutch conflict was also about liberty of conscience, in England that became pre-eminent only from 1646–7, and in Scotland it never did so. What followed in England in 1649 was not a Dutch-style patchwork of localized toleration for a myriad of faiths, but liberty for radical, or non-magisterial Protestantism only.

By the army this was taken to be the cause for which 'God hath so often and wonderfully declared himself'. Concerning the Dutch 'Interest of the Protestant Religion: True it is that it hath been there for many years professed, and exercised . . . and they have been a place of Refuge to many precious Saints, from the bitter persecutions of the Enemies of God, and true Religion'.[87] English republicans had reason to remember this, since so many of them had availed themselves of this shelter. But they were not prepared to replicate in England a situation where 'all other Religions, have had their professions there as well as the Protestant'.[88]

English republicanism, like English empire, was confessional. By contrast the fundamental premises of the Dutch republican ideology of 'true liberty' were economic.[89] Had Anglo-Dutch republican union eventuated this would have been a major problem. However, it is not the least important feature of the Anglo-Dutch revolution that liberty of conscience for Protestants arrived in England for the first time in 1649, the only such provision outside the Low Countries; or that it was made permanent with Dutch assistance in 1689.

ENGLISH REPUBLICANISM IN EUROPEAN CONTEXT

The architects of the Anglo-Dutch revolution applied themselves creatively rather than copying. The differences between English and Dutch institutional and social environments were highly significant in the making of a new great power. Unlike Holland, England remained in 1649 predominantly rural; it was governed not by a complex of cities but by one; its fiscal and political institutions were not federal but national and centralized; and, the moral ambitions of the revolution notwithstanding, there remained alongside negotiation an old-regime culture of command. Nor in England, unlike in the Netherlands, was the army during this period under secure political or social control. However, from 1649, the government was radical, republican, dominated by the interests of the city, unusually well-resourced, internationally ambitious and impatient for reform.

Under these circumstances, across the fields of religion, politics, social morality, political economy, and commercial and naval policy, the Dutch republic provided the model for the modernization of the English state. Although the republic lasted for only four and a half years it achieved a radical and permanent break with the past. Its military achievements in particular attracted Europe-wide attention and concern. Partly for this reason the new policies and administrative reformation survived the Protectorate and the restoration of monarchy. 'Charles II's . . . government declared its intention to reverse changes that it identified as incendiary. The reality saw little reversal but much obfuscation of the original source of the many improvements.'[90] A second Navigation Act was passed in 1660 and a second Plantation Act in 1663. A commercial revolution picked up speed from the 1670s. When, in 1689, the Stuarts were replaced by a Dutch king, William of Orange, the Anglo-Dutch revolution was completed as conflict gave way to fiscal, political and military collaboration.[91]

Such a process of borrowing and adaptation was not new, particularly in the context of war and revolution. Historians of the Dutch republic have also deployed 'the notion of the Netherlands as a *transport and diffusion country*, which took over knowledge, technology, and insights from other countries and cultures, appropriated them through a creative process of adaptation to local circumstances, and subsequently passed them on to others as their "own" Dutch products and values'.[92] To this they add the

> classical notion of *translatio*, or cultural transference. Already in 1650 the Dutch lived with a strong sense that the old power, knowledge and wealth of southern Europe were being handed on to the north and that the centre of European culture had moved to the Batavian Athens, as Leiden called itself, or the Batavian Rome that Amsterdam aspired to be. But transference did not involve a complete break. Venice inspired reflection on government, Rome remained the Mecca for painters, drawers, and sculptors; and for sciences . . . Italy, from Florence to Naples, proved to be an inexhaustible source of knowledge . . . The Town Hall of Amsterdam, with its direct allusions to the imagery of ancient Greece and Rome, illustrates in a highly concrete way this appropriation of forms and symbols and values.[93]

English classical republicanism, the revolution's richest theoretical and literary legacy, emerged from the same context.[94] England's republican governors understood their experience, and achievements, in these same terms. Algernon Sidney, who later lived in exile in Rome, finding there persons 'excellent in all sciences', claimed that it had been 'the design of the English . . . to make a Republic on the model of that of the Hebrews, before they had their kings, and on that of Sparta, of Rome, and of Venise, taking from each what was best, to make a perfect composition'.[95] This was the design destroyed by Cromwell, leaving another Italophile, John Milton, to famously enquire in 1660: 'Where is this goodly tower of a Commonwealth which the English boasted they would build to overshadow kings, and be another *Rome* in the west?'[96]

Above all, the United Provinces taught English republicans what good government could achieve. This was a lesson about the superiority of art (or artifice) and culture to nature, a theme to which we will return in Chapter 16. From 1649 the application of this insight to economic and social as well as political life began a transformation of the capacities of the state. The result, by 1702, was an economy led by a state capable of drawing upon all of the resources, moral and material, of the people by whose consent it ruled.

CHAPTER EIGHT

—— ◆ ——

THE REPUBLIC WAS AN EMPIRE

In the midst of all strife, never tired of raging,
Your city [Amsterdam] heaves its crown unto the very heavens,
And goes through fire and ice to find another world,
Guns thundering in all four directions of the wind.
                    Joost Van Den Vondel, *Gijsbrecht Van Aemstel* (1637)[1]

Is this, saith one, the Nation that we read
Spent with both Wars, under a Captain dead?
Yet rig a Navy while we dress us late;
And ere we Dine, raise and rebuild their State.
What Oaken Forrests, and what golden Mines!
What Mints of Men, what Union of Designes! . . .
Theirs are not Ships, but rather Arks of War,
And beaked Promontories sail'd from far;
Of floting Islands a new Hatched Nest;
A Fleet of Worlds, of other Worlds in quest . . .
That through the Center shoot their thundering side
And sink the Earth that does at Anchor ride.
                    Andrew Marvell, *The First Anniversary
                    of the Government under O.C.* (1654)[2]

The government of the English republic ushered in the second of three
early modern periods of unusual Anglo-Dutch proximity. These constituted
a sequence involving elements both of alliance and emulation, and of
conflict. That of 1649–54 was the most intense and creative, producing

139

THE ANGLO-DUTCH REVOLUTION

a proposal for political union giving way to the first of three Anglo-Dutch wars.

Why was an English revolution so comprehensively informed by Dutch example the harbinger of an Anglo-Dutch war? The question contains the answer. For the Dutch republic, in possession at last of its internationally recognized independence, the appearance on the other side of the North Sea of a new state committed to similar policies, targeting many of the same resources, and supporting them with a revolutionary augmentation of naval power, was a nightmare. The danger was compounded by the not-coincidental proposal for political union. For the English republican Ralph Maddison the revolution of 1649

> transformed relations with the Dutch, making that neighbour republic . . .
> a model to be emulated and a rival to be feared . . . in a Commonwealth,
> new avenues for economic improvement had opened up . . . like the banks
> and free ports of the United Provinces. They should look there for examples
> of best practice . . . Yet the Dutch were also competitors, and likely to
> monopolize all the trade of Europe unless . . . they were 'incorporated one
> nation with us', a prospect they had refused to contemplate.[3]

Having seen off one existential threat the Dutch republic now faced another. The union proposal of 1651 was not, like the Dutch offer of sovereignty to Elizabeth of 1584, or the crowning of William and Mary in 1689, a partly dynastic project. Dynastic confederations, like the Stuart union of crowns of 1603, were relatively common in early modern Europe. A proposed union between two sovereign republics was far more unusual. Caroline parliamentarians had long demanded 'a more strict alliance with the states of the United Provinces'.[4] But how did what Edward Ludlow called 'the coalescence so much insisted on . . . by the Parliament' come to take such an extreme form, and why was the proposal, which may have been a demand, followed by war?

Approaching these questions two themes will be emphasized. In the first place, from the moment of its foundation the English republic was, and behaved like, an empire. Second, it was the product not only, as in the Netherlands, of a rebellion and fiscal/military revolution which built the state. More than its Dutch model the English republic entailed a sharp, indeed spectacular, break with the past, accompanied by a revolutionary as well as an imperial ideology.

REVOLUTION AND EMPIRE

The English republic was an empire partly because of the circumstances from which it emerged: a regional war which displaced traditional power structures in three Kingdoms, and across the Atlantic. Before anything else the new government had to secure itself militarily within that context. But the republic was also an empire by virtue of the ideological forces by which it had been created and which developed in response to its startling military achievements. It was in light of both of these circumstances that English republicanism was distinguished by its imperial bellicosity.[5] The revolutionary government revived with unprecedented vigour a Western design envisaging the establishment of 'a single transatlantic state [incorporating the] British isles and every English colony'.[6]

One component of what became the republican ideology of empire consisted in the social concerns which had informed Tudor and Stuart commonwealth literature. John Streater and Marchamont Nedham developed Hakluyt's perception of Western Planting as a cure for overpopulation and unemployment. More broadly plantation figured as a manifestation of industry, the opposite of sloth and military inactivity. Ants sent out colonies of workers and soldiers, 'It being in Plantations of Men, as in that of Bees, amongst whom one *Swarm* sends out another, that begets a *Castling*, till the whole ground or Garden grow too small to hold them.'[7] In the later words of Algernon Sidney, developing a theme from Machiavelli:

> He that builds a city, and does not intend it should increase, commits as great an absurdity, as if he should desire his child might ever continue under the same weakness in which he is born. If it do not grow, it must pine and perish; for in this world nothing is permanent; that which does not grow better will grow worse.[8]

The second strand of imperial argument was religious. Hakluyt had explained that it was Elizabeth's duty to rescue indigenous Americans from heathen and popish idolatry. This was one component of a global confessional war against Spain. Before his death Sir Philip Sidney had drafted a 'heroical' plan for 'Planting upon the Main of America', and attempted to join Francis Drake's voyage of 1585. Fulke Greville said of Sidney, in words published, significantly, in 1652: 'To Martiall men he opened wide the door of sea and land, for fame and conquest. To the nobly ambitious, the far stage of America, to win honor in. To the Religious divines . . . a calling of the last heathen to the Christian faith . . . [and] a large field of poor Christians, misled by the Idolatry of *Rome* . . . To the curious, a fruitfull womb of innovation.'[9] English empire, tempered to a slicing edge in Ireland, had always been confessional. In this respect it more nearly resembled its Spanish than Dutch counterpart (see Chapter 9). This underpinned the 'Planting', in Ireland and North America, of people and culture rather than (merely) things.

The third component of imperial ideology was classical. The empires of Athens and Rome had advertised their brilliance. In the words of Pericles: 'Mighty indeed are the marks and monuments of our empire . . . Future ages will wonder at us, as the present age wonders at us now.'[10] The Elizabethan Thomas Smith explained: 'nations . . . that be politic and civil do master the rest . . . The empires of the Greeks and Romans do that declare.'[11] Yet not until 1649 did England acquire either the military power or the republican political form appropriate to such ambitions. It did not take the new 'Free State' long to begin thinking about its situation in these terms. Nedham explained in the first book-length defence of the Commonwealth in 1650:

> Livy . . . tells us so many quarrels and tumults arose about division of lands that the Senate knew not which way to prevent them till they disburdened the commonwealth by sending forth colonies and satisfying them with lands in the remote parts of Italy and other places.[12]

In the terms developed by Machiavelli's *Discourses upon . . . Livy* England was a Commonwealth for Expansion (like Rome) rather than merely Preservation (like Venice), a claim subsequently developed in detail by James Harrington and Algernon Sidney.[13]

In practice, following the regicide, the first task of the New Model Army was the long-delayed subjugation of Ireland. This was accomplished in 1649 with unheard-of speed and infamous brutality. There was more than a touch of the Duke of Alva in Cromwell's confessionally informed massacres of civilians at Wexford and Drogheda. As Clarendon remarked, Cromwell's Irish settlement could not have been achieved by a " "virtuous prince and more quiet times" ' . . . confiscating half the island and transferring . . . a third of it, some seven million acres, from Catholic to Protestant ownership'.[14] A subsequent mapping and survey, distinguishing between 'profitable' and 'unprofitable' lands, were the work of Benjamin Worsley and William Petty, both members of Hartlib's network.[15]

The army then turned to Scotland, which had been outraged by the regicide and was now pre-emptively invaded. John Milton subsequently praised Cromwell who 'in one battle . . . broke the power of Hibernia' and 'in . . . one year . . . completely subdued and added to the wealth of England that realm [Scotland] which all of our kings for eight hundred years had been unable to master'.[16] By 1653 legislation was in progress 'in order to the Uniting of Scotland into one Commonwealth with England'. Henry Neville, a member of that committee, remembered:

> The Union of that nation was then calculated for a Commonwealth, and not for a Monarchy. England was then, by the blessing of God, governed by its own representatives . . . You promised it to them, to take them into your bosoms and make them one with you. The Romans never did well till they did so.[17]

Thus the republican union proposal made to the United Provinces in 1651 was the first of two, and it was made again, and refused again, at the conclusion of the war in 1654.[18] Meanwhile the impact of the English republic's internationally expansive understanding of its political remit was also felt elsewhere. In 1652 the Venetian ambassador to France reported: 'The opportunity enjoyed by the English of going yearly to Bordeaux in order to ship wines, has given them ample means . . . of impressing their own opinions on the inhabitants of that city . . . This seems to have led to speeches in favour of liberty, advocating the expulsion of the parliament and the forming of a more popular one . . . in short governing themselves.'[19]

As to its longer-term impact the most important context for consolidation of the new government's imperial claims was maritime. The regicide and associated events of 1649–50 sent shock waves across the Atlantic. Antigua, Barbados, Bermuda, Maryland, Newfoundland and Virginia responded by declaring for Charles II. Thus the security of the republic required an imposing presence at sea, as well as on land. 'While subduing rebels . . . the Commonwealth articulated an aggressive imperial agenda. It envisioned the state controlling the governance of the individual plantations as well as their trade, in this respect as in others departing from earlier royal policies. Revolution . . . thus stimulated the creation of a more centralized and rationalized . . . approach to the Atlantic plantations.'[20]

THE MARINE REPUBLIC AND THE NEW ATLANTIC ECONOMY

In early 1649 the nation possessed fifty warships, a slight increase in the number inherited by James VI and I in 1603. Between 1649 and 1654, 147 were added in pursuit of 'the revolutionary goal of constructing a permanent fleet'.[21] Many but far from all of these were captured prizes. The programme consumed 20 per cent of the total government budget. This was the first step towards a situation whereby 'between 1689 and 1763 annual investment in the army and navy nearly always accounted for two-thirds of government expenditure', with investment in the navy much higher than in the army.[22]

This was the work – while Cromwell and the army were attending to Ireland and then Scotland – of an alliance between what Robert Brenner called 'new merchants' and 'imperialist republicans'. Whereas during wartime Charles I had built one or two new ships a year, the English republic built tens and dozens – twenty-two in 1654. While it had taken the early Stuart Crown a year to plan 'a peaceful summer cruise in the narrow seas', the republic patrolled the Channel, the Mediterranean and Caribbean simultaneously.[23] Between 1649 and 1650 Admirals Blake and Penn imposed the republic's naval writ upon the North Sea, Irish Sea, the Atlantic coast of Portugal and the Mediterranean. 'England's rights, or reparation for her wrongs, were demanded by her fleets throughout the world – in the Baltic, in the Mediterranean, against the Barbary States, in the West Indies.'[24]

Behind this naval revolution lay more than money and ships. At its heart stood administrative reconstruction and moral renewal. In February 1649 the fleet was put into the hands of commissioners who 'proved indefatigable'.[25]

Reforms followed under a new Admiralty Committee headed by Sir Henry Vane. Officers' pay was substantially increased, rules were imposed to secure a fairer share of prizes for crews, and shipboard discipline tightened. Corruption was targeted and emphasis placed in recruitment on both experience and adherence to the cause. The result was a fleet led by 'well-trained and politically committed officers . . . including ideologically driven radicals at less exalted ranks':[26]

> Another advantage possessed by the English navy in 1652 . . . [was] the high morale of the sailors . . . their conditions were vastly superior to those endured by their unpaid, half-starved predecessors of Charles I's navy. The Commonwealth had resources of taxation and fines and sales of property unknown to the first Stuart kings and they laboured hard to pay their sailors and to care for the sick or wounded and for the dependents of the slain. The sailors repaid this solicitude by very low rates of desertion compared with the Dutch fleet . . . Finally they were well led and they knew it. Robert Blake was a legend among his men long before the Dutch war.[27]

Apart from Vane the political architects of this marine republic included Henry Marten, Thomas Chaloner, Thomas Scot, Henry Neville and (from 1652) Algernon Sidney. Their 'confidence and competence in . . . commercial and foreign affairs' were assisted by their alliance with 'new merchants [who] played a very direct . . . role in the processes of commercial and foreign policy making . . . conditioned by their extraordinary penetration . . . of all levels of militia, naval and financial administration within the commonwealth'.[28] This alliance was recognized by a Venetian observer in 1651: 'Owing to the care of parliament they have 80 men of war, which are certainly the finest now afloat, whether for construction, armament, or crews. They can increase these numbers with incredible facility to 150, 200 or more sail . . . [In addition] trade . . . has made great strides for some time past, and is now improved by the protection it receives from parliament, the government of the commonwealth and that of its trade being exercised by the same individuals.'[29]

It was this leadership that formulated the government's response to the Revolt of some American colonies. The Plantation Act of October 1650 did more than merely vow to 'reduce [militarily] all . . . parts and places [in America] belonging to the Commonwealth of England'.[30] It forbade them in future to trade – for slaves, food, plantation produce or anything else – with foreigners, which meant in practice with the Dutch. Far from being merely a temporary measure this was intended to be permanent. The idea was to establish 'English merchant hegemony throughout the British Empire'. Because 'Commonwealth commercial policy was . . . an expression of the aims of the imperialist republicans and the new-merchant leadership . . . support for commercial development tended . . . to be raised almost to the level of a principle'.[31] Colonists protested vociferously. 'All the old *Planters* [of Barbados] well know how much they have ben houlding to the *Dutch* for their subsistence, and how difficult it would have been (without their assistances) ever to have settled' the island.[32] 'If the Hollanders must not trade to *Virginia* how shall the Planters dispose of their Tobacco . . . [if] The English *will* not buy it?'[33]

This legislation did indeed precede the ability of English colonies to survive without Dutch supply and markets. In addition to addressing the republic's security concerns it was a response to the resurgence of Dutch mercantile activity in the Baltic, the Mediterranean and the Americas following the peace with Spain in 1648.[34] Soon the government's ships were in the Caribbean and in Virginia and the new arrangements were being imposed. Twenty-four Dutch ships were seized in Barbados in 1651–2 and the same number again in 1655–6.[35] Together the Plantation and Navigation Acts established the framework for the navally protected Anglo-American commercial system. Over the following century this would become the most important basis of British global commercial and military power.

The Acts were the work of 'an influential . . . association of London merchants, which included parliamentary committee members, whose ambition was to drive back Dutch competition and advance English trade . . . through the device of a national monopoly. In the past foreign trade in England had been a matter for corporate monopolies . . . [but] these new men were in favour of the very liberalisation and reform which had earlier fuelled Dutch expansion'. The legislation instituted

an early form of . . . 'imperial preference' . . . goods imported into England must be brought directly from the country of origin and in English ships or in ships of the country of origin. Moreover no goods of Africa, Asia or

America were to be imported in foreign ships . . . the target is clearly the Dutch entrepot trade. The monopoly companies had wanted the Dutch restricted by increases in their own privileges, but the government had listened to the 'free' traders and made the terms of the act general, a significant departure from precedent which heralded the beginning of a gradual decline in the significance of these companies in the nation's commerce.[36]

The result was a sharp correction to previous commercial practice, informed by Dutch example, which had supported national monopolies like the VOC and WIC with the full military weight of the state, and which did not suffer anyone else to thus monopolize regional trade. At the same time administrators like Worsley noted other keys to Dutch success, such as their 'singular and prudent care in preserving the Credit of most of those Commodities which are their own proper Manufactures; By which they keep up the Repute and Sale of them abroad, taking hereby a very great advantage of the contrarie Neglect in us.'[37]

The system at which these Acts took aim was global, with 'Amsterdam the commercial capital of an empire with trading posts and colonies in North America, the Caribbean, West Africa, around the Indian Ocean and through the East Indies'.[38] The result over the next century and a half would include replacement of the global commercial pre-eminence of Amsterdam by that of London:

> Protectionism, coupled with a powerful navy, a strong state, and the funding to prosecute war, became part of the 'inseperable connections' that combined to forge Britain's rise to global power over the course of the eighteenth century. Protection afforded by the Navigation Acts and the Royal navy was an essential feature of the pursuit of mercantilist objectives. The five Navigation Acts implemented between 1651 and 1696, and the three Anglo-Dutch Wars of 1652–1654, 1665–67 and 1672–74, eliminated the Dutch from much of the carrying trade and ensured that Amsterdam did not become a greater trading entrepot than London.[39]

Thus a key result of the Anglo-Dutch revolution of 1649–1702 was a sharp reorientation of global maritime and mercantile power away from the

Netherlands and towards Britain. While initially involving war, this process was continued by means of peaceful co-operation as the two countries became allies against France from 1689, with London's money markets now attracting large-scale Dutch as well as English investment. Analyzing the eclipse of the United Provinces by England as the world's leading naval and commercial power, Thayer Mahan placed emphasis upon the policies of the Anglo-Dutch government of 1689–1702:

> When William III came to the throne, the governments of England and Holland were under one hand, and continued united in one purpose against Louis XIV until the Peace of Utrecht in 1713 . . . The English government more and more steadily . . . fostered the growth of her sea power [and] sapped the power of Holland afloat. The treaty between the two countries provided that of the sea forces Holland should furnish three eighths, England five eighths . . . [and] made Holland keep up an army of 102,000 against England's 40,000 . . . and at the peace, while Holland received compensation by land, England obtained, besides commercial privileges in France, Spain and the Spanish West Indies, the important maritime concessions of Gibraltar and Port Mahon in the Mediterranean; of Newfoundland, Nova Scotia, and Hudson's Bay in North America.[40]

AN ENGLISH PROPOSAL FOR EUROPEAN UNION
(INCLUDING FREEDOM OF MOVEMENT)

In the spring of 1651 William Strickland and Oliver St John led a large delegation to The Hague for the new republic's first major diplomatic overture. This requested a 'comprehensive and permanent alliance' between the two states for the mutual defence of their 'protestant religion and republican liberties'. When the Dutch replied affirming the 'ancient friendship' between the two nations, the English countered by demanding 'a nearer union than formerly hath been . . . with all speed'.[41] We should be in no doubt about the novelty of what was here proposed. The idea, explained the newspaper *Mercurius Politicus*, was that 'These two great republics . . . equally hated by all monarchies in Europe . . . [should] become as one entire body.' The resulting 'Confederacy and Union' would have allowed any citizen of either republic, 'being of the Reformed religion', to 'freely dwell and inhabit', own and inherit property, and enjoy full legal rights in the other.[42] In the words of Jonathan Israel this was a proposal for union 'of the sort which Parliament had recently imposed, by force, on Scotland'.[43]

Israel has emphasized the damage such a union would have caused to Dutch primacy in trade.[44] Historians of English politics have pointed out that the United Provinces was not simply a sympathetic republic, but contained a large constituency of pro-royal Orangists, to say nothing of the royalist exiles who vilified the regicide republic, and screamed abuse at their 1651 delegation.[45] More importantly, having only three years earlier won an eighty-year-long struggle for their freedom, the Dutch could hardly have been expected to hand over in friendship what they had won by the sword. Indeed in January 1651 the seven United Provinces reaffirmed a constitutional Union which carefully protected the internal sovereignty of each of its members.

The proposal was an English political project. Even externally it had little to offer the Dutch, whose international relationships hinged primarily upon securing concessions concerning trade. There is no evidence that any of the seven Provinces seriously considered it, and neither have Dutch historians.[46] In the formulation of one Dutch pamphleteer in 1651:

Commerce and traffic are often . . . mixed with great Jealousy, especially between neighbouring republics. As two twins, they constantly fight and wrestle with each other over profit. Therefore it can also be compared to connected waters, where the growth of one place is the erosion of another. For this, many wise and far-sighted persons have judged that commerce would be handled with more profit and security by their state if England would remain a kingdom, than if it turned into a republic.[47]

Thus the Dutch had less incentive to co-operate with the new regime in England than to challenge it, or at least hope it would go away. Accordingly, in the gleeful formulation of Edward Hyde, St John returned from The Hague with 'extreme indignation . . . which he manifested . . . to the Parliament; who, disdaining likewise to find themselves undervalued (that is, not valued above all the world besides) presently entered upon counsels how they might discountenance and control the trade of Holland, and increase their own.'[48] In the drafting of the subsequent Navigation Act, St John played a key role. Yet as we have seen, and Hyde did not, the Act only built upon revolutionary colonial and trading policies which had already been developed.

The English republic, too, had emerged from a remarkable recent war. This had swept away not only the opposing armies but monarchy itself, and with it English military impotence. English security required an end to the Dutch haven enjoyed by royalists, a key demand of the union proposal, and to the liberties taken – in practice the near monopoly of local shipping enjoyed – by Dutch merchants protected by their navy. If the Dutch would not recognize the benefits of peaceful union, they could be made to experience the consequences of independent English power.

Specifically the Navigation Act directed its attention to the imbalance between English and Dutch carrying within English territorial waters. This had been a long-standing subject of mercantile complaint, leading to a Proclamation by James I in 1624 attempting to prohibit the import of commodities of third-party origin in anything other than English ships.[49] Proclamations, however, were cheap. What was required for any such measure to be effective – and the Navigation Acts went further – was a transformation in the size and nature of England's merchant fleet, and a national navy capable of enforcing the new regulations. This was a matter not only of military capacity but of political will. It was the arrival of both of these things between 1649 and 1652 which made the situation, or showed it to be, revolutionary. In the view of Jonathan Israel this was such a spectacular initiative, with such huge economic implications, that the Dutch had little choice but to oppose it.

THE FIRST ANGLO-DUTCH WAR, 1652–4

Thus the first Anglo-Dutch war was not fought, as Steven Pincus once argued, because the Dutch republic was believed to have become corrupt.[50] Rather it was fought, as the government's public defence of it proclaimed, because England had ceased to be so. This was a necessary component of the attempt to make the English government and economy more like those of the Dutch. When England too had a republican-mercantile government contriving 'laws and orders' at home and making treaties abroad 'to the securing and promoting of their traffic', then the wealth of the world would have (at the least) to be shared.[51] In this as in other respects the English revolution had to be militarily secured, regionally.

Thus the longest-standing explanation of this conflict, expounded by Charles Wilson, adapted by Christopher Hill, and still adhered to by Jonathan Israel, has correctly focused upon trade. This was, however, from the English side – and this entire sequence of events was initiated in England – merely the economic component of a political and military project.[52] It was an assault upon Dutch mercantile hegemony which emerged in the context of revolutionary political and imperial ambitions. History showed that it was republics rather than principalities which understood the value of maritime power and trade (and banks and money). Liberty and prosperity, material and moral, were intertwined. Thus the replacement of English monarchy by a republic in 1649 was a fundamental precondition for the complete reorientation of the country's economic history which unfolded over the subsequent century and a half.

There was a history of Anglo-Dutch economic grievance, particularly from 1609. Within that context England's long-standing claim to sovereignty over the Narrow Seas, though it had economic content, had been a political claim, and the Dutch response to it showed rigidity or flexibility (the striking of sail) according to calculation of the likely impact of both claim and response. Everything changed following the arrival of serious English mercantile ambitions with the full military backing of the state. Nedham explained:

Now the *Dutch* refusing to strike, do deny our Title, and . . . would fain make the striking of the Flag a frivolous thing; yet it is of as much concernment to us, as the Dominion of those Seas . . . And this together with the managing of our Trade for our best advantage, held forth in the Act for *Navigation* . . . may be strongly presumed to be the true grounds for their quarrel . . . The truth is . . . through the negligence of former Kings . . . these people . . . had not only got a Staple of Trade . . . but had almost ingrost all our Trade, and thereby spoyled us of our Navigation and Maritin Defence, Our long voyages about the world . . . being curted to their borders, and mostly in their own ships, to fetch from their stores at the second hand, and to retail it in *England*.[53]

Things would now be different 'in a Commonwealth well ordered'.[54] On the eve of the first clash between Lieutenant-Admiral Maarten Tromp and Blake off Dover on 19 May 1652 the Venetian ambassador Lorenzo Paulucci reported: 'The negotiations with the Dutch ambassadors are incessant, as the ministry is well aware that by a good understanding with them the security of the present government will be to a great extent established . . . The Dutch insist on the repeal of the Act of Parliament forbidding them to import foreign merchandise. This meets with great, not to say insurmountable difficulties.'[55] English sources described the encounter as a treacherous Dutch attack. All agreed that it was unexpected. Paulucci described Tromp being saluted by Blake 'in token of amity, but still more as a hint to strike [sail]':

> The Dutch General not being inclined to admit this, contented himself with returning the compliment by firing a single gun . . . [Blake] then repeated the warning by another discharge, and as that also was disregarded, he desired a shotted gun to be pointed at the flag itself. This so incensed Tromp that he began to fire shot after shot at the English.[56]

This account largely agrees with that by Nedham. The encounter appears to have been an attempt by Tromp to test English resolve to defend both the flag and the Act. Since the English squadron was heavily outnumbered the result might have come as a surprise. Richard Gibson later claimed that the Dutch had dared 'to make war on us' on the assumption that England had 'but a small navy, like him that had one pair of breeches, which when torn, would oblige us to lay a bed till mended'.[57] But the English navy was no longer small and neither were its ships. 'No less than fourteen ships carried an equal or far greater number of guns than Tromp's *Brederode*, the most formidable Dutch warship.' Well might Adriaen Pauw, Grand Pensionary of Holland, have observed: 'The English are about to attack a mountain of gold; we are about to attack a mountain of iron.'[58]

War was declared by England on 8 July. The first major battle, on 30 November 1652 at Dungeness, resulted in a Dutch victory. The second, a crucial and bloody encounter at Portland on 30 January 1653, went the other way. So did the third off Texel on 31 July. Thus, in between the two, Cromwell ejected the republic at the point when it looked as if the war was beginning to be prosecuted successfully. Later Thomas Scot claimed that at the time of the dissolution: '[W]e intended to have gone off with a good savour and provided for succession of Parliaments, but we stayed to end the Dutch war. We might have brought them to a oneness with us. Their ambassadors did desire a coalition. This we might have done in four or five months.'[59] This is another basis for seeing the union negotiations and war as intertwined, and the English war effort, at least in the minds of those responsible for its management, as not only a defence of the Navigation Act, but a pursuit of union or coalition by military means.

England's victory in the first Anglo-Dutch war had far-reaching consequences. It altered the country's European and global military standing. The legislation which had been successfully defended became the foundation of a revolution in English maritime power. Beyond this it provoked a European naval revolution during the 1650s and 1660s. This saw a change in fighting tactics, the size of fleets, and their administration.[60] The Dutch, caught unprepared against 'an English fleet . . . expanded by a major building programme of heavy, well-equipped and purpose-built men of war', ceased to rely on armed merchantmen and made the transition to a permanent state navy. The States-General provided two million guilders to build sixty new warships.[61] In France and Sweden as well as England and the United Provinces 'the building and maintenance of permanent purpose-built war fleets required much more sophisticated naval institutions than had previously existed, such as specialised shipyards, dry and wet docks, large-scale storage facilities, and a bureaucracy capable of administering such facilities'.[62]

Meanwhile England's merchant marine was transformed by the vast haul of Dutch prizes. The United Provinces lost 1,000 ships between 1652 and 1654; the English about a quarter that number.[63] Some of these gains were then counteracted by the commercially disastrous consequences of Cromwell's subsequent war against Spain. But the period 1660–89 saw the most dramatic expansion of English trade and shipping of the early modern period. One component of this consisted in imports from Norway and the Baltic – England's own bulk trades – including timber and other shipbuilding materials, carried primarily, initially, in captured Dutch ships.[64]

All three Anglo-Dutch wars were predatory English campaigns against a neighbour not only wealthy, but strategically vulnerable, in that it depended upon trade – from the Baltic, Mediterranean or East Indies – passing through or near the Narrow Seas. In the words of Richard Gibson, all 'French, Flemings, Dutch, Hamburgers, Danes, Swedes, Poles + must . . . pass in sight of our

Islands to France Spaine Portugal, the Streights, Guinea, East and West Indies or fetch a Circum=Navigation round Scotland + Ireland'.[65] Notwithstanding their disparate military outcomes these conflicts were cumulatively effective in undermining Dutch maritime dominance:

> At sea, the Dutch were gradually losing to the English. The latter had reorganized their navy more efficiently. They were able to mobilize resources on a bigger scale because of the centralization of state institutions, coupled with favourable developments in their economy and population.[66]

THE REPUBLIC AS AN EMPIRE REVISITED

In the policies of these years may be discerned the prehistory of the eighteenth-century British Empire.[67] This intertwined land and sea power with commercial, political and fiscal reform. In particular it hinged upon a close relationship, unmatched elsewhere in Europe, between an expansive, outwardly directed manufacturing and commercial economy and its exceptionally expensive state and naval protection. In Britain industrialization and eventually industrial revolution emerged in the context of an imperial state almost constantly at war, the needs of which supplied large-scale economic stimulus and the power of which was used to suppress competition.[68] In policy terms this arrangement originated not in 1689 but 1649, acquiring a stable basis during the financial revolution of the 1690s, on the basis of which 'the economy was driven forward by the state rather than the state being driven by the economy':[69]

> From the time of the Commonwealth in the 1650s onwards, British merchants, shippers, bankers and other intermediaries played an ever more important role in the co-ordination of global commerce. Their endeavours received strong support from the Navigation Acts, enforced by the Royal Navy, which protected them against foreign competition, particularly from Dutch middlemen.[70]

This chapter has argued that the Anglo-Dutch union project and war of 1651–4 can usefully be understood in imperial terms. Certainly both can be seen to have emerged from an English republican vision with political, religious and economic dimensions. The political ambition was to extend and defend European republicanism (or liberty) territorially by establishing it in a single confederation or state straddling the North Sea. Speaking to the States-General in 1651 the English delegation emphasized the two states' shared Protestantism and commitment to liberty 'against royal usurpation'.[71] 'For the Interests of Liberty, it is true, they are in a condition of a Free State.'[72] It was because the United Provinces were governed as a Free State while England languished under monarchy that the gap between their power and prosperity had become so great. Yet the Dutch enjoyed this liberty only selfishly, and were

> so far from establishing others in the same condition, who have groaned under the sad oppression of Tyrants; that it is known to *Europe*, how their great designe hath been to be Free Men themselves, and to make the world ... their slaves ... So far have they been from the true Principles of Freedom, which is ready to make others as free as itself.[73]

The English republican understanding of liberty, by contrast, was imperial. Being God-given, liberty was compulsory 'till the whole *Creation* that is now groaning under the exorbitant and wicked lusts of Kings and great ones, whether in *Monarchies* or *States*, be delivered into freedom'.[74] This also helps us to understand the religious content of England's Anglo-Dutch imperial scheme. It was true that the United Provinces had been a bastion of safety for persecuted Protestants. But it also tolerated Catholics, Episcopalians, Muslims and Jews. For the safety not only of republicanism but of Protestantism, liberty of conscience had to be for Protestants only.

To this broader project the English republic's economic agenda was central. Extraordinarily, within an economy and society which remained overwhelmingly agrarian the new government's policies were urban and commercial. This reflected the understanding of its mercantile-republican leadership, informed by contemporary observation as well as by a classical republican reading of history, of the basis of the prosperity and security of free cities and states. It also reflected the dominance of London. By underpinning the construction of a new naval power, these policies would change the history not only of Britain, the Netherlands and Europe, but of the Atlantic and wider global economy.

CHAPTER NINE

THE EMPIRE WAS UNIQUE

In the Islands of the West Indyes the English keepe the Negros theyr slaves in such servitude and misery that they being weary of theyr Lives have found a way to . . . kill themselves . . . [which] they keepe . . . secret among them-selves . . . This I heard from Aulgernon Sydney 17 Feb 1652 . . . from the relation of one Liygen, who hath lived much in these islands . . . the masters of these Negros, keepe from them all knives or other weapons, [but] . . . they make them-selves away whensoever they can.

Robert Sidney, Second Earl of Leicester, 1651[1]

The Dutch republic was born of a revolt against imperial – experienced as tyrannical – power. During this struggle the rebels devoured works such as Bartolomé de Las Casas' *Short Account of the Destruction of the Indies*, first published in Dutch in 1578. This described the inhuman crimes in the New World of 'Spaniards who call themselves Christian' but act as 'ravening wild beasts'. 'The pitiless slaughter of over twenty million innocent Indians who did [Spain] no harm . . . [demands] God's righteous judgement.'[2] Subsequent editions added illustrations by Theodore de Bry and accounts of additional Spanish atrocities committed in France and the Netherlands.[3]

This laid the basis for what Benjamin Schmidt has called the Dutch cultural geography of empire. The fate of the Indians was an object lesson and doom to be avoided. Schmidt contrasted the attitude of William the Silent towards indigenous Americans as fellow sufferers and potential allies with that of James VI and I, who regarded them as hapless barbarians.[4] But James came later, from Scotland, with a pro-Spanish perspective which might have aligned him with De Las Casas' Thomist opponent Juan de Sepulveda and which alienated him from many English and Scots subjects. By contrast Richard Hakluyt's 'Discourse', composed in the year of William's death, echoed his claim that 'the Spaniardes have executed . . . more then Turkishe cruelties in all the west Indies, whereby they are . . . become most odious unto them, whoe woulde joyne wth us or any other moste willingly to shake of[f] their moste intolerable yoke'.[5] De Las Casas' work had been translated into English the year before (1583) as *The Spanish Colonie*. As the Dutch and English were drawn together by the struggle against popery and Spain, the fate of the Indians showed what could be expected if resistance failed.[6]

In practice English and Dutch relationships with native peoples in Atlantic North America both became violent, though there were important differences. Employees of the West Indies Company in New Amsterdam, eschewing either a civilizing or Christianizing mission – exhibiting, to that extent, cultural indifference – invited local Algonquian-speaking peoples into a trading relationship. Only gradually did the situation deteriorate into a war (the 'Indian War' of 1640–5), resulting in hundreds of native deaths.[7] English settlers moving south from Massachusetts into the 'Connetticott Plantation' were seeking not simply trade but – in terminology reminiscent of Hakluyt's 'Discourse' – 'land abounding with rich and profitable meadows along all the rivers, various species of good wood . . . varieties of fish . . . [and] fowle in abundance'. These settlers did have a Christian mission, both for themselves and for the natives. This was confronted by the Pequots, who 'sought to make peace with the Narragansetts . . . argu[ing] . . . that the English were strangers and began to overspread their country, and would deprive them thereof in time, if they were suffered to grow and increase'.[8]

The Narragansetts sided with the English, who then responded to Pequot hostility with a war of extermination.[9] When during the burning of a village at Mystic River in 1637, killing between 400 and 700 Pequots, the survivors fled, they encountered English soldiers who received them 'with the point of the sword. Down fell men, women and children.'[10] During this atrocity the Narragansetts 'stood round about . . . aloof from all danger . . . and left the whole execution to the English':

With the wind, all was quickly on a flame, and thereby more were burnt to death than was otherwise slain . . . Those that escaped the fire were slain with the sword; some hewed to pieces, others run through with their rapiers . . . It was a fearful sight to see them thus frying in the fire, and the streams of blood quenching the same, and horrible was the stink and scent thereof; but the victory seemed a sweet sacrifice, and they gave the praise thereof to God.[11]

While Donna Merwick perceives in both of these conflicts the predatory brutality towards civilians characteristic of Europe's Thirty Years War, Mystic River unmistakably recalls English conduct in Ireland.[12] In the words of John Underhill: 'We had sufficient light from the word of God for our proceedings.'[13]

Thus second-stage European colonization – English, Dutch and French – furnished all the materials necessary for a second Black Legend had anyone wished to compile one. Yet only English settlement became the basis for a long-term, large-scale trans-Atlantic transfer of people and culture. This necessitated expropriation not only of resources but territory, a process executed where necessary with savagery, assisted by the impact upon native peoples of introduced diseases, especially smallpox. This made possible the later explosive eighteenth-century settler population growth which would be a key stimulant of the Industrial Revolution. To this extent the Anglo-Dutch-American archipelago was mapped in blood.[14]

DUTCH EAST INDIES (AND WESTERN PACIFIC)

The United Provinces acquired the Dutch East Indies as part of a frantic process of wartime state formation. The harbours and shipyards of Zeeland and Holland equipped themselves as urgently for long-distance voyaging as they had a century earlier for development of the bulk trades. The East Indiamen, however, were expensive, the East Indies voyage long and dangerous, and the vessels heavily armed. This projection of power across space could not have succeeded without the commissioning of massive private investment by the state. 'It was on sea that the Dutch superiority to the former Habsburg overlords became most apparent, and the foundation of the East and West India Companies in the first decades of the seventeenth century allowed the state to transform an essentially defensive "war of liberation" into a war of conquest and empire-building'.[15]

By 1601, three years after the reimposition of the Spanish embargo against Dutch shipping, fourteen Dutch East India fleets totalling sixty-five ships had sailed. The following year the trade was regulated under the VOC, which began a string of conquests in the Malay archipelago:

> The company was funded with a capital of 6.4 million guilders, of which 57 per cent was supplied by 1,100 participants from Amsterdam, with a substantial share of this coming from immigrants from the southern Low Countries . . . From the outset, the VOC was involved in the political-military ambitions of the Dutch oligarchy and the republic and it received a monopoly of Asian trade in order to achieve these ambitions. The VOC became an instrument of power, for instance in subordinating the spice-producing areas in the East Indies by brute force.[16]

The most important conquest was Jakarta, renamed Batavia, which became the foremost European military and commercial base in Asia. This eastern empire became much larger and more economically important than its later western counterpart. Hundreds of thousands, many foreigners, travelled to the parts of Asia and South Africa controlled by the VOC.[17] The population of Batavia grew from 8,000 in 1624 to 80,000 in 1700, including 6,000 Europeans. The city had canals, houses and bridges built of stone imported as ballast from the Netherlands. Dutch residents were permitted to marry locals and to have children, but not to take them back to the Netherlands. The Dutch East India Company sought a monopoly on European supplies of pepper, nutmeg, cinnamon, and later coffee. In time its empire, protected by forts, stretched from the Indian subcontinent (Malabar) and Ceylon in the west, through Sumatra, Java and Peninsular Malaysia, to the north-eastern islands of Ternate, Tidora and Amboina.

Batavia waged a battle with the jungle, and diseases, in particular malaria. From here there were further expeditions north, to China (where the Portuguese were established at Macau), Taiwan (from which the Dutch were expelled in 1661) and Japan. Following the ejection of Europeans from Japan the Dutch only were allowed to remain in a single location because they had not attempted to prosyletize. As already noted concerning New Netherland, the absence of a confessional mission was a striking feature of Dutch empire, distinguishing it from Spain, Portugal, England and France.[18] This was, however, perhaps an unsurprising aspect of a colonial venture under the control of a privately funded mercantile company rather than the direct government of the state.

While the Portuguese had hugged the East African coast, the VOC created a new fast route to Java from Cape Town across the Southern Indian Ocean (the roaring forties), turning north short of Western Australia. Occasionally this went wrong. When the brand-new *Batavia* departed Texel Island on its maiden voyage with 340 aboard on 29 October 1628 it sailed immediately into a storm and ran aground on Walcheren sandbanks. Recovering, the ship reached Cape Town five months later. On 3 June 1629, after a fast five-week crossing of the Southern Ocean, it was travelling at full speed after dark when it struck a coral archipelago not recorded on any charts: Houtman's Abrolhos, off the west coast of Australia. Three hundred people (including some women and children) survived the impact. Over the next few days, as the wreck broke up, over two hundred made it onto the surrounding atolls where they survived on fish, birds and rainwater.

Forty-eight others rowed east in a thirty-foot longboat looking for water. Arriving in the Western Australian desert there was none. Astonishingly, after drifting in the open ocean for three weeks, surviving on rainwater, on 3 July they arrived in Java. In Batavia the VOC was informed that the *Batavia*, which had been carrying twelve money chests containing 400,000 guilders (about $50 million in today's terms), was destroyed. While the survivors were cast into the company's dungeons another vessel was dispatched to find the wreck. When it was found on 10 September it was discovered that in the Abrolhos a reign of terror had resulted in the murder of 120 people. There were seventy-seven still alive, including five women. The conspirators were captured and several tortured and executed on the spot. Others were returned to be executed in Batavia. A third group were taken to the Australian mainland and marooned without food and water. Meanwhile salvage efforts around the wreck, using Malay divers, recovered ten of the *Batavia*'s money chests.[19]

Batavia also became a base for southern voyaging. In 1615, seeking an alternative route outside the VOC monopoly Jacques Le Maire became the first European to enter the Pacific by rounding Cape Horn (rather than navigating the Straits of Magellan) and then the first to encounter Tonga and Futuna before arriving in Batavia in October 1616.[20] Twenty-seven years later, leaving Batavia in search of the unknown southern continent (see Chapter 12), the Dutch commander Abel Tasman explored the Southern Indian Ocean and then entered the Pacific at deep southern latitude from the west, south of Australia. At 42 degrees south, after discovering Tasmania, which he called Van Diemen's Land ('Too cold for spices'), Tasman continued east, where after several days he encountered Staten Landt.[21] 'This . . . looks like being a very beautiful land and we trust that this is the mainland coast of the unknown south land.' To a Maori challenge issued 'in a rough loud voice', Tasman's crew responded by attempting to communicate in the language of Futuna as recorded by Le Maire. When the natives 'blew many times on an instrument which gave a sound like a Moorish trumpet', Tasman 'made one of our sailors (who could play the trumpet a little) play them some tunes in reply'.[22] When the following day Tasman was unwise enough to launch a cockboat, it was attacked with astonishing speed, leaving four dead. After this 'monstrous happening and detestable affair' New Zealand did not see more Europeans until the arrival of Captain Cook a century and a half later.[23]

Beyond such events what should be emphasized is the human cost of long-range seafaring. During the early seventeenth century up to 20 per cent of the adult male Dutch population were at sea at any one time. Charles Boxer estimated that crew on seventeenth-century Dutch East Indiamen had a 'not much more than even chance of returning alive'. Ship-board punishments included the death sentence for murder, mutiny and sodomy; 'keel-hauling; ducking from the yard-arm . . . nailing the culprit's hand to the mainmast; flogging with anything from ten to five hundred lashes'.[24] Disease was rife, exacerbated by the extraordinarily cramped and insanitary conditions, and the 'fleas, lice and other vermin abounding in men's filthy clothing', and feeding 'on the rotting provisions in the ship's stores'.[25] In 'unrefrigerated, often sweltering' conditions 'food spoiled rapidly, and sailors were obliged to share it with rats, worms, spiders and cockroaches – but they could not allow themselves to throw it away'.[26] Prevailing diseases were scurvy, typhus, dysentery, colds and pneumonia. Seasickness was ever-present and serious accidents were common.

This was only one aspect of the eye-watering human cost of early modern European empire in general, particularly in Africa and the Americas.[27] For victims of the slave trade the notorious 'middle passage' between the Atlantic coast of Africa and the Americas was merely one of a sequence of horrors. A European-sponsored outgrowth from traditional African practice, it was the objective of this trade to supply a tropical plantation labour force to replace the 50 million indigenous Americans wiped out by introduced European diseases between 1492 and 1560.[28] Of the millions of Africans captured perhaps a third died before embarkation and another 20 per cent of passengers during the ocean crossing.[29] Scenes reported by European observers at African slave ports were harrowing and revolting. Survivors then subjected to brutal conditions on Brazilian or Caribbean plantations (poor food, harsh discipline, unrelenting work) were lucky if they survived a few years. For Europeans the tropical disease regime in the Caribbean was such that as a percentage of the total arriving (rather than an absolute number) their annual mortality exceeded even that of slaves.[30] Almost 14 million captives had crossed the Atlantic Ocean by the early nineteenth century. This was the nature of the larger world system within which the Industrial Revolution became possible.

DUTCH WEST INDIES AND ATLANTIC

On their way to East Asia the Dutch displaced the Portuguese in West Africa in the trade in gold and ivory. In the second quarter of the seventeenth century they moved into the Atlantic slave trade. From 1598 Dutch ships began to appear in significant numbers in the Caribbean and northern South America. In 1621 the Dutch West India Company was founded. There followed the conquest of Curaçao, St Eustatius and St Maarten in the Caribbean, and Surinam in Guyana. In North America, New Netherland was established in 1624 and was also a base for assaults upon Spanish and Portuguese shipping: by 1636, 547 prizes had been taken.[31] Most spectacularly, in 1628, east of Havana, the commander Piet Hyn captured the entire Spanish New Spain fleet. It was carrying silver, gold, silk, hides, dyewood, indigo and cochineal worth 11.5 million guilders.[32] Buoyed by this success, in 1630 the WIC took a large area of north-eastern Brazil and renamed it New Holland, with its capital at Recife.

By the mid-1630s the company controlled much of the Brazilian sugar trade to Europe. In 1640 it ended Portuguese dominance of the slave trade and conquered Angola (losing Luanda again, however, in 1648). Dutch slavers supplied Angolan and other African captives to English colonies at Virginia, Barbados and Boston.[33] From 1637 Johan Maurits of Nassau-Siegen, governor of New Holland, was 'patron to the single greatest assemblage of artists and scientists in the early modern New World, [and] a superb administrator . . . of Recife . . . where Portuguese and Dutch, Christian and Jewish, African and Brazilian men and women . . . all intermingled . . . [in] one of the most impressive Baroque societies, in the Old World or the New'.[34] Johan Maurits persuaded forty-six scholars, scientists, artists and craftsmen to relocate from Holland. Among their achievements was Willem Piso's exquisitely illustrated *Historia naturalis Brasiliae* published in Leiden and Amsterdam in 1648. Maurits also built an astronomical observatory and founded a Botanical and Zoological Garden.[35]

Yet the fall of the colony to the Portuguese in 1654 illustrated one limitation of the Dutch western empire, and perhaps Dutch empire in general. It did not involve, or aspire to, large-scale domestic emigration and settlement. In England the period 1620–40 completed a century of population growth, and the export and gainful employment of surplus bodies had been an objective of Western planting since Hakluyt. The Dutch republic was crowded, but had by contrast achieved something close to full employment; indeed only immigration, both permanent and seasonal, sufficed to service the labour needs of the booming economy.[36] New Holland collapsed partly because it could not attract immigrants. A similar problem beset New Netherland:

> New Netherland never approached the promise, style or glamour of New Holland . . . Land claims in North America – colonization in general – had never been one of the West India Company's serious concerns. That enormously ambitious body, a trading not a settling organisation, had little interest in the few primitive trading shacks that had been thrown together at the coastal edge of the mid-Atlantic forests . . . on the Hudson, Delaware and Connecticut rivers; nor was it otherwise interested in territorial conquest in North America.[37]

First settled in 1609 by Walloons (French speakers from the Spanish Netherlands) to access the fur trade, New Netherland survived in uneasy interaction with native Americans. Conditions were challenging and mortality was high. A distinguishing feature of the colony – as in New Holland – was its extreme heterogeneity, in nationality, ethnicity, language and religion. As the Governor Pieter Stuyvesant complained to the WIC, neighbouring English and French colonies were 'populated by their own nation and countrymen and consequently bound together more firmly and united, while your honors' colonies in *New-Netherland* are only gradually and slowly peopled by the scrapings of all sorts of nationalities'.[38] This was a general feature of the Dutch Atlantic:

> A highly diverse European population inhabited WIC settlements . . . The[y] . . . demonstrate[d] the ability, willingness, and, often, eagerness of the Dutch to assimilate other people, not necessarily into a single Dutch culture, whatever that might be, but into a Dutch political dominion and commercial operation.[39]

This was a distinction of degree. All European Atlantic colonies, including England's, were fluid and culturally complex by comparison to the home country.[40] Nevertheless, when the fall of New Holland led to an influx of settlers, including New Netherland's first Jews, the governor asked for permission to expel them, which was refused by the company, who ordered that they be not only tolerated but welcomed, as they were in Amsterdam. When the first Quakers arrived from New England, causing mayhem, and the governor's punitive response proved ineffective, Stuyvesant was instructed to 'shut [your] eyes, at least not force people's consciences but allow everyone to have his own belief, as long as he behaves quietly and legally . . . and does not oppose the government'.[41] Over the last decade of its existence immigration to New Amsterdam (on Manhattan Island) increased, but on nothing like the same scale as in neighbouring English plantations, so that encroachment from New England became constant. In 1650 Thayer Mahan pointed out, in their establishment of colonies:

> in the East Indies, in Africa, and in America . . . the Dutch . . . were far ahead of England . . . But though the origin of these colonies, purely commercial in its character, was natural, there seems to have been lacking to them a principle of growth . . . This placid satisfaction with gain alone,

unaccompanied by political ambition, tended, like the despotism of France and Spain, to keep the colonies mere commercial dependencies upon the mother-country, and so killed the natural principle of growth.[42]

Yet as this European comparison suggests, in their adherence to this so-called 'natural principle of growth' England's global colonies were singular. Here Mahan was attempting to understand, from a nineteenth-century viewpoint, 'the fact of England's unique and wonderful success as a great colonizing nation'.[43] The demographic expansiveness in question could hardly be more important to the present study, being an immediate catalyst of the Industrial Revolution (see chapter 15). Most important in this respect were the thirteen North American colonies, initially founded by mass migration. To the extent, however, that their subsequent eighteenth-century expansion was endogenous, what helped to spark the Industrial Revolution was a post-migrational 'principle of growth' which was American, rather than simply British, though one protected by, connected to, and instrumental in sustaining British imperial power.

In 1664 New Netherland fell to the English, after which, claimed one study, 'New Englanders were largely responsible for the foundational omission of Dutch Americans from the master narrative of United States history'.[44] Yet a subsequent account has identified New Amsterdam's 'Babel of peoples – Norwegians, Germans, Italians, Jews, Africans (slaves and free), Walloons, Bohemians, Munsees, Montauks, Mohawks' as the prototype not only for the 'cultural fusion' of New York City, but for the whole 'multi-ethnic, upwardly mobile' modern American republic.[45] A review in *The New York Times* celebrated the arrival of this 'new foundation myth', recognizing that 'our ancestors came to this land for material as well as ideological reasons' and that 'the legacy of tolerance from the Dutch colony in Manhattan would be extended into the very heart of the continent'.[46] There seems no present-day reason for complacency about tolerance in the heart of the continent. However, there are indeed historical reasons for understanding the American republic to have been an Anglo-Dutch creation. As for New Netherland, perhaps it is also the role of historians to rescue a pre-modern Atlantic rim community, with its distinctive cobweb of seventeenth-century mentalities, from master narratives of any kind.[47]

PLANTING PEOPLE (DESPERATE FOR LEMONS)

England's first theatre of empire was Ireland. The effort to conquer Ireland intensified during the 1590s in response to confessionally motivated rebellion. Like the Dutch Revolt, this undertaking was seen as an essential defence against popery (Counter-Reformation). But it was also a war of extermination against a people held to be 'more uncivill, more uncleanly, more barbarous and more brutish in their customs . . . then in any other part of the world'.[48] In the early Stuart period it was Ireland, rather than America, that was the primary site for English and Scots plantation – a planting of people and culture rather than things.[49] 'In the twelve years after 1630, 120,000 Englishmen and Scots are estimated to have migrated to Ireland, double the number of those who went to the West Indies in those years, six times more than went to New England.'[50]

From the outset British empire, unlike Dutch or French, entailed large-scale domestic migration. The 1630s 'was the beginning, in the British Isles, of an extraordinary period of emigration, a demographic phenomenon that would not be matched until the 1760s, when again there was a sense that an entire new world had suddenly been flung open for settlement by land-hungry migrants'.[51] The Iberian settlements had also elicited emigration: by the end of the sixteenth century 250,000 Spaniards had travelled to the Americas. This was, however, a quarter of the seventeenth-century English total, and settlers in the tropics had to contend with exceptionally high mortality.

Looking back from the late nineteenth century, Britain may have been unique in its consistent use of empire for the purposes of large-scale settlement of surplus population, combined with a willingness and ability to support that process with military power. When Captain Cook arrived in New Zealand in 1769, the Maori population stood at 86,000–100,000. At the time of the signing of the Treaty of Waitangi in 1840 there were about 2,000 resident Europeans.[52] At this time Britain was among maritime powers 'the only one then at all active in colonising. Of the two chief rivals . . . in Pacific shipping . . . the New Englanders were not interested in colonies, and the French were only mildly interested, whereas the British were migrating in thousands annually.'[53] A flood of British immigration began around 1850 and accelerated following the subsequent crushing of Maori military resistance. Between 1900 and 1915, 300,000 migrants arrived and by 1970 the population was

3.3 million.[54] But by comparison with North America, and even Australia, New Zealand was a secondary or tertiary destination for the 22 million British and Irish emigrants during the century after 1815.

Thus one force driving early English Atlantic settlement was population growth, combined with unemployment and economic stagnation. Thomas Scott reported in *Vox Populi, Or News from Spayne* (1622) that England's 'West indian voyages . . . serve for draines to unloade [its] populous State, which else would overflow its own bancks by continuance of peace, and . . . make a body fit for any rebellion.'[55] Another factor was the economic hunger of merchants and adventurers excluded from the Mediterranean (until 1604), pestered by piracy, and unable to make inroads into the deepening Dutch stranglehold on the East Indies. A third was religion, as we have seen a force for emigration across the North Sea, Irish Sea and Atlantic.[56]

In all of the early American theatres of settlement colonies faced an uphill battle for survival. A process of experimentation was aborted at Roanoke (twice), and became the subject of desperate struggle at Jamestown.[57] In the early years of the Virginia plantation the London directors of the company made good dramatic settler population losses by sweeping the city clean of the young, vulnerable, under-employed and defenceless. These included military veterans, vagrants and (between 1618 and 1620) 337 inhabitants of Bridewell Hospital, a jail for vagrant children.[58] In 1635 five more boys were sent from Bridewell and fourteen prisoners from Newgate Jail.[59] When in 1788 Australia was saved from the grasp of France by transportation of 1,030 captive convicts (see Chapter 12), we should not be surprised, particularly since Britain was experiencing another demographic explosion.[60] The English way of empire entailed a profuse outlay of cannon fodder.

Like the settlement at Roanoke, the renewed attempt at Jamestown in 1607 was charged to identify valuable commodities, preferably mines, and to search for waterways west to the Pacific and so Asia. What saved Virginia was tobacco: 1,250 pounds shipped to England in 1616; 10,000 pounds in 1617; 60,000 in 1620; 400,000 pounds in 1625.[61] This was despite the 1622 massacre which almost wiped out the settlement, and such action by native Americans at a time of rapid appropriation of land for tobacco farming was not a coincidence. The lucrative crop gave a vital incentive both to colonial emigrants and to private investors in the company. It also proved extremely attractive to Dutch merchants who brought to the colony 'sugar, strong waters, lemons, hats, shirts, stockings, frying pans' and other supplies 'for which Chesapeake planters were always desperate'.[62] Before 1650, when English merchants could not meet colonists' needs, Anglo-Dutch trade was crucial to the survival of English settlements both in North America and in the Caribbean.[63] As late as the 1770s continental European markets – often accessed via the British re-export trade – were vital for the American colonies, purchasing 85 per cent of their tobacco, much sugar and sugar by-products, New England fish and Southern rice.[64]

Other plantations followed, in Plymouth, New England and Maryland, after which, having damaged their lungs, the English set about ruining their teeth. During the 1620s and 1630s Caribbean settlements were founded in St Christopher, Nevis, Antigua, Montserrat and Barbados. From Barbados, George Downing wrote to John Winthrop junior, advising the planting of sugar with indentured labour from England until 'you shall be able . . . to procure Negroes (the life of this place) out of the increase of your own planta-tion'.[65] Historians used to believe that early planters in Barbados were dependent upon the Dutch (based in Recife) for instruction in sugar cultivation. This was not the case, though Dutch merchants did supply both slaves and a market for the sugar in Amsterdam.[66] As English naval power was transformed from 1649 there followed the capture in 1655 of Jamaica, which was to become the region's largest sugar producer. English involvement in the slave trade preceded the foundation of the Royal African Company in 1660, the Dutch counting seventy-five English slavers on the Gold Coast between 1652 and 1657.[67]

Thus in the search for precious metals and lucrative plantation agriculture the English in America were not unlike their European rivals and competitors. Where such commodities could be accessed they were, both in Asia (the Indian subcontinent) and the West Indies. The unique component of their empire, with no Spanish, Dutch, Russian or French equivalent, was plantation of culture and people. All empires, of course, involved the movement of people and culture. But what distinguished some British settlements was their confes-sional, and sometimes political, rather than merely economic motivation. This is not to understate the importance of economic migration, nor to suggest that the settlements which resulted were culturally uniform. It is, however, to identify a crucial outcome of the English settlement process which, by estab-lishing colonies that were not only economic but cultural and ideological constructs, helped to lay the foundations for both the American and Industrial Revolutions.

The cultural motivations of settlers help to explain why they planted in cool and temperate North America, beyond the scope of tropical plantation production, and (as it transpired) without access to precious metals. The same circumstances put these colonies outside the zone of mosquito-borne tropical diseases. Historians are familiar with the idea that environmental factors were frequently the most powerful determinants of the success or failure of imperial enterprises which by their nature transcended the boundaries of what was controllable and known.[68] The early modern world was a laboratory within which the architects of Europe's empires aspired to raise their projects to the status of experiments. Thus, in the Dutch republic, Britain, Spain and France, colonies were an engine of the scientific revolution.[69] But before the eighteenth century the laboratory was also a lottery through participation in which, although riches were available, the chances of disaster were higher.

In England's boom-town tropical colony, Jamaica, between 1661 and 1788 the population rose from 4,000 to 255,000. This required immigration of 600,000 people as compared (until 1780) to 900,000 to all of British North America. Of that 1788 population 90 per cent (226,000) were slaves. Because of malaria and yellow fever 50,000 white immigrants were required to increase the settled white population by 5,000. English and Scots planters continued to flock to this graveyard because for most of the eighteenth century Jamaica was the wealthiest economy in British America.[70] What made the North American colonies different was their capacity to attract migration which was voluntary (rather than enslaved) and culturally rather than simply economically motivated (400,000 from England in the seventeenth century, 300,000 more in the eighteenth, plus Dutch, French Protestants and at least 100,000 Germans).[71] What made them a force in global history was their ability to sustain themselves locally and then grow rapidly, demographically and territorially.

REPUBLICAN COMMERCIAL AND IMPERIAL POLICIES
SURVIVE THE RESTORATION

It has been argued that England's civil wars were decisive for the development of its American colonies in causing a breakdown in metropolitan authority which 'gave emerging settler leaders enhanced confidence in their ability to manage their own affairs, a confidence seemingly justified by their consolidation of local power in the 1640s and 1650s at the expense of proprietors and the crown'.[72] Subsequently, in exchange for acceptance of the centrally imposed commercial monopoly of the Atlantic trading system the metropolitan government accepted a good deal of colonial political autonomy. Under this mutually beneficial arrangement 'Britain's Atlantic possessions after 1660 would be commercial and diverse . . . and committed to the rights of local landowners'.[73] It was partly the perception of a design to renege on this arrangement with respect to taxation which would provoke the American Revolution.

With the naval victory of 1654 and the capture of Jamaica in 1655, England's imperial potential began to attract attention in Europe.[74] This helps to explain why the restored Stuarts made the navy and empire a personal project. James Duke of York became Lord High Admiral. Most of the large ships of Charles II's navy (the *Naseby* being renamed the *Royal Charles*, the *Dunbar* the *Henry*, and the *Marston Moor* the *York*) had been built between 1649 and 1653.[75] During secret negotiations with France between 1668 and 1670 the one interest of state Charles II showed himself determined to defend was English maritime power. The navy remained the most expensive department of state, accounting for over 20 per cent of government expenditure.[76] Employing the group of civil servants around Samuel Pepys, it was also one of the most reform-minded.[77]

Interregnum figures such as Anthony Ashley Cooper, Edward Lord Montagu and George Downing were kept on. In 1660 Downing rewrote and strengthened the Commonwealth's Navigation Act, specifying that foreign ships could carry into English ports only goods originating in their own country. In 1663 his 'Act for the Encouragement of Trade', or Staple Act, 'stipulated that products from English colonies might only be exported via English ports and shipped in English vessels. In this way England would become an entrepot for colonial goods which could be distributed all over Europe. It was obvious that English mercantilists had taken the Dutch staple as their example.'[78] These developments imposed real hardships on the sugar and tobacco colonies, who petitioned in vain to be allowed 'to transport their produce to any port in amity with his Majesty' and who continued to covet Dutch supplies.[79] One result was the establishment of an illicit trade network linking English and Dutch colonies, particularly through the island of St Eustatius. Even so, 'Between 1650 and 1665 . . . a policy aimed at bringing the plantations more completely under the domination of the state was relentlessly pursued.'[80]

American settlement continued: after Jamaica (1661), the first new Crown colony since Virginia, came Carolina (1663) and Pennsylvania (1681). While the king's wish to establish liberty of conscience in England was twice frustrated (1662, 1672), enough of the new colonies did so to furnish destinations for nonconformists and to reinforce the pattern of confessionally motivated, often Anglo-Dutch-Swedish-German settlement.[81] Charles II also explored further afield. In 1669 Sir John Narborough was secretly commissioned to sail through the Straits of Magellan and up the Pacific coast of Chile.

Narborough's instructions to 'make a Discovery . . . of the Sea and Coasts of that part of the World, and if possible to lay the foundation of a Trade there' bore a resemblance to those issued a century earlier to Francis Drake. They would be echoed a century later by those of Captain Cook, except that Narborough's voyage was for 'the Honour of our Prince and Nation' and Cook's for 'the Honour of this Nation as a Maritime Power'. Narborough's project was to establish the southern limits of Spanish American occupation and ascertain the potential for England beyond them. He was ordered not to touch the Atlantic coast of South America north of the Río de la Plata, and after that to make the '*Indian* Inhabitants . . . sensible of the great Power and Wealth of the Prince and Nation to whom you belong'.[82]

The Patagonians were disinclined to interact with Narborough's crew, who wintered over in St Julien, on the Atlantic coast, where both Magellan and Drake had also anchored. Narborough's record of his excursions inland from there later inspired a proposal for Patagonian plantation. According to Daniel Defoe, Narborough had confirmed that the climate was temperate (unlike Spanish America); the earth covered in grass (unlike North America); the grass fed wild sheep and cows; there were no snakes or crocodiles; few Indians; few Spaniards; and if there was gold on one side of the Andes there must be gold on the other ('Sir *John Narborough* . . . found several small pieces').[83]

In truth, however, despite making it through the Straits to Chile the following year, and aside from the suspiciously English-sounding claim that penguins would queue in order to be clubbed to death, Narborough reported relatively little of interest save finding a plaque of 'Sheet-Lead' left by the 1615 circumnavigation of Jacques Le Maire.[84] Drake had reported 'fowl that could not fly, as big as geese, whereof they killed three thousand, which was good provision'.[85] In 1772 a member of Cook's crew recorded ninety penguins on an iceberg 'set erect on their Leggs ranged in regular lines, which with their Breasts forms a very Whimsical appearance we fired two 4 pounders at them but Mist them after which they wheeld off three deep and March down to ye water in a Rank'.[86] These voyages were tough on penguins, and on the causes of penguins.

Settlement in the Caribbean and North America helped to develop maritime as well as commercial expertise and infrastructure.[87] If the restored Stuarts were not sufficiently merchant-minded to abolish customs revenues, there was no attempt to restore parliamentary subsidies (or Crown lands). Assessment and excise were lowered but retained and supplemented by new taxes like 'chimney money' (1662). The republic's Council of Trade was retained. In 1673 an improved Plantation Act gave Customs Commissioners and their deputies enhanced powers in relation to colonial governments in line with the republic's legislation of 1649–51:[88]

> It is no exaggeration to see these years as a turning point in England's economic destiny, when the old monolithic conception of the export trade in half-manufactured cloth gives way to a new conception – a foreign trade growing in scope and variety to which the new colonial regions added their new commodities. This in turn became the basis of refining and manufacturing industries in London and the west-coast ports and of a large re-export trade. The whole system rested on a growing mercantile fleet, and slowly the necessary commercial and financial mechanisms were evolved for facilitating its operations.[89]

From the beginning of the Restoration period the quantity and value of English colonial imports began to increase rapidly. By 1669, with Barbados in its heyday and slaves now being supplied directly by the Royal African Company, annual English imports of sugar totalled 8.5 million kilograms. By 1690 they had doubled, to 13 million kilograms, and by the 1750s this had become 58 million kilograms per year. Now the port specializing in Jamaican sugar and slaves was Bristol. These totals included sugar by-products like molasses and rum, 40 per cent of which were re-exported, mainly to other European markets. At the same time, imports of finished goods boomed, especially from Asia:

> . . . silks, japanned ware, porcelain and a host of minor curiosities – in addition to French luxury goods. Chinaware was an ideal complementary cargo to go with tea, and heavy porcelain chests provided the necessary ballast for the East India Company's ships. The 1660s saw the acceleration of an import-led phase of commercial growth, occurring at a time when London's population was expanding much more rapidly than that of the rest of the country.[90]

Imports, both of colonial raw materials and of manufactured items, fed into a broader commercial and manufacturing revolution driven by rising domestic consumption. Now, as earlier in the Dutch republic, the developing economy was putting items imported or manufactured on a large scale – paintings, books, porcelain, pipes, newspapers, cutlery, mirrors – into non-aristocratic hands.[91] In the process

> aristocratic taste was adapted to the more modest aspirations of the gentry and middling sorts . . . the spread of polite taste coincided with an improvement in standards of domestic comfort for the London middle class . . . Post-Restoration interiors became much brighter, with the increased use of mirrors, sash windows, candlestands, high ceilings and plastered walls, set off with lighter furnishing fabrics, including silks and cottons. By the 1690s, pictures, prints and chinaware proliferated in many houses of the 'middling sort'.[92]

Colonial expansion and the maritime voyaging upon which it depended fed economic expansion in other ways:

> The Discoveries disrupted the accepted wisdoms of the ancient canonical texts . . . and pushed [Europe] onto a path of systematic observation and experiment . . . Ocean navigation, mapping and surveying required mathematical skills and improved measuring instruments . . . new processes required experiments with the use of heat and the development of new

types of machinery and equipment; new and desireable commodities changed tastes and encouraged efforts at import substitution . . . Overseas expansion depended on a massive technological thrust which opened up a large and profitable market for inventive activity.[93]

Thus a transformation in the scale of English shipping, the diversification of its nature, and the development of its global range between 1649 and 1702 did more than alter the economy. Assisted by the dramatic political developments discussed in the following two chapters, they helped to move the country, and especially London, to the forefront of an early modern European and global geography of invention.

CHAPTER TEN

ISLE OF PINES

The terror that the city of London was possessed with, when a few Dutch ships came to Chatham, shews that no numbers of men, tho naturally valiant, are able to defend themselves, unless they be well arm'd, disciplin'd and conducted.

Algernon Sidney, *Discourses Concerning Government* (1698)[1]

ANGLO-DUTCH RESTORATION

The revolution of 1649 had resulted in a sharp alteration in English political administration, military expenditure, and economic and commercial policy. In none of these areas did the Restoration bring any attempt to reverse course. On the contrary there was consolidation, legislative amplification and an acceleration of mercantile and colonial growth. Politically and religiously, however, restoration brought change, and also contestation and instability. The fall of the republic opened the way to reaction, and to the government of a reinstated royalist and Anglican ruling elite.

In the short term a struggle between this elite and the king it recalled from exile resulted in the displacement of what had appeared likely in 1660 to be a mild, ecumenical settlement. But the less forgiving Restoration elaborated by the Cavalier Parliament between 1661 and 1665 was then itself destabilized by the calamities accompanying the second Anglo-Dutch war of 1665–7. These included the plague of 1665, the Great Fire of London the following year, and the Dutch burning of the English fleet at anchor at Chatham in 1667. All of these biblical judgements visited upon what was now the largest city in Europe acted as stimuli to reform across the economy, political and military

175

administration, and urban architecture and planning. More immediately they exposed an unconfident and incompetent restored regime. This left the king to be blown by the winds of European geopolitics into the arms of France. There followed an Anglo-French-German attack on the United Provinces in 1672, which brought down the government and almost destroyed the state. This Dutch disaster in turn prepared the ground for a spectacular military intervention in England in 1689, which would reset the terms of restoration in a way that completed the Anglo-Dutch revolution initiated in 1649.

The king's own blueprint for restoration was published in his *Declaration* from Breda in the Netherlands in 1660. People being 'engaged in parties and animosities against each other', matters would 'be better composed . . . when they shall hereafter unite in a freedom of conversation'. To this end Charles offered a 'liberty for tender consciences', which he hoped would quickly be given statutory form: 'we shall be ready to consent to such an act of parliament as, upon mature deliberation, shall be offered to us, for the full granting of that indulgence'.[2] Had this intention prevailed the English republic's religious policies might have been developed in a Dutch direction. William Temple's commentary on Dutch religious arrangements captured the kind of settlement with which the new king would have been content:

> in this Commonwealth, no man having any reason to complain of oppression in Conscience; and no man having hopes by advancing his Religion, to form a Party . . . They argue without interest or anger; They differ without enmity or scorn . . . Men live together like Citizens of the World, associated by the common ties of Humanity, and by the bonds of Peace, Under the impartial protection of indifferent Laws, With equal encouragement of all Art and Industry, and equal freedom of Speculation and Enquiry.[3]

Temple inhabited an early Enlightenment intellectual world within which religious difference was less important than 'Speculation and Enquiry'. So did Charles, patron of the new Royal Society under the banner of which Anglo-Dutch-French collaboration in experimental philosophy blossomed. Following a decade spent in exile Charles II could not take seriously the claim of the Church of England to be the only true Church. More problematically the king may have been a secret Roman Catholic. This further endangered the already parlous situation of European Protestantism between 1670 and 1690. But Charles was not the only Englishman who saw the re-establishment of religious uniformity as a bolting of the stable door after departure of the spiritual horse. For Temple religious belief was no more within the command of a person's will than 'their Stature, or Feature'. William Petty agreed. '[N]o man can believe what he himself pleases: and to force men to say they believe, when they do not, is vain . . . and without honour to God'. Indeed 'if one-fourth of the people were heterodox, and . . . [could] be removed . . . one fourth of the remainder would again become heterodox . . . it being natural for men to differ in opinion in matters above Sense and Reason'.[4]

The contrary thinking behind the Act of Uniformity was articulated by Gilbert Sheldon, Archbishop of Canterbury: ''Tis only a resolute execution of the law that must cure this disease, all other remedies serve and will increase it; and its necessary that they who will not be governed as men by reason and persuasions should be governed as beasts by power and force, all other courses will be ineffectual, ever have been so.'[5] In 1662 (though not in 1680 or 1689) this view commanded majority support in Parliament, despite leaving many Protestants outside the pale of legal worship. From The Hague, George Downing lamented the Act's economic consequences. 'Every passage still great numbers come from England of handycraft people under ye notion yt they cant enjoy their meetings and do sett up their trades hear. There is one, who is a silk stocking weaver, and is lately come from London and has brought with him and sett up foure of those engines at Amsterdam, which is a great pity.'[6] Downing's response was a Bill for the Naturalization of Foreigners ('Invite Foreigners in') and an 'Act encouraging the manufacture of Linen cloth and Tapestry'.[7] Resident aliens could benefit from the greater religious leeway given through stranger churches. Within the growing manufacturing economy the leading sector was still woollen textiles, and observers during the 1670s and 1680s noted its indebtedness to Flemish, Dutch and Huguenot immigrants.[8]

That religion and the economy were linked, and that both operated within a competitive regional context, was a long-standing lesson of Dutch experience. In this and other respects Slingsby Bethel argued that England and the United Provinces shared a fundamental identity of 'interest'.[9] That called for Anglo-Dutch amity, English liberty of conscience and prioritization of trade.

Downing's Bill was one of a series of attempts during the period to promote immigration, most vociferously opposed by supporters of the Act of Uniformity. From about 1640 English population growth had paused and then been followed by a slight decline. Others concerned about the economic implications of this situation included the king (and his successor James II – see Chapter 14), the demographic theorist William Petty, and the commercial advocate Sir Josiah Child.[10] The most important restoration immigrants were Huguenots, who became key participants in an increasingly cosmopolitan commercial and intellectual world. Between 1680 and 1700, 35,000 Huguenots settled in the Dutch republic and 40,000 in England, mainly in London. In 1681 Child was among seventy sponsors of a Huguenot settlement in Ipswich for the establishment of a linen manufacture. By 1689 an Anglo-Dutch monarchy and an Act of Toleration had smoothed the path for large-scale immigration, though this still faced Tory opposition which could be sharpened by particular political circumstances.[11]

In *England's Present Interest Discover'd* (1675), Quaker leader William Penn, whose mother was a native of Rotterdam, drew attention to the destructive social and economic impact of religious persecution in England while the '*Land already swarms with Beggars*':

And it is but some prudent Forreigners proclaiming Liberty of Conscience within their Territories, and a Door is opened for a Million of People to pass out of their Native Soil . . . especially at this Time of Day, when our Forreign Islands yearly take off so many necessary Inhabitants from us . . . so let the Government of *England* but give that prudent Invitation to Forreigners, and she maketh her self Mistress of the Arts and Manufactures of *Europe*: Nothing else hath hindred *Holland* from truckling under the *Spanish* Monarchy, and being ruin'd above threescore Years ago, and given her that Rise to Wealth and Glory.[12]

Six years later Penn secured a charter for the colony of Pennsylvania.[13] Promoting this project in Germany and the Netherlands as well as Scotland and England, 'He preached in Dutch, and won thousands of converts and settlers, inviting them to his Christian commonwealth.'[14] From Philadelphia, Gabriel Thomas reported in 1698 that the climate was fabulous, 'bearing mighty resemblance to the better part of France'; good health general so that doctors were unnecessary; food cheap and game abundant; wages triple those in England and Wales; 'the Earth so fertil', and available for ten to fifteen pounds for ten acres; 'fine and delightful Gardens and Orchards in most parts of this Countrey'.[15] The natives were peaceable and dignified; the 'first Planters' had been Dutch, who, however, 'made little or no Improvement (applying themselves wholly to Trafique in Skins and Furs, which the Indians . . . furnish'd them with . . . for Rum, Strong Liquors and Sugar) . . . Soon after them came the Swedes and Fins, who apply'd themselves to Husbandry, and were the first Christian People that made any considerable Improvement there.'[16] Lutherans continued in the present colony, alongside Quakers and Presbyterians.

THE SECOND ANGLO-DUTCH WAR, 1665–7

Restoration, by re-establishing monarchy and the Church, also altered the ideological relationship between the English and Dutch governments. As usual, however, the broader situation was complicated, and by 1689 many aspects of the 1660–5 religious and political reaction were being softened or undone. Meanwhile, retaining the republic's navy and its aggressive commercial and colonial policies helped to set in place the contexts for the second Anglo-Dutch war. Envy of Dutch prosperity was not new, accompanied by a desire to emulate it or forcibly reassign 'market share'. '[T]here is but a certain proportion of Trade in the world, and *Holland* is prepossessed of the greater part of it'; 'the trade of the world is too little for us two, therefore one must down'.[17] Competition was sharpened by the foundation of the Royal African Company, which immediately took a large share of the slave trade (40,000 African captives in the first six years).[18] The new restoration ingredient, embodied by that company's patron, the Duke of York, was a hostile royalist perspective upon a neighbouring republic.

Among royalist Anglicans during the early 1660s, far from being a model for imitation, the United Provinces was a religious and political antitype. In the parlance of the day it was a 'fanatic' (radically heterodox) republic. That also made it the embodiment of a painful and traumatic English past. To the fact that royalists lived with the memory of regicide, usurpation, expropriation and exile the Act for Indemnity and Oblivion (1660) had been a legislative response. Real forgetting, however, would require generational change.[19] Meanwhile, not least by sheltering English republican exiles, the Dutch republic posed the question of whether restoration could succeed in one country. In the words of the English courtier Philalethes in Sidney's *Court Maxims*, 'we . . . look on their power and . . . happiness . . . as a most pernicious example to England . . . By destroying Holland we shall show the world that their prosperity is but a blaze soon going out.'[20]

From The Hague, Downing assured the English government that this hostility was reciprocated. He reported that 'De Witt [and his party] do not love the king and make it their study to make him little esteemed and accounted of . . . I assure you they do already looke upon his majesty through a diminishing glasse and themselves through a multiplying glasse':[21]

[They] discourse very publicly . . . we shall wholly destroy the English in the East Indies, we are masters of Guinea, we shall ruin the English trade in the caribee islands, and western parts, and we doubt not but now by the orders sent to Cadiz and the Streights, to be masters of those seas and to take and ruin all the English shipping there.[22]

What most animated the ambassador was the possibility of loss of the English republic's maritime and mercantile gains.[23] Initially Clarendon instructed him to cool his jets. 'I pray remember the streights and necessitys we are in for money, the emptiness of all our stores and magazines.'[24] However, as the regime consolidated itself Charles II became tempted by memories of the previous conflict. Another naval triumph would confer prestige, further prizes, and any increase in English trade would augment customs revenues. It was the belief of Downing, in view of the damage the earlier war had inflicted upon Dutch shipping, that De Witt would go to considerable lengths to avoid a repetition. Moreover, the seven Provinces were not united on this or any other issue. Thus by force, or the threat of force, concessions could be extracted, and if war did result the Dutch were much more vulnerable than the English.

Yet the Dutch were far better prepared, navally, in 1664 than in 1652.[25] The second and third Anglo-Dutch wars were fought not only around the North Sea but in West Africa, the East Indies and North America.[26] The war arrived in practice before the formal declarations (Dutch in January 1665,

English in February). In Guinea in West Africa the English Royal Company had initiated an English thrust for a share of the slave trade.[27] In May 1664 Captain Robert Holmes seized a Dutch-controlled island, a fort, a castle and several ships. To this the Dutch response proved far more resolute than Downing's prediction ('Go on in Guinea; if you bang them there they will be very tame').[28] Admiral De Ruyter was dispatched from the Mediterranean and by December Pepys had received 'fully the news of our being beaten to dirt at Guinny . . . to the utter ruine of our Royall Company'.[29]

In between these two clashes, on the other side of the Atlantic, on 29 August 1664 four English ships appeared to demand the surrender of New Amsterdam. This Governor Stuyvesant, despite citing Grotius in support of 'first discovery, uninterrupted possession, and Purchase' of the colony, found himself incapable of resisting, particularly after English settlers on Long Island declared themselves obliged to assist the invaders.[30] From Massachusetts, John Winthrop celebrated the 'way made for the inlargement of his Maties Dominions, by filling yt vacant wildernesse, in tyme, wth plantatios of his Maties subjects'.[31] The capture of New York, though less immediately lucrative than control of the Guinea coast, had more important long-term consequences. Formally it removed the last continental American base for evasion of the terms of the Navigation and Staple Acts.

In the short term, with encouragement of the new English government, there remained a considerable Dutch mercantile and cultural presence in New York, and relationships with Dutch networks remained close. Following Anglo-Dutch peace in 1674, textiles, paper and tiles were imported from the Netherlands and 'Dutch city inhabitants were entitled to receive letters of denization which gave them the right to send vessels from the British North American colonies to the Netherlands provided they entered an English port . . . to observe British customs procedures under the Navigation Acts'.[32] Informally, through most of the late seventeenth and eighteenth centuries there was vigorous illicit trading between New England, New York and the Dutch Caribbean, particularly the islands of St Eustatius and Curaçao.[33] This relative Anglo-Dutch continuity contrasted with the situation in Surinam, ceded to the Dutch in 1667, where English planters and merchants were driven out.[34] Over the following century the exchange of New York for Surinam proved as beneficial for the Dutch as it was for the English.[35]

Throughout 1664 the Dutch were engaged in a vigorous programme of shipbuilding. When in December all Dutch shipping in English ports was seized, the ground was prepared for war.[36] The United Provinces were now allied to France. In addition there was the question of whether the English republican naval effort of 1652 could be repeated under monarchy. That war had been the nautical wing of a moral and material revolution. It had called upon unheard-of resources within a reformed and politically animated administrative structure. As Alfred Thayer Mahan put it, 'a stern, enthusiastic religious government . . . grounded on military strength, had made its mark both on the fleet and army . . . This superiority in tone and discipline gradually disappeared under the corrupting influence of court favour in a licentious government.'[37] Reintroducing gentleman officers to the fleet the king explained: 'I am not for the imploying of men merely for quality, yet when men of quality are fit for the trade they desire to enter into, I think it is reasonable they should be encouraged at least equally with others.'[38]

In the short term the English fleet more than held its own. What would lose England the war was not want of skill or valour on the ships, but corruption and incompetence on land. The conflict was, by Stuart standards, adequately funded, the House of Commons voting the unheard-of supply of two and half million pounds.[39] Moreover, Downing persuaded the king to pass the Act for the Additional Aid (1665). By its 'technique of raising Orders, registered and repayable in course . . . an entirely new credit structure was erected'. This marked 'the acquisition by the Commons of the power of appropriating its supplies, the first significant limitation of the freedom of the action of the executive' and 'the most important constitutional development of Charles II's reign'.[40] This was the kind of legislative guarantee which had enabled the provincial estates of the Low Countries to revolutionize public lending in the mid-sixteenth century.[41] The Earl of Clarendon was appalled:

> Downing . . . told them . . . by making the Payment with Interest so certain and fixed, that . . . it should be out of any Man's Power to cause any Money that should be lent To-morrow to be paid before that which was lent Yesterday . . . he would make [the] Exchequer (which was now Bankrupt and without any Credit) the best and greatest Bank in Europe . . . and all

Nations would sooner send their Money into [it] . . . than into Amsterdam or Genoa or Venice. And it cannot be enough wondered at, that this Intoxication prevailed so far that no argument would be heard against it . . . without weighing that the Security for Monies so deposited in Banks is the Republick itself, which must expire before that Security can fail; which can never be depended on in a Monarchy, where the Monarch's sole word can cancel all those formal Provisions . . . upon that and the like Acts of Parliament.[42]

This principle of appropriation was regularized and applied to the ordinary revenue from 1667, with Downing as Secretary to the Treasury Commissioners and later a commissioner himself. All of this made the further steps taken in 1694–5, resulting in the establishment of a permanent National Debt, much more likely and straightforward.[43] The result would be a system of public credit which 'enabled England to spend on war out of all proportion to its tax revenue'.[44] This worked on a Dutch model in that it 'used a public bank to handle the loans, based the debt on long-term redeemable annuities, and spread the debt amongst a substantial number of borrowers'.[45]

The outbreak of war saw a barrage of anti-Dutch publication, much of it (like Marvell's *Character of Holland*, now published for the first time) recycled from 1652–4. By writers lacking Marvell's wit readers were informed that the Dutch '*Were First Bred and Descended from a Horse-Turd which Was Enclosed in a Butter-Box*'; 'An Hollander . . . is a low-lander for he loves to be down in the dirt and wallow therein.'[46] The first year of the war was closely fought, despite the worst outbreak of bubonic plague in London's history, killing a quarter of its population (100,000 people). The first battle, off Lowestoft in Suffolk on 13 June 1665, produced 'a continued terrible thunder', heard by both Downing in The Hague and Pepys in London.[47] It was an English victory, resulting in the death of the Dutch Admiral Obdam and the loss with almost all hands of his ship *Eendracht*. Also killed, however, were three senior courtiers standing on deck next to the Lord Admiral James, Duke of York. York was replaced by Edward Montagu, Earl of Sandwich. There followed a skirmish off Bergen, and then the following year the Dutch reappeared off the Thames. An encounter on 1 June 1666 was inconclusive, though English losses were greater. In another, on 25 July off Suffolk, England prevailed.

Yet there was no substitute for the capacity, financial, organizational and mental, to continue the war until it was won. On 2 September, London was devastated by fire (described by Clarendon as 'the highest calamity this nation hath ever felt').[48] In late 1666, having made 'exacting and haughty . . . demands' as conditions of a peace treaty, Charles II failed to fit out a fleet. 'Instead of that, poverty, the result of extravagance and of his home policy, led him to permit it to decline; ships in large numbers were laid up.'[49] The Dutch, meanwhile, continued to build more ships.[50] Then, on 14 June 1667, under De Ruyter, and piloted by English republican exiles, 'a force of sixty or seventy ships-of-the-line' entered the Thames. It sailed 'up as high as Gravesend, destroying ships at Chatham and in the Medway, and taking possession of Sheerness. The light of the fires could be seen from London, and the Dutch fleet remained in possession of the mouth of the river until the end of the month'.[51] England's flagship *Royal Charles* was towed back to the Netherlands, 'the greatest ever English naval humiliation to date'.[52]

WE NEED TO TALK ABOUT CHATHAM

'The dismay that is upon us all in the business of the kingdom and Navy at this day,' wrote Pepys, 'is not to be expressed.'[53] In the words of Jeremy Bentham:

> There is general consternation and wonder that we were in no readiness to receive the enemy . . . how strangely were all our counselors lulled into a dead sleep of security that nothing less than so mortal a blow and irreparable loss should awaken them.[54]

More than the Glorious Revolution, Chatham was England's anti-1588. With the loss of fourteen great ships, including some of the best in the fleet, the raid was a military as well as political catastrophe.[55] What the prospects were for an administration that could not send its fleet to sea in wartime, or defend it on the edge of its own capital city, was far from clear. It was lucky for all concerned that the government of Johann De Witt saw fit to exploit this triumph by making peace. It was the doctrine of the De Witt regime, expounded in a tract of which a manuscript translation survives in Pepys' papers, that the lifeblood of the Dutch republic was trade, for which the imperative was peace.[56]

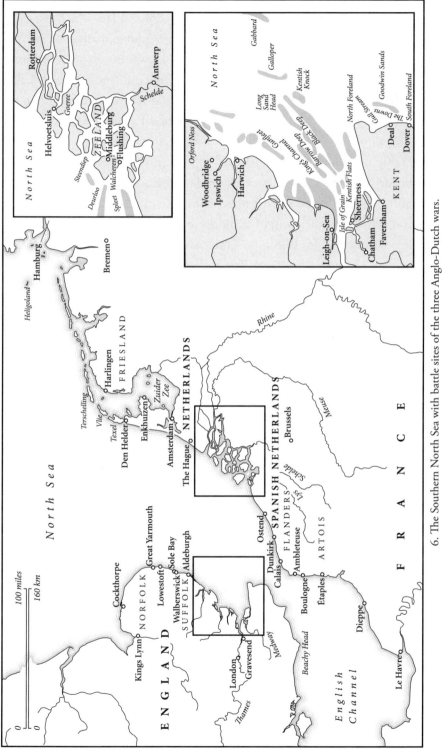

6. The Southern North Sea with battle sites of the three Anglo-Dutch wars.

Nevertheless the descent on Chatham underlined a fact which remained lodged in minds on both sides of the Channel. Without 'mastery of the seas' the most important fact about English geography was not its supposed insularity. It was the location of the Thames estuary opposite those of the Scheldt, the Maas and the Rhine, creating a single maritime zone of cultural, economic and military interaction.[57] When Dutch political circumstances changed, adding alongside the pro-French, peace-mongering regents a reinstated and militarily ambitious Stadtholder, the consequences for England would be dramatic. Thus as North America became less Anglo-Dutch, and more securely English, England revealed itself to be vulnerable to Dutch invasion; an invasion which, in a further twist of archipelagic history, would establish the eighteenth-century basis for British pre-eminence and Dutch decline.

After Chatham, Pepys' secretary Richard Gibson composed a blistering analysis. This repudiated charges which had been levelled at inferior officers within the naval administration such as himself.[58] These directed blame 'either for not bringing up the great shipps, especially the Charles, in ye midst of the consternation . . . or for using his Mats boates to save theire goods at such a time as . . . those very Boates being well mann'd might have preserved his Mats Shipps from burning'.[59]

Gibson found little merit in these criticisms, 'nor matters it much in wch stable ye Horses stood when ye Principll Doore leading to every roome was left open'. Nobody 'imagined that ye Enemy would have sent up 5 or 6 Fireshipps above Upnor Castle without some men of Warr to defend them'.[60] What then was the explanation for this astonishing audacity, or perhaps intelligence? The most important problem was the negligence of 'Principll Officers' in preparing and fortifying the waterway. Core defence was 'Five Guard shipps & a Chaine the meanest contrivance against an Ennemy wth a Briske Easterly winde that could ever bee thought on'.[61] 'Fireshipps . . . would have proved of great use but they were (by whose Councell I know not) sunk under pretence of stopping up the River wch also proved frivolous.' A 'Fort at ye Ness' ordered to be built a year earlier was three days before the raid 'to ye Seaward . . . not 12 inches high' equipped with eight guns without firing platforms. At Tilbury 'the carriages being rotted & the Guns dismounted' there was anyway 'a very insufficient quantity of powder'. All of this suggested 'supineness, insufficiency or treason in some of our Prime Officers'.[62]

Anticipating 'ye enquirys that would best become ye wisdome sagacity & grandure of our king & Parliamt', the republican veteran became specific:[63]

Who braged of ye Strength & safety of that Port in ye midle of Aprill in case ye Enemy attacks it wth 40 Men of Warr; who wrott . . . to Sr Wm Coventry ye beginning of June assureing ye strength and safe condition of that place; Who permitted a Vessell of Flaunders with . . . 15 Pipes of choice Canary Wines . . . whereof ye licencer had one pipe for his share wch hee sold for 55 pounds to come up that River contrary to Orders from ye Councell . . . who was ye author of sinkeing our 5 Fireshipps. . . . in such places as did not at all hinder ye Enemys approach . . . Who should have provided Boates to have saved the many hundreds of Brave Men aboard ye Guardshipps . . . Who carried away ye Henrietta & Jemmy pleasure Boates wth a few gazeing Principll Officers & other Idle Spectators at ye very moment when those Boates might . . . have saved ye life of many a brave Man who for want thereof was either drowned like ye Old World or burned like Gomorra.[64]

Decades earlier the possibility of just such a disaster at Chatham had been predicted by Sir William Monson, should the Dutch 'become enemies to us'.[65] Monson had counselled powerful coastal fortifications, constant vigilance and heavily armed ships. Several aspects of Gibson's post-mortem, with names added, were echoed by Andrew Marvell's excoriating *Last Instructions to a Painter*. This reversed the same author's earlier celebration of republican naval power in *First Anniversary of the Government Under Oliver Cromwell*. *Last Instructions* mourned the Thames, where

... our sick Ships unrigg'd in Summer lay,
Like molting Fowl, a weak and easie Prey . . .
Once a deep River, now with Timber floor'd,
And shrunk, lest Navigable, to a Ford.
Now (nothing more at *Chatham* left to burn)
The *Holland* Squadron leisurely return:
And spight of *Ruperts* and of *Albemarles*,
To *Ruyter's* Triumph lead the captive *Charles* . . .

When aged *Thames* was bound with Fetters base,
And *Medway* chast ravish'd before his Face . . .
Sad change, since first that happy pair was wed,
When all the Rivers grac'd their Nuptial Bed;
And Father *Neptune* promis'd to resign
His Empire old, to their immortal Line![66]

The 'captive *Charles*' was a painful image, as was the ravished '*Medway* chast'. Marvell portrayed the king tormented by visions of his murdered predecessors Henry IV and Charles I:

Harry sits down, and in his open side
The grizly Wound reveals, of which he dy'd.
And ghastly *Charles*, turning his Collar low,
The purple thread about his Neck does Show:
Then, whisp'ring to his Son in Words unheard,
Through the lock'd door both of them disappear'd.[67]

The best-selling satire inspired by Chatham was Henry Neville's *The Isle of Pines . . . A late Discovery . . . near Terra Australis Incognita* (London, 1668). George Pines was an Elizabethan book-keeper shipwrecked on an uninhabited island in the East Indies with four women: his merchant Master's daughter, two maids and an African slave. '[T]hey were all handsome Women, when they had Cloathes', which was not for long, and they clung to George excessively, he 'being now all their stay in this lost condition'. Their condition could have been worse, since the island was large, 'ever warm . . . always . . . green', devoid of harmful animals, and blessed with food. It could have been much worse for George, for whom 'Idleness and fullness' led to sex, first with two women, and then with all, initially in private, and then 'more openly'.[68] By the time the island was rediscovered a hundred years later its population was two thousand. Readers trying to determine whether Neville's anonymously published story was a spoof might have found their first clue here: such a rate of increase is not possible in a human population where the children are being breastfed. The same readers would have been on solid ground in deducing that the author was male.[69]

This story found a lively market. It was quickly translated into Dutch, French, Italian, German and Danish. While one German scholar considered learnedly the moral status of Pines' *menage a cinq*, another unscrambled the title as *Penis Island*.[70] While laughing all the way to the bank, Neville's point was serious. Like Marvell and Gibson he was a product of the Interregnum. Like Henry Vane and Algernon Sidney, Neville had been a member of the republican government which had run, and won, the first Anglo-Dutch war.

The ship by which Pines' island was rediscovered was Dutch. The author of the published account was its captain. What Henry Cornelius Van Sloetten's crew found was a people who, although they 'could speak *English* . . . yet go naked'. Great numbers 'flock . . . about us . . . admiring . . . our Cloaths . . . [and] wondering at our ship, as if it had been the greatest miracle of Nature'.[71] Their 'Prince' William Pine, grandson of George, was a good-natured imbecile who lived in a 'Pallace' made of 'rough unhewn pieces of Timber'. His hundred-year-old axe was 'blunt and dulled', he ate like a 'peasant', drank only water, and was 'altogether ignorant [of] . . . ships, or shipping'. His people lived in a state of 'Nature' without 'the benefit of Art'.[72] When they saw someone playing bagpipes they thought he was blowing into 'a living creature'.[73] When the Dutch came 'to discharge a piece of Ordnance, it struck him into a wonder . . . to behold the strange effects of Powder'. When William faced domestic disorder and persuaded the Dutch to intervene, they countered 'Clubs and Stones' by 'discharging . . . three or four Guns', which caused the offenders to run away.[74]

Neville's account recalled Columbus' description of the inhabitants of Hispaniola as 'naked . . . with no experience of arms and very timid'.[75] The Dutch could enter Penis Island at any time. Since Elizabethan settlement it had reverted to the military stone age. Devoid of art, industry or technology, Charles II cavorted with his mistresses. These semi-public couplings produced no legitimate issue. In another reversal of Elizabethan and republican dispensations, royal sexual promiscuity signified military impotence. Marvell made more of this conjuncture, including spectacular ridicule of the Duchess of York, daughter of the Lord Chancellor:

Happy'st of Women, if she were but able
To make her glassen *Dildoes* once *malleable*!
Paint her with Oyster Lip, and breath of Fame,

Wide Mouth that Sparagus may well proclaim:
With *Chanc'lor's* Belly, and so large a Rump.
There, not behind the Coach, her Pages jump.[76]

Chatham revealed the government's nakedness. It caught Captain Penis of the *Royal Charles in flagrante* on the beach. This was a humiliation from which Charles II's reign would not recover. Eighteen years later, not long before his death, the king recounted the episode to Henry Sheres 'alone in his Closet':

> with Soe feeling a Sense of ye Misfortune, Such Admirable Observations upon the Motives the Enemy had to the Attempt . . . together with what was done and Attempted on Our Part, What false Stepps and Judgements were made and by whom, Descending to every Remarkable Particular . . . That a Stranger to the Story would by ye Relation have Guess'd It to have just then hapned; soe lively and lasting an Impression had that fatall Success made in his Mats Mind . . . [A]s his . . . Matie . . . observed to me . . . the People on the Occasion of . . . [that] Attempt . . . were frighted almost out of their Obedience, and the Successe of that action threatened even a Convulsion of the State.[77]

Pepys reported that 'people make nothing of talking treason in the streets openly'.[78] There followed predictions of another civil war. Should such a thing occur, '(which God forbid)', Sir William Coventry told Pepys:

> that which must save the Crown in every other particular will do it also in this, namely, the securing to itself the City of London, the being master of that and of the River . . . particularly the fleet, which cannot reasonably be supported by any power of this nation that hath not London . . . And in proof of this he very well observed that the losing of London did not discover itself of prejudice to the late King in anything more than in his fleet.[79]

FLIGHT TO FRANCE

The government's first reaction was to make peace. Dutch anxiety now pivoted to France, which had invaded the Spanish Netherlands. Thus the Treaty of

Breda, signed on 21 July 1667, was followed by the Triple Alliance (1668), an Anglo-Dutch-Swedish project for the containment of France. In response Louis XIV applied himself to the cultivation of Charles II.[80] Two years later, in the Treaty of Dover, Charles II abandoned this agreement for an alliance with France itself, with one objective of destroying the United Provinces. In the accompanying Secret Treaty, which was not a very good secret, the king being forced to deny in Parliament the existence of any 'secret articles of dangerous consequence', Charles undertook to support Louis XIV's European ambitions, in exchange for annual pensions; to follow the attack on the Netherlands with an announcement of his own Roman Catholicism; and to convert his whole kingdom to that religion, using 'six mille [French] hommes de pied, s'il est besoin'.[81]

Comments John Miller: 'Now that he was firmly established as the king of a strongly anti-Catholic country, the idea of [Charles] turning Catholic would seem bizarre to the point of lunacy.'[82] Indeed, the French ambassador Colbert de Croissy informed Louis XIV: 'He . . . told me . . . he [supposed] that . . . I considered that he . . . [was] crazy to claim to be capable of re-establishing Catholicism in England; that . . . everyone apprised of . . . the disposition of its people had to have the same thought; however . . . he hoped that with the support of your Majesty this great undertaking would have a favourable outcome.'[83] What was going on?

Approaching his own conversion in 1668, James, Duke of York had discussed it with Charles 'knowing that the King was of the same mind'. There followed a meeting on 25 January 1669 with the Duke of York, Lords Arundel and Arlington, and Sir Thomas Clifford. The king explained:

How uneasy it was to him not to profess the Faith he beleev'd, and that he had call'd them together to have their advice about the ways . . . fittest to be taken for the settling of the Catholick Religion in his Kingdoms . . . That he was to expect . . . many and great difficultys . . . and that he chose rather to undertake it now, when he and his Brother were in their full strength . . . This he speake with great earnestness, and even with tears in his eyes . . . the Consultation [concluded] . . . that there was no better way for doing this great work, then with the assistance of his Most Christian Majesty.[84]

James had an interest in talking up his brother's Roman Catholicism.[85] Yet every aspect of the project thus described is verified by the record of the subsequent negotiations. They underscored Charles' interest in a 'reconciliation' with Roman Catholicism and a 'stricter alliance with France then there has hitherto been'.[86] What the negotiations make clear, indeed, alongside sharp bargaining over French subsidies, is that whereas Louis' primary interest was English assistance in the war on the United Provinces, that of Charles concerned French support for 'Catholicity'.[87] *Le Roy de la grand Bretagne estoit convaincu de la verite de la Religion Catholique et resolu de se declarer Catholique et de reconcilier avec l'Eglise de Rome.*'[88] This conversion was to be the centrepiece of a dramatic reorientation of Stuart religious, political and foreign policy to establish a 'paix, union, vraye confraternite' and 'confederation perpetuelle' with France which would secure the future of the monarchy.[89] This was a dynastic inversion of the proposed Anglo-Dutch republican union of 1651.

Here was the height of the European Counter-Reformation, with Louis XIV's France the new superpower. After Charles, James would follow the same course. The subsequent Dutch breaking of the Anglo-French alliance in 1688–9 was an axis upon which European and global history turned. Notwithstanding the importance to the Dutch of economic motives, if the Glorious Revolution was about anything it was about religion.[90] It was religious anxieties that underpinned English collaboration, both with the invasion and in the subsequent European war. Those anxieties, which had also sustained Anglo-Scots collaboration between 1640 and 1646, were as old as the Dutch Revolt, but were reignited by the events of 1670–2. Economic historians have argued that industrialization was able to follow an Anglo-Dutch (rather than Spanish or French) line of development because the United Provinces and Britain avoided absolutism. They would not have done so, however, without the stunning events of 1688–9, made possible because long-standing religious connections remained much more important than economic rivalries.

Part of Charles' motivation for Dover was to take military revenge against the Dutch.[91] But this does not explain the Treaty's religious clauses, or the king's apparent indifference to the probable domestic reaction to this destruction of a key Protestant ally.[92] However, fear not only of popery, but for the security of monarchy, had been a constant of seventeenth-century English politics.[93] How much more reason for this was there in the mind of a king, once a hunted fugitive, then a penniless exile, whose father had been publicly murdered by the people over whom he now reigned? 'We are bound to *honour* our Kings and Princes . . . and how have we done it? *Murder the Father! Banish the Son!*'[94]

This may explain why, when he was forced in 1673 to withdraw his *Declaration of Indulgence*, and to pull out of the third Anglo-Dutch war, Charles spoke as if he had narrowly escaped a rebellion. When parliamentary anger intensified over unabated French military expansion, Charles asked Louis why he couldn't give up a town or two to save him from his father's fate, or from being 'chased from his kingdom' again. As alarm mounted, Charles refused to change course because his opponents were out to 'take over the government' and so he could not abandon France as 'the only security he has'.[95] The Secret Treaty promised French military support for the English monarchy against Parliament and people 'should they rise against it'. The Marquess of Normanby ascribed the king's throwing 'Himself into ye hands of a Roman-Catholick Party, so remarkable of late for their Loyalty' to 'his being tir'd . . . with those bold Oppositions in Parliament' and thereupon 'lulled . . . asleep with those inchanting Songs of Soveraignty and Prerogative'.[96] Soon, however, the alarm clock sounded, interrupting both enchantment and sleep.

CHAPTER ELEVEN

THE REVOLUTION COMPLETED, 1672–1702

> The people are so generally dissatisfied . . . in relation to their religion, liberties and properties (all of which have been greatly invaded) . . . that your Highness may be assured there are nineteen parts of twenty . . . who are desirous of a change, and who . . . would willingly contribute to it if they had such a protection . . . as could secure them from being destroyd before they could get to be in a posture to defend themselves.
>
> Lords Shrewsbury, Devonshire, Danby, Lumley, Compton, Sidney and Russell to William of Orange, 30 June 1688[1]

> Charles II had been Louis XIV's satrap; William III was his hammer.
> T. C. W. Blanning, *The Culture of Power*

RESTORATION UNRAVELLING

The king's first priority in 1670–2 was to undo the religious settlement of 1662 and make his own Roman Catholicism public. A second was to bolster the English Crown by alliance with the most powerful monarch in Christendom. The third objective was a war of annihilation against the United Provinces which would yield some cross-Channel territory and erase the memory of Chatham. In addition to being insanely irresponsible, geopolitically (when the French cat had eaten the Dutch canary would it turn vegan?) this project was, domestically, a desperate gamble.

For of course these measures were not only opposed but 'abhorred' by an overwhelming majority of the king's subjects. Hence Charles' extraordinary protest to the French ambassador Ruvigny in 1674 that he 'alone was standing up for France's interests, against his entire kingdom'.[2] Fear of France had been building rapidly since 1667. The fire of London had been attributed to Jesuit incendiaries; the raid on Chatham had coincided with a French invasion of the Spanish Netherlands, and the fear of popery which deepened in England throughout the 1670s was unmistakably reminiscent of the 1580s and 1620s. Meanwhile the actual precariousness of Protestantism in 1670 was much greater. In 1590 Protestant territories had comprised almost one-half of the land area of the European continent; by 1690 the Protestant share was about one-fifth.[3] During the period 1670–1702 the survival of Protestantism was actually at stake.

So was that of the United Provinces. In 1672 Charles issued Declarations of *War*, and of *Indulgence* granting liberty to worship to Roman Catholics as well as to Protestant dissenters. Assisted by a drought which made rivers fordable, France invaded, crossing the Rhine on 12 June, overwhelming southern and eastern defences and occupying Utrecht on 27 June.[4] A measure of control was restored by flooding the Water Line, on the border of Utrecht and Holland, halting and partly drowning the Bishop of Munster's army.[5] Under the mercantile leadership of Holland, and during the course of two Anglo-Dutch naval wars, the republic's land defences had been neglected.[6] In his final chapter, 'The Causes of their Fall in 1672', William Temple criticized the exclusion of the Stadtholder, the disbandment of many of the foreign troops in Dutch service, and the addiction of the 'Commonwealth-Party' to France, occasioned by the republican priority of peace in order to facilitate trade. Amid the ensuing crisis the De Witt brothers were lynched by a furious mob.

Temple added that De Witt had also failed to predict this calamity because the Dutch 'could not imagine a Conjunction between *England* and *France* for the ruin of their State; for, being unacquainted with our Constitutions, they did not forsee how we should find our Interest in it . . . Nor could they believe that other Princes and States of *Europe* would suffer such an addition to be made to the Power of *France*, as a Conquest of *Holland*.'[7] They did not understand, this was to say, that England's king could, if he wished, conclude a treaty against the interest of his own country. Yet even allied with France, Charles' second Dutch war also failed. In three naval battles between June and August 1673 De Ruyter successfully defended the United Provinces from a planned landing of English and French troops, and reopened Dutch ports to trade.[8] The House of Commons refused to support the war, and in the same year Charles was forced to withdraw the *Declaration of Indulgence* and replace it with a Test Act reinforcing the Anglican monopoly on office holding.

Meanwhile the Dutch had to absorb the implications of the near-destruction of their state. On 3 July 1672 the Perpetual Edict setting aside the office of Stadtholder was revoked and six days later William of Orange was made Stadtholder of Holland.[9] As the occupation continued, a priority became to detach England from its French alliance and from the war. That would be the purpose of the invasion of 1688 when it could not be achieved in any other way. From 'the spring of 1673 onwards, Dutch pamphlet propaganda hawked on the streets of London began to insinuate that the French alliance was not in England's true interests, and that there was more in the friendship between the English court and Louis XIV than met the eye'.[10] The arguments of Pierre Du Moulin's *England's Appeal from the Private Cabal to the Great Council of the Nation* (1673) were echoed in House of Commons debates, that '*This is a war of religion, undertaken merely for the propagation of the catholic faith*, and as the French minister at Vienna expressed it . . . the Hollanders being heretics . . . all good Christians are bound to join and unite to extirpate them'.[11] This was the language of the Popish Plot which had driven English political anxieties in 1585, 1621 and 1641, and which would usher in a new crisis from 1678 to 1683. The English had long considered the Low Countries the fortified 'outworks' of their religion. This was the last stage of a 'Holy War . . . not only here, but in Christendom: for Popery or Protestanisme must fall.'[12]

RESTORATION CRISIS, 1678–83

By 1674 the parliamentary uproar had forced Charles, for public consumption at least, to adopt a new policy. In February, England withdrew from the war. The new minister in charge was Thomas Osborne, Earl of Danby, and one of his achievements was the marriage between William of Orange and James' daughter Mary, under discussion from 1674 and completed in November 1677. This was facilitated by William Temple, who completed a second posting to The Hague from 1675, and then to Nijmegen where a Franco-Dutch peace was signed in 1678, rather to the satisfaction of the Amsterdam regents than of

William. In fact Charles had not abandoned his relationship with France. The crisis of 1678–83 was triggered by the revelation in Parliament of ongoing secret negotiations, and payments, between Louis and Charles. Those revelations were orchestrated by Louis to punish Charles for attempting to extract more money while allowing the marriage of William and Mary. By 1679 this Anglo-French rupture and the political uproar in England necessitated a new Parliament, a new government ministry and a new foreign policy.[13]

Amid the ensuing crisis, in November 1680, the House of Commons published an *Address* documenting the return of popery and arbitrary government to England. This detailed the 'Attempts of the Popish Party, for many years last past . . . not only within this, but other your Majesties Kingdoms, to introduce the Romish, and utterly to extirpate the true protestant religion':[14]

> After some time [these Jesuits] . . . became able to influence matters of State and Government . . . Ministers of England were made Instruments . . . to make War upon a Protestant State . . . to advance and augment the dreadful power of the French King . . . [and] When in the next Parliament the house of Commons were prepared to bring to a legal Tryal the principal Conspirators in this Plot, that Parliament was first Prorogued, and then Dissolved. The Interval between the Calling and Sitting of this Parliament was so long, that now they conceive hopes of Covering all their past Crimes.[15]

The following month Louis was advised by his ambassador Paul Barillon that the Crown was in danger of being swept aside by the enraged Parliament, raising the possibility of a second English republic. Charles had been telling Louis since mid-1679 that he needed to decide whether he wanted a monarchy or a republic in England. The problem with a popular government would be that the English were passionately anti-French. Barillon took the point and reported: 'I do not think a republic in England would be in the interests of France; one saw by experience how powerful the nation became under such a united government.'[16] In December 1680 Louis agreed to resume financial support for the Crown.

After one more abortive parliament called to Oxford for presentational purposes, this enabled Charles to govern for the remainder of his reign without parliaments, and so gradually to bring the crisis under control.[17] Still, it took more than two years to pacify the capital city, and the respite proved temporary. In 1685 Charles was succeeded by James. England's third and final seventeenth-century crisis of popery and arbitrary government was provoked by the new king's reckless confessional policies, amid a European religious crisis. In 1685 Louis XIV revoked the Edict of Nantes, which had protected French Protestants for almost a century, turning an existing trickle of Huguenot refugees into a flood. Over the following two years the Roman Catholic James, presiding over a court replete with Catholic ministers including one Jesuit priest, promoted Catholics in the army and the universities, and issued his own Declaration of Indulgence for the benefit of Roman Catholic as well as Protestant dissenters in 1687. When in early 1688 seven bishops who had petitioned against the king's dispensing power and been charged with sedition were acquitted, public political allegiance began to disintegrate.

THE GLORIOUS REVOLUTION, 1688–9

On 5 November 1688, in the largest naval operation ever mounted in Atlantic waters, a Dutch-European fleet and army landed unopposed at Torbay in south-west England. It included 500 ships (53 warships), 40,000 men (including 15,000 soldiers and gunners, 5,000 volunteers and 19,000 crew) and 500 horses.[18] A month earlier John Evelyn had written of the 'hourly expectation of the Prince of Orange's invasion'. The people looked upon the Prince 'to be their deliverer from Popish tyranny, praying incessantly for an East wind . . . The apprehension was (and with reason) that his Majesty's forces would neither at land or sea oppose them with that vigour requisite to repel invaders.'[19] This was to say that English troops might prove as reluctant in 1688 as they had been between 1638 and 1640 to defend popery at home against a Protestant invasion.

Over more than a century Dutch and English Protestants had come to regard the fortunes of their countries and their religion as interdependent. Edward Seymour explained in 1689: 'England has done formerly for Holland, as Holland has now done for England.'[20] One European observed: 'The Dutch are convinced that they will be as fortunate in their plan to attack England as

Philip II was unfortunate . . . There are few among them who are unaware of this period of history and who do not know by heart the inscriptions on the medals which were struck at that time.'[21] In June 1688 William had been assured by seven English lords that a Dutch military intervention in England could expect widespread support. Nevertheless the size of the Dutch Armada, five times that of its Spanish predecessor, left little to chance. It contained a variety of European, including English, Protestants. It proved militarily self-sufficient, which was just as well, since the crisis-weary West Country elite hedged their bets. From Exeter after the landing William's adviser Hans William Bentinck reported:

> I doubt not the Good God will bless the cause, the people appear every-where here extremely well disposed, it is only the gentlemen and the clergy who are somewhat more cautious, and do not espouse our cause. I am surprised at the latter, it seems to me that fear of the gibbet has more effect on their minds than zeal for religion.[22]

How had the invasion transpired? As in 1678, the crisis seems to have been precipitated by an aggressive French king. By 1687 the trade concessions granted to Dutch regents by the Treaty of Nijmegen, and the haven offered to fleeing Huguenots, had become intolerable to Louis. There followed, in violation of the Treaty, the imposition of tariffs, and by September the arrest of all Dutch shipping in French ports. The same measure, enacted by England in December 1664, had precipitated the second Anglo-Dutch war. Alienating the regents, this made it possible, on 29 September, for Caspar Fagel to lay before a secret session of the states of Holland an extraordinary plan:

> France had grievously damaged Dutch trade, shipping and fisheries; war with France was . . . unavoidable; if the Republic remained in a defensive posture, France, in alliance with England . . . would overwhelm [it]; the only way, in these circumstances, in which the Dutch state could be made secure was to break the 'absolute power' of James II quickly, suppress the Catholic pro-French influence in England, convene Parliament and restore its authority, and turn England round against France . . .

> This . . . objective . . . could not conceivably have succeeded without the concerted, unified, support of all sections of the Dutch state – something exceedingly rare in seventeenth-century Dutch history – but this was now assured thanks to the actions of Louis XIV.[23]

Nothing but a Dutch emergency can explain either the scale or the risk of what was undertaken. This involved a financial and military outlay greater than that between 1598 and 1602 which had resulted in the conquest of the Portuguese East Indies. The invasion was financed by the same Amsterdam bankers who would soon be investing heavily in the reformed public finances of the English state.[24] It cannot be understood as a dynastic adventure by William, which would not have been supported by the republican states of Holland. Rather it was the first act in a war for survival against France which immediately provoked a French declaration of war. The Dutch had been watching English parliamentary politics since 1673. They knew that if the summoning of a parliament could be achieved there was every reason to expect it to support war against France. Thus William's carefully worded *Declaration*, issued on landing, promised restoration of 'a free and legal parliament':

> It is . . . evident to all men, that the publick peace and happiness of any state or kingdom cannot be preserved where the law, liberties and customs, established by the lawful authority in it, are openly transgressed and annulled; more especially, where the alteration of religion is endeavoured, and that [in favour of] a religion, which is contrary to law . . . those counsellors, who have now the chief credit with the King, have overturned the religion, laws and liberties of these Realms, and subjected them . . . to arbitrary government.[25]

This was the language of England's troubles, and William had many advisers (like Gilbert Burnet, William Temple and Henry Sidney) with whose help to perfect it. James drew together his army, but from the moment of the Dutch landing English officers began defecting. In the end James' army fell apart – 'disgraced . . . humiliated . . . defeated . . . However much the English generals and senior officers tried to cloud the issue, the . . . truth was that their army had been smashed in the field.'[26] In a further development which could not have been predicted (the king had a distinguished record of military service), on 11 December 1688 James fled the country.

Meanwhile there was a revolution within the government of the City of London. On the day of James' flight, William, 'called by the Voice of the People', was invited by the new Lord Mayor to enter the City. At the request of the City and an Assembly of Peers William undertook the de facto government of the kingdom. Following his formal entry on 18 December, 'to the loud acclamations of a vast number of people of all sorts and ranks', Dutch troops restored order in the capital. English soldiers were required to leave the city, and in early January 1689, under the terms of the Treaty of Nijmegen, 10,000 left for training alongside the remainder of the Dutch army in the Low Countries.

ANGLO-DUTCH RESTORATION, COMPLETED

In late December William summoned a never before heard-of body called an Assembly of Commoners. This was composed of members of the City of London government and any surviving members of the Houses of Commons of the reign of Charles II. Thus it brought back into being the anti-French City–Commons political alliance which had led the opposition to Charles II during the crisis of 1678–81. The Assembly advised William to call a Convention (a parliament in the absence of a king). Such a body had been the instrument of restoration in 1660.

The Convention met on 22 January 1689, and in early February produced its first important amendment to the restoration settlement: 'That it hath been found by Experience, to be inconsistent with the Safety and Welfare of this Protestant Kingdom, to be governed by a Popish Prince.' It was accordingly resolved on 6 February, 'That no Popish successor shall be capable to inherit the Crown, and no Papist capable of succeeding to the Crown'. In 1680 a similar bill had been resisted not only by Charles II but by a House of Lords understandably more protective of the hereditary principle than was the Commons. Now, however, with the king absent, London under Dutch military occupation, the House under siege by crowds and by five petitions from the City government, opposition in the Lords was overborne. Thus after more than a century of struggle, beginning with the crisis surrounding Mary, Queen of Scots, dynastic criteria were permanently subordinated to confessional ones in respect of the succession.

In the same context the Lords acquiesced in the present settlement of the Crown. James being absent, the Commons wished to proceed on the basis that the throne was vacant. The Lords begged to 'differ . . . about the Words Abdicated and Deserted . . . upon the Account of the Consequence . . . in . . . your vote, *That the Throne is thereby Vacant* . . . which we say will make the Crown *Elective?*'[27] However, France threatened, and William offered to leave England to fight another civil war if that was what the Lords preferred. William and Mary were crowned joint sovereigns on 14 February.

The next amendment of the terms of settlement of 1660 was the Convention's refusal to vote the Crown more than sufficient revenue for the current financial year. In the words of Sir William Williams, 'Because King Charles II was called home by the Convention, and nothing settled, you found the consequence. Charles II was a young man, in the strength of his youth, and you know, how much Money was given him, and what became of it.' 'In the great joy of the King's Return', added the no more sprightly Mr Sacheverell, 'the Parliament overshot themselves so much, and to redress a few Grievances they got so much Money, that they could live without you.'[28] As necessary as security for Protestantism was security for parliaments.

The third key restoration institution was the Church. In 1689, in place of the Act of Uniformity, which had been opposed by successive Declarations of Indulgence, Parliament passed an Act for Toleration. This did not permit Roman Catholic worship; and it approved only Trinitarian Protestant dissent. Most importantly the Act was a parliamentary statute, rather than an attempt by the Crown to dispense with the same. In this carefully contrived compromise, also, the lessons of experience were applied in a controlled Anglo-Dutch political and military context. The result was a revised restoration settlement which limited the Crown, secured annual parliaments and established religious toleration. This was further adjusted over the period 1689–1701, in the context of practical governmental experience in wartime. For the Dutch, who needed to confront France militarily quickly, a supported rather than imposed settlement was imperative. Then, for the war to be successfully led and funded, more than a century of English political dysfunction had to give way to a new era of negotiation and co-operation.

THE ANGLO-DUTCH REVOLUTION COMPLETED, 1689–1702

Although England declared war on France in May 1689 the preparatory troop movements and training began before William and Mary were crowned. What the Nine Years War achieved was not only a halt to French expansion. It gave rise to a vigorous period of military-fiscal state-building which completed the Anglo-Dutch revolution inaugurated in 1649 and so the emergence of a new world power. As in 1649 the revolution had to be secured militarily.[29] Again this process began in Ireland. The defeat of James in Ireland, which re-established the Protestant ascendancy imposed between 1649 and 1652, was the work of a European army including 2,000 Huguenots, with Swedish and Dutch as well as English commanders. Speaking before William in Belfast, the royal chaplain George Royse emphasized the European Protestant cause: 'how much the general interest of the reformed Church and Religion does depend on the present Juncture . . . [how William] had come from saving Holland's reformation, to save England's, and had now come to promote God's cause in Ireland'.[30] In this and other respects, this revolution and the state that emerged were more than merely national achievements, with regional and global consequences explored in Part Three of this study.

The war against France was fought by a European alliance. When Henry Sheres considered 'the Danger of one mighty United Power which like a Comet at this day threatens ye World' and 'what a Rope of Sand Confederacys of such diversified Ends & Interests as those are which compose ye present League', his conclusion was 'that our joint Safety is contained . . . in an inviolable Concord and sincere union of our Strength & Councils; and by postponing all Competitions and Jealousys whatsoever . . . conspiring to fix our Comon Safety on its Proper Basis'.[31] Under Dutch tutelage and international command the English army was made an effective fighting force.[32] This was one component of a broader Anglo-Dutch military-political-fiscal modernization. Experience had shown that it was English parliaments that had the capacity to make war. 'Our dear bought experience has taught us what Vast Taxes are necessary to maintain the armies and the Fleet, which are requisite, and for the defence of our religious and civil rights.'[33]

One historian credited to Dutch influence a 'revolution in English attitudes to Europe' during the war of 1689–97. '[A] substantial body of English opinion, much of it concentrated in the Whig party, had at length come to accept the "Williamist" view of the kingdom's destiny . . . the outward-looking view that the only real safety for the English nation and for the Protestant religion lay not in disengagement from the continent but in her involvement.'[34] Yet as we have seen this view had been general among England's Protestant political elite since the Elizabethan period. What was new, from 1689, was a Dutch monarch determined to give it military expression. In 1698 an English writer reflected:

> our late *Kings* half undid us, and bred us up as narrow spirited as they could
> . . . we seldom were permitted to cast an eye farther then *France* or *Holland*,
> and then too we were carefully watched: but at present matters are other-
> wise; we have a *Prince* that has raised us to our natural station, the eyes of
> most part of the World are now upon us, and take their measures from our
> Councils: we find every day occasion to inform ourselves of the strength
> and interests of the several Princes of *Europe*.[35]

With the advice of managers, this new leadership deepened its institutional foundations by sometimes painful concessions limiting royal, and augmenting parliamentary, autonomy. The Triennial Act of 1694 subjected the calling and dissolving of parliaments to statutory regulation, and the Act of Succession of 1701 accepted parliamentary oversight of several monarchical functions and powers. Yet the military rewards were enormous. By 1694 the Commons was voting annual funding approaching five million pounds. The security made available to lenders by Parliament's legislative guarantee made possible completion of the Anglo-Dutch financial revolution prefigured by the Act for the Additional Aid (1665). Establishment followed of the Bank of England (1694), other banks, the London stock exchange, a burgeoning insurance sector and a proliferation of joint-stock companies.

These were milestones along a road that was not only about institutions and money. Fear of popery and arbitrary government, which had fuelled the troubles, was now directed outwards, against France, to drive construction of the fiscal-military state. One result was growth, not only of public investment, but public trust. Parliamentary monarchy, with security for Protestantism and parliaments, religious toleration, open debate through the press (the Licensing

Act lapsed permanently in 1695) and at the hustings (triennial elections from 1694), combined with continuous input into policy by parliamentarians and ministers, all contributed to this. So earlier the success of the Dutch republic had been built upon 'certain cultural preconditions' including 'a strong information network, widely shared commercial habits . . . cooperation on all fronts relating to social interaction, and confidence in the institutions' of commerce and government.[36]

These developments were part of a broader cultural process, initiated by the revolution of 1649–53 despite its military origins, whereby by speaking for the political nation at large the state came to be capable of drawing fully upon its resources, moral and material. One historian has discerned the presence between 1689 and 1815 of 'a mainstream of widely diffused approval across social ranks for the state's foreign and commercial strategy', which had 'not existed under the Tudor and Stuart regimes'.[37] In the words of the third Earl of Shaftesbury, reminiscent of Milton's earlier praise of republican manners:

A PUBLICK Spirit can come only from a . . . *Sense of Partnership* . . . Now there are none so far from being *Partners* . . . as they who scarcely know *an Equal*, nor consider themselves as subject to any Law of *Fellowship* or *Community*. And thus Morality and good Government go together. There is no real Love of Virtue, without Knowledge of *Publick Good*. And where Absolute Power is, there is no PUBLICK.[38]

The associated 'depersonalizing of public credit' made possible by the Bank of England 'began the creation of a properly managed national debt, whose collateral was nothing less than the landed and commercial wealth of the country itself, represented in Parliament'.[39] Concerning this fiscal revolution John Brewer remarked that 'the similarities are so great, the obsession of English ministers with Dutch methods so well known, and the arrival of William III with his Dutch advisors so timely, that it is hard to believe that contemporaries were wrong when they described the new fiscal arrangements as "Dutch finance" '.[40] But the same finance also had English characteristics, some reflecting the political and urban context within which these developments were occurring.

Unlike the Bank of Amsterdam, controlled by the government of that city, the Bank of England 'came to be . . . a *central, national,* and *note-issuing* bank'.[41]

In the United Provinces most government borrowing had been negotiated at local level, guaranteed by the provincial estates. The most important feature of the English financial scene was the importance to national public lending, as well as to investment in trade and manufactures, of the joint-stock companies which proliferated from the mid-1680s. These included the venture which established the Bank of England, lending 1.2 million pounds to the government at 8 per cent interest.[42] Such returns resulted in large-scale Dutch investment 'attracted to British securities by the high return on English bonds and by the convergence of Dutch and English public debt institutions'.[43] Daniel Defoe commented: 'Necessity, which is allow'd to be the Mother of Invention, has so violently agitated the Wits of men at this time . . . [as] to call it, *The Projecting Age*'.[44] Even the 'Royal Academy of Musick' founded in 1719 was, in 'a neat demonstration of the mixed nature of London's cultural scene . . . organised as a joint-stock company, with leading members drawn from the peerage . . . and the gentry, and was meant to be run at a profit for its shareholders'.[45]

Annual parliaments from 1689 affected the entire economy because of the volume of economic legislation into and throughout the eighteenth century. One foreign visitor commented in 1700: 'One can infer that it is the frequent Parliaments which England has enjoyed during this reign that has given rise to an infinity of Acts made for the public good.'[46] By contrast the Dutch republic was a decentralized federation with each of its seven provinces protecting its sovereignty. Moreover, Temple explained,

> each of these Provinces is likewise composed of so many little States or Cities, which have several marks of Soveraign Power within themselves, and are not subject to the Soveraignty of their Province; Not being concluded in many things by the majority, but only by the universal concurrence of Voices in the Provincial-States. For as the States-General cannot make War or Peace, or any new Alliance, or Levies of Money, without the consent of every Province; so cannot the States-Provincial conclude any of those points without the consent of each of the Cities, that by their Constitution has a voice in that Assembly.[47]

In exchange for his well-judged political concessions, in England William III could deal with a single source of military funding capable of voting taxes and agreeing that government loans would be guaranteed against tax yields.[48] No less important were the resources of a single city which by 1700 dwarfed all others:

> The entire economy of England was ruled from London. Political centralization, the power of the English Crown, the highly concentrated nature of trade, all combined to make the capital great. But this greatness itself imposed an order on the area it dominated and throughout which it set up a wealth of administrative and trading connections . . . London was a good hundred years ahead of Paris in the organisation of her supplies. Moreover London was also a very active port (handling at least four-fifths of England's foreign trade) as well as . . . the centre of luxury and . . . of culture.[49]

The Anglo-Dutch revolution was enabled by London as a corporate political entity, as a partner in war and government, and as a transnational economic, social and cultural world. By the early eighteenth century it contained not only dozens of Dutch and French churches but three German ones, one Greek, and several synagogues.[50] After the Act of Union in 1707 it received increasing numbers of 'domestic foreigners' from Scotland and Ireland. All these immigrants, 'religious refugees, adventurers, uprooted victims of war, artisans in search of new markets', found their place in a metropolis which had been transformed over the previous century and a half by constant migration from within England as well as beyond it. Even before it began to follow in Amsterdam's footsteps as a 'foreigners' mecca', London was a migrational construct on an unprecedented scale.[51]

The same developments 'helped to prise open London's commercial culture' in a way which made it more attractive to many Dutch and Huguenot investors than its more tightly controlled Dutch urban competitors:

> For more than half a century after 1689, a large cluster of Dutch and Huguenot firms played a disproportionately large role in London's financial and commercial life . . . Dutch and Huguenot families frequently intermarried and pursued joint business ventures. Many acted as attorneys for Dutch and other foreign investors in English government stocks, while a small elite stood at the heart of government finance, as bankers and military contractors.[52]

In 1724 it was observed: 'Mr Walpole manages all. He has raised his reputation and interest exceedingly by his dealings with the Dutch . . . [who] are willing to trust their money in his hands at three per cent . . . and consequently . . . is become absolutely necessary to the King.'[53] Tapping such resources the national debt increased from 16.7 million pounds sterling in 1697 to 744.9 million in 1815.[54] 'In 1744, at the time of the city's declaration of loyalty to George II, 542 merchants added their signatures . . . [of whom] at least one-third . . . . . . were of non-British descent. The Dutch numbered 37, another 40 were Jewish, almost all Sephardim, while over 100 were Huguenot.'[55] The cosmopolitanism of London attracted not only compliments but criticism. According to the author of *The Rights and Liberties of Englishmen*, immigrants were 'scum', 'caterpillars' and 'vermin' who should be sent on their way before there was 'little or no English blood left amongst us'.[56] Anti-Dutch sentiment accusing that state of 'seizing control of English affairs and raiding English resources for their own ends' was a staple of Jacobite rhetoric.[57] In 1745 the Anti-Gallican Association was founded 'to oppose the insidious arts of the French nation . . . [and] discourage the introduction of French modes . . . and the importation of French commodities':[58]

> In Days of Old, when Englishmen were – Men
> Their Musick, like themselves, was grave and plain . . .
> Since Masquerades and Operas made their Entry,
> And Heydegger and Handell ruled our Gentry;
> A hundred different Instruments combine,
> And foreign Songsters in the Concerts join . . .
> All league, melodious Nonsense to dispense,
> And give us Sound, and Show, instead of Sense.[59]

While the United Provinces was a republic Britain remained a monarchy. Yet this was no longer a government of men but of laws. Institutional structures regulated the economy, the state and their relationship. This was the only monarchy in Europe with a legislatively governed national bank. Dynastic continuity had been subordinated to confessional and military security. Montesquieu called Britain a republic disguised as a monarchy. The republican component had arrived in 1649; between 1660 and 1702 the monarchical disguise was applied and then refined. In Spain and France dynastic prevailed over commercial thinking and decision-making. 'In contrast, both in bourgeois republics like Venice and the Dutch republic and in the British constitutional monarchy, bureaucrats and capitalists engaged on a much more equal footing.'[60]

Andrew Fletcher considered the Glorious Revolution to have brought to bear an Anglo-Dutch blueprint in not only state but empire formation. According to Fletcher, under Philip II an obstinate determination to retain the Spanish Netherlands had been accompanied by the depopulation and enervation of both Iberia and the Americas. Philip did not

> introduce among the people of Spain . . . any sort of industry, whether in agriculture, in manufactures, in commerce or in navigation . . . Instead the little ships of the English traversed his seas with impunity; [and] attacked his greatest carracks, which his subjects did not know how to sail . . . That King and his Spaniards lived entirely on the mines of the Indies; the gold and silver of which, passing out of their hands, served only to enrich their enemies, the English, the French and the Dutch, who provided the Spanish with their manufactures, and other necessities of life.[61]

The present solution to the Spanish Empire's problems was twofold. First it required territorial rationalization in the form of abandonment of what remained of the Spanish Netherlands and consolidation of control of the strategic corridor between the Mediterranean Straits and the Americas. One contribution to this might be the ceding of Flanders to England in exchange for Jamaica. The Low Countries were still the outworks defending English religion and liberties. In the view of Fletcher geographical proximity, economic and military ties, and a foothold on both sides of the Channel still counted for much more than Caribbean sugar.

The other necessity for Spanish recovery was an 'increase of population [which] will in turn lead to an increase in agriculture, the mechanical arts, commerce and navigation'. This Fletcher described as 'imitating the orders of the English, the Dutch and [until recently] the French'.[62] Following the Glorious Revolution, England had at last taken the correct Dutch path, while in 1685 the French had followed Spain, making 'this fatal error of government, of tormenting and persecuting peoples on account of their religion, and not wishing to have subjects who differ in their opinions on the highest and most difficult mysteries'.[63] In the later words of Fletcher's countryman William Robertson:

> It was towards the close of the seventeenth century, before toleration, under its present form, was admitted first into the republic of the United Provinces, and from thence introduced into England. Long experience of the calamities flowing from mutual persecution, the influence of free government, the light and humanity acquired from the progress of science, together with the prudence and authority of the civil magistrate, were all requisite in order to establish . . . [this] regulation.[64]

After 1689 London was a regional and imperial hub, its stock market attracting international investment, its trade networks spanning the world. No such metropolitan prodigy would have been possible without Dutch-sponsored religious toleration. Only under that protection could Voltaire have joked in his *Letters concerning the English nation* about a London stock exchange where 'people of all nations and religions happily do business together and only those who go bankrupt are regarded as infidels'.[65]

PART III

✳

ARCHIPELAGIC STATE FORMATION

Public liberty, with internal peace and order has flourished almost without interruption: Trade and manufactures, and agriculture, have increased: The arts, and sciences, and philosophy, have been cultivated . . . and the glory of the nation has spread itself all over Europe . . . Nor is there another instance in the whole history of mankind, that so many millions of people have, during such a space of time, been held together, in a manner so free, so rational, and so suitable to the dignity of human nature.

David Hume, *Essays and Treatises on Several Subjects* (1772)

Legend:

(1606) Date of settlement

Dutch settlement

English settlement

French settlement

Spanish settlemen

CREEK Native peoples

Lake Superior

Lake Huron

Lake Michigan

Lake Ontario

Lake Erie

Gulf of St Lawrence

St Lawrence

Quebec *(1608)*

PENOBSCOT

Port Royal *(1606)*

ABENAKI

KENNEBEC

Fundy Bay

Montreal

NEW FRANCE

MOWHAWK

NEW HAMPSHIRE

MASSACHUSETTS BAY *(1629–30)*

HURON

ONEIDA

NARRAGANSETT

OTTAWA

ONONDAGA

CAYUGA

SENECA

IROQUOIS

TUSCARORA

DELAWARE

WESTERN DELAWARE

SHAWNEE

Boston

PEQUOT

Providence

Hartford

PLYMOUTH *(1620)*

RHODE ISLAND *(1636–43)*

NEW NETHERLAND *(1624)*

CONNECTICUT *(1636–9)*

New Amsterdam

PENNSYLVANIA *(1681)*

Wilmington

Philadelphia

NEW SWEDEN *(1638)*

Baltimore

MARYLAND *(1634)*

THE CHESAPEAKE

Henrico

VIRGINIA *(1606–7)*

Williamsburg

Jamestown

Ohio

UPPER CHEROKEE

CATAWBA

Raleigh expedition to Roanoke Island *(1585)*

YAMASEE

MIDDLE CHEROKEE

CAROLINA *(1663)*

UPPER NATCHEZ

LOWER CHEROKEE

Charles Town (Charleston)

GEORGIA *(1732)*

Savannah

CREEK

Atlantic Ocean

Gulf of Mexico

0   300 miles

0   500 km

Bahamas

7. European settlement in North America.

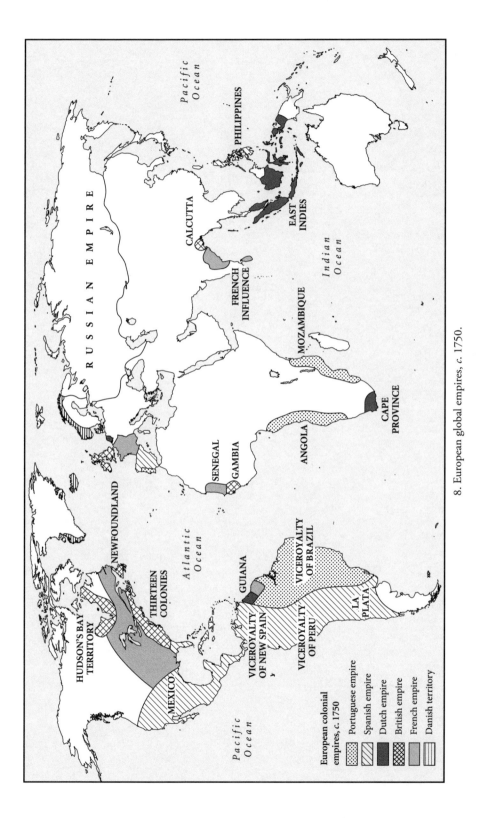

8. European global empires, *c.* 1750.

European colonial
empires, *c.* 1750

- Portuguese empire
- Spanish empire
- Dutch empire
- British empire
- French empire
- Danish territory

RUSSIAN EMPIRE

*Pacific
Ocean*

PHILIPPINES

CALCUTTA

EAST
INDIES

FRENCH
INFLUENCE

*Indian
Ocean*

MOZAMBIQUE

SENEGAL
GAMBIA

ANGOLA

CAPE
PROVINCE

NEWFOUNDLAND

HUDSON'S BAY
TERRITORY

THIRTEEN
COLONIES

*Atlantic
Ocean*

GUIANA

VICEROYALTY
OF NEW SPAIN

VICEROYALTY
OF BRAZIL

MEXICO

VICEROYALTY
OF PERU

LA
PLATA

*Pacific
Ocean*

CHAPTER TWELVE

A MARITIME MONARCHY

I shall close these Essays with a Scheme and Modell of a Maritime Monarchy. Wherein I shall shew how . . . this Nation has by nature all the materials necessary to lay the Foundation of such a Power by Sea, as to entitle us not only to a Dominion of the Narrow Seas, but to the wide Ocean. That having nature so much in our favour, nothing but want of Genius, Art and Application can be thought to frustrate so vast a Designe.

Sir Henry Sheres, 'Navall Essays' (1691)[1]

A SOCIAL, ECONOMIC AND CULTURAL REVOLUTION

As a social and political system monarchy was terrestrial and aristocratic, a fact reflected in the command of its armies. But the government of ships required a highly specialized form of expertise, distinct from, whether or not antithetical to, the breeding of a gentleman. There was no connection between the ability to ride horses and the skills required to 'ride the great Wooden Horses of the Navy'. 'There is no comparison betwixt ye sea service + ye land service. It . . . is absurd to think that a gentleman . . . (who in foule weather is sicke, or if not sicke, cannot stand . . .) should be an Able Seaman or commander.'[2] This partly explains why most early modern commentators associated maritime culture – naval power and trade – primarily with cities and republics.

The potentially fraught relationship on board ship between gentlemen and mariners became an issue as soon as Elizabeth's war with Spain introduced large-scale privateering. It underpinned the risky execution by Francis Drake of gentleman volunteer Thomas Doughty in Patagonia in 1578. 'Gentlemen are verye necesarye for governments sake in the voyadge . . . but I must have the gentleman to hayle and draw with the mariner, and the mariner with the gentleman.'[3] By the 1620s, with the navy crippled in wartime by incompetence and corruption, aristocratic command had become a burning issue. The culture of aristocracy and monarchy was about idleness and display. But facing 'ye ruine of ye Navigation of this kingdome; + the discipline + honor thereof wch is almost lost', most mariners were 'borne of poore or meane parentage':

> None but hard Bodies + bould spirits will endure it . . . being enured to eminent daungers, + escaping many tymes the peril of ye sea (beyond hope) . . . after they betake themselves to the sea [the mariner] Is hardy, daungerous and painefull, They must undergoe hunger, thirste, heate, could, wett, watching . . . It is the stormes + Tempest that doth discover ye able seaman from ye Idler and ignorant.[4]

In 1649 the tension between maritime and monarchical culture was eliminated. Under the leadership of a republican-mercantile alliance both the policies and the material resources of the state were reoriented around maritime power. Building upon the Self-Denying Ordinance the same naval revolution was driven by an anti-aristocratic social reformation of military command. In 1653–4 the military results echoed around the world. But to these developments subsequent events would put a broader question. Whether or not liberty and industry were inherently maritime qualities, were they compatible with aristocracy? If not, could a mid-century revolution in government and culture, which was helping to create the conditions which would make the Industrial Revolution possible, survive the Restoration?

To rephrase the question, was it possible to make a maritime monarchy? Across a wide field of policy and practice Charles II gave every indication that this was his ambition. Although he found it expedient to readmit gentleman officers they did not dominate at the expense of utility to the extent that had been the case.[5] This was a major issue throughout the career of Samuel Pepys, whose sympathies lay on the tarpaulin side. Accordingly the debate about tarpaulin versus gentleman commanders was still being vigorously conducted during the early 1690s.[6] Under its terms the government of a ship was a model for government in general. 'As every Sea Comander being Head of that little Comon Wealth should be a Man of example in all the nice Points of discipline, so every ship should be a Seminary ... of Virtue and Instruction ... 'Twas not among the [Romans] a Point of debate between Patrician and Plebean in actions of Glory ... virtue was considered for her own single sake.'[7] So what of this state, which was not, like Rome or the United Provinces, a republic? Could an agrarian monarchy be governed in a way which was compatible with industry, liberty and trade?

This was the crowning achievement of the Anglo-Dutch Revolution. Early modern Europe was governed by territorial monarchies and small, sometimes maritime, republics and/or cities. The former were culturally and socially aristocratic and the latter mercantile. But in the later seventeenth century a new European great power emerged that was a territorial monarchy within which a landed aristocracy, enriched by the economic changes of the period, beginning with those revolutionizing agricultural productivity, became fully participant in its new commercial economy. The way in which Britain's ruling class in both Houses of Parliament intertwined hereditary nobility and a mercantile, manufacturing and financial oligarchy had no European parallel.[8] The strict separation of the world of work from socially mandated aristocratic idleness which applied elsewhere had disappeared (though not the distinction between money and land, with its status implications). In the view of one scholar:

England in 1600 already had an elite which was both fully engaged in improvement of land and far from hostile to the progress of industry and commerce ... In England more than any other country, the interests of land and trade, though never identical, were acknowledged to be closely allied.[9]

This difference from other European monarchies, and France in particular, became a cultural point of pride. Thayer Mahan noted the ineffectiveness of Louis XIV's ordinance, issued under Colbert, 'authorising all noblemen to take an interest in merchant ships, goods and merchandise, without being considered as having derogated from nobility' in the face of the 'public opinion, universally prevalent, that maritime commerce is incompatible with nobility'. By contrast in England, as in Holland, 'Wealth, as a source of civic distinction, carried with it also power in the State ... The nobility were proud; but in a representative government the power of wealth could be neither put down nor overshadowed ... in England, as well as in Holland, the occupations which were the source of wealth shared in the honor given to wealth itself.'[10] In the words of a Richard Steele character (Mr Sealand): 'I know the Town and the World – and give me leave to say, that we Merchants are a species of Gentry, that have grown into the World this last Century, and are as honourable, and almost as useful, as you landed Folks, that have always thought yourself so much above us.'[11] 'Nor,' wrote Thomas Sprat,

> ought our *Gentry* to be avers from the promoting of *Trade*, out of any little jealousy, that thereby they shall debase themselves, and corrupt their Blood. For . . . *Trafic*, and *Commerce* have given mankind a higher degree than any title of *Nobility*, even that of *Civility*, and *Humanity* . . . In former ages . . . The Seats of *Empire*, and *Trade* were seldom . . . the same . . . but now so many *Nations* being Civiliz'd, and living splendidly, there is a far greater consumption of all *forein Commodities*; and so the gain of *Trade* is become great enough to overbalance all other strength.[12]

During the eighteenth century, wrote Charles Tilly, the increasing scale of war 'eventually gave the war-making advantage to those states that could field great standing armies; states having access to a combination of large rural populations, capitalists and relatively commercialised economies won out.'[13] France had the rural population and the United Provinces the commercial economy, but no state combined the two in the same way, or to the same degree, as Britain. Anchoring this brilliant hybrid, in Europe's largest city, was a Dutch stadtholder-king co-opted by a Protestant political and an Anglo-Dutch mercantile elite. The result was a monarchy both parliamentary and maritime, which was to say (to adapt Hume) doubly free.

Between 1660 and 1760 a series of published works supplied this political and cultural development with a geography and history. Sprat remarked upon 'this advantage of our island . . . lying . . . as it does, in the passage between the *Northern* parts of the World, and the *Southern*; its *Ports* being open to all Coasts, and its *Ships* spreading their Sails in all Seas; it is thereby necessarily made, not only *Mistress* of the *Ocean*, but the most proper *Seat*, for the advancement of *Knowledg*.'[14] After the third Anglo-Dutch war John Evelyn similarly argued that Britain was so situated between the Baltic, North Sea, Mediterranean and Atlantic:

That if the *Hollanders* themselves (who . . . are best skill'd in making Canales and Trenches, and to derive Waters) had joyn'd in Consultation, how the scatter'd parts of the Earth might be rendred most Accessible, and easie for Commerce; They could not have contriv'd, where to have made the In-let with so much advantage, as GOD and Nature have done it for Us, Since by means of this Sea, we have admission to no less than Three Parts of the habitable World.[15]

Evelyn's historical model for Charles II was Roman. After describing the struggle between Rome and Carthage from Polybius, Evelyn turned to Suetonius to sketch an Augustan golden age of maritime power. Rome, learning the lesson that they 'Onely might be said to speed Conquerors of the World, when they had Conquer'd the Sea, and subdu'd the Waters', it was under Augustus that 'the World by Sea . . . [was] first subdu'd to the Empire of a single Person'.[16] Augustus had one fleet

at *Ravenna*, as a constant Guard of the *Adriatic*; and another riding at *Misenum*, to scowr the *Tyrrhen*-Sea . . . The *Misenian*-Fleet lay conveniently for *France, Spain, Morocco, Africk, Aegypt, Sardinia,* and *Sicily*; That at *Ravenna*, for *Epirus, Macedon, Achaia, Propontis, Pontus*; The *Levantine* parts, *Creete, Rhodes*, and *Cyprus*, &c.

Thus this monarchy was maritime and imperial. '*Marine* Laws and Customes they also had', and foreign vessels were required 'to strike Sail to the Ports of the Empire . . . So early was the claim to the Flag, and the ceremonies of Naval-Honour stated.'[17]

During Charles II's reign references to the Punic Wars, and to Holland as Carthage to England's Rome, became common.[18] But after the Glorious Revolution, Daniel Defoe felt able to set aside the Augustan model, decrying 'the cruel Romans' as having 'but little Genius to Trade, and but few merchants among them'. In Defoe's geopolitical framework Rome was France. By contrast the model for 'a trading, improving Nation' like Britain was Carthage itself. Defoe's Carthaginians were the inventors of commerce and the original settlers of America. That at the height of its power the empire of Carthage had included North and West Africa, Sicily, Sardinia, Spain and the Americas was clear from the 'Similitude of Manners and Customs, between the *Carthaginians* and the *Americans*'.[19] Hanno 'I take to be the Carthaginian Sir *Walter* Raleigh, as afterwards Sir *Walter* Raleigh was called the *English* Hanno.'

THE COMMERCIAL REVOLUTION

A history of navigation published in 1732 looked back on the transformation of early modern Europe's global trade. The 'improvement of navigation on this side the world since the discovery of the magnetical needle . . . having made known to us as much of the coasts of *Africk* and *Asia*, as . . . amounts to about five thousand leagues . . . The benefit we reap is so visible':

> For now all *Europe* abounds in all such things as those vast, wealthy, exuberant eastern regions can afford; whereas before those discoveries it had nothing but what it received by retail, and at excessive rates from the *Venetians* . . . But now the sea is open, every nation has the liberty of supplying itself from the fountain-head . . . and . . . these parts . . . supply the Christian world with all gums, drugs, spices, silks and cottons, precious stones, sulphur, gold, salt-peter, rice, tea, *China*-ware, coffee, *Japan* varnished works, all sorts of dies, of cordials, and perfumes, pearls, ivory, ostrich-feathers, parrots, monkeys, and an endless number of necessaries, conveniences, curiosities, and other comforts and supports of human life.[20]

It was during the reign of Charles II that the gap began to close between the comparative value of imports of the English and Dutch East India Companies. Although the EIC imported some pepper, it faced a Dutch monopoly on the supply of cloves, nutmeg and mace. Forced to diversify it had, from the 1620s, been importing Indian cotton calicoes. Enhanced by the acquisition of Bombay in 1661 these imports boomed, totalling 200,000 pieces a year during the late 1660s, 578,000 a year during the 1670s, and 707,000 during the 1680s.[21] It was partly because of the resulting customs revenue that Charles was able to do without parliaments between 1681 and 1685. This trade first established cotton clothing as a fashionable alternative for all classes to wool and linen. From 'the greatest Gallants to the meanest Cook-Maids' all now supposed that 'nothing was . . . so fit to adorn their persons as the Fabricks of India'.[22] It also accessed technology for the mass manufacture of cotton textiles which would be improved during the eighteenth century, to become the leading sector of the Industrial Revolution. Meanwhile there was an export trade in English woollen broadcloth to the Levant, in exchange for silk, until 1725 when it was eroded by French competition.[23]

From the 1690s came an import boom in coffee and tea. In 1724 the English East India Company imported 1,213,000 kilograms of coffee, 21 per cent of the value of EIC imports, from Mocha as later from Java and then the West Indies.[24] This was the golden age of the London coffee shop, selling an array of drinks hot and cold, alcoholic and otherwise, liberally infused with sugar and spices. From the 1720s the total value of EIC imports exceeded those of the VOC. Helping to drive the figures was the British love affair with tea. In 1690 the EIC imported 38,000 pounds of tea from Canton. By the 1710s the quantity was 401,000 kilograms a year, and during the 1750s a staggering 1,688,000 kilograms per year. Yet the trade did not really hit its stride until the Commutation Act of 1784, which reduced the import duty on tea from 119 to 12.5 per cent. Between 1784–6 and 1814–16 the average annual value of imports from Asia rose from 4.9 million to 11.8 million pounds.[25] By this time the American Revolution had been provoked in part by a tax on tea. This was also a period of deepening British military intervention in India, which eventually became the major supplier of this combustible leaf.[26]

From the West, the Chesapeake, came tobacco; from the Caribbean, sugar, and from New England, fish and furs. As we saw in Chapter 9 many of these commodities yielded re-exports to Europe. As in the Netherlands, this surge in imports was feeding a growth in manufactures. Although the Nine Years War (1688–97) depressed trade and led to major losses of shipping, the military needs of the state stimulated shipbuilding, metalworking, textile manufacture and other industries. Extended and regular sittings of parliament facilitated economic lobbying and legislation became increasingly commercially informed. Duties on exports were lowered, and during the wars high tarriffs against imports, in particular but not only from France, provided protection behind which domestic manufactures including cotton and silk weaving, paper-making and alcohol distilling flourished. Meanwhile, as also in the Netherlands, this boom in commerce and manufacturing was being driven by a developing domestic culture of consumption. An array of foodstuffs, types of clothing, household furnishings, ceramics and glassware, books, watches and pipes found their way into the hands of an urbanizing population ready to work longer hours to buy them.

In the same period (1690–1710) appeared inventions facilitating the more efficient mining of coal and tin, and smelting of iron ore (including Newcomen's steam pump). In the period 1663–9 England's gross commodity trade had been worth 7.9 million pounds a year; in the years 1722–4 the figure was 14.5 million.[27] Between 1689 and 1750, supported by a parliamentary bounty, the farms of East Anglia and the Midlands exported grain (wheat and barley), which undercut the Dutch trade from the Baltic to the Mediterranean.[28] In the same period, as in the Dutch staple system, particular towns became manufacturing centres, Birmingham of guns and swords, Sheffield of cutlery, Nottingham of stocking-frame knitting, and, reported Defoe in the 1720s, government policy succeeding where Anthony Jenkinson's camels had failed, the West Riding of Yorkshire 'prodigiously encouraged and increased by the great demand of their kerseys for clothing the armies abroad'.[29] As Delftware had emerged in response to the market for imported Chinese porcelain, so in Staffordshire potteries proliferated until in 1766 Josiah Wedgwood could report that in one town, Burslem, 'there are 500 separate potteries for stoneware and earthenware. They provide employment for 7,000 and export to Liverpool, Bristol, Hull and from there to America and the West Indian colonies and every port in Europe.'[30]

Driving domestic consumption, and supported by increased agricultural productivity, the eighteenth-century British population doubled. Urbanization was spread coastally by the maritime commercial economy and then inland by the industrializing North Midlands and North (Derbyshire, Yorkshire and Lancashire). Parliamentary leadership and public and private investment constructed a national turnpike road system. 'Fifty-two percent of the total mileage constructed between 1696 and 1836 was authorised between 1750 and 1770.'[31] 'Britain's infrastructure – its roads, rivers, canals, bridges and ports – was radically overhauled by the use of locally initiated acts of parliament.' After turnpike mania came 'the canal age'.[32] Again modifying Dutch example, the island of Britain created a multifaceted system of transport and communications connecting itself internally, and to the world. Within this circulated the advertising and news which stimulated a society of consumers:[33]

Cities, particularly capital cities . . . played a crucial role in the . . . changes affecting consumption in the early modern period . . . Material wealth, power, and knowledge were concentrated [there] . . . Cities were communication and transport hubs. They served as centres of material and intellectual exchange . . . they were open to innovation.[34]

But as in the Netherlands the countryside too participated in the same culture. In late seventeenth- and early eighteenth-century Cornwall and Kent yeoman farmers, themselves producing for the market, were purchasing clocks, books, plates, padded furniture, tea and coffee sets and mirrors.[35]

LONDON AS A WORLD CITY

Until the mid-eighteenth century these developments were led, though not solely enabled, by London. Conducting his *Tour Thro' The Whole Island of Great Britain*, Defoe commented upon the incredible market magnetism of the metropolis. Grain was barged, fish ferried, cheese shipped, bullocks driven, coal sailed, iron moved, logs floated and geese driven towards its all-embracing maw. All were available in 'amazing Plenty and Cheapness' from the markets at Billingsgate, Smithfield, Covent Garden and the Corn Exchange.[36] Around the outskirts 'above a Thousand new Foundations have been erected, besides old Houses repaired, all since the Revolution'.[37] Discussing the Thames ('The whole River . . . from *London*-Bridge to *Black Wall* is one great Arsenal, nothing in the World can be like it'), Defoe considered, before dismissing, the suggestion 'that there are more Ships . . . seen at *Amsterdam*'.[38]

'Pre-eminent among European ports, Hanoverian London was, first of all, a shipping center.'[39] In 1667 John Dryden (who called London 'Empress of the Northern Clime') had written: 'Instructed ships shall sail to quick Commerce/ By which remotest Regions are alli'd/ Which makes one City of the Universe/Where some may gain, and all may be suppli'd.'[40] If the universe could be imagined as one city that was in part because between 1660 and 1760 one city was becoming 'the center of world commerce' within which could be found 'countrymen and foreigners consulting together upon the private business of mankind, and making this metropolis a kind of emporium for the whole earth'.[41] Defoe concluded:

In a Word, nothing can be more Beautiful; here is . . . a rich fertile Soil, cultivated and enclosed to the utmost perfection of Husbandry, then bespangled with Villages . . . and . . . Houses surrounded with Gardens, Walks, Vistas, Avenues . . . the Country adjoining fill'd with the Palaces of the *British* Nobility and Gentry . . . looking North, behold . . . the whole City of *London* it self; the most glorious Sight without exception, that the whole World at present can show, or perhaps ever cou'd show since the Sacking of *Rome* in the *European*, and the burning the Temple of *Jerusalem* in the *Asian* part of the World.[42]

By 1700 London stood at the apex of an Atlantic European economy, a Protestant Enlightenment culture, and a global trading empire. It had presided over the breaking and remaking of the fiscal-military state. Alongside its port and ships it offered networks of information, exchange and expertise. The institutional development of the city catered to the increasing accumulation of international capital so that if by 1730 Dutch commercial supremacy had been superseded by that of Great Britain, this was partly financed by Dutch and Huguenot immigrants and investors.[43] In 1689 there were fifteen joint-stock companies, including the East Indies Company, Eastland, Muscovy, Royal African and Hudson Bay Companies, with a total value of 0.9 million pounds. By 1695 there were 150, with a value of 4.3 million pounds.[44] '[A] great many *Stocks* have arisen since this War with *France*; for Trade being obstructed at sea, few that had Money were willing it should lie idel, and a great many that wanted Employments studied how to dispose of their Money, that they might be able to command it whensoever they had occasion.'[45] Thereafter came insurance companies, particularly marine insurance, and ancillary professions such as stockbrokers and stockjobbers. The Sun Fire Office, Royal Exchange Assurance and Phoenix Assurance were founded in 1708, 1719 and 1782 respectively.[46]

This fiscal infrastructure grew in a symbiotic relationship with the power of the state. Britain's expanding commercial economy fed a burgeoning state revenue from customs and excise which spawned a vast bureaucracy, colonial and metropolitan. Manufacturing and mercantile capital supplied the loans to the Bank of England and other joint-stock companies which allowed the government to engage in military spending out of all proportion to its revenue. That spending performed an essential economic function, as it had earlier for the Dutch state.[47] After 1689 came 'an amplified and permanent Board of Trade, the most comprehensive Navigation Act to date, and a new system of vice-admiralty courts':[48]

> Naval protection was an essential backup for the pursuit of mercantilist objectives. During the eighteenth century the Royal Navy became more efficient than the rival French Navy and was the beneficiary of generous government funding . . . The Navy fought pirates, privateers and *guarda costas* . . . Naval dockyards were augmented in the eighteenth century to provide a regular flow of new and repaired vessels. Chatham, Portsmouth and Plymouth thus became important centres for the British merchant marine and among the largest industrial sites of employment in Hanoverian Britain.[49]

This was the apotheosis of the private–public partnership which had underlain English maritime and imperial endeavour since Tudor privateering. Then it had proved an inadequate rival to Dutch public investment. What had changed was not only the extent and profitability of English trade, but the nature of the relationship in question. From 1649 an alliance between the Crown and chartered monopoly companies gave way to a more direct, diverse and potent partnership between parliamentarians and merchants pursuing imperial and commercial policies of mutual benefit under the military protection of the state. As mechanisms of public credit developed, private lending and so public military spending became simultaneously prolific.

In the process London became, arguably, the first world city.[50] Other cities performed unique global roles: Rome in relation to the aspirations of Roman Catholic Christianity; Amsterdam as a community of immigrants and entrepot for trade; Peking as a magnet for silver bullion; and Mexico City as a unique point of geographical connection between the Atlantic and Pacific. But if none of these were global cities of the kind that by the eighteenth century London had become, this was partly because they remained subordinate to a larger Church or state. Only London created, or fundamentally altered, a state and empire to serve its own interests, and then wielded the power of that state to advance them. In 1667 Sprat argued that Babylon, Memphis, Athens, Carthage, Rome, Constantinople, Vienna, Amsterdam and Paris all had their particular strengths:

But it is *London* alone, that enjoys most of the others advantages, without their inconveniences. It is the head of a *mighty Empire*, the greatest that ever commanded the *Ocean*: It is compos'd of *Gentlemen*, as well as *Traders*: It has a large intercourse with all the *Earth*: It is . . . a City, where all the noises and business in the World do meet: and therefore this honour is justly due to it, to be the *constant* place of *residence* for that *Knowledg*, which is to be made up of the Reports, and Intelligence of all Countreys.[51]

Later extending such universalizing claims, James Boswell:

often amused myself with thinking how different a place London is to different people . . . A politician thinks of it merely as the seat of govern- ment in its different departments; a grazier, as a vast market for cattle; a mercantile man, as a place where a prodigious deal of business is done upon 'Change; a dramatic enthusiast, as the grand scene of theatrical entertain- ments; a man of pleasure, as an assemblage of taverns; but the intellectual man is struck with it, as comprehending the whole of human life in all its variety, the contemplation of which is inexhaustible.[52]

In 1687 William Petty subjected the metropolis to demographic and historical comparison. He observed that before 1660 'the People of *Paris* were more than those of *London* and *Dublin* put together, whereas now, the People of *London* are more than those of *Paris* and *Rome*, or *Paris* and *Rouen*'.[53] London was superior, he argued, not only demographically but physically, so 'the People do not live at *London* so close and crouded . . . but can afford themselves more room and liberty', despite the fact that Paris was 'the Seat of the great *French Monarchy*', which had a revenue four times that of England, and Rome was 'the Seat . . . of the Papacy'.[54]

Petty asked if, in addition to being the leading city in Europe, London might be the largest in the world. There was no evidence to support a belief in the greater size of '*Pequin* in *China* . . . *Dely* and *Agra* belonging to the *Mogull* . . . *Constantinople* or *Gran Cairo*'.[55] Beyond being 'the . . . most considerable City of the World', London was 'manifestly the greatest Emporium'. Indeed reviewing 'the 4 great Emporiums, London, Amsterdam, Venice and Rouen', London was almost twice the size of the other three combined; four times the size of Amsterdam, and in the quantity of its houses and people two-thirds the size of the 'whole Province of Holland'.[56] Yet perhaps this dominance was not unprecedented. 'At the birth of *Christ* old *Rome* was the greatest City of the World, and London the greatest at the Coronation of King *James* the Second, and near 6 times as great as the present *Rome*.'[57] But Petty believed the population of 'Old *Rome* . . . to have been half as big again as the present London'.[58] If the historical framework was imperial then London's growth could be expected to continue, as of course it did.

As the world came to London so Londoners increasingly inhabited the world. By 1720 newspapers which had a century earlier catered for an insatiable appetite for European news were now reporting politics, scandal, satire, cultural reviews, shipping news (cargos arriving and for sale, or departing, with room still available), news from the Plantations and the rest of the habitable world, and new global geographic and navigational discoveries.[59] Feeding into the same arena of coffee-house conversation and both public and specialist knowledge was an avalanche of printed pamphlets, compilations, monographs and fictions, including globetrotting bestsellers such as Defoe's *Robinson Crusoe* and Swift's *Gulliver's Travels*.

In 1694 two 'Printers to the *Royal Society*' published *Several Late Voyages to the South and North*, dedicated to Pepys. Like other such compilations this had an eye to the market for exotic voyage accounts and focused on expeditions which had extended the boundaries of existing geographical knowledge. Its Preface set the four featured expeditions – two each to the north and south – within their historical context, taking its readers around the world, including on the circumnavigations of 'Magalines' and Drake. It exalted '*The Advantages of taking judicious and accurate Journals in Voyages and Itineraries . . . as the Improvements of* Geography, Hydrography, Astronomy, Natural *and* Moral History, Antiquity, Merchandise, Trade, Empire, &c [testify, so] *that few books can compare with them either for Profit or Pleasure*'.[60]

To the south through the Straits of Magellan had been found 'Flying Fishes, Dolphins, Albacores, Bonito's, Sharks, Tropick Birds; *The* Sea Weeds *called* Sargasso *and* Tromba; *the* Aromatick Tree *bearing* Winter's Spicy Bark . . . *Infinite Numbers of* Penguins, Seals, Muscles, Whales, Ostriches'.[61] In the 'Islands *on the* South Sea' there were 'Coco-trees, Plantanes, Bonana's, Pine Apples . . . Monkeys, Goats, Turtle, Almonds *of four sorts*, Sugar Canes, Oysters *on Trees, &c.'* To the north-west the Elizabethan John Davis had encountered fur-bearing animals like beavers:

> *and in the Moss, grew a Shrub whose fruit was very sweet, full of red juice like*
> *Currans, perhaps 'tis the same with the* New-England Cranberry . . . [and]
> *marvellous store of Sea Fowl, and Cod, Woods of Pine-Apple, Spruce, Elder, Ewe*
> *. . . Birch, Geese, Ducks, Black-Birds, Thrush, Jayes, Partridge, Pheasant . . .*
> *Salt, kerned upon the Rocks, white and glistering; Unicorn, and other Whales.*[62]

The empirical veracity of these observations was on a different level from Richard Hakluyt a century earlier. Even 'Oysters *on Trees*' do exist on the leaves of mangroves growing in the South Pacific.[63] This reflected thirty years of assiduous information seeking from remote geographical outposts by the Royal Society (within which oysters are a recurring theme, as they are in Pepys' *Diary*).[64] Concerning current geographical knowledge, the publishers noted:

> *The* Hollanders *have indeed made the greatest Discoveries towards the South*
> Terra Incognita, *which they have not yet divulg'd.* Dirk Rembrantse *about 15 or*
> *16 years ago published, in* Low Dutch, *a short Relation out of the Journal of*
> *Captain* Abel Jansen Tasman *upon his Discoveries of the South* Terra Incognita
> *in the year 1642, to the Southward of* Nova Hollandia, Vandemen's Land, &c.[65]

They described Tasman's voyage as '*more considerable, in that 'tis the* Discovery *of a* New World, *not yet known to the* English' and speculated from what information was available that New Guinea, New Holland, Van Dieman's Land and New Zealand were one '*vast prodigious Island*'. For it was one purpose of this publication to furnish the first account of Tasman's voyage in English.

THE ANGLO-DUTCH GEOGRAPHICAL FRONTIER

This English connection to the Dutch south-western Pacific discussed in Chapter 9 would culminate in the ultimate, multiple circumnavigation. In 1769 a copy of *Several Late Voyages* belonging to Joseph Banks travelled south on board James Cook's *Endeavour*.[66] Britain was now the pre-eminent global maritime power. Its century-long struggle for military supremacy with France

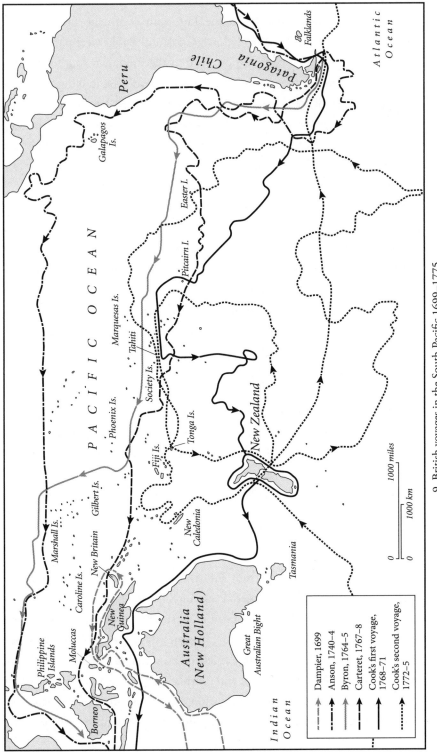

PACIFIC OCEAN

Atlantic Ocean

Indian Ocean

Peru

Chile

Patagonia

Falklands

Galapagos Is.

Easter I.

Pitcairn I.

Marquesas Is.

Tahiti

Society Is.

Phoenix Is.

Fiji Is.

Tonga Is.

New Caledonia

New Zealand

Tasmania

Great Australian Bight

Australia (New Holland)

New Guinea

New Britain

Gilbert Is.

Marshall Is.

Caroline Is.

Moluccas

Borneo

Philippine Islands

Dampier, 1699
Anson, 1740–4
Byron, 1764–5
Carteret, 1767–8
Cook's first voyage, 1768–71
Cook's second voyage, 1772–5

0   1000 miles
0   1000 km

9. British voyages in the South Pacific 1699–1775.

was being conducted primarily on the European continent and in North America (see Chapters 13 and 15 below). Cook and Banks were participating in another Anglo-French competition, to find the unknown southern continent (*Terra Australis Incognita*) for which Tasman had been looking 127 years earlier. In respect of this, anticipation and urgency had been intensified by advances in European navigation. The key to these, especially in the vast Pacific, was the ability to determine longitude (East–West position). This had been the subject of fierce Anglo-French competition since the 1670s (see Chapter 14 below).

In 1766–7 a circumnavigation by Samuel Wallis resulted in the discovery of Tahiti. A few months later Louis De Bougainville arrived, claiming 'New Cytheria' for France. Back in London, Wallis was able to provide the admiralty with Tahiti's precise location, latitude and longitude. Wallis' discovery provided a destination for the Royal Society's expedition the following year to observe the transit of Venus from the Southern Hemisphere. But astronomical observation was not the primary purpose of James Cook's voyage. The Admiralty's choice of Tahiti was informed by Wallis' report of a high land visible to the south.[67] Cook was instructed that

> Wheras there is reason to imagine that a Continent or Land of great extent, may be found to the Southward of the Tract lately made by Captn Wallis . . . You are to proceed to the southward in order to make discovery of the Continent until you arrive in the Latitude of 40 degrees . . . [and then] proceed in search of it to the Westward . . . until you discover it, or fall in with the Eastern side of the Land discover'd by Tasman and now called New Zealand.[68]

Hence the dramatic jag south from Tahiti that caused such consternation to Tupia, the ship's Raiatean passenger, 'a very intelligent person' who knew 'more of the Geography of the Islands situated in these seas . . . then any one we had met' and who implored his European colleagues to go west.[69] A new capacity to determine longitude as accurately as latitude was strikingly illustrated by the vigour of Cook's movements north and south as well as east and west. This was a pivotal moment of navigational invention, being applied in search of a non-existent figment of the European geographical imagination, before relocating the archipelago discovered by Eastern Polynesians (Maori) in about 1380, and Tasman 260 years later.[70]

Rounding New Zealand's South Island to the south-east in early March 1770, Banks recorded the division of the *Endeavour*'s crew into 'Continents' and 'Islanders . . . one who wishd that the land in sight might, the other that it might not be a continent; myself have always been most firm for the former tho sorry I am to say that . . . the rest begin to sigh for roast beef.'[71] Five days later a fresh wind 'carried us round the Point to the total demolition of our aerial fabrick calld continent'.[72] At least Banks was fulfilling a larger ambition: 'every blockhead' did the European tour, but 'my Grand Tour shall be one around the whole globe'.[73] Despite 'Proving New Zealand to be an Island . . . [and] the land seen by Juan Fernandes . . . by the Dutch squadron under Hermite, signs of Continent seen by Quiros, and the same by Roggewein', he continued 'firmly [to] believe' in the existence of a southern continent. This was not to accomplish 'the Balancing of the two poles, which always appeard to me to be a most childish argument'. Indeed, 'if ask'd why I believe so, I confess my reasons are weak'.[74]

Cook made a careful analysis of the geographical knowledge accumulated by his own just completed Pacific crossing added to that of Pedro Fernández de Quirós, Jacob Roggeveen, Abel Tasman and Jacques Le Maire. He concluded that there was now such a reduced space of ocean 'where the grand Object can lay, I think it would be a great pitty that this thing which at times has been the object of many ages and Nations should not now be wholy clear'd up' by one further voyage. Should that reveal that 'after all no Continent was to be found' then its Captain 'might turn his thoughts towards the discovery of those multitude of Islands which we are told lay within the Tropical Regions to the South of the line [equator], and this we have from very good Authority'.[75] In thus beginning to turn his mind from the shrinking continent to an expanding world of islands, Cook's geographical thought was evolving in a Polynesian direction.[76]

On his way home Cook claimed the east coast of Australia for Britain, finding it to be low-lying, though 'indifferently well watered' and 'indifferently fertile'.[77] After being holed on the Great Barrier Reef the *Endeavour* limped home via Batavia, where many of the crew fatally contracted malaria. The possibility of a southern continent lingered until the astonishing Antarctic sailing of Cook's second voyage (1772–5), which also proved the accuracy of John Harrison's chronometer.[78] Now circumnavigating in the opposite direction, Cook's two ships, *Resolution* and *Adventure*, after calling at Cape Town, proceeded south to the edge of the polar ice pack and then east across the Southern Ocean. Anders Sparrman recorded: 'On the 26th [December 1772] . . . one of the icebergs . . . was transformed into the loveliest scene imaginable. The glow of the setting sun fell upon this iceberg, which was as clear as crystal, so that its many thousand crevices and chasms shone like gold, in a clear scintillating yellow, while the rest of the mass reflected a rich purple colour.'[79]

After defrosting in New Zealand the *Resolution* again sailed to the Antarctic, this time in the Pacific, and crossed the entire ocean at extreme southern latitudes. Thereafter Cook repaired to Tahiti, and then discovered many islands to the west, as Tupia had first intended. Only once he had rounded Cape Horn and re-entered the temperate Atlantic could it be certainly said that a great southern continent did not exist.[80] None, at least, other than Australia, upon which, in January 1788, Banks' overly optimistic testimony about Botany Bay (south of modern Sydney) would inform the establishment of a new penal colony.

The first Australian fleet contained eleven small vessels carrying 1,030 people, including 548 male and 188 female convicts. It had been organized by the commissioners of the navy and only 48 people died over its 252 days. The second fleet, which did not arrive until three years later, when the colony was starving, was different. It had been contracted by the government to slavers Camden, Calvert & King, who equipped the three ships with slave shackles: short rigid bolts between the ankles which locked bodies together in pairs and prevented them from moving. Throughout the voyage the 'starving prisoners lay chilled to the bone on soaked bedding, unexercised, crusted with salt, shit and vomit, festering with scurvy and boils'.[81] The contractors were paid a fee per head which was the same whether people arrived alive or dead. Of the 1,006 passengers who embarked, 267 died at sea and another 150 after landing. Upon arriving the contractors opened a market on the shore, selling food that had been withheld from passengers to starving settlers at famine prices.

To change the world in the early modern period it was necessary to take to 'the wide Ocean'. This involved empire, manufactures and trade. It required knowledge of the world (natural philosophy), including of geography and navigation. Most extraordinarily, in this case, it entailed social and political change. This reinforces a general suggestion of this study. This is that to understand something like the Industrial Revolution, which changed everything, we need to examine every aspect of the life of the societies it changed.

CHAPTER THIRTEEN

ARCHIPELAGIC STATE FORMATION, 1578–1783

New England, New York, New Jersey ... Virginia ... What then are these Colonies, tho' Great in themselves, and Powerful and Potent ... compar'd to the vast Continent of *North America*? Whose extent North I have describ'd a little, and whose Western Coast is not yet discover'd? neither do we yet know whether ... it is bounded by the Sea *yea* or *no.*

Daniel Defoe, *A General History of Discoveries and Improvements* (1725–6)[1]

AN ATLANTIC AGE OF REVOLUTION

The first product of Anglo-Dutch-American early modernity, understood as a process of invention, was an agricultural revolution emanating from the world of the 'half-anders ... half wet, half dry'. Crossing to the west coast of the North Sea, this made possible a doubling of the English and Welsh population between 1540 and 1640, and its doubling again between 1700 and 1800. It underpinned the explosive demographic growth of London, and the economic and social diversification of Britain. By 1670 only 60 per cent of the English population was engaged in agriculture; in 1750 that figure was 46 per cent.[2] One result was the major pool of labour available for subsequent exponential industrialization.

Then in England, from 1649, followed a political and military revolution with equally profound economic and cultural consequences. Its course was punctuated by partial and superficial reversals and intertwined with three Anglo-Dutch wars. Yet over the second half of the seventeenth century the creation of a new military-fiscal great power, with parliamentary government, transformed commercial and imperial policies and Dutch-style mechanisms of public credit, was rapid and spectacular. By 1700 the value of England's trade was five times what it had been in 1600.[3]

Without the transformation of agriculture and urban demography there could have been no English commercial revolution. Without the wealth this created there could have been no such debt-funded imperial superpower. Upon protection by the state, in turn, and its willingness to intervene militarily and politically in defence of the economic interests of its subjects, that economy became dependent. The emergence of Britain as a world power was an event in global, not simply Atlantic history. The same was true of the first Industrial Revolution. Yet to explain how the old world ended, our focus here and in remaining chapters is upon economic, political and cultural processes which were trans-Atlantic in scope.[4]

The first was a sequence of republican revolutions. The Anglo-Dutch revolution of 1649–1702 was part of a broader process of Anglo-Dutch-American state-making spanning two centuries. Across the Atlantic, between the Dutch Revolt and the American War of Independence, a series of states emerged which were new not only in fact, but nature. These were products of an Atlantic Age of Revolution which is sometimes located only in the eighteenth century, but which had clear origins in the sixteenth.

Although the new states in question were three in number, the 'Age of Revolution' involved four political and military upheavals of global importance. The first and third of these, in the Netherlands and North America, took the form of successful wars of independence within global empires. The second and fourth saw the fall of ancient European monarchies, in England and France. However, the Dutch War of Independence (1565–1648), Anglo-Dutch revolution (1649–1702), American War of Independence (1775–83) and French Revolution (1789–98) were all intertwined. They constituted a single interconnected sequence by virtue of their practical contexts, and also their cultural and political objectives.

The Dutch and English troubles emerged from connected religious and political contexts, addressing the same grievances. Thereafter the American and French upheavals were equally intertwined. Exhausted by the imperial struggle with France, and driven to impose new taxes in America to pay for it, the government of George III provoked a colonial rebellion it could not contain. Exhausted by the same struggle against Britain, involving the loss of the Seven Years War and subsequent support for the American rebels, the French government collapsed. Over two centuries the contexts of all of these revolutions linked old worlds and new. They coincided with, and helped to bring about, the decline of Iberian and the rise of Anglo-Dutch-French (North-West Atlantic) imperial power. They exploited and exacerbated military-fiscal overstretch, the risks attending which became increasingly grave between the sixteenth and eighteenth centuries as empires, states and armies grew larger, and the wars in question became global. The result was a political dynamic which was both destructive and creative, rooted in the making and breaking of both states and empires.

All of these revolutions were linked by culture (including cultures of communication) and ideology. The Dutch and English troubles were as closely bound by news and ideas as by military co-operation and conflict. The Dutch rebels against Philip II took up arms in defence of political and religious freedoms and rights as they had been protected by a government both customary and legal, involving a complex of representative institutions. Following their own rebellion against Stuart popery and arbitrary government, English parlia-mentarians and then republicans acknowledged the inspiration furnished by the Dutch.

When more than a century later thirteen American colonies rebelled against British imperial tyranny they also did so in defence of a Protestant 'Free State'. This had been partially secured by the Anglo-Dutch revolution of 1649–1702. Accordingly the American Revolution asserted a need to return to the first principles of England's republican moment: 'of Aristotle and Plato, of Livy and Cicero, and Sidney, Harrington and Locke; the principle of nature and eternal reason; the principles on which the whole government over us now stands.'[5] This belief system was imbibed by the American rebels from the authors of the radical commonwealth tradition, in particular Sidney and Locke.[6] Accordingly the ideology of the American Revolution, as of the Dutch and English, was republican:

So absorbed were the Americans in the Commonwealth tradition of English radicalism that even the destruction of monarchy and the institution of republicanism did not clearly signify a repudiation of the ancient constitution; for the spirit of republicanism, the spirit of the great men of the seventeenth century, was 'so far from being incompatible with the British constitution, that it is the greatest glory of it'.[7]

In the view of one historian, for their role in furnishing a republican ideology capable of felling monarchy and empire simultaneously, the English civil wars of the 1640s were 'the essential precondition of American independence'.[8] Yet of course while felling monarchy, the English republican moment of 1649 had dramatically consolidated and expanded empire, in America in particular. It had done so in response to royalist rebellions in six American colonies, and in Ireland.[9] Moreover, the association of republicanism with imperial expansion was hard-wired into the English republic's Machiavellian ideological DNA. It is therefore not surprising that some American patriots took aim at the actions of 'the Commonwealth parliament', in particular the Navigation Act of 1651, for asserting with unprecedented vigour a 'usurped . . . supremacy over the Colonies of *America*'.[10] For these rebels the American was a necessary revolution against what had become, between 1649 and 1776, a tyrannical parliamentary power.[11] Yet whether understood as republican, royalist, or neither, the American was a war of independence indebted to Dutch and English precedent on behalf of liberty, leading to the establishment of a Protestant 'Free State'.

In *The Machiavellian Moment* J. G. A. Pocock described the ideology linking the English and American revolutions as classical republicanism.[12] Pocock's was a history of political thought rather than of republican revolutions in practice. Its European focus was Anglo-Florentine rather than Anglo-Dutch; its leading lights Niccolò Machiavelli, who wrote to lift the spell cast over Italian republicanism by Venice, and James Harrington, who wrote to offer Oliver Cromwell an agrarian alternative to the commercial policies of the English republic of 1649–53 which he abhorred.[13] One result was an account of classical republicanism as in fundamental tension with commerce. The present study, by contrast, has emphasized the predominantly maritime and commercial nature of early modern republicanism, in theory and practice, in Italy, the Netherlands and England. That is why the Industrial Revolution has a specifically republican prehistory, and also (partly) why it was an Anglo-Dutch-American phenomenon.

When England became a republic its government thought in terms of ships, banking and trade. Yet the new regime also explained and promoted itself, in the works of Marchamont Nedham, John Streater and John Milton, with a full array of classical, religious and renaissance sources. Pre-eminent among these, as later channelled by Sidney, was Machiavelli:

> Hobbes indeed doth scurrilously deride Cicero, Plato and Aristotle . . . But 'tis strange that this anarchy . . . should overthrow all the monarchies . . . within their reach . . . I desire it may be considered whether it were an easy work to conquer Switzerland: Whether the Hollanders are of greater strength since the recovery of their liberty, or when they groaned under the yoke of Spain: And . . . whether the entire conquest of Scotland and Ireland, the victories obtained against the Hollanders when they were in the height of their power, and the reputation to which England did rise in less than five years after 1648, be good marks of the instability, disorder and weakness of free nations?[14]

The English republic sought not to choose between Venice and Rome, as Machiavelli had insisted was necessary, but (as we have seen in Chapter 6) to combine from each, and from Israel and Sparta, what was best to form a 'perfect composition'. Subsequently the 'Commonwealth tradition', augmented by Neville, Sidney, Locke, and *Cato's Letters*, intertwined classical republicanism and natural-law theory.[15] Partly from this synthesis emerged the American claim 'that all men are created equal, that they are endowed by their Creator with certain inalienable Rights, that among these are Life, Liberty and the pursuit of Happiness'.[16] When subsequently revolutionaries in Paris declared that all were 'by nature free and equal in respect of their rights' they were articulating their version of the same cause. 'The aim of all political association is the preservation of the natural rights of man. These rights are liberty, property, security, and resistance to oppression.'[17] Many American and English republicans were involved in the French upheaval. Recent historians have underlined the direct impact of seventeenth-century English upon French republican thought.[18] One scholar sees the English, American and French revolutions as culminating in a single 'Revolutionary Enlightenment, 1776–1800'.[19]

THE GEOGRAPHY OF CONSTITUTIONAL INVENTION

If, in these and other respects, the more than two-century-long Age of Revolution was one, our focus in the remainder of this chapter is upon three of its constitutional products. These emerged from a process of state formation which was trans-Atlantic in scope. The Anglo-Dutch revolution was part of a larger archipelagic upheaval which saw the invention of three new states. These were the United Provinces of the Netherlands (1579), the United Kingdom of Great Britain (1707) and the United States of America (1783). All were similarly culturally and constitutionally articulated, being composite (federal or multi-national), Protestant, religiously tolerant, and republican or parliamentary. All were not only new states, but new kinds of state, created by elected representatives demonstrating their right and power to make something new.

This was the most important *political* product of Anglo-Dutch-American early modernity as a process of invention. On the one hand it involved the conscious imitation of previous models. Regarding America's federal constitution, for instance, John Adams explained that no one initially thought 'of consolidating this vast Continent under one national government'. Instead, 'after the Example of the Greeks, the Dutch and the Swiss . . . [it was to be] a Confederacy of States, each of which must have a separate Government'.[20] On the other hand, during the eighteenth century, attention to precedent combined with Enlightenment exultation in change and discovery:

Is not the Change We have seen astonishing? Would any Man, two Years ago have believed it possible, to accomplish such an Alteration in the Prejudices, Passions, Sentiments, and Principles of these thirteen little States as to make every one of them completely republican, and to make them own it? Idolatry to Monarchs, and servility to Aristocratic Pride, was never so totally eradicated, from so many Minds in so short a Time.[21]

Although built upon prior developments, these new states were inventions, or innovations, as much as the *fluit* or the spinning jenny. And like those they emerged pragmatically, as a result of experimentation, as responses to specific opportunities and emergencies. In particular they emerged in response to the demands of war. Following the assassination of William the Silent in

July 1584, leadership of the Dutch Revolt fell to the States of Holland. The militarily crucial 1590s consolidated not only the geography but political shape of the republic as a federation of seven provinces which protected a large measure of autonomy. The origins of this autonomy lay in the medieval period. 'It was the lack of a strong overbearing state and the peripheral position of especially the Northern provinces to the composite states that gained control over them that allowed their towns and capitalists to develop relatively unhindered.'[22]

However, the result was more than a defence of the status quo. Within the context of a protracted military emergency there emerged a new level of economic prosperity, and a new kind of state, as the Revolt swung a pendulum between alternative social, economic, political and confessional worlds. 'Freed from the centralising aims of the Habsburg crown and the essentially feudal world-outlook of the . . . nobles that stood behind it, the seven northern provinces . . . became the territory of a new state that concentrated political and economic power to an extraordinary extent in the hands of a coalition of large-scale international merchants and smaller scale urban and rural oligarchs.'[23]

During the 1690s, similarly, the modernization of the English state was completed pragmatically and urgently, in wartime. Thus a remodelling of the first restoration settlement gave way to reconstruction of the army and navy, the institutional elaboration of the financial revolution, and the ceding of some royal powers to Parliament in exchange for military funding. Such concessions were much easier for a Dutch ex-stadtholder to make than they would have been for a Stuart king (though William still resented the necessity). Within such a political relationship the financial role of the English House of Commons in wartime unlocked a game-changing military-fiscal dynamic. Setting the agenda were the military priorities of the king himself. These had to do, in the short and long term, with the struggle against France.

This dominated English and British geopolitical thinking until 1815. After the Hanoverian succession this imperative acquired a German dimension. At the same time it had an imperial, and in particular an American, theatre. By the 1760s Britain and France were competing in the South Pacific as well as for domination of the North American continent. The British understood their empire to be 'Protestant, commercial, maritime and free'.[24] This was to say that, as the product of the revolution of 1649–1702, it followed a Dutch, rather than French or Spanish, model. Yet it was also agricultural, and in this respect different not only from the Spanish and French, but also from the Dutch:

> Elizabethan . . . colonization in North America . . . rested explicitly on . . . planting and cultivating the land, as a justification for possession of thinly peopled territories quite different from the empires and cities which the Spanish had encountered in the south . . . The conquistadors . . . were not farmers, and the English were already practising agrarian improvement at home.[25]

The seventeenth-century improvement of English agriculture was powerfully indebted to Dutch example. Yet this was not an example the Dutch exported to their colonies. As Josiah Child observed, they 'did never much thrive in planting'. They were interested only in war and trade, 'not in clearing, breaking up of the ground, and planting as the English have done'.[26] Agriculture was the basis, though not the totality, of the English North American (and Irish) plantation of people and of culture.

The constitutional outcome of the Dutch struggle against Spain was unique. During the 1590s Dutch rebels facing a vigorous imperial monarchy had had to create a rival military-fiscal structure. That this took the form of a federated republic reflected the urban demography as well as the provincial political structures of the north. William Temple wrote that within the resulting 'Confederacy of Seven Soveraign Provinces . . . the Freedom of the Cities' amounted to an '*Oligarchy* . . . very different from a Popular Government'.[27] Moreover, 'though they retain'd the Name of a Free People, yet they soon lost the ease of the Liberties they contended for, by the absoluteness of their Magistrates in the several Cities and Provinces, and by the extream pressure of their Taxes, which so long a War with so mighty an Enemy made necessary'. Even after the war, Temple explained, 'at Amsterdam . . . when, in a Tavern, a certain Dish of Fish is eaten with the usual Sawce, above thirty several Excises are paid'.[28]

The contrast between the dispersed Dutch federation and the London-centred English government is important not only for our understanding of the Anglo-Dutch revolution. That revolution involved the reapplication of Dutch processes and policies within a very different constitutional environment. The

American Revolution began partly as a reaction against a perceived British imperial abuse of power, and therefore of a British (Anglo-Dutch-Scots) constitution held to be free. But it was also a reaction against the highly centralized British imperial state itself. The English republic had been imposed upon a war-ravaged country without consent and had created a new imperial power by force. It was against the eighteenth-century offspring of this power that the American rebels brought to bear principles of liberty and of radical popular sovereignty which had their own origins in the civil war radicalism of the period 1646–9 as articulated by the Levellers.[29] In 1649 such aspirations had been crushed by the New Model Army. In 1776, however, as they were successfully defended across the Atlantic, they were given a decentralized anti-imperial constitutional form indebted to the Dutch.

THE INVENTION OF BRITAIN

When in 1707 the search for military security produced another new state – the United Kingdom of Great Britain – it took a very different form. It was a product not of rebellion, dynastic federation, or conquest. It was an 'incorporating union' insisted upon by the English negotiators against the federal proposal preferred by the Scots. 'Underlying . . . [this] position was a deep distrust of federalism, which during the [English] republican period had been referred to contemptuously as "cantonising".'[30] It was another version of the union imposed by the English republic upon the Scots and successfully resisted by the Dutch, at a price. It created a new representative body, a Parliament of Great Britain, while leaving most other Scots and English legal and ecclesiastical institutions intact.[31]

The most important English motivation to the union of 1707 was protection of the Hanoverian succession provided for in the Act of Settlement of 1701. The need for this had been underlined by passage by the Scots Parliament in 1703 of legislation asserting the country's independence in respect of the succession, and of peace and war. Thus Parliament's overriding priority was, as it had been consistently from 1585 to 1689, confessional security. The resulting Treaty of Union replaced what had been a Stuart Union of Crowns with a unified parliamentary state. This was made possible by the augmentation of Scots as well as English parliamentary power between 1689 and 1702. It was also encouraged during his life by a Dutch monarch who had served his own political apprenticeship within a composite constitution. For William III co-operation between what had been distinct sovereign assemblies was not a threat, but the means to wielding effective executive power; and federation, beginning with the 'Closer Union' between Holland and Zeeland in 1576, the route to Great Power (including imperial) status and functionality.[32]

In the United Kingdom this federation took a more centralized constitutional form. Creation of a parliamentary state with a monarch at its head reduced the insecurities which had attended early Stuart attempts to deepen Anglo-Scots union, both political and religious. Equally important was the emergence of parliamentary government as the system through which the Crown satisfied its appetite for military expenditure in exchange for economic as well as political favours granted to members of the elite.[33] In this respect the United Kingdom involved more than the union of two previously separate parliaments. It was again a new kind of state, Anglo-Dutch, Anglo-Scots and about to be Anglo-Scots-German, a process under accelerated development since 1689 but with its origins in the period 1642–53, or earlier, that of the Dutch Revolt.

By 1707 such a settlement did not need to be imposed by force. After more than a century of Scots resistance to such incorporation it was agreed to in the context of guarantees concerning Scots religious, institutional and cultural autonomy. Above all it was accepted in exchange for the right to trade with every part of Britain and its empire. In this respect, like the English republic upon the achievements of which it built, the United Kingdom of Great Britain was a product not only of state but of empire formation.[34] Attracted by the economic and cultural benefits of empire, Wales and Scotland became core participants in its extension and administration. 'I might enlarge here,' wrote Defoe,

> Upon the Honour it is for *Scotland* to be part of the *British* Empire, and to be incorporated with so Powerful a People under the Crown of so great a Monarch . . . enjoying all the Privileges of . . . a Nation who have the greatest Privileges, and enjoy the most Liberty of any People in the World. But I should be told, and perhaps justly too, that this was talking like an *Englishman*.[35]

This was a good joke, but by the early eighteenth century it wasn't only Englishmen who spoke this way. Radical Whigs praised that 'civil and religious liberty . . . which . . . [is] the glorious inheritance of Freeborn Englishmen'.[36] Conservative Whigs claimed defence of 'our liberties and properties' as the major achievement of 1689.[37] The French observer Montesquieu described Britain as the 'one nation in the world whose constitution has political liberty for its direct purpose'.[38] The Scot David Hume, a sceptic upon all other subjects, attributed to 'our mixed form of government' a degree of personal and political liberty unique in Europe.[39] An inhabitant of Virginia lauded what is 'by the confession of the wisest men in Europe, the freest and the noblest government on the records of history'.[40]

Yet if the empire helped make the Union, there remained on both sides of the Atlantic those for whom it remained an affront to national identity. Jonathan Swift wished 'a pox on the modern phrase *Great Britain*, which is only to distinguish it from Little Britain [the London neighbourhood], where old cloaths and books are to be bought and sold'.[41] In 1774 a Virginian denounced the word 'Britain' as an unfortunate 'Scotticism'. 'What chance can England or America have for a continuance of their liberty or independence when not only the principles, but phraseology of that accursed country is prevalent everywhere?'[42] In 1773 Samuel Ward of Rhode Island opined that 'the Liberty of America is the Life of Britain, and if Slavery takes place in this Country, Britain will fall a sacrifice to her own tyranny'.[43]

The Treaty of Union was a political (but not religious or legal) incorporation which was highly unusual in European terms. Although the reasons for Scots assent were not simply economic, the country had endured an arduous period including famine followed by the collapse of an attempted colony at Darien. Now the Union brought into being 'the biggest free trade area in a Europe bristling with both international protectionism and the jealous defence of local economic privileges'.[44] For England in the context of the European wars of 1689–97 and 1704–11, military insecurity within the archipelago was a luxury it could not afford. The fall of the early Stuart monarchy had been initiated by rebellions in Scotland and then Ireland. In the words of a pamphleteer of 1679: 'Scotland and Ireland are two Doors, either to let in Good or Mischief upon us.'[45] As the changes of the revolution were consolidated and as the reach and power of the state expanded, its first priority was to lock those doors (not achieved immediately, as the Jacobite risings of 1715 and 1745 demonstrated).

In the same European context the differences between Scots and English reformations began to look less important than their connections. Since both nations 'are Protestant, both Orthodox in Principle, and equally opposite to Popery . . . inhabit[ing] one Island, neither separated by dangerous Seas or unpassable Mountains . . . the on-looking World has beheld with no less Wonder than Pleasure, that they have not to this Day been able to unite in one Body'.[46] In the event of a successful French invasion those opposed to Union would 'see things with a different Aspect, will have their Opticks extended, and see the Gulphs and Precipices, which they, blinded by Ignorance and Prejudices, are now willing to push the Nations upon'.[47]

THE UNITED STATES OF AMERICA

Constitutional construction of the United States also took place amid the pressing exigencies of war. Although the American process was remarkable and in some respects unprecedented, it did not, as has been claimed, produce 'the first new nation', nor was 'the Revolution the world's first successful revolt against colonialism'.[48] In their early modern context both of those descriptions would better apply to the United Provinces. More broadly the constitutional history of the new republic fell primarily into two phases. During the first, in 1776, in a reaction against imperial tyranny the federation had a distinctly Dutch-style constitutional colouring. During the second, when the mechanisms were put in place for a stronger federal union, there was a much greater willingness to learn from British experience. Referring to the first of these phases one historian has commented:

> The government of the United Provinces . . . bears a curious resemblance to the government which the former American colonies temporarily adopted under the articles of Confederation while fighting their war of independence. The Dutch and the Americans after them regarded their states (seven in the Netherlands, originally thirteen in America) as sovereign but in order to achieve victory in a long war and to preserve their independence in peace they formed a union whose constitutional expression was the States General

in the Netherlands and the Constitutional Congress in America. In both these bodies each state was equally represented for the larger states had no more representatives than the smaller states.[49]

According to one contemporary, Ezra Stiles, the Confederation achieved in 1776–7 was not believed or meant to be 'a body in which resides authoritative sovereignty; for there is no real cession of dominion, no surrender or transfer of sovereignty to the national council, as each state in the confederacy is an independent sovereignty'.[50] The Declaration of Independence spoke on behalf of thirteen 'Free and Independent States they have full power to levy war, conclude peace, contract alliances, establish commerce, and to do all other acts and things which independent States may of right do.' 'No confederacy in history, the Germanic, the Helvetic, the Dutch, had ever dissolved the parts into one common mass.'[51] Once the war was over, however, this level of decentralization proved inadequate to the challenges of constructing a viable and independent modern polity.

There followed the Philadelphia Constitutional Convention of 1787 – the contrivance of a convention being the same as had accomplished the English Restoration of 1660 and the Revolution Settlement of 1689. It fell to this body to establish the mechanisms of a functional and durable federal union. In so doing, argues Brendan Simms, it borrowed from the Treaty of Union of 1707. The Act of Union was 'a parliamentary, debt and foreign policy partnership' for military security. Although the outcome of the Philadelphia Convention had some unique features, it was in its 'essence, and was understood by contemporaries to be an improved variant of the Anglo-Scottish Union. Americans soon pooled their debts, created a treasury bond, a national bank and, in due course, a strong military.'[52]

The constitution that emerged was not parliamentary but republican (the president elected, the Senate not hereditary, but elected proportionately from the states, and the House of Representatives elected directly). 'Our President is not a King, nor our Senate a House of Lords.' 'No lords strut here with supercilious hautiness, or swell with emptiness . . . All dignities flow from the people.'[53] Nevertheless the constitutional focus had shifted from protection of liberty to 'a creation of power'. 'There is hardly an instance where a republic trusted its executive so long with so much power.'[54] For James Wilson of

Pennsylvania the investiture of an executive presidency with sweeping powers was consistent with a revolution which did 'not oppose the British King but the parliament – the opposition was not against an Unity but a corrupt multitude'.[55]

Thereafter, one historian has claimed: 'To an almost incredible degree, American developments after 1789 mimicked or even repeated English developments of a century before. America's Revolution Settlement resembles the remake of an old movie classic, except that the new producer has altered the ending to suit the changing tastes of his audience.' These repetitions included brutal party conflict accompanied by foundation of the 'Bank of the United States, America's direct copy of the Bank of England [England's copy of the Bank of Amsterdam]', a great recoinage as during the 1690s, and the foundation of the New York Stock Exchange.[56]

From the standpoint of the history of political thought David Armitage has analyzed the Thirteen Colonies' Declaration of Independence (1776) as a new kind of political document marking 'the transition from subordination within an empire to independence alongside other states'.[57] What was new was its 'appeal to the tribunal of the world', and specifically to that world of independent modern states to membership of which it laid claim.[58] It was thus not simply a claim to rights, individual or collective, against a previous colonial master, let alone a justification of rebellion. It was an announcement of the creation of a new state, directed to the existing community of states, a declaration of independence and interdependence.

In this respect Armitage recognized that one possible precedent was the United Provinces. The Dutch Revolt too had resulted in the successful military defence of a new state. In the Netherlands, as later in America, 'A great revolution ... happened – a revolution made, not by chopping and changing of power in any one of the existing states, but by the appearance of a new state, of a new species.'[59] The document which founded the United Provinces allowed for the incorporation, by unanimous agreement, of other provinces which should seek to join the Union, just as the United States eventually incorporated other states (for instance Vermont).[60] Like the United States, the United Provinces was not only a federation, but a republic. Thus it was free, both religiously and politically, and was sometimes in English called 'the united States of the Low Countries'.[61]

Armitage's textual basis for distinguishing between the two revolutions is to show the difference between the American Declaration of Independence and the Dutch Act of Abjuration of 1581, which renounced allegiance to Philip II, to offer it to the Duke of Anjou. In light of this effort to replace one prince (who had become a tyrant) with another, it could be said that the United Provinces had not yet become a republic, and on that basis that it was not independent and/or not declaring its independence. Thus the Abjuration did not furnish a 'specific generic precedent' for the Declaration.[62]

Yet in fact the foundational agreement of the new Dutch state was not the Act of Abjuration but the Treaty of Utrecht (1579).[63] Over time the Union of Utrecht 'transformed from a temporary alliance into the political foundation of the Dutch republic. The document came to be seen as a substitute constitution.'[64] William Temple agreed. This '*Union . . .* was the Original Constitution and Frame of that Common-wealth, which has since been so well known in the World by the Name of *The United Provinces*'.[65] When, following the peace of 1648, a Great Assembly convened in The Hague in 1651 'to settle issues of the Union, religion and the militia', its first measure was to 'solemnly renew . . . the Union of Utrecht' as the basis of a 'Further Union'.[66]

Like the Declaration of Independence the Treaty of Utrecht agreed articles of confederation, mutual defence and aspects of the internal government of the seven provinces which came to constitute the new state. The earlier Abjuration had added 'nothing new to what had already been said many times before . . . Of course Philip II did not forfeit his sovereignty on 26 July 1581; he had clearly lost it well before that date. On 26 July the States General confined themselves to stating this as a fact; they did not proclaim independence, they did not decide on any revolutionary innovation.'[67] This was because the basis of independence had already been declared by 'The Union signed at Utrecht . . . a formal alliance of provinces acting as if they were independent states, and deciding to integrate their foreign policies and war efforts through a fairly loose federation in order to defend their individual independence and traditional customs.'[68]

It is true that the Treaty of the Union did not declare independence from the 'General Union' of the Netherlands.[69] That is because the military struggle to incorporate the rest of those provinces had not yet been abandoned, not because an independent United Provinces of the Netherlands had not yet been conceived. It is also true that independence was not recognized by Spain or the rest of the international community until 1648. But if the Dutch military struggle for independence was the first in a modern succession of such struggles, it is that much less surprising that it was incremental. Nevertheless, without the extraordinary actions by which seven provinces progressed from a treaty of union (1579), to the fact of an independent republic led by Holland (1590s), to an international treaty recognizing that independence (1648), the possibility of such an achievement might never had been entertained, let alone repeated later.

There was an important presentational difference between the two revolutions. The American Revolution was comfortable underlining and perhaps exaggerating its novelty. It was a product of the insistence by Tom Paine, Thomas Jefferson and others that no generation was bound by the precedents, let alone errors, of its predecessors. By contrast Dutch liberty was defended as a continuation of the local self-government, both urban and provincial, which had been the foundation of Dutch harmony, community and prosperity since medieval times.[70] Yet such differences in modes of legitimation do nothing to diminish the importance of the Dutch precedent in practice. John Adams claimed that 'The Origins of the two Republicks are so much alike, that the History of the one seems but a Transcript from that of the other'; and Abigail Adams spoke of 'an indissoluble bond . . . between the united States of America and the united Provinces who from a similarity of circumstances have each arrived at Independence disdaining the Bondage and oppression of a Philip and a G[e]orge'.[71] Concerning the Dutch republic Benjamin Franklin recorded, 'in love of liberty, and bravery in defense of it she has been our great example'.[72]

Thus the Anglo-Dutch-American geography of invention was not only agricultural, or commercial, or religious, but also political and constitutional. Moreover, the insistence upon religious and political self-government in the Netherlands, England, America and France was a moral demand the making good of which had powerful material as well as cultural consequences. Thus classical republicanism arrived in England from the Netherlands, on its way to America and France, in the moral service of a radical Protestant reformation of manners. But its result went beyond reformation, to inform a revolutionary remaking and then new foundation of modern states and empires from the competitive struggles among which there emerged (among other things) the first global economy.

———•◆•———

CHAPTER FOURTEEN

ANGLO-DUTCH-AMERICAN
ENLIGHTENMENT

If it be lawful for us . . . to build houses, ships and forts better than
our ancestors, to make such arms as are most fit for our defence, and
to invent printing, with an infinite number of other arts beneficial
to mankind, why have we not the same right in matters of government, upon which all others do almost absolutely depend?

Algernon Sidney, *Discourses Concerning Government* (1698)[1]

Every age and generation must be as free to act for itself . . . as the
ages and generations which preceded it . . . It is the living and not
the dead, that are to be accommodated . . . There was a time when
kings disposed of their crowns by will upon their death-beds, and
consigned the people, like beasts of the field, to whatever successor
they appointed. This is now so exploded as scarcely to be remembered, and so monstrous as hardly to be believed.

Thomas Paine, *Rights of Man* (1789)[2]

THE GEOGRAPHY OF CULTURAL INVENTION

This study has explored a process of invention involving modernizations of
the economy (agricultural, then commercial), of political economy and the
military-fiscal state and empire, and of public culture, including religious and
political freedoms. Some historians have related early modern economic innovation to the competitive behaviour of Renaissance Italian and Dutch cities.
Another has identified an English cultural rhetoric of improvement deriving
from the 'profitable agrarian innovation' of the late Tudor and early Stuart

periods.[3] More broadly historians have placed invention, its identification and celebration, at the heart of the North-Western European cultural movement called Enlightenment.

Enlightenment refers, in the first place, to a description by European intellectuals of what they took to be an advanced present state of moral and natural knowledge by comparison to that of the ancients. With related self-confidence, in the heyday of their empires, some described their culture as possessed of a dynamic modernity to be distinguished from the 'oriental' lethargy and backwardness existing elsewhere.[4] Yet Enlightenment also originated as European self-criticism. One context for that was the comparative perspective acquired by discovery of non-European cultures. This was harnessed for purposes of contemporary social criticism by Sir Thomas More and Michel de Montaigne.[5] In this and in other ways the origin of Enlightenment, including its 'conviction that progress had become unstoppable', lies in the period when Renaissance and Reformation combined with printing and natural philosophy to establish the culture of the European North-West.[6]

Thus Paul Hazard's *The European Mind, 1680–1715* depicted William Temple 'studying the moral and political history of China, Peru, Tartary and Arabia. With an eye on a map of the New World he examines once again the principles that governed and directed the Old':[7]

> Travel ... meant comparing manners and customs, rules of life, philosophies, religions; arriving at some notion of the relative ... divers civilisations, each one of which boasted that it, and it alone was perfect – what a School for Sceptics was there! Blind are they, and ignorant of life, who suppose that Europe is self-sufficing; that she has nothing to ask from her neighbours.[8]

One result was a taste for toleration which until recently seemed a secure feature of Western modernity. Was there an Anglo-Dutch-American Enlightenment? What did Anglo-Dutch-American experience contribute to this perspective? How did it relate to the broader geography of invention which helped to make the Industrial Revolution possible?

For much of the twentieth century the historiography of Enlightenment was dominated by a national contest between France and Germany.[9] Recently, however, national history has come to enjoy a utility and status comparable to that of the shoe collection of Imelda Marcos. Taking its place, multiplicity, liminality and hybridity have ushered in an Atlantic, Pacific, American, Christian and Global Enlightenment.[10] Yet it is too soon to close the wardrobe in Manila. While acknowledging the inadequacy of national approaches, Roy Porter attempted to correct what he took to be surprising neglect of the British Enlightenment.[11] Mapping the supranational contours of Radical Enlightenment, Jonathan Israel nevertheless identified a lode-bearing seam in Spinozism which shifted the focus to the Netherlands.[12] For Paul Slack discourses of improvement 'became a particular way of thinking, a turn of mind, which distinguished the English from everyone else'.[13] None of these historians has recognized the Anglo-Dutch Enlightenment, which actually looms like a colossus over the cultural history of the period. Thus England's Toleration Act (1689), the abandonment of press licensing (1695) and parliamentary monarchy (1689–1701) were all achievements of an Anglo-Dutch government completing an Anglo-Dutch revolution. To understand its intellectual significance we need to return to its European, and in particular its confessional, context.

For Paul Hazard, Enlightenment was a reaction against the prospect of a Europe dominated by France, the French language and Roman Catholicism. The high point of Counter-Reformation was the revocation of the Edict of Nantes in 1685. The gates of Enlightenment were thrown open by the flood of Huguenot refugees who fled to the Netherlands and England before and during the 1680s. In collaboration with their hosts they established a transnational Anglo-Dutch-French Protestant assault upon the old order. Into this were swept English exiles like John Locke, sheltering in Rotterdam from 1683, and the Huguenot Pierre Coste, prevented by the Edict from returning from Geneva to France, enrolled at the universities of Lausanne, Zurich and Leiden, accepted as a student by the Walloon church in Amsterdam, emigrant to England in 1697, Fellow of the Royal Society, and translator into French of the third Earl of Shaftesbury's *Essay on the Freedom of Wit*, Isaac Newton's *Optics*, and Locke's *Essay concerning Human Understanding*.[14]

Hazard underlined the importance of the Glorious Revolution's successful military confrontation of France. Only when the power and culture of Versailles had been contained, and a safe space created for its transnational Protestant alternative, could Enlightenment take hold. In this context he discussed what he took to be the extraordinary transformation of English literature, thought and science from about 1700, while acknowledging the crucial prior role of Holland as a haven for intellectuals, book publishers, exiles and refugees. In this role the United Provinces served as bridgehead for the establishment of something similar in England, alongside the growing commercial and military power of which, 'after 1688, she began to look rather like a dinghy alongside a big ship'.[15] This culture became transatlantic, so that Benjamin Franklin was raised with as keen a resentment of the Revocation as any native European.

Yet all of these developments had a long history. England before 1700 had hardly been a cultural wasteland. As noted in Chapter 6, the imaginative literature of the English Revolution was astonishing in size, range and quality. In 1600, 259 English books were printed; in 1640, 577; and 'when control of the press lapsed during the middle decades of the . . . century some years saw up to 2,000 titles appearing'.[16] Anglo-Dutch co-operation against the Counter-Reformation began during the 1570s, not the 1680s. Accordingly the roots of Anglo-Dutch-American enlightenment are visible from the late sixteenth and early seventeenth centuries.

THE ANGLO-DUTCH CULTURE OF INVENTION

In Chapter 3 we noted Jonathan Israel's observation that visitors to the Dutch republic were struck by a range of novelties. These included an apparent subversion of the proper relations between men and women, Christians and non-Christians, nobles and commoners. They included 'a military revolution . . . characterized not only by innovations in artillery, tactics, fortifications, siege techniques, and military transportation, but by a vast improvement in . . . discipline and orderliness'. They embraced a philosophical and political commitment to liberty, accompanied by an outburst of intellectual creativity comparable to that of 'classical Athens or Renaissance Florence'.[17] As in those cities, 'it is . . . striking that the sustained creativity is confined to a remarkably small geographical space'.[18] These innovations paved the way for a Radical Enlightenment which

> severed the roots of traditional European culture in the sacred, magic, kingship, and hierarchy, secularizing all institutions and ideas . . . and . . .

effectively demolished all legitimation of monarchy, aristocracy, woman's subordination to man, ecclesiastical authority, and slavery, replacing these with the principles of universality, equality and democracy.[19]

Meanwhile Mark Kishlansky reflected upon the 'astonishing . . . achievements' of seventeenth-century England. These included 'New ideas, new forms of entertainment, new theories of government'. There was the intellectual and literary production of Shakespeare and Jonson, of Donne, Milton and Marvell, of the King James Bible (1611) and Bunyan's *Pilgrim's Progress*, of Thomas Hobbes, James Harrington and Locke. During the same century was 'inaugurated nearly every element of modern commerce and finance. The Bank of England was founded in 1694, the Bank of Scotland in 1695. Cheques, banknotes and minted coins made possible an economy based on money. The creation of the Stock Exchange and the national debt made possible an economy based on credit. The excise and land tax revolutionised government finance.'[20] To this magazine of modernity Kishlansky added the scientific revolution and the invention of cricket, a renaissance in architecture and the transformation of Britain from 'an isolated archipelago' into a pre-eminent global power. For Kishlansky, too, the site of this explosion of creativity was small ('little more than 5 million people in the entire world spoke English'). For him also the results reached heights 'unattained since the Golden Age of Athens'.[21]

In fact, as we have seen, a number of these English developments originated in the Netherlands. These even included cricket, introduced to sixteenth-century England by Flemish weavers ('O lorde of Ipocrites/Nowe shut upp your wickettes/And clape to your clickettes A! Farewell, kings of crekettes!').[22] Many features of Dutch and English society and culture remained distinct. There was no English Vermeer or Rembrandt (but, instead, Van Dyck at the court of Charles I, and at least twenty-two Dutch artists in Restoration London).[23] Nor was there a Dutch Shakespeare, or a Milton. 'While Amsterdam was outstanding in the Netherlands for its drama, London was far ahead of the Dutch . . . London's first permanent public theatre dated from 1576 and its repertoire was impressive . . . In musical performances London also rose high above Amsterdam.'[24] Speakers of each vernacular language found it difficult to learn the other, and even to understand the other conversing in Latin.[25] Yet in the early seventeenth century both Dutch and English scholars also remarked on the 'neernes' of English to Dutch, and William Camden, Richard Verstegan and Thomas Scott all asserted a common ethnic origin on the basis of linguistic kinship, 'as our speech witnesseth'.[26] Moreover, in creativity – cultural, economic, political, technological and scientific – these societies collectively constituted the seventeenth-century European cutting edge.

Underpinning an Anglo-Dutch proto-Enlightenment, accompanying proto-industrialization, were numerous connective tissues. They included geographical proximity, Protestantism, religious and political liberty, a migrational presence in both countries, relationships between universities and other learned institutions, material prosperity (wages in London and Amsterdam in 1700 had twice the value of those in other capitals), high levels of literacy, extensive trade, maritime culture, global empire, and advanced experimental science.[27] The Dutch and then English troubles challenged the status quo, stimulated debate, spurred innovation, and created a rich print culture. In the Dutch republic 'in 1650 there were 265 printers, publishers, and booksellers . . . spread over 38 localities – twice as many as twenty years earlier'.[28] London had fifty-three printing houses in 1661–2, twenty-three in 1675, and sixty-two in 1705.[29] During the Restoration 'Dutch houses could reprint London books for less than it cost to import them, and they were not slow to do so.'[30] Before 1700 the Dutch republic was the print shop of Europe; after 1700 the same was true of London.

There were many manifestations of what was more broadly an Anglo-Dutch-German-French world of intellectual collaboration and debate. They included the early Stuart exchange between Grotius and Selden concerning the laws of the sea; and Milton's defence of the regicide against Salmasius, a French expatriate living in Leiden, which caused Dutch scholar Vossius to exclaim: 'I had expected nothing of such quality from an Englishman'.[31] They involved the impact upon Dutch new (post-Aristotelian) philosophy of Bacon before Descartes; the uptake of French-influenced Hobbes by Dutch republicans Pieter de la Court and Spinoza; and the literary and philosophical criticism of Pierre Bayle, Jean Le Clerc and Locke.[32] Following foundation of the Royal Society's *Philosophical Transactions*, the editor Henry Oldenburg was plunged into a fruitless struggle to prevent unauthorized Latin and vernacular editions from being produced in Amsterdam, Copenhagen and Hamburg.[33]

Anglo-Dutch collaborations facilitated by the Royal Society included the construction of spring-regulated clocks and watches to be used for the determination of longitude; and lens-grinding, microscopy and telescopy. Christiaan Huygens, the first overseas member of the Society, exchanged visits, letters and books with Robert Hooke, the Curator of Experiments.[34] Like the Anglo-Dutch relationship in general this resulted in both creativity and acrimony, Hooke eventually claiming to have unlocked the 'secret concerning the longitude' seventeen years before his rival.[35] Yet as Sprat pointed out with pride, these exchanges were maintained even during the second Anglo-Dutch war. Into the eighteenth century scientific and scholarly collaboration continued which was Anglo-Dutch-American in scope.[36]

Restoration English culture combined renewed emphasis upon the classics in education, literature and architecture with the dominance of natural philosophy in technology and the natural sciences. Exemplars of this blend of humanism and experimental science were virtuosi like John Evelyn, William Petty or Christopher Wren.[37] Yet according to its first historian, by virtue of its universal ambitions the Royal Society to which these men belonged could not be the product of any one kingdom. Here Sprat's language linked the intellectual life of the Society to the economic argument about naturalization discussed in Chapter 10:

> By their *naturalizing* Men of all Countries, they have laid the beginnings of many great advantages for the future. For by this means, they will be able, to settle a *constant Intelligence*, throughout all civil Nations; and make the *Royal Society* the general *Banck*, and Free-Port of the World: A policy, which whether it would hold good, in the *Trade* of *England*, I know not: but sure it will in the *Philosophy*. We are to overcome the mysteries of all the Works of Nature; and not onely to prosecute such as are confin'd to one Kingdom, or beat upon one shore.[38]

Nor is it a coincidence that this image of the Society as a 'general [philosophical] *Banck*' resembled the Earl of Clarendon's outraged description of Sir George Downing's contemporaneous scheme to turn the kingdom's Exchequer into 'the best and greatest Bank in Europe'. Sprat's 'perfect Philosopher' would be a composite of 'several Countries', combining 'the *Industry, Activity, and*

Inquisitive humor of the *Dutch, French, Scotch*, and *English'* with the '*circum-spect*, and *wary* disposition of the *Italians*, and *Spaniards'*.[39] Thus the Society was the product, not of a kingdom but a city, and not any city, but one which was a microcosm of the world:

> By this they have taken care, that nothing shall be so remote, as to escape their reach: because some of their *Members* are still scattered abroad, in most of the habitable parts of the Earth. By this, they have provided, that no profitable thing shall seem too mean for their consideration, seeing they have some amongst them, whose life is employ'd about *little* things, as well as *great* . . . Thus they have form'd that *Society*, which intends a *Philosophy*, for the use of *Cities*, and not for the retirements of *Schools*, to resemble the *Cities* themselves: which are compounded of all sorts of men, of the *Gown*, of the *Sword*, of the *Shop*, of the *Field*, of the *Court*, of the *Sea*; all mutually assisting each other.[40]

ANGLO-DUTCH-AMERICAN RESISTANCE

The first basis of Anglo-Dutch-American collaboration remained religious and political. When William Penn drafted Pennsylvania's 'Frame of Government' in 1681 he received comments from Benjamin Furly, an English Quaker living in Rotterdam, and Algernon Sidney, a political ally whose attempts to be elected to Parliament in 1679–80 he had assisted. Penn was introduced to Furly by Sidney. Sixteen years earlier the English government spy Aphra Behn had reported from Holland that the republican exile 'Collnll Sidney is often in Consultation with Benjamin Turly the quaker . . . He is att present writing a Treatise in defence of a Republique, & ag.st Monarchy, & designes it soone or late for ye presse.'[41]

This was Sidney's *Court Maxims*. Responding to the persecutions unleashed by the Act of Uniformity, it made a pioneering case for the repulsion of force with force. This anticipated the resistance theories of Locke's *Two Treatises of Government* (1689) and Sidney's own *Discourses Concerning Government* (1698).[42] Sidney used Hugo Grotius's *The Law of War and Peace* (1625) to insist that resistance was not so much a right as an imperative of justice.[43] For 'Grotius, though a gentle-spirited man . . . against force that is unjustly imposed just force has to be opposed.' 'Whoever acts unjustly breaks the common pacts by which human society is established, renders himself a delinquent, and gives him that is offended . . . an unlimited moral right against him.'[44] The appropriate action depended upon the extent of the injury, but 'I think nobody will say any injury is greater than to compel me to a profane worship or banish or kill me for refusing'. Sidney spoke personally when he added:

> Those that by violence are brought to the hard necessity of sinning against God [by worship against their conscience] or suffering their families to be ruined and persons perpetually imprisoned, banished, or murdered, may seem enough to justify those who by force seek to repel such violence.[45]

Later allowed to return to England, and writing in London between 1681 and 1683, Sidney issued a call for revolution:

> The ways of preventing or punishing injuries are judicial or extrajudicial. Judicial proceedings are of force against those who submit or may be brought to trial; but are of no effect against those who resist, and are of such power that they cannot be restrained . . . Legal proceedings are therefore to be used when the delinquent submits to the law; and all are just, when he will not . . . if the lusts of those, who are too strong for the tribunals of justice, cannot otherwise be restrained, than by seditions, tumults, and wars, those seditions, tumults and wars, are justified by the laws of God and man.[46]

Arrested in possession of this manuscript in 1683, Sidney was beheaded for treason, thus launching the *Discourses'* glittering Enlightenment career. Editions followed in eighteenth-century Holland, France, Germany, England, Scotland and the United States. Fleeing following Sidney's arrest, John Locke took refuge with Furly in Rotterdam.[47] His own *Two Treatises of Government*, also using Grotius, and like Sidney's refuting the *Patriarcha* of Sir Robert Filmer, was published after his return to England in 1689.[48] It was in Rotterdam that Locke formed his associations with Pierre Bayle, Jean Le Clerc, Philip van Limborch and other early Enlightenment luminaries.[49]

Benjamin Furly was a merchant who teased Locke – a medical doctor – for being 'unversed in matters of exchange'. Locke's biographer was struck by this since his subject was to become 'such a notable economist'.[50] Perhaps, like Benjamin Worsley and Slingsby Bethel, he became one in Holland. '[I]n the beginning,' the *Two Treatises* announced, 'all the World was *America*.' Yet as ' 'tis *Labour* . . . that *puts the difference of value* on every thing . . . Land that is left wholly to Nature, that hath no improvement of Pasturage, Tillage or Planting, is called . . . *wast* . . . This shows how much numbers of men are to be preferred to largeness of dominions.'[51] Labour was the basis of property (or 'dominion') and as 'different degrees of industry were apt to give men possessions in different proportions, so [the] invention of money gave them the opportunity to continue or enlarge them'.[52] Here too Locke used Grotius to explain how, by the application of labour, private property came to be appropriated from the common stock. It originated in the industry of man, himself the property of a God whose workmanship he was.[53]

The idea that labour rather than land was the basis of prosperity was widespread in the later seventeenth century, in France and Germany as well as in the Netherlands and England. 'Labour is the father and active principle of wealth,' wrote William Petty in 1662.[54] Adherents of this view were also boosters for the immigration and naturalization of foreigners. For Josiah Child the influx of Huguenots was beneficial in part because 'it is multitudes of people [that] principally enrich any country'.[55] In 1751 Josiah Tucker summarized the argument:

What are the riches of a country? – Land? Money? Or Labour? What is the value of land but in proportion to the numbers of people? . . . Is not that country wealthiest which has the most labour? And hath not that country the most labour which hath the most people to create mutual employment for each other? Was a country thinly inhabited ever rich? Was a populous country ever poor?[56]

This was also the explanation offered by William Temple for Dutch industry and prosperity in 1673. The spur to both was population density, occasioned principally by migration, not only from the southern Netherlands, but 'The long Civil-Wars, at first of *France*, then of *Germany*, and lastly of *England*... [which] serv'd to increase the swarm in this Countrey'.[57] 'Tis evident to those who have read the most, and travel'd farthest ... That no Countrey can be found either in this present Age, or upon Record of any Story, Where so vast a Trade has been managed, as in the narrow compass of the Four Maritime Provinces of this Commonwealth.' This was not a consequence of natural resources (poor), geographical advantages for trade (in Temple's view limited), or land area (tiny). Instead:

> I conceive the true original and ground of Trade, to be great multitude of people crowded into small compass of Land, whereby all things necessary to life become dear, and all men who have possessions, are induced to Parsimony; but those who have none, are forced to industry and labour, or else to want. Bodies that are vigorous, fall to labour; Such as are not, supply that defect by some sort of Inventions or Ingenuity. These Customs arise first from Necessity, but increase by Imitation, and grow in time to be habitual in a Countrey.[58]

To this example Temple contrasted Ireland, where he had also lived, in which sparse population and ample resources meant that 'an industrious man, by two days labour, may gain enough to feed him the rest of the week; Which I take to be a very plain ground of the laziness attributed to the people: For men ... will not take pains if they can live idle.'[59] Thus industry, 'Inventions or Ingenuity', all had their origins in necessity.[60] They occurred in spite, rather than because of the availability of local resources. Dutch agricultural inventions had been applied in England in the context of population increase. Now commercial expansion offered a response to demographic decline. 'Religious freedom and the encouragement of immigration had made the Netherlands wealthy and strong, while intolerance ... and aversion to manufacture and trade conspired ... to draw Spain into an eddy from which it could not escape.' For writers like William Temple, 'Dutch commercial success figured more prominently in the English imagination than any other economic fact of the seventeenth century.'[61]

By 1689 English policy-makers thinking in these terms included James II, whose attempt to establish liberty of conscience in 1687 was accompanied by proposals for 'a public registry of lands, and a general naturalisation of all foreign immigrants in England, including Jews'. In line with the earlier policies of his brother, the king argued to his privy council: 'nothing Can more Conduce to the Peace . . . of this Kingdom, and the Increase of the Number as well as Trade of His Subjects (wherein the greatness of a Prince does more Consist then in the Extent of His Territories) then an intire Liberty of Conscience'.[62] James was advised on this point by William Penn. Here as elsewhere the Dutch invasion of 1688–9, though profoundly important for European and world history, did not inaugurate so much as complete a revolution of thought and practice which was already under way.

The principal beneficiary of such beliefs was the North Atlantic dissenting, manufacturing and mercantile community whose culture early Enlightenment was. Having survived the Spanish and then French Counter-Reformation assault, and helped to settle North America, by 1689 this Protestant diaspora was turning London into a bulwark against France. There emerged a world of manufacturing and commerce, stocks, coffee houses, booksellers and news, for which toleration and a free press were necessities.[63] By the 1690s Huguenot immigrants, a 'massive injection into England's industrialisation', constituted 8–10 per cent of London's population, settling in Spitalfields, Soho, Leicester Fields and Wandsworth, supporting forty-five churches, developing silk-weaving, paper-making and metal-working, and strengthening intellectual and cultural links with the Netherlands, Amsterdam in particular. In 1709, after the passage of the General Naturalization Act, the Huguenots were followed by 13,000 German Palatine Protestants fleeing persecution.[64] This sudden influx overreached the resources of the state, and of social tolerance, resulting in failure and a political backlash.[65]

By accepting immigrants Britain was following Dutch example, but it was also continuing its own practice since the sixteenth century (and earlier). New arrivals could face hostility: there was a rich xenophobic lexicon of insult available for the French, Dutch, Irish, Scots and Jews. The most likely grounds for welcome was religious; the commonest cause for complaint the perception of economic burden, or competition. By the early eighteenth century cosmopolitanism was not only a feature of London life, but a (Whig) political position.[66] It was, that is to say, both a feature of the culture and a contested cultural position (as it remains today). Thus if improvement had indeed been a 'turn of mind, which distinguished the English from everyone else' – which seems doubtful – it was so at a time when national identity and economic development were profoundly influenced, not only by foreign example, to say nothing of invasion, but by ongoing immigration.

Montesquieu and Voltaire saw the cosmopolitanism of London as anchored in religious toleration. The international economic and cultural capital the city attracted fed into the 'industrial enlightenment . . . a keen interest in the application of scientific ideas and methods to solve practical problems, institutionally supported by forums for the exchange of ideas such as journals and learned societies'.[67] Huguenots settled around Soho included goldsmiths and silversmiths, clock and instrument makers, sculptors and gun makers.[68] By the early eighteenth century, Britain may have had a European edge in its 'abundance of literate, skilled and experienced mechanics and craftsmen . . . Some inventors emerged directly from this class; all . . . depended on its abilities to make their ideas a reality.'[69]

ANGLO-DUTCH-AMERICAN LIBERTY AND EMPIRE

Alongside Protestant internationalism the other core tenet of Whiggism was liberty. Indeed, by the early eighteenth century, adherence to this political totem transcended the party divide. Liberty in the Dutch republic had as much to do with social, commercial and cultural relationships as with its equally distinctive religious and political arrangements. 'The most important characteristic common to the Dutch . . . was their active involvement in society. They considered it their own affair, not a system shaped by others and imposed from above.'[70] By contrast the English republic had indeed been so imposed – if not by others, then from above – and its understanding of the cause was militant and expansionist. Whereas Dutch empire concentrated on commerce, omitting to export religious or political values, English plantation in North America was driven by just such an attempt. The result was a trans-Atlantic theatre of religious and political liberty which could not have been acquired in any other way. This fact would have momentous economic as well as political consequences.

Within England, too, the Anglo-Dutch revolution of 1649–1702 yielded a distinct ideological product, forged by the militant alliance of English

Parliament and anti-French stadtholder. In the words of the third Earl of Shaftesbury:

> We are now in an Age when LIBERTY is once again in its Ascendant. And we are ourselves the happy Nation, who not only enjoy it at home, but by our Greatness and Power give Life and Vigour to it abroad; and are the Head and Chief of the EUROPEAN *League*, founded on this *common Cause*.[71]

Mid-century English republicans had stressed the self-government of the person as well as of the state. This moral philosophy had been inspired by Dutch example and by (among other things) Erasmian Christian humanism. At the same time, from Plato's *Laws* English republicanism derived the formula that a commonwealth was a government of laws and not of men. These laws might be framed by the popular single assembly advocated by Marchamont Nedham and John Streater; or by a mixed constitution, advocated by James Harrington, and later Algernon Sidney. For Harrington constitutions supplied the public interestedness which could not be expected from the selfish actions of individual persons.[72] This sceptical constitutionalism informed Hume's understanding of the virtues of the Hanoverian constitution. In Hume's opinion Britain owed its liberty, not to the moral accomplishments of its citizens, but to the constitution itself.[73]

Nedham's democratic model emerged as an attack not on monarchy, but upon parliamentarian oligarchy. A republic was free not when dominated by its senate, but only when the people had most power. In *The Excellencie of a Free State* (1656), a favourite text during the French Revolution, he extolled frequent elections, non-extension and rotation of office.[74] At the same time he insisted upon the right to political change. 'What if *England* will change yet seven times more? What is that to Scotland? *It being a Right inherent in every Nation, to alter their particular Governments, as often as they judge it necessary for the publick weal and safety.*' Sidney elaborated: 'If men are not obliged to live in caves and hollow trees, to eat acorns, and to go naked, why should they be forever obliged to continue under the same form of government that their ancestors happened to set up in the time of their ignorance?'[75] A century later Thomas Paine thundered: 'Every age and generation must be as free to act for itself . . . as the ages and generations which preceded it. The vanity and presumption of governing beyond the grave is the most ridiculous and insolent of all tyrannies.'[76]

There was no necessary tension between liberty and empire. The empires of Athens and Rome had been products of their liberty, and emblematic of their greatness. There was, however, potential for American colonists to begin to question their status when the political cultures of Britain and France were placed under intolerable pressure by the cost of global war. Captain Cook crossed the Pacific speaking the Enlightenment languages of science and of commerce, rather than conquest, with instructions requiring his people to behave towards native peoples as guests, rather than proprietors. Yet both Britain and France were seeking territory, and so both states became proprietors in practice in Tahiti, Tonga, Australia and New Zealand, by whatever means became possible or necessary.

English and Scots writers sought to distinguish a liberty characteristic of maritime cultures (including Athens) from continental despotism. This argument might separate Carthage from Rome, or the Netherlands and Britain from France. Thus William Falconer (a Scot) quoted Montesquieu to the effect that 'The inhabitants of islands . . . have a higher relish for liberty than those of a continent . . . the sea separates them from great empires, and tyranny cannot reach them.'[77] The surrounding seas rendered islands temperate, and so the people 'less timid indolent and servile'; on an island a standing army ('always necessary to the support of a despotism') was impractical, and the people on the contrary 'employed on fleets and a maritime force', a circumstance favourable to liberty, as in Holland, Venice and Athens:

> Thriving and independent nations were accordingly scattered on the banks of the Pacific and Atlantic oceans; they surrounded the Red-sea, the Mediterranean, and the Baltic; whilst (a few tribes excepted, who retire among mountains bordering on India and Persia, or who have found some rude establishment among the creeks and shores of the Caspian and Euxine seas) there is scarcely a people in the vast continent of Asia that deserves the name of nation.[78]

This last passage Falconer lifted without acknowledgement from Adam Ferguson's *An Essay on the History of Civil Society*, first published in 1767. Its context lay in the revival of an ancient maritime orientalism, and anti-continentalism, by means of which Athens had once distinguished itself from Sparta (and claimed credit for defeating Persia).[79] The purpose now was to appropriate for Western Europe what Athens had seen in itself: cultural superiority based on a geographic and cultural relationship to the sea. Quoting Xenophon to the effect that had Athens been an island it might have kept its liberty and power indefinitely, Falconer added: 'One would imagine, says Mr. Montesquieu, that Xenophon was speaking of England.'[80]

For another Scots proponent of maritime orientalism, James Dunbar, empire and civilization ('refinement and the liberal arts') were 'repugnant' to one another.[81] To be imperial was to be continental; and to be continental was to be uncivilized and unfree. In the ancient Near East, the Arabic and Ottoman Middle East, and Tartary, the open spaces of Asia had set the scene for despotism:

> The voice of liberty will be heard no more ... The monarch of a great empire sits secure upon the throne, and sets at defiance the murmuring of the people ... Such consequences then may be traced to a geographical source ... The torrent which covered the plains rolls on with increasing violence, and the best fenced territories are no longer able to resist its progress. Nations ... whose frontiers seem little exposed to external annoyance, may have these advantages more than balanced by a dangerous vicinity to a growing empire.[82]

For their cultural achievements civilized nations could thank their limited territorial scope. 'Happy, in this respect, were the governments of antient Greece. Happy, on a larger scale, the governments of modern Europe.'[83] Thus Dunbar agreed with Ferguson and Gibbon that 'The division of Europe into a number of independent states ... is productive of the most beneficial consequences to the liberty of mankind.'[84] As late as 1968 this Enlightenment anti-continentalism found brilliant expression in the response of Hugh Trevor-Roper to the Soviet crushing of the Prague Spring:

> I hate the thought of being driven back into the mindless postures of the Cold War. Like Jacob Burckhardt, if I must die in the ditch, it will be for

the civilisation of old Europe, with its complexities, its hierarchies, its rich and varied cuisine, its wines; not for either of those two vast blank, faceless, uniform continents, with their insipid viands and deplorable beverages.[85]

In the end its vast empire had destroyed Rome's liberty, its political culture, and finally its power. From this perspective Europe's discovery of America posed a grave danger. 'Instead of augmenting their territorial possessions at home . . . [the powers] began, from that aera, to form distant establishments by conquest or colonization, and to erect, in another hemisphere, a new species of empire.'[86] Colonies were 'regarded in the light of subordinate provinces, as appendages to government', when in fact the 'relation of a colony to the antient country, rightly understood, is a relation of perfect equality . . . The one country is no more the mother, than it is the daughter. They are both the children of the same political parent, and that parent is the government to which they owe equal allegiance.'[87]

In such colonies 'Jealousies ripen into disaffection. Political independency figures in the imagination, and is aspired after as an elevation of rank.' Moreover, 'The geographical divisions of the American continent are certainly auspicious to civil liberty; and seem to oppose the establishment of such extended governments as have proved, in the antient hemisphere, a source of the most destructive and debasing servitude.' In any case, 'to recall American allegiance by the power of our arms, if not an impracticable, is certainly a most hazardous attempt'.[88]

Thus the British-American crisis became a context within which to understand the continued passage of liberty West. Nor did it disturb the deeper cultural ties underpinning the Industrial Revolution, as we will see.

CHAPTER FIFTEEN

AN EMPIRE OF CUSTOMERS

A great empire has been established for the sole purpose of raising up a nation of customers who should be obliged to buy from the shops of our different producers, all the goods with which these could supply them. For the sake of that little enhancement of price which this monopoly might afford our producers, the home consumers have been burdened with the whole expense of maintaining and defending that empire.

Adam Smith, *The Wealth of Nations* (1776)[1]

REVOLUTION AND EMPIRE, REVISITED

The Navigation Acts of 1651, 1660 and 1689 regulated England's trade with its plantations and possessions all over the world, in Africa and Asia as well as America. They extended to this global system the obligation to use English or local shipping that had hitherto applied to the internal English coastal trade. One immediate effect was to exclude from this English-speaking world of trade the Dutch carriers whose number and cost-efficiency had previously secured their dominance, not only in American but even in English ports. Another was to provide a boost for English domestic and eventually colonial shipbuilding and maritime trades. Accompanied by a dramatic augmentation of naval power, this transformed the scale and profitability of English trade over the following century and a half.

At its inception this system was shaped by the determination of English republicans and their merchant allies to eclipse the Dutch by emulating the means of their success. More broadly, until the late seventeenth century the nature of English global trade was a recognizable variant upon that of its European rivals. It was dominated by colonial and other imports: tobacco, sugar, textiles, furs, timber, spices, coffee and tea, both for domestic consumption and re-export. Assisted by the boom in imports after 1660, Britain exported grain, coal, textiles and other manufactured goods, and it played a major role in the Atlantic slave trade.

It was in the mid-eighteenth century that the value of British exports entered an unprecedented period of expansion. One factor facilitating this was a relative abundance of raw materials and of energy. Thus one reason the Industrial Revolution occurred in Britain had to do with access by British merchants and manufacturers to coal, iron, tin, flax, wood and wool as well as sugar, tobacco and eventually cotton. But the other and more decisive factor concerned the size and growth of the markets, especially imperial markets, for British exports. As the most dynamic such market North America is the focus of the present chapter. But in relation to the development of the economy as a whole, this should not be prematurely abstracted from its broader relationship to the empire.

When the first water mills were built in Lancashire and Derbyshire they adapted Indian technology to weave cotton imported from the Caribbean and the American South. They derived part of their incentive to innovate, harnessing new sources of energy to newly developed machinery, from global competition with India, where the cotton industry was larger and labour costs much lower. Accordingly British textile imports from India had been restricted by Parliament since the 1720s. The capital to build these factories had been accumulated by participation in global trade, and the other incentive to innovate derived from the relatively secure profits to be made in the protected cloth markets of North America. Although the core processes driving the economic changes under examination here were Anglo-Dutch-American, the Industrial Revolution was more broadly enabled by the global infrastructure which bound together the eighteenth-century British imperial economy and equipped the state to defend it militarily.[2] One recent study has correctly underlined 'the central place of an aggressive and interventionist state'.[3] More broadly, 'The early modern Atlantic was . . . nested within a globalizing world.'[4]

Exports to the West Indies included slaves, of whom British merchants became the largest carriers during the eighteenth century, transporting approximately three million between 1660 and 1807.[5] Slaves were purchased in Africa with manufactured goods, including between 150,000 and 200,000 guns per year.[6] It has been argued that the capital accumulation from slavery explains the Industrial Revolution in Britain, and the country's emergence as the world's leading economic power. Yet other European powers also sold and owned slaves for centuries. The British slave trade was part of a larger and more unusual commercial and imperial picture. Certainly the slave trade was a vital link in the chains both of British Atlantic trade and of British global power.[7] But these were necessary rather than sufficient preconditions of the first Industrial Revolution. In asking why this occurred in Britain we need to pay attention to what was unique about Britain's colonies and their economic relationship to the home country.

Between the first and second halves of the eighteenth century, European markets for British manufactures were overtaken in importance by imperial ones. During the second quarter of the century, when the value of exports to Europe was almost flat, that of those to the East Indies multiplied by six, those to the West Indies more than doubled, and those to the continental North American colonies almost quadrupled.[8] 'Between 1700 and 1773 official exports from England to British America rose six-fold in value . . . [to exceed] sales to Europe.'[9] By 1800, as we have seen, the North American market accounted for 57 per cent of all exported British manufactures. Over the same period London was joined by increasingly dynamic ports on the Atlantic coast, in particular Bristol, Liverpool and Glasgow:[10]

> The main development in English trade in the eighteenth century was the expansion of trade with America. In 1700 the American colonies had only 300,000 inhabitants, by 1776 nearly three million. Colonial purchasing power . . . increased fivefold and American purchases from England grew even faster . . . Colonial imports were of immense variety and served almost all the needs of the colonial population . . . Woollen cloth found a big colonial market after mid-century, so that . . . English woollen exports began to rise again after remaining stationary for over sixty years.[11]

This rapidly developing export economy involved an increasingly specialized relationship between manufacturers, merchants and their local agents. The core manufactured product for export (as for domestic consumption) remained textiles, within which sector cotton competed increasingly with wool, accompanied by silk and linen, the latter a manufacturing speciality of Scotland. This was not only clothing. 'Enhanced levels of domestic comfort raised demand for bed and table linen, window and door curtains, floor and table rugs, while traders and agriculturalists depended on sails, sacks, and strainers all made of fabric':[12]

> Overall, England's textile exports and re-exports (of which more than three-quarters of the cottons and some of the silks were Asian) grew less than twofold between 1699-1701 and 1772-4 – but they rose more than sixfold to the Americas and West Africa . . . [British] Exports and re-exports of cottons and calicoes more than quadrupled, of woollens and linens more than sextupled, of silks jumped nearly sevenfold.[13]

From the middle of the eighteenth century this growth of the colonial export sector distinguished the mercantile activity of Britain from that of other European powers.

THE ANGLO-AMERICAN CULTURE OF CONSUMPTION

In 1750, while the military contest for territory was fierce, there was no comparison demographically between French and British North America. One was an empire for access to North American commodities, especially furs; the other was 'based on farming settlement and transatlantic commerce'. '[W]heras . . . the whole French population of North America amounted to about fifty-five thousand, the white colonists of the British mainland provinces numbered at least 1.1 million, and owned an additional quarter-million enslaved African Americans.' To the disgust of Monsieur Trepagny in Annie Proulx's novel *Barkskins,* 'The English send thousands to their colonies but France cannot be bothered.'[14] Still more important than this 'numerical advantage of twenty to one over their rival' was the dynamic growth of the British colonies: in the early eighteenth century, 'a rate of growth sufficient to double their population every twenty-six years'.[15] When in 1751 Benjamin Franklin exulted that even without further migration the population of North America would 'in another Century be more than the people of England', he under-stated the case. The rate of increase in British North America was four times that in Britain.[16]

Between 1520 and 1640 a doubling of the population of England and Wales had put that society under extraordinary pressure. It had resulted in a fivefold increase in prices; it provided a key impulse behind the emigration to America begun in 1607; it contributed to the religious and political explosion of 1638–51. It took a pre-industrial agricultural society to the limit of its resources, above all of land and food. Mid-eighteenth-century British America, too, was a pre-industrial agricultural society, though an unusually prosperous one. Thus this rate of population increase could only be sustained by territorial expansion.

That meant expansion west. The fastest-growing colony was Pennsylvania, the population of which was increasing by 150 per cent per decade. 'There was, inevitably, a price to be paid for so much growth. The colony's white farmers, with their large families and burgeoning livestock herds, needed space to expand, and hence ever more Indian land.'[17] It was this dynamic which helped to provoke the Seven Years War, or French and Indian War (1747–54), not only with native Americans but with France as expansion over the Appalachians into the Ohio river valley threatened the links between French colonies in Canada and the lower Mississippi.

It was this war, in turn, which transformed both the territorial scale of British America and the established means of governing it in ways which would provoke colonial rebellion against Britain. The same unprecedented demographic expansion drove the growth of Britain's protected market for exports. Within this context, the Industrial Revolution constituted the third in a three-hundred year-long sequence of Anglo-Dutch-American demand-driven innovations. For the first, the Dutch bulk trade in grain (and alongside it the fishery), market stimulus had come from the exceptionally urbanized Netherlands, and then from the large cities of the Mediterranean. The second, England's seventeenth-century importation of the Dutch-pioneered agricultural revolution, accompanied by expansion of its commercial economy, was driven by the extraordinary tenfold growth of London. In this third case the explosive demand in question was not for food, but for manufactured produce.

America produced its own food. What it could not supply on the scale, of the quality, or at the price available from British merchants, was a rich array of manufactured produce. This was no accident. Essential components of Britain's mercantilist system were the 'pieces of legislation . . . intended to restrict the level of manufacturing so that the colonies did not compete directly with manufactured goods supplied by the mother country'.[18] By the middle of the eighteenth century the basis of British power in North America was a massive trans-Atlantic military system funded by the British government in exchange for the profits from this monopoly trade. Thus for Adam Smith the growth and prosperity of the North American colonies had two causes: 'Plenty of good land, and liberty to manage their own affairs their own way.' To this liberty, however, there was one important exception:

> In everything except their foreign trade the liberty of the English colonists is complete. It is in every respect equal to that of their fellow-citizens at home, and is secured in the same manner, by an assembly of the repre-sentatives of the people . . . The government of the English colonies is perhaps the only one which, since the world began, could give perfect secu-rity to the inhabitants of so very distant a province.[19]

'Perfect security' was a considerable exaggeration, particularly on the Western frontier. Yet it was a formidable system, driven by constantly increasing American demand. Furniture, kitchen utensils, clothes, farm tools, firearms, tea, liquor and books were not essentials in the same way as food. Yet for such items eighteenth-century America was becoming part (with Britain, and urban Western Europe) of the first cheap mass market in world history.[20] This had a lot to do with the kind of society British America was.

Beyond population growth two other factors made the North American market exceptionally dynamic. The first was a certain, not high but wide-spread, level of prosperity above subsistence. According to Jack P. Greene, the things that contemporaries thought 'distinguished the societies of colonial British America from those of the Old World' were:

> comparative religious and ethnic diversity . . . extraordinary demographic and economic growth after 1715 . . . the presence of racial slavery . . . [and] most distinctive and most significant . . . the remarkably wide distribution of property among free people. A much higher proportion of the free colo-

nial population owned real property than was the case in England or in any other Old World society.[21]

Bas van Bavel observes:

> The English settlers were obsessed with acquiring their own land, prefer-
> ably by way of ownership of a family-sized farm. It was the ideal of many
> to become an independent yeoman, an ideal . . . imported from Britain,
> where this status had become much harder to realize . . . in New England
> and other parts of the north, freeholding . . . became widespread . . . Also,
> income inequality in the colonies was much lower . . . [with] the richest 1
> per cent of households only having 7 per cent of total income, colonial
> America in 1774 was the most equal society in the documented parts of the
> eighteenth-century world.[22]

Thus British Americans had the numbers, the growth in numbers, and the means to help spark a manufacturing revolution. But it was even more important that they had the inclination. For the purchase of manufactures is an event in the history of culture (the culture of consumption). Britain's North American colonies had been distinct in European terms as primarily cultural foundations. By the middle of the eighteenth century, notes Trevor Burnard, there was 'considerable and growing ethnic and religious diversity, especially in the Middle Colonies of New York, New Jersey, and Pennsylvannia'. Yet these nevertheless shared some dominant characteristics which derived from the mode of plantation peculiar to the seventeenth-century English empire, and initially focused upon Ireland:

> [W]hat impresses most about this period of remarkable and sustained growth
> in all areas is the degree to which these diverse societies developed along
> similar lines and converged culturally. One means by which this convergence
> was achieved was through the expansion of the world of goods and the devel-
> opment of a commercial culture based on the extensive importation of
> consumer goods from Britain that gave a stylistic uniformity to British
> American culture. Just as important was the rise to authority in every colony
> of creole elites . . . anxious to show their credentials as English gentlemen.[23]

British America was a cultural community, and in addition to its agricultural, religious and political components, this culture was shaped by trans-Atlantic consumption.[24] 'Throughout Pennsylvania,' claimed one visitor surprisingly, men's clothing 'is very costly, among the farmers as well as among persons of rank; they all wear garments of fine English cloth or other materials, also fine shirts. Every one wears a wig, the peasant as well as the gentleman.'[25] It was an effect of the climate that in temperate North America 'dress regimes . . . were less syncretic and more oriented to European norms than those found in warmer areas'.[26] All of this occurred within a no less homogeneous ideological and institutional framework:

> Not counting Newfoundland, which remained a fishing settlement without regular participatory government, the British empire, on the eve of the American War for Independence, had twenty-nine colonies in America, eleven in the islands, and eighteen on the continent, only one of which, Quebec, was not a regular British-style polity with representative institutions. This proliferation of polities represented an astonishing spread of English common-law culture and modes of representative government across the Irish Sea and the Atlantic and provided abundant evidence of their adaptability to radically different physical, social and economic contexts.[27]

When it came, the American War of Independence was fought (like the Dutch before it) in defence of a cultural, including political and social, identity. Most white English-speaking Americans considered themselves respectable, independent and free, which is to say governed by laws rather than men. They also identified as English (or less commonly British) with a sensitivity perhaps peculiar to Americans, hence the revolution against an imperial parliament which seemed to have decided that they could be treated as slaves. At the same time, Adam Smith observed, 'There is more equality . . . among the English colonists than among the inhabitants of the mother country. Their manners are more republican, and their governments.'[28]

Thus British exports to English-speaking America boomed partly because it was populous, and that population was expanding faster than any other in the world. It was prosperous, with that prosperity uniquely widely spread.

Exports were also booming because the cultural identity of this market made English imports not only most acceptable, but to some extent essential. The English in America had not gone there to become American (though that eventually happened) but to achieve a distillation of Englishness, Protestantism, and proximity to roast beef (or bison) which could not have been achieved in any other way.[29] Even without these factors the Navigation Acts made this a captive market. But by excluding other Europeans for a century and a half this system had also reinforced English American colonial identity. Thus by 1780 this relationship between supply and demand had become sufficiently robust to survive independence.

THE BRITISH CULTURE OF SUPPLY

These were the factors which made North America the fastest-growing, and by 1800 the most important, market for British manufactures. This requires us to consider not only the American culture of consumption, but its impact upon the British culture of supply. As American consumer demand shaped British manufacturing, so manufacturers and merchants 'both fed and shaped consumer demand in the colonies'.[30] Thus John Smail's study of the woollen textile trade 'ask[ed] not only what merchants, manufacturers . . . and consumers were doing, but how they thought about what they were doing, and . . . argues that the crucial changes which brought about industrialisation were cultural rather than narrowly technical or organisational'.[31]

Smail stressed 'the contributions of the export trade and of product innovation to the growth of the eighteenth century economy'. This 'demand for particular kinds of products, in relatively large quantities, to be supplied on a tight deadline . . . contributed to industrialization by influencing the ways in which producers and merchants went about their business'.[32] What must be appreciated is 'the impact which the *quality* of foreign demand, rather than [just] its quantity, had on the pace of economic growth in this period'. The transformation of the English woollen textile industry during the early Industrial Revolution is 'best characterised as an intensification of economic effort'. Alongside technological innovation – machines, water, steam, factories – 'intensification of economic effort . . . involved many smaller, demand-induced, innovations'. These were developments *within* the economic environment which amounted to a qualitative transformation.[33] Driving this intensification was the 'interplay between the mode of production and the mode of marketing', and this under-pinned the Industrial Revolution more generally.[34] Within the American export trade

> rapid growth in the range of products required more complex and more adaptable modes of marketing to pass information about these new prod-ucts between producer and consumer. Product innovation also required more complex and more adaptable modes of production to invent, adapt and then make these new kinds of cloth . . . In a way which was not true of the domestic trade, shipping cloth to foreign markets required much closer links between producer and consumer and more flexible and adaptive production systems because merchants had to secure the particular assort-ment of cloth they needed for the many different regional markets they served.[35]

This was in addition to assigning the 'correct assortment of cloth – type, colour, quality, finish' to the right location, reliably and quickly, while attending to 'regularity of shipping, the cost of insurance, the reliability of remittances'. In general the early Industrial Revolution was not about 'mass production of a standardised product'. Rather it was about scale, speed, flexibility and adapta-tion in response to a large, regionalized, evolving and lucrative captive market. Technological invention did not arise in a vacuum. Rather, in England, as earlier in Holland, it emerged as a process in response to new and specific opportunities as long as they lasted. This is to say that it came to constitute a *culture* of invention standing at the heart of a broader revolution which was also cultural and which depended upon opportunity, flexibility and develop-ment. This was a matter, first, of modes of thought, information and commu-nication. Within the British Atlantic trading system

> [a] single act, such as the exchange of East Indian cloth for West African slaves, required years of preparation and coordination in the markets of India, England, Holland, France, Africa, and the Americas . . . A merchant's expanded commitments required him . . . to communicate with other merchants . . . around the globe. And they forced him to improve and raise

the level of commercial communication – not only to keep in touch with the collection and distribution networks of existing peripheral areas but also to penetrate those of new ones as he had never done before.[36]

The Industrial Revolution was made possible by multiple and complex contexts evolving over three hundred years. But as its most dynamic catalyst the British American market uniquely combined the logistical demands of long-distance international trade (mitigated by the imperial monopoly) with the opportunities not only of the scale of that market but of communication across what remained a shared if evolving cultural and linguistic space. Even after the demise of the Navigation Acts, British merchants 'had the advantage of very strong commercial networks, a common language, culture and legal system which provided a strong edge in these markets, as the French found to their disappointment after the American Revolution'.[37]

For Jan de Vries, 'trying to disentangle the relations between demand and supply . . . The Industrial Revolution, with its technology-driven, hence supply-driven, economic growth, long stood as a formidable barrier to any effort to search for economic growth based on any other factors or in any earlier period.'[38] But the fact that the Industrial Revolution was enabled by new technology did not make it 'supply-driven'. To the contrary, economic, including technological innovation was stimulated and made possible by explosive demand. Discussing cotton, the fastest-growing sector, which employed 340,000 people by 1795, Sven Beckert remarked: 'the true boom . . . was . . . an export boom'.[39] The larger apparatus of Britain's empire facilitated the appropriation of Indian technology, a ban on the subsequent import of Indian calicos, and a supply of American cotton. But the sequence of innovations which revolutionized production was motivated and funded by the profits to be made serving 'British trade networks and the institutions in which they were embedded – from a strong navy creating and protecting market access to bills of lading allowing for the transfer of capital over large distances':[40]

It was the indisputable rise in total demand in the course of the eighteenth century that created the 'bottlenecks' . . . in manufacture that encouraged the well-known experiments in new methods in both metallurgy and spinning. Just as British market demand helped create the plantation economies of the West Indies and the . . . south . . . so did overseas demand make necessary . . . the technological transformation of several long-established branches of British industrial life.[41]

THE AMERICAN REVOLUTION, REVISITED

For all of these reasons:

> It is difficult to overestimate the economic importance of the American colonies to the British Empire on the eve of the Revolution . . . more than forty percent of exports of British-made goods went to the colonies. Forty-seven of the rising industrial towns were largely involved in producing goods for the rapidly expanding American market. As America demanded goods especially adapted to local conditions, entire districts were engaged solely in supplying that market . . . When orders from America for British manufactures ceased, thousands of labourers and skilled workers . . . were thrown on the poor rates and thus increased the already heavy land taxes which the landed gentry had to pay.[42]

By 1764 the expansion of the colonies, and the cost of defending them, had outgrown the capacity of existing fiscal structures to cope. By its end the Seven Years War – a conflict fought around the world – was costing 20 million pounds a year. One response was a body of colonial legislation of which the most notorious component became the Stamp Act imposing duties on legal transactions, newspapers and dice. Until this time the colonists had enjoyed an exemption from the payment of tax to the mother country in exchange for compliance with the commercial and navigation system of such profitability to British merchants and manufacturers.

They responded with outrage and by organizing an embargo on the importation of British goods. This spooked the British Parliament, which repealed the Act in 1765. The following year, however, it approved the Townshend duties which imposed a tax on imports from Britain of glass, lead, paint, paper and tea. 'The duties were cunningly devised to meet American objections. Benjamin Franklin had given the Commons the impression, during his influential testimony against the Stamp Act, that the colonies would not oppose taxes which arose from the regulation of trade, only those directly levied on American property. Though their plain intention was revenue, Townshend's duties could be presented as commercial regulations.'[43]

This was a distinction reiterated in Parliament by William Pitt, who had as 'friend to America' led opposition to the Stamp Act:

> As an *Englishman*, I recognise to the American their supreme unalterable right to property. As an *American*, I would equally recognize to England, her supreme right of regulating commerce and navigation . . . property is private, individual, absolute; the touch of another annihilates it. Trade is an extended and complicated consideration; it reaches as far as ships can sail, or winds can blow . . . To regulate the numberless movements of its several parts . . . requires the superintending wisdom and energy of the supreme power of the empire.
>
> On this grand practical distinction, then, let us rest; taxation is theirs, commercial regulation is ours.[44]

In fact property was either private or public, as in the case of the tax-derived wherewithal of the state. But this high-flying rhetorical baloney articulated the basis upon which Britain's American empire had long been governed. The colonies taxed themselves and were not subject to British tax, in exchange for which their imports and exports remained subject to the Navigation laws, which were a source of such prosperity that they functioned as a substitute for direct taxation. However, this arrangement could no longer meet the cost of contemporary global war. The colonists were not fooled by an attempt to disguise new taxes as commercial regulation. In 1768 British Customs Commissioners in Boston were confronted by a mob, and then in Boston, New York and Philadelphia a non-importation campaign resumed.[45] In May 1769 the British Cabinet agreed to rescind all the Townshend duties except one – that on tea, in order to defend the principle of Parliament's right to tax.

When war came in 1775 it was supported by many Britons because 'For merchants . . . there was a real fear that America would end by throwing off parliamentary regulation of trade along with parliamentary taxation. It was widely assumed that the Navigation Acts were the basis of British prosperity.'[46] '[I]f you give up this tax it is not here that you must stop, you will be required to give up much more'; 'Would not the Americans be encouraged to insist on a repeal of the Act of Navigation, the principal source of the wealth, power and glory of England?'[47] This was a claim explicitly denied by Franklin:

> It has been said that we refuse to submit to the restrictions on our commerce. From whence is this inference drawn? Not from our words, we having repeatedly declared the contrary, and we again profess our submission to the several acts of trade and navigation passed before the year 1763 . . . And we cheerfully consent to . . . the regulation of our external commerce for the purpose of securing the commercial advantages of the whole empire to the Mother-country . . . excluding every idea of taxation internal or external, for raising a revenue on the subjects of America without their consent.[48]

Indeed, 'The protectionist mercantile system was largely accepted by colonists in north America and the West Indies' because of 'the benefits that . . . [it]brought to colonial living standards and economic development'.[49] The Patriots therefore opposed new taxes in favour of adherence to the traditional arrangement. The British defended the principle of new taxation partly in case a display of weakness opened the empire to the dismantling of the Navigation system as well.

Meanwhile, the principle upon which both parties to this conflict agreed was that Britain, including its empire, was free. In this respect the cultural identity for which the colonists were fighting had its origin in the empire's seventeenth-century founding, a point made by Edmund Burke. "Three thousand miles of ocean lie between you and them . . . Seas roll, and months pass . . . [T]he people of the colonies . . . are descendants of Englishmen. England, Sir, is a nation, which still I hope respects, and formerly adored, her freedom. The colonists emigrated from you when this part of your character was most predominant.'[50] In the event, just as the Navigation system had not been particularly controversial in the Americas, so the economic relationship which it had created emerged from the conflict intact. Once French and Spanish entry into the war forced Britain to accept American independence the terms it agreed in Paris in 1783 were relatively generous in the hope of 'an era of renewed Anglo-American co-operation based on commercial collaboration'.[51]

'When expansion resumed in the mid-1780s it took place on the basis of the new British manufactures.'[52]

It was in Britain that the system had been opposed, by free traders like Adam Smith who lamented its distortion of the national economy solely around the interests of exporters. 'It cannot be very difficult to determine who have been the connivers of this whole mercantile system; not the consumers, we may believe, whose interest has been entirely neglected; but the producers, whose interest has been so carefully attended to; and among this latter class our merchants and manufacturers have been by far the principal architects.'[53] One of Smith's primary concerns was the prohibitive military cost of maintaining this arrangement:

> A great empire has been established for the sole purpose of raising up a nation of customers who should be obliged to buy from the shops of our different producers, all the goods with which these could supply them. For the sake of that little enhancement of price which this monopoly might afford our producers, the home consumers have been burdened with the whole expense of maintaining and defending that empire.[54]

By 1789 the 'whole expense' of war between the world's two superpowers had undone not only Britain's control of the Thirteen Colonies but the ancient monarchy of France. Yet what Smith didn't acknowledge was the profound historical impact of what he so slightingly termed 'that little enhancement of price which this monopoly might afford our producers'. Around the Navigation system had grown a post-agricultural (manufacturing and mercantile) economy in Britain, modelled on that of the Dutch; a uniquely dynamic and prosperous colonial society in North America, which had no model and was to some extent an ecologically and climatologically assisted accident; and from this combination would emerge the American Revolution on one side of the Atlantic and the Industrial Revolution on the other.

Smith did not know that exponential industrial growth was possible. He expected British industrialization to encounter its ceiling and then flatten, as had happened in the Netherlands. He could not have predicted the new alchemy unleashed between 1780 and 1850 by a combination of global markets, state protection and military domination, technological innovation, and the lifting of previous limits upon available sources of energy and land. This process was not interrupted by American independence and it happened in the United Kingdom, rather than in the United Provinces or France, partly because it was supported by rapid population growth within a long-standing, navally patrolled, English-speaking empire of customers.

***

In the words of one French observer: 'England has only arrived at the summit of prosperity by persisting for centuries in the system of protection and prohibition.'[55] A recent study concurs:

> British industrial divergence was not the product of a new science of the enlightenment or any peculiarly British proclivities, skills or knowledge that produced innovative and productive superiority . . . Instead it developed out of a long era of . . . state protectionism and regulation, war, colonization and labour exploitation . . . the state was crucial to the Industrial Revolution.[56]

The American War of Independence had called forth the greatest military effort in British history and defeat was shattering. 'The collapse of Britain's international position after 1763 was shocking to contemporaries.' But 'the long-term strategic consequences were much more ambiguous. To be sure, Britain lost a continent, but the feared commercial decline did not take place. Indeed British exports to and imports from America massively *increased* after Independence . . . By contrast, France, resurgent in 1783, soon fell into a terminal decline.'[57]

In fact, having lost, in thirteen colonies, much less than a continent, Britain stood on the threshold of more than a century of global domination.

CHAPTER SIXTEEN

———◆———

CULTURES OF INVENTION

He [Blake] was the first Man that declined the old Track . . . and despised those Rules which had been long in Practice, to keep his Ship and his Men out of Danger . . . as if the principal Art requisite in the Captain . . . had been . . . to come home safe again . . . He was the first that infused that Proportion of Courage into Seamen, by making them see by Experience, what mighty Things they could do, if they were resolved . . . he was the first that gave the Example of that kind of Naval Courage, and bold and resolute Atchievements.

Reasons for Giving Encouragement To The Sea-Faring People of Great Britain (1737)[1]

GEOGRAPHY AND CULTURE

This final chapter revisits the most important general question underlying this study. In a pre-modern society, before the old world ended, what made fundamental change possible? The answer given so far has been multifaceted, involving water, people, events, ideas and commodities: an early modern society in motion, and that motion discernible, in retrospect, as what might be called a process of cultural invention. But what sustained that process over centuries, territories and oceans?

There could have been no Industrial Revolution without the doubling of agricultural output per head which occurred in Britain between 1600 and 1800, 'a necessary, though not a sufficient cause of the complex of changes which gave birth to the modern world'.[2] Only that permitted the improved prosperity and broader diversification of the economy into services, trade and manufactures. In this respect '[t]he great bulk of the advance made [in Britain] relative to continental countries before 1800 was due to much the same causes as had earlier allowed a much smaller country to achieve a brilliant period of commercial and economic dominance and a notable degree of naval and military success'.[3] However, the Anglo-Dutch relationship was not merely one of imitation, but was creative and ultimately transformative. England's agricultural improvers applied Dutch methods within a rural environment characterized by less occupational differentiation than in the north-western Dutch provinces, to larger landholdings predominantly worked by copy or leaseholders. To new crops, methods of rotation, intensive plant nutrition, changes in land use, and the interrelationship of livestock, cereal and vegetables, they added inventions like the seed drill. Nor was this transformation, which would establish a global presence in Britain's colonies, simply Dutch or English. In several European countries agricultural improvement drew upon global and imperial experimentation and exchange.[4] In revolutionary England the campaign was led by three Protestant migrants from Prussia and Bohemia: Samuel Hartlib, John Dury and Johann Amos Comenius.[5]

The first finding of this book has been that the source of Anglo-Dutch-American early modernity – of that particular Danube – lay in the Dutch water world.[6] For thousands of years cities had imported grain. During the Peloponnesian War, Athens made the fatal mistake of invading Sicily partly to secure its grain supply. But there is no example before the sixteenth century of a national or regional agricultural sector enabled to serve a large and lucrative urban market by entire liberation from the rigidities of grain production. In this sense the Baltic grain trade, or Dutch 'mother trade', anchored the entire Anglo-Dutch-American process. It was one outgrowth of a North Sea economy alternative, not only to traditional agriculture, but to the Mediterranean rich trades. In addition to facilitating a transformation of agriculture this created in Amsterdam a new, post-Italian, mercantile culture and technological infrastructure, based upon the passage of bulk goods (grain, wood, fish, salt). To this were added the resources and networks brought by merchants and manufacturers from Antwerp. The result was commercial empire on a new scale, inhabiting a water world linking Amsterdam to goods and markets 'in the White Sea and the Russian Empire, Italy, North Africa and the Levant, West Africa, South America, the Caribbean and . . . North America, and the Indonesian Archipelago, India and East Asia'.[7]

The resulting wealth furnished a spectacular urban society with books, paintings, shops, and accommodation for its economic and political institutions. From the 1590s Amsterdam grew, employing strict geometric principles copied from Antwerp.[8] New buildings included the Amsterdam Stock Exchange (built 1608–11), the municipal Exchange Bank (1609) and the Grain Exchange (1617).[9] To such financial institutions, which had originated in Italy, Holland added a state-wide waterborne transport network, and a vigorous, commercially competitive Protestant print culture. Amid the material splendour the most important invention was moral, a product of the difference between rich and bulk trades, and therefore more broadly between the Mediterranean and Baltic. By comparison with Venice and Florence the United Provinces was a relatively meritocratic state ruled by commoners rather than nobles, and manifesting a high degree of equality; 'a society in which the horizontal ties of power sharing were more important than vertical ties leading to monopolization of power . . . in which the dominant form of communication . . . was not command but negotiation'.[10]

Enabling the North Sea fishery William Monson identified one invention in 'ye year 1307 to their un measurable wealth + our shame, and for ye Honor of him that first found out the secret of Pickleing of Herrings, wch was one Wm Backalew'.[11] Others followed, including the herring *busse*, the grain carrying *fluit*, and all the attendant processes developed on ship and shore. All depended upon social changes deriving from the agricultural challenges and environmentally imposed obligations of life in the rural North-West. In Holland

> a transition had occurred from agrarian farming to stock-breeding, while diking and poldering . . . made possible . . . the vast reclamation of the fens. [This] . . . resulted in the emergence of an independent peasantry free from feudal obligations and free to settle wherever they liked. Many people freed from the land began to earn a living in shipping and trade, particularly the grain trade.[12]

The resulting culture of invention developed in response both to opportunity and necessity. One aspect of the opportunity for the bulk trades lay in established

Hanse markets for Dutch herring, salt and textiles which could be exchanged for grain (and timber). The most important was a market for grain underpinned by a level of urbanization unprecedented in any pre-industrial agricultural economy. In 1477 the population of Flanders was 64 per cent rural/36 per cent urban; of Brabant 69 per cent/31 per cent; and of Holland 55 per cent/45 per cent.[13] The third component of opportunity was the potential for bulk transport furnished by the Dutch water world. 'It was . . . Holland's urbanization . . . and . . . the high degree of interconnectedness of the cities that distinguished the coastal provinces most clearly from other maritime trading areas of western Europe.'[14] Assisting all was regional location. Unlike the Hanse to the north and French to the south, Dutch shippers could complete three round trips in a year, transporting wine and salt from Brittany to the Baltic, grain and textiles to the Mediterranean, and then luxury products back home. Unlike the Hanse on the one hand, and Venice on the other, the Dutch economy combined bulk and rich trades in interdependence.[15]

On the side of necessity, meanwhile, stood the agricultural poverty of the north relative to Brabant and Flanders, the richest agricultural as well as urban economy in Europe. Faced with the challenges of deteriorating land hard up against the sea many northerners turned for a livelihood to the sea itself. Amsterdam's grain trade initially outgrew that of regional rivals by supplying, within Holland alone, Leiden, Haarlem, Dordrecht, Delft, Amsterdam, Gouda and Rotterdam. But the magnitude of growth – fivefold in sixty years – documented its rapid expansion beyond the Netherlands to the Mediterranean.

As in the case of the eighteenth-century British Atlantic export trade, to which this rate of increase is very comparable, such an expansion required development of these markets by a sensitive and adaptive culture of supply. While invention was stimulated by the presence of the market, the ability of suppliers to respond creatively was facilitated by the presence of some (Amsterdam, municipal) institutions, and the absence of others (inhibiting guild or federal regulations, whether Hanseatic or Habsburg). Within this context 'the inventiveness of the shipwrights of Holland stands behind much of Dutch commercial expansion in the sixteenth century . . . these largely anonymous innovators were spurred to their efforts by the vigorous growth in the demand for ships'.[16]

NATURE AND ART

In 1609 the Englishman Thomas Overbury put the Dutch economic achievement in historical and geographical context. By their domination of the Baltic then East Indies trades the republic now combined the previous roles of the Hanse towns and of Venice:

> There belong to that State twenty thousand vessels . . . all the commodities that this [northern] part of the world wants and the Indies have, as spice, silk, jewels and gold, they are become the conveyors of them for the rest of Christendom . . . as were the Venetians of old. And all those commodities that those northern countries abound with and these Southern stand in need of they like wise convey thither, which was the ancient trade of the Easterlings . . . And to this purpose the situation serves fitly; for the rivers of the Rhine, the Maese and the Schelde end all in their dominions and the Baltic sea lies not far from them; all which affords them whatever the great continent of Germany, Russia and Poland yields; then they . . . lying between Germany and the sea do furnish it back with all commodities foreign.[17]

Sixty-four years later William Temple reiterated the economic importance 'of those two great Rivers of the *Rhyne* and *Mose*, reaching up, and Navigable so mighty a length into so rich and populous Countreys of . . . *Germany*; which as it brings down all the Commodities from those parts to the Magazines in *Holland*, that vent them by their Shipping into all parts of the World where the Market calls for them'.[18] Yet as to regional location he added: 'For their commodious seat as to the Trade of the *Streights*, or *Baltique*, or any other parts of the Ocean, I see no advantage they have of most parts of *England*; and they must certainly yield to many we possess, if we had other equal circumstances to value them.'[19] Unlike England the Dutch had to contend with the 'Westerly-winds, which drive upon this Shore . . . much more constant and violent than the East'. By working against the silt distributed into the ocean by the rivers, these helped to account for the treacherous Dutch coastal waters, only made navigable by dredging. 'This I presume is . . . the natural reason of so many deep and commodious Havens found upon all the *English* side of the Channel, and so few (or indeed none) upon the *French* and *Dutch*: An advantage . . . given us by Nature, and never to be equal'd by any Art or Expence of our Neighbours.'[20]

Samuel Pepys' secretary Richard Gibson, reading Temple, agreed: 'the Winds blowing westerly for more than 3 quarters of the year makes all our Cape lands and Bayes, opposite to the French and Dutch= coast, good Roades for All our great Shipps to ride with Security any winter storme beyond any port of Flanders, France or Holland.'[21] The sea bottom in English harbours was superior for anchoring to the French; the Flemish and Dutch coast was too shallow for 'Great Shipps', and 'choak'd up with Quicksands . . . Their Ports alsoe are oft Frozen up 2 months or more in a yeare.'[22] These features of climate and geography were of course constant. What changed between 1609 and 1673 were the 'other circumstances' causing England to 'value' the maritime advantages it had.

In 1629 the total tonnage of English shipping was 115,000. In 1660 it was 200,000 and in 1686, after three Anglo-Dutch wars, 340,000.[23] Moreover, its nature was changing. Ships clearing London for North America in 1664 numbered 43, and in 1686, 114; and for the West Indies in 1664, 45, and in 1686, 133. In the same years the numbers for the Baltic were 22 and 65 and for Norway 26 and 111.[24] Dominating the latter between 1677 and 1687 were imports of timber, hemp, flax, pitch, tar, turpentine and rosin. Driving England's own newly thriving bulk trades was the importation of shipbuilding materials – in exchange for colonial commodities – in the kind of unarmed, lightly manned bulk carriers which had been the basis of Amsterdam's rise to greatness. During the 1670s and 1680s these materials were used not only to build ships, but to rebuild London after the Great Fire of 1666. To support this trade Dutch prizes were supplemented by the purchase of Dutch-built ships until bulk carriers were built, initially around Tyneside and Scarborough, and then in London.

Thus what counted was not unimproved nature, but its exploitation by art (meaning artifice). 'In thriving Arts long time had Holland grown,' wrote Dryden; 'Crouching at home, and cruel when abroad . . . Our king they courted, and our Merchants aw'd.'[25] The Dutch republic was a spectacular work of art erected in an otherwise intractable water world. 'Whereby it plainly appeareth,' wrote one Elizabethan commentator,

That as the Excessive Expence of the Low Countryes bestow'd on *Havens*, hath not Impoverish'd, but the clean contrary, greatly Enrich'd them by Incomparable Wealth and Treasure, with number of Rich, Fair and Populous Towns; So our Sparing Mind, or rather greedy Getting, Gaining and Enriching Land from your Majesty's *Havens* and Navigable Channels, hath utterly Destroy'd and Spoiled many good *Havens* by nature left us, and thereby wrought very Beggary, Misery and Desolation on these your Frontier Towns.[26]

Over the seventeenth century this situation changed. One stimulus was Dutch economic competition, experienced within the context of a broad confessional alliance. One result was the direct application of Dutch ingenuity to English needs, as in the drainage of the Fens. But what particularly drove the rise of English shipping, and the associated broader transformation of the economy, was the Anglo-Dutch revolution of 1649–1702. Guided, and goaded, by Dutch example the English republic ruthlessly modernized the state's political economy and transformed its military-fiscal power. In the process it created a maritime *culture* of imperial and global reach. This received its legislative direction from the Plantation, Navigation and Staple Acts (1649, 1651, 1660 and 1663). Another requirement was the elevation to primary status amid the strategic priorities of the state of mercantile and colonial interests simultaneously. Most important was a transformation in naval resources and power. Thus 'the abolition of the monarchy and advent of a republic . . . produced institutions vital for England's subsequent economic performance and the character of its political economy'.[27] This involved:

funding a standing navy as well as army, passing a Navigation Act, confiscating large parts of Ireland, conquering Scotland and Jamaica, and setting a precedent and a model for the effective protection of the country's commercial interests in Europe and across the oceans. The model remained in place after 1660 because it was in the interest of both the landed and the commercial elite that it should do so.[28]

In this context we may see the new English legislation and policies as a Dutch-style infrastructure of artifice. Yet the republic's aspirations also involved, and could only be achieved by, a revolution of culture (men and manners). The first intimation of this came with Van Tromp's naval clash with Blake on 13 May 1652. The English victory of 1652–4 sent an alarm across Europe and created an imperial military theatre which made the subsequent conflict of 1665–7 trans-Atlantic and global.[29] This had one basis in institutional reform of the Admiralty. But informing that was an ideological and moral commitment which also manifested itself in the conduct of men on ships:

> He [Blake] was the first Man that declined the old Track . . . and despised those Rules which had been long in Practice, to keep his Ship and his Men out of Danger . . . as if the principal Art requisite in the Captain . . . had been . . . to come home safe again . . . He was the first that infused that Proportion of Courage into Seamen, by making them see by Experience, what mighty Things they could do, if they were resolved . . . he was the first that gave the Example of that kind of Naval Courage, and bold and resolute Atchievements.[30]

In this Blake might have taken as his model Tromp himself, described by Algernon Sidney as 'the best captain at that day in the world'. A similar resolution had been demonstrated in 1637 by Tromp's total destruction of a Spanish fleet sheltering in the English Downs, ignoring Charles I's threat to protect them.[31] The republican policies that created an English naval superpower were comprehensively indebted to Dutch example. But they were also grounded in the novel 'Experience' of king-less government in England, which gave those involved an opportunity to see 'what mighty Things they could do'. The result set new standards in naval administration, shipbuilding and 'line-ahead' fighting tactics. Also, as in Amsterdam during the 1590s, though by very different means, it secured and established the basis of a new global economy and empire.

This was part of the broader attempt by English republicans to achieve a reformation of manners, applying the post-aristocratic values of industry, meritocracy and utility. Elements of a wider culture of improvement, agricultural, mercantile and intellectual, had been initiated during the Elizabethan and early Stuart periods.[32] But when, after 1649, and in particular 1653, the aristocracy returned to government, they did so on the basis that they were modern, useful and busy. '[O]ur own *Nobility*,' wrote Sprat in 1667, are now bred up, and live in a quite different fashion . . . they are ingag'd in freer rodes of *Education*: now the vast distance between them, and other orders of men is no more observ'd: now their *conversation* is large, and general: now the *World* is become more *active*, and *industrious*: now more of them have seen the use, and manners of men, and more apply themselves to *Trafic*, and business than ever.[33]

Accordingly the Royal Society, which was an attempt to institutionalize a culture of invention, rejected 'amplifications, digressions and swellings of style', aspiring to 'return . . . to . . . primitive purity, and shortness, when men deliver'd so many *things* . . . [as] *words* . . . a . . . naked, natural way of speaking . . . preferring the language of Artizans, Countrymen, and Merchants, before that, of Wits, or Scholars'.[34] Elsewhere the revolution re-oriented national policy away from the territorial and dynastic priorities of monarchy and towards the mercantile and maritime concerns of the city. It was within this context that London took its place among the North-Western European cities which were (in the words of David Hume) 'doubly free'.

In 1568 London had erected the Royal Exchange, its first building devoted exclusively to mercantile activity. An 'architectural copy of Antwerp's Nieuwe Beurs [completed 1531–2] . . . it was a material outgrowth of the shuttling of people, products and capital between these two northern European cities'.[35] Described in Stow's *Survey of London* (1698) as 'The Eye of London', the Exchange became a hub for the city's international, especially Dutch, commercial society. It was then the model for the new Bourse constructed in Amsterdam between 1607 and 1611. In Amsterdam

many stores for luxury products, such as booksellers and art dealers, were located there. Within a minute's walk of the Town Hall (which housed the famous Bank of Exchange) were the Bourse, the Corn Exchange, the Weigh-house, several market-places and a multitude of shipping connections. No more than five or ten minutes away one could meet renowned painters . . . get a drink at the Doelen (the inns of the militia . . .) go out shopping for maps or curiosities, visit the (public) theatre or look up some books in the public library.[36]

Drawing upon his personal experience Hugh Peter insisted in 1651 that London 'should be improved by broader streets, cleaned and paved, houses of brick and stone, plentiful almshouses and hospitals, a fire brigade, and a large Thames-side quay like that in Rotterdam'.[37] London's Royal Exchange was destroyed by the Great Fire of 1666. Attending Restoration festivities in 1660, Christiaan Huygens reported: 'I had little pleasure in my visit . . . The stink of the smoke is unbearable . . . the city poorly built, with narrow streets having no proper paving and nothing but hovels . . . There is little going on and nothing compared with . . . Paris.'[38]

This was hardly fair: in 1629 London had seventeen theatres, including 'the Swan, the Rose, the Globe, the Hope, the Red Bull . . . whereas Paris had only one'.[39] But John Evelyn also returned to Restoration London from Rome and Paris depressed by the architectural barbarity of the city. It 'is from the assymetry of our Buildings, [and] want of decorum and Proportions of our Houses, that the irregularity of our humors and affections may be shrewdly discerned'. The Great Fire of 1666 made it 'possible to imagine a new city relieved of its Gothic buildings and turned into classical magnificence'.[40] Although the plans of Evelyn and Wren were blocked by the 'obstinate Averseness of the great Part of the Citizens to alter their Old Properties', in the longer term the fire did see a cramped wooden city give way to something grander constructed in brick and stone.[41]

During the 1680s, resolving a cure for the 'ill disposition and gross temperament of the air', one citizen took comfort that Amsterdam had 'showed that through "vast toil and industry" how human art could improve on nature'.[42] In 1724 Defoe recorded with satisfaction that 'the buildings of this great city are chiefly of brick . . . the most commodious of all other materials . . . [and] the safest . . . from fire'. '[N]o where in the world is so good care taken to quench fires as in London' by means both of extensive water piping and 'admirable engines'.[43] A mid-eighteenth-century *History* concluded:

> whatever the unfortunate Citizens . . . suffered by the late dreadful Fire . . .
> a greater Blessing could not have happened for the Good of Posterity; for,
> instead of very narrow, crooked and uncommodious streets (fitter for a
> wheel-barrow than any nobler Carriage) dark, irregular and ill-contrived
> wooden Houses, with their several Stories . . . hanging over each other . . .

Whereby the Circulation of the Air was obstructed . . . and verminous pestilential Atoms nourished . . . since the Enlargement of the Streets, and modern Way of Building . . . there is such a free Circulation of Sweet Air . . . the City [has been] freed from all pestilential Symptoms for these eighty-nine Years.[44]

CULTURES OF INVENTION

By the application of such arts, accompanied by a revolutionary reformation of culture, England modernized along Dutch lines. Explanations of the subsequent Industrial Revolution begin with further 'advantage[s] . . . given us by Nature'. In an organic economy energy came primarily from the muscle-power of humans and animals, supplemented by wind and water, harnessed by ploughs, mills, ships and sails.[45] Before being stored in the muscles of people and animals this energy had been created by photosynthesis, for consumption in the form of grain and other vegetables. After the early Dutch lead in mobilizing wind and water the most important additional British resource was coal, created by photosynthesis in a previous historical era, and providing more energy by volume than wood or peat (four times as much as peat). In addition there were abundant British supplies of lead, tin and iron.

Not only improved agriculture but coal was essential to the super-growth of London, for heating and manufacture, including that of building materials. Between 1580 and the 1640s imports of coal to the capital multiplied sixfold, from 50,000 to 300,000 tons per year.[46] Because 'no other city in the world . . . burned nearly as much dirty coal as London', nowhere else lived in such a 'smoke, rolling in a thick heavy atmosphere . . . a cloud . . . which suffers the sun to break out only now and then'.[47] Around the country coal facilitated industries like brewing, dyeing, sugar and salt refining, soap boiling, glass making and the smelting and casting of metals.[48] With peat stocks dwindling, by the 1720s the United Provinces was importing 100,000 tons of British coal a year.[49] By 1800 'British coal output . . . exceeded the output of the whole of continental Europe' by a multiple of seven.[50] Coal did not cause the Industrial Revolution, and other countries, including Germany, had comparable reserves. But in the eighteenth century outside the Netherlands only Britain had the framework of advanced agriculture, manufactures and trade which made coal so valuable.

293

Concerning the other reason for British take-off from the plateau attained by the Dutch economy by 1750 there is less historiographical agreement. Tony Wrigley described 'an abrupt acceleration in the overall rate of growth of the economy in the period 1780–1840', accompanied by an enormous increase in British power by 1800 of an order only normally made possible by an increase of territory.[51] Yet he concluded that Britain's empire was not the explanation, because all the elements informing Britain's divergence from every other European economy except the Netherlands had been present for two hundred years. To the question of how we explain Britain's divergence from the Netherlands – from a capitalist, industrialized economy with a plateau, to one where growth was 'exponential, and unbounded', Wrigley's answer was energy, not only coal but the steam engine.[52] For Ken Pomeranz this energy advantage also involved the empire. Britain and China both had coal, but as China had far greater population pressure on its resources, so British coal and timber came to include the enormous reserves of North America.

That the Industrial Revolution had long-term causes, or preconditions, seems beyond dispute. From the length of the runway, however, it does not follow that the circumstances enabling take-off were equally long term. Since Britain and the Netherlands only diverged after 1750, that need not be the case. When that divergence happened the overall ratio of resources to people – even without the empire – was sharply in Britain's favour. Whatever else occurred, late eighteenth-century Britain saw the consequences of the application of Dutch measures – religious, political, fiscal, economic – over a long period, without Dutch natural resource constraints. But could that acceleration have occurred in the absence of an equally rapidly growing and protected imperial market? What we know is that it did not. Since such growth had never before been seen – just as the equally explosive growth of the Dutch bulk trades had never before been seen – this is not a small matter. So here it might help us to return to earlier comparative questions concerning the circumstances in which cultures of invention arise.

The grain trade and fishery helped to revolutionize the Dutch economy by creating a mercantile infrastructure and culture alternative to those of the rich trades, and by supplying staple foodstuffs from outside the region. Their development suggests that where a new super-market is identified, in the presence of a temporary monopoly of supply, and given enabling institutional structures, the result may be a process of invention. Responding to the difficulties confronting traditional agriculture, and to the commercial potential of the physical environment, Dutch innovations in shipbuilding, harbour maintenance and ship-supply, voyage design, commodity processing and delivery, all drew upon an evolving economy of knowledge. This was informed first by an understanding of the needs of consumers (the culture of demand). But what equally impressed William Monson was the size of the herring fleet, the precise timing and co-ordination of its annual operation, and its ability to pursue and find the fish in bulk every season (all aspects of the culture of supply).

In Britain we saw the development of an equivalent economy of knowledge in the context of the booming and complex North American market for manufactures. Enabling the technological breakthroughs which transformed the ability to mass produce (water-mill, steam engine, spinning jenny) was an accumulation of human capital from communication, relationships and experience, leading to adaptation, diversification and niche product development. Supporting both was the financial and structural stability deriving from long-standing monopoly access to a growing market capable of rewarding large-scale, reliable supply. In both Dutch and British cases game-changing technological inventions occurred in the context of a larger system called into being by market opportunity which made investment in innovation attractive. Also in both cases these were motivated by an imperative to reduce labour costs.

The essence of the resulting system was a commitment to mass production, which required four things. One was resources, in the British case not simply energy but raw materials (wool, linen, cotton, wood, iron). Another was a market, or complex of markets, great in scale, and growing and diversifying rapidly, something which the ever-diminishing unit costs of successful mass production helped to sustain. The third was capital, both human and material. This furnished not only occasional breakthrough inventions. It established a climate of ends-directed tinkering and problem-solving and the mentality necessary for that to exist and be sustained: a mentality which identified challenges and invested in solutions that were believed to be possible. Thus:

[t]he flying-shuttle loom (1733), steam condenser (1764), spinning mill (1771), steam engine (1775) . . . and cotton gin (1793) changed manufacturing techniques, which in turn led to changes in the organization of

industry. Practical and enlightened international merchants were enamoured of these new discoveries, inventions, and systems, attempted to acquaint themselves with their benefits wherever feasible, and even introduced them into their daily lives.[53]

The inventions in ship design necessary to make the Dutch bulk trades profitable were the work of 'largely anonymous innovators' over a period of time. They were products not so much of individual genius as of a culture of invention. Now eighteenth-century Britain became, as it were, an oceanically oriented Hollandish shipyard equipped with an Enlightenment culture believing and investing in the future. It may be true that 'The great minds of the Industrial Enlightenment had shown how the useful knowledge they were accumulating could be used to improve ... to innovate.'[54] But invention preceded the Enlightenment, in China, Italy and the Netherlands, and was as often the product of local cultures responding to specific opportunities as of 'great minds'. Nor is it clear that 'It was ingenuity and innovativeness that drove exports and trade, not the other way around.'[55] As trade developed within the context of a long-term Anglo-Dutch-American process, so many features of British culture, economic and political, adapted in response. The final move to factory production – beginning in the North Midlands, Lancashire and Yorkshire – happened incredibly quickly. This demonstrated a capacity for adaptation and ingenuity but it also drew upon long-term developments, including a navally protected imperial market, a growing non-agricultural labour force, and globe-spanning resources of both materials and knowledge.[56]

Joel Mokyr has questioned the importance of empire to the Industrial Revolution on the grounds that by the time it occurred the thirteen colonies had already attained their independence.[57] Yet what is instructive is the lack of impact of the American Revolution on the Anglo-American economic relationship. That relationship was the product of a long-term process of migration, settlement and protection. By 1780 its durability rested less on formal power than on cultural ties of language, thought and taste. The inventions which occurred supplied what was necessary to make the new trades profitable on the basis of their scale. Beyond that, the chronological simultaneity of American and Industrial Revolutions is partly attributable to the demographic and geographic expansions which so powerfully contributed to both.

Invention was not confined to the export trades. 'The great innovations in steam power and cotton spinning were cost-effective at small scales of operation, easily accommodated in the domestic market. Steam engines were employed at hundreds of individual mines and mills . . . productivity growth through technical change was not limited to the export industries.'[58] Yet this is what a culture of invention looks like. It develops over time and becomes widespread. It accumulates intellectual and financial capital. Technological invention in the iron industry, which 'was anything but an overnight solution', involved 'the adoption of coal-fired refinery methods drawing upon innovations in other British industries, most notably malt'.[59] Moreover, 'the most famous technological breakthroughs came in cotton production, which was transformed by a series of inventions after 1765' and was almost entirely export-driven. 'Over half of output was exported from the first and there was a dizzying expansion in overseas sales which increased by 2,283% between 1784/6 and 1814/16.'[60] More broadly:

> If we think of the industrial revolution as being about structural change, foreign markets may have had a more important role. A rapidly growing industrial sector marketing its entire output domestically would find its internal terms of trade deteriorating rapidly . . . Foreign markets relaxed this constraint . . . Exporting may also have generated greater spillover effects for the rest of the economy . . . for example through the development of insurance and finance.[61]

Concerning the importance of the empire David Ormrod agrees with Pomeranz. The exponential increases in British prosperity and power noted by Wrigley did not in fact occur in the absence of a dramatic increase in territorial resources:

> Abolition of the 'land constraint' was achieved with the most dramatic results by British imperial power and coercion. If the annual energy output of the British coal industry in 1815 represented the equivalent produced by 15 million acres of forest, the land area required to produce the cotton, sugar and timber imported from North America in 1830 would have amounted to between 25 and 30 million acres.[62]

Here Ormrod's focus is upon explaining British divergence from the United Provinces. In this respect he correctly emphasizes the ability of the British state to militarily protect its colonial trade routes and their lucrative commercial monopoly. A similar investment of state resources had created and maintained the Dutch East Indies trade. It must be remembered how important colonial imports had been to establishing the economic circumstances of the Dutch Golden Age. Thus up to a point, particularly in the case of its tropical plantation colonies, the British Empire was performing an economic function comparable to that earlier of the Dutch, and before that of other European colonies. Moreover, that function was being managed on a model already established (military protection of a monopoly, in territory seized by force, in this case from indigenous Americans). Alongside its sugar islands, Britain's North American colonies supplied many other vitally useful resources like timber, coal, furs, fish, rice and cotton.

The distinguishing British invention was Industrial Revolution as a product of manufacturing, rather than of trade and services. Its most dynamic engine was a North American market originating in the plantation of people and culture rather than things. The location of this outside the tropics allowing for a ninefold increase in population across the eighteenth century had no parallel elsewhere in the European colonial world. This expansion, territorial as well as demographic, was assisted by the devastating impact of European diseases upon indigenous Americans, and it was accompanied by continuing migration from the British Isles.[63]

Understood in this way the Industrial Revolution had both short- and long-term causes. It was the product of centuries of arduous and extraordinary human endeavour, and suffering. But it was not the outcome of any plan.

***

There were three key components of that transformative process – both creative and destructive – called Anglo-Dutch-American early modernity. One, the bulk trades, owed nothing to England but drew upon the resources and earlier trading practices of the Dutch North Sea coast and Hanseatic towns. Another, Britain's North American plantations, were primarily Anglo-Scots-Irish Protestant in inspiration, but indebted to the United Provinces for their spiritual and physical establishment, as well as for their early supply. Their imposition in practice, deploying the might of the English confessional state, was trialled in Ireland. The other factors were modernizing revolutions (agricultural, commercial and fiscal-political-military) pioneered in the Netherlands and then applied and adapted in Britain.

Thus the process which made Industrial Revolution possible was regional, transnational and trans-Atlantic; a revolutionary product of the Anglo-Dutch-American archipelago, with the consequences of which the world is still coming to terms.

1649: REVOLUTIONARY TURNPIKE

Global warming is the issue of our time, perhaps the biggest . . . in all of human history. Every one of us is now in the position of the indigenous Americans when the Europeans arrived with guns and smallpox: our world is poised to change vastly, unpredictably, and mostly for the worse . . . My only hope is that we can accept reality in time to prepare for it humanely, and . . . that facing it honestly . . . is better than denying it.

Jonathan Franzen, 'Is it too Late to Save the World?',

Guardian (4 November 2017)

The Industrial Revolution was the transformative event of modern world history. It created modernity, permanently ending a previous way of life. Without it we would still be peasant farmers living in a village rather than inhabitants of a city. Our lives would still be governed by the seasonal agricultural calendar, and the constantly evolving daily cycle of light and darkness, rather than the never-ending flow of hourly work time, glow of electricity, and electronic devices which never sleep, accompanied by aircraft which fly us from one season to another. This book has asked what made possible this emergence of urban modernity from another world with different rules of conduct and habits of mind which had lasted for thousands of years.

One factor was a component of the British Empire in North America that was unique in European terms. It was unique in the circumstances of its foundation and in its eighteenth-century cultural character and demographic growth. But neither of these things would have triggered the Industrial Revolution had

Britain's economic relationship with those colonies not been weaponized by an Anglo-Dutch revolution beginning in 1649.

Comparing the English and Dutch abroad, Thomas Sprat wrote that the former 'carried their way of life with them, establishing it in the new communities they encountered'. Dutch merchants, by contrast, 'keeping themselves most within their own Cells, and Ware-houses . . . mind[ed] . . . their gain alone'.[1] Eighteenth-century France and Spain also had large-scale Atlantic and global empires, and large and sophisticated cities. But their colonies were not equipped to play a similarly dynamic role as markets for manufactures, nor had the French and Spanish economies served a two-century-long Dutch-style economic apprenticeship. For that what was requisite was not only a maritime neighbourhood but the shared cultural (especially religious) affiliation which made interaction and co-operation not only possible but essential.

The Anglo-Dutch revolution of 1649–1702 stood at the centre of a succession of wider transformations which were agricultural, political and commercial. All of these had their origins in the Netherlands before spreading to south-eastern England and across the Atlantic. Understanding their development and diffusion has required attention to religion, migration and war as well as to economic, social and cultural life. The result connected a series of unique local human environments, including the Dutch water world, the city of London and the American frontier into a world-altering imperial system. By the later eighteenth century the Atlantic reorientation of the European economy had thrown the Baltic into relative decline, sparking the dramatic growth of Liverpool, Manchester and Glasgow while Stockholm, Copenhagen and Amsterdam stagnated.[2]

Anglo-Dutch-American early modernity was not self-contained, temporally or spatially. The changes which were making parts of Europe wealthier than China began in the medieval period; the subsequent relocation of Europe's economic and cultural engine-room from the Mediterranean to the North-West was informed by a change in Europe's relationship, not only to the Atlantic, but to the world. It was also informed by the geographic, ecological and cultural specificities of the region connecting the Baltic and the North Sea.

Some developments within this Anglo-Dutch-American process were steady and slow-moving. Others were explosive. To accounts of how pre-industrial history ended which are primarily about incremental process, this study has added an emphasis upon the importance, and contingency, of some events (as of some particular inventions). These were only one layer within a web of causation, enablement and possibility. But that does not make political less important than economic or social history: they cannot and should not be separated. The Dutch Revolt and English Revolution were complex upheavals in cultural and intellectual as well as economic, political and military history. They cost hundreds of thousands of lives in payment for the exchange of one mode of life and belief for another. They inflicted savage punishment upon their foes, from Ireland to South-East Asia. We do not say that the military defeat of fascism in 1945 was icing upon an historical cake which was already being baked.

Concerning the growth of the seventeenth-century English economy it is possible to take the view that

> [i]f Charles I had defeated parliament in 1643, or James II defeated William of Orange in 1688, or if France had won the War of the Spanish Succession after 1701, things would certainly have been different in the short term . . . But it is difficult to believe that ultimate outcomes would not have been broadly the same because they depended on the distribution of wealth and other resources, on assumptions about property, and on norms of behaviour normally untouched by single events.[3]

Yet none of these wars or revolutions was actually single, as opposed to complex, events. None hinged only upon developments in England. They and other upheavals like the eighty-year-long Dutch war for independence were protracted transnational and often global conflicts themselves frequently determined by 'the distribution of wealth and other resources', while also helping to determine them. They were, that is to say, part of the warp and weft of economic and social, as well as of political and military history. Similarly, that the first Industrial Revolution did not occur in China, despite the exceptional productivity of late medieval Chinese agriculture, the richness of Chinese culture and the splendour of the Ming and Qing courts, was as much the result of imperial military history and political decision-making as of any other cause.

Within the early modern period the present study identifies a tipping point beyond which the end of pre-industrial history became possible, though not inevitable. Political historians of seventeenth-century England over the past half-century have been relatively unmoved by the idea of 1649 as any significant climacteric. The republican experiment only lasted eleven years, with the monarchy restored in 1660 remaining in place to this day. Even during those years, it is suggested, the government was not really a republic, being installed by a military coup, never calling elections, and giving way in 1653 to Oliver Cromwell's Protectorate, a military proto-monarchy. On these grounds England's sole experience of government only by elected representatives has been subjected to an historiographical version of the fate envisaged by the Act of Indemnity and Oblivion (1660), which commanded that people, upon pain of severe punishment, put the revolution out of their minds.[4]

By bending the knee before this political injunction historians may have overlooked the key turning point, not only in British, but modern world history. The year 1649 can be seen to have constituted a kind of turnpike of revolutions, both those it absorbed and imitated and those it initiated. The English climacterics of 1649 and 1689 were parts of a single Anglo-Dutch process which permanently changed the structures and policies of the English and then British states and created a new world power. That made 1649 the hinge upon which the wider Anglo-Dutch-American process turned. This was, in the first place, because it was one component of an Atlantic-wide process of state and empire formation which created three new composite states. It was so, secondly, because the revolution of 1649 set in train a whole series of other decisive changes across the Atlantic which helped to make the Industrial Revolution possible.

The architects of restoration in 1660 saw no reason to unsettle the commercial and naval revolutions in progress, or the attendant and enabling transformations of political economy and public administration. Accordingly these were further developed during a period the inglorious military record of which was compensated for by its commercial and cultural vibrancy. As Christopher Hill noted, 'After 1660 the republican . . . foreign policy of active support for English trade and navigation was continued . . . The navy and the system of taxation which had made possible the Navigation Act and the first Dutch War were taken over by post-Restoration governments; the second and third Dutch wars would have been impossible without them.'[5] Hill's argument was that, restoration notwithstanding, the revolution had made the country safe for capitalism.

In this respect what interested him even more than commerce and the navy was the commercialization of agriculture. Following this, including the

> abolition of feudal tenures and the Court of Wards (1646, 1656, confirmed 1661) . . . landowners were set free . . . and their land became a commodity which could be bought, sold and mortgaged; thus, long-term capital investment in agriculture was facilitated. This was 'the decisive change in English history, which made it different from the continent'. From it every other difference in English society stemmed.[6]

Here Hill quoted H. J. Perkin on the long-term contexts of the Industrial Revolution. Both authors had other things to say about emerging 'difference[s] between England and the continent'.[7] These arguments derived from a still vigorous mode of English historiography which attributed national patterns of development to an insular exceptionalism.[8] Neither Hill nor Perkin noticed the essential role of Dutch example in the revolution in productivity which drove the commercialization of English agriculture, or in inspiring and provoking the commercial, maritime and imperial policies of 1649–53 which laid the basis of the Anglo-American 'closed colonial system'.[9] However, there is now a long-range comparative literature which sets these developments in context. After the Anglo-Dutch revolution:

> At the beginning of the eighteenth century, about a quarter to a third of the British national debt . . . and the stock in the East India Company was held by Dutch investors . . . Monopolies, tarrifs and privileges were further removed . . . highly dynamic and well organized factor markets sustained entrepreneurship and technological innovation . . . agriculture had been revolutionised, with the commodification of land and labour, and the growth of commercialised production . . . factor and output markets offered the infrastructure to combine the labour of workers released from agricultural work, the surpluses of food, and the accumulated capital in order to boost industrial production and . . . services.[10]

Following the invasion of 1688–9, to prosecute war against France, there was every reason to accelerate this revolution in military, fiscal and commercial power. In the service of this confessional and political objective Dutch and English elites co-operated. What English Whigs called the Glorious Revolution involved much more than the defeat of one king by another. By building, in a particular way, upon the European history of the preceding century and a half it helped to set the course, not only of England, but of the world.

At the heart of this Anglo-Dutch process were not simply co-option and adaptation, but competition and conflict. In *The Rise of English Shipping* Ralph Davis wondered whether the Industrial Revolution could have taken place without the maritime and colonial policies of 1649–51 and the three Anglo-Dutch wars which followed. In line with their intention the Navigation Acts transformed the scale of English shipping and also therefore the availability of sailors in times of war. In addition they 'secured a monopoly of English colonial trade and its profits for English merchants' and protected 'English industry's colonial markets from the effective competition of European manufactures'. If instead of these developments 'the Dutch had been permitted, in the seventeenth century, to trade freely with the English colonies', so that these 'sea links' had remained 'in Dutch, not English hands', could England have prevailed against France in the eighteenth-century struggle for North America?[11] Might that not have left

the English colonies, if still English, a fringe on the east coast of French America? If colonial America had been lost or whittled away; if during its lifetime it had been a Dutch commercial province; where would have been the merchant fortunes, the crown revenues, accumulated in England through colonial trade? Where would the English industries have found room for massive expansion? . . . The needs of the state for naval power reinforced the demands of merchants and shipowners in securing legislation to preserve the merchant marine, and so . . . the colonies; and colonial monopoly was one of the bases . . . for industrial expansion. When colonial monopoly was broken after 1776 the work was done; the wealth had been accumulated, and the dependence of the American economy on England established too firmly to be undone in less than another century.[12]

If this story has a chronological so it also has a spatial centre of gravity. The Anglo-Dutch-American transformation was enabled by London as a corporate political entity, as a partner in war and government, and as an economic, social and cultural world. London was a site for domination of the archipelago; for institutional copying and development, and for international migration, investment and trade. As London anchored the transnational and global process which made the British imperial and eventually industrial state, so it was made by that process into the first world city.

Small wonder that between 1600 and 1760 domination by London caused anxiety and resentment.[13] One of the first consequences of the industrializing process was to create a national urban economy capable of contesting it. '[F]or all of London's influence on the first Industrial Revolution . . . the great shock cities of the Industrial Age were Birmingham, Leeds, Sheffield, Preston, and above all, Manchester.'[14] 'The extent to which new industrial centres developed into large cities in Britain has no counterpart elsewhere in Europe before the mid-nineteenth century.'[15] One contemporary claimed:

> Manufactories that begin about the center of the kingdom, push on to the north . . . the east and west; but particularly the west, in a most astonishing way. Thus, from Leeds to Liverpool – through Bradford, Halifax, Rochdale, Manchester, Warrington and Preston – the population is wonderful. The workmen are like to many ants employed about their heaps; but they are so different from those in London, that while the ants of the north labour for the *general benefit*, the other pismires work hard for the general confusion.[16]

In June 2016 Britain shocked the world by voting to leave the European Union. But perhaps what had occurred was that parts of England had voted to secede from the transnational and global world to which the city of London had attached them. Still today 'London alone has almost five times the foreign-born population of Scotland, Wales and Northern Ireland put together'.[17] The Brexit campaign was led by ex-Minister of Education Michael Gove, who had earlier reformed the history curriculum to emphasize 'one of the most inspiring stories I know – the history of our United Kingdom'.[18] The referendum result might bring that history to an end, in part because the United Kingdom was one product of a transnational and global process. To consider it 'ours', a comfortable item of domestic political upholstery capable of being rescued from Brussels on the eagles' wings of resurgent nationalism, suggests that the history curriculum may require further revision.

The nationalism informing Brexit was English. Scots nationalism, also alive and well, does not entail the same hostility to the European Union. Nor was there a majority for departure from the EU in Northern Ireland. If the purpose of Brexit is recovery of national sovereignty and autonomy, this can only be achieved for England by denying the same thing to the other components of the Union. In this respect Brexit, which is in its motive power Exit, constitutes a threat to a United Kingdom which is no less a European federation than the European Union itself. Such arrangements have been a feature of the history examined in this book. From this perspective the proponents of Brexit do not oppose all transnational European federations, but only ones which England does not control.

It is not clear that the historical experiment of the EU, originating in a post-WW2 peace process, has made Germany less distinctly German, or France less French. To the extent that all national governments are confronting limits to their power and autonomy these are primarily consequences of globalization. The EU is hardly perfect, as the crushing of Greece in 2015 showed. It needs reform, and faces dangerous challenges. However, amid a current line-up of global great powers it looks like a model of civility. Within its European framework Northern Ireland, and the rest of Ireland, benefit from a peace process of their own. The EU's future is not predetermined; it will be determined by a complex dialogue within which Britain used to have an important voice.

In one sense the dream of an autonomous but global Britain, riding the waves of trade, harks back to the mercantilist rupture of 1649–53. Yet that was an achievement, not of negotiated international agreements or of global openness, but of brutal state power. It was the product of a republican revolution which accessed unprecedented material resources by confiscating and selling Crown, Church and aristocratic land. Britain secured its empire in Ireland, America, India and Australasia by blood and terror.[19] This is a history rather to be studied than repeated. The current British state, in conflict with Russia, partially unmoored from the EU, and in alliance with a United States weathering its own period of political danger, lurches from one crisis to the next.

Brexit may have been partly a response to the impact of freedom of movement upon the only EU member state within which the local language is also the world language, making it a uniquely attractive, or at least accessible, migrant destination. This was one of the grounds upon which Margaret Thatcher's Education Secretary Kenneth Baker secured from Brussels a British exemption from the EU requirement that students learn a second language (many learn several). The world language thus functioning as an instrument of cultural parochialism is a problem all over the English-speaking world. Ironically, as we have seen, English became the world language as a result of historically unique levels of British out-migration. The gravest damage of Brexit may be generational, as baby boomers foreclose for their children and grand-children the capacious transnational future which they had themselves enjoyed. Participation in the EU improved British life. In this respect Brexit looks like an act of self-mutilation, like the Revocation of the Edict of Nantes.

In John Le Carré's *A Legacy of Spies* retired British intelligence chief George Smiley asks himself what all the sacrifice was for:

> So was it all for *England* then? . . . There was a time, of course there was. But *whose* England? *Which* England? England all alone, a citizen of nowhere? I'm a European, Peter. If I had a mission – if I was ever aware of one beyond our business with the enemy, it was to Europe. If I was heartless, I was heart-less for Europe. If I had an unattainable ideal, it was of leading Europe out of her darkness towards a new age of reason. I have it still.[20]

Twenty-first-century Britain does not need to find or rejuvenate its historical and political identity. It already is the North-Western European state which, over the last five hundred years, has played a – and for a while the – key role not only in European, but global history. Enabling that was the intensity, complexity and quality of its relationships with its neighbours. Informing this was, not distinction, let alone isolation, but proximity and movement, including the unprecedented movement south and north, as well as east to west, of James Cook's *Resolution* in 1772–5, and the large-scale trans-European and global movement of peoples.[21]

Of this European, trans-Atlantic and global entanglement the most impor-tant product was the Industrial Revolution. The consequences of that continue not only to make the weather, but to change it. To the extent that this story is not over, its history cannot yet be written.

ENDNOTES

INTRODUCTION

1. Quoted by Joseph Levine, *Between the Ancients and the Moderns: Baroque Culture in Restoration England* (New Haven, CT, 1999), pp. xii–xvii.
2. Quoted by Alain de Botton, *The Art of Travel* (London, 2003), p. 97.
3. Christopher Clark's *The Sleepwalkers: How Europe Went to War in 1914* (London, 2012) also tells the story of how Europe went to war, rather than why, and James Vernon's *Distant Strangers: How Britain Became Modern* (Berkeley, CA, 2014) is 'less interested in *why* societies become modern than in *how* they do so' (p. 7).
4. Winstanley et al., *The True Levellers' Standard Advanced, or, The State of Community opened, and presented to the Sons of Men* (1649), in Christopher Hill (ed.), *Winstanley: The Law of Freedom and Other Writings* (Harmondsworth, 1973), pp. 78–9.
5. Jonathan Scott, *England's Troubles: Seventeenth-Century English Political Instability in European Context* (Cambridge, 2000), p. 16. In relation to the present study see the discussion of Karel Davids and Jan Lucassen (eds), *A Miracle Mirrored: The Dutch Republic in European Perspective* (Cambridge, 1995), pp. 489–90.
6. Jonathan Scott, 'What the Dutch Taught Us: The Late Emergence of the Modern British State', *Times Literary Supplement* (16 March 2001), pp. 4–6.
7. Jonathan Scott, *Commonwealth Principles: Republican Writing of the English Revolution* (Cambridge, 2004), p. 357. This use of the word 'achievement' now strikes me as naff and it has been abandoned.
8. Scott, 'What the Dutch Taught Us', p. 4.
9. Scott, *England's Troubles*, pp. 8–16 and thereafter.
10. T. C. W. Blanning, *The Culture of Power and the Power of Culture: Old Regime Europe 1660–1789* (Oxford, 2002); Tombs, *The English and Their History* (London, 2015); Carla Gardina Pestana, *The English Atlantic in an Age of Revolution 1640–1661* (Cambridge, MA, 2004); Alison Games, *Web of Empire: English Cosmopolitans in an Age of Empire* (London, 2008); David Hancock, *Citizens of the World: London Merchants and the Integration of the British Atlantic Community, 1735–1785* (Cambridge, 1995); Brendan Simms, *Three Victories and a Defeat: The Rise and Fall of the First British Empire, 1714–1783* (London, 2007); Nicholas Canny, 'Atlantic History and Global History', in Jack P. Greene and Philip D. Morgan (eds), *Atlantic History: A Critical Appraisal* (Oxford, 2009).
11. I have asked myself how I ever became involved in such a mad, hubristic undertaking, before rediscovering this account of a Research Fellowship interview in 1984: 'At Pembroke I explained that in Algernon Sidney we found the causes of the English, French and American revolutions; the preconditions for the industrial revolution; and the essence of the transition from early modern history to modern. Before the next interview I had five hours in which to wonder if I had overstated my case.' Jonathan Scott, *Harry's Absence: Looking for my Father on the Mountain* (Wellington, 1997), p. 144. The interview was unsuccessful.

12. Thus my *Commonwealth Principles* examined a body, not only of political but religious, moral and social thought pertaining to the 'Commonwealth'. See in particular Chs 2–3 and Scott, 'What were Commonwealth Principles?', *Historical Journal* 1, 2004.

13. Jan Luiten van Zanden, *The Long Road to the Industrial Revolution: The European Economy in a Global Perspective, 1000–1800* (Leiden, 2009); Stephen Broadberry, Bruce M. S. Campbell, Alexander Klein, Mark Overton and Bas van Leeuwen, *British Economic Growth 1270–1870* (Cambridge, 2015).

14. Winstanley in G. H. Sabine (ed.), *The Works, with an Appendix of Documents Relating to the Digger Movement* (Ithaca, NY, 1951), pp. 242, 569.

15. Winstanley, *True Levellers' Standard*, in *Law of Freedom*, p. 80.

16. Scott, *England's Troubles*, Chs 1, 10, Part 2 in general, and p. 23 in particular.

17. Patrick Collinson, *The History of a History Man: Or, the Twentieth Century Viewed from a Safe Distance* (Woodbridge, 2011), p. 137.

PROLOGUE

1. In this respect its most important predecessor is K. H. D. Haley, *The British and the Dutch: Political and Cultural Relations through the Ages* (London, 1988).

1 THE ANGLO-DUTCH-AMERICAN ARCHIPELAGO

1. Van Zanden, *Long Road*, p. 1.

2. Ibid., p. 5.

3. Jan de Vries, *The Dutch Rural Economy in the Golden Age* (New Haven, CT, 1974); Jan de Vries and Ad van der Woude, *The First Modern Economy: Success, Failure, and the Perseverance of the Dutch Economy, 1500–1815* (Cambridge, 1997); Jan de Vries, *The Industrious Revolution: Consumer Behaviour and the Household Economy, 1650 to the Present* (Cambridge, 2008).

4. Van Zanden, *Long Road*; Bas Van Bavel, *The Invisible Hand? How Market Economies have Emerged and Declined since AD 500* (Oxford, 2016).

5. Davids and Lucassen (eds), *A Miracle Mirrored*; Oscar Gelderblom, *Cities of Commerce: The Institutional Foundations of International Trade in the Low Countries, 1250–1650* (Princeton, NJ, 2013).

6. Karel Davids describes an Anglo-Dutch-American community of knowledge which began by studying oceanic winds and currents (when Isaac Vossius collaborated with Edmond Halley in England during the 1670s and 1680s) and subsequently enabled the work in Philadelphia announced in Benjamin Franklin's *Experiments and observations upon electricity* (London, 1751). Davids, 'The Scholarly Atlantic: Circuits of Knowledge between Britain, the Dutch Republic and the Americas in the Eighteenth Century', in Gert Oostindie and Jessica V. Roitman (eds), *Dutch Atlantic Connections, 1680–1800: Linking Empires, Bridging Borders* (Leiden and Boston, MA, 2014), pp. 233–4, 239–40.

7. Hakluyt, *The Principall Navigations, Voiages and Discoveries of the English Nation*, 2 vols (London, 1589), vol. 1, title page.

8. Max Weber, *The Protestant Ethic & the Spirit of Capitalism: New Introduction and Translation by Stephen Kalberg* (Los Angeles, 2002), pp. 8, 10.

9. Andrew Marvell, *The Character of Holland* (London, 1672), pp. 3–4. The poem was written in 1653, as England began to prevail in the first Anglo-Dutch war, but not published until 1665. For the texts and contexts of all of the Marvell poems used here (*Character of Holland, First Anniversary* and *Last Instructions*) see Nigel Smith (ed.), Andrew Marvell, *The Poems of Andrew Marvell*, rev. edn (Harlow, 2007).

10. Ibid., p. 1.

11. Alison Games, 'Conclusion', *Dutch Atlantic Connections*, p. 371.

12. Sir William Temple, *Observations Upon the United Provinces of the Netherlands* (London, 1673), p. 126.

13. John Evelyn, *Navigation and Commerce, Their Original and Progress* (London, 1674), p. 17.

14. Jonathan Scott, 'Maritime Orientalism, or, the Political Theory of Water', *History of Political Thought* 1 (2014).

15. Temple, *Observations*, p. 121; 'As many environmental historians have shown, the natural world has not been a static backdrop for human actions, but is rather made up of elements and creatures with their own complex histories, which have intertwined with people's affairs'. Ryan Tucker Jones, *Empire of Extinction: Russians and the North Pacific's Strange Beasts of the Sea, 1741–1867* (Oxford, 2014), p. 9. On recent early modern European environmental histories see William Cavert, *The Smoke of London: Energy and Environment in the Early Modern City* (Cambridge, 2016), pp. 7–10.

16. Thucydides, *History of the Peloponnesian War*, ed. M. I. Finley, trans. Rex Warner (Harmondsworth, 1975), pp. 76–7.

17. Davids and Lucassen (eds), *A Miracle Mirrored*, pp. 439–40.

18. Alfred Thayer Mahan, *The Influence of Sea Power Upon History 1660–1783*, 12th edn (Boston, MA, 1918), p. 25.

19. Lisa Jardine, *Going Dutch: How England Plundered Holland's Glory* (New York, 2008), pp. xvii–xviii.

20. Jonathan Scott, *When the Waves Ruled Britannia: Geography and Political Identities, 1500–1800* (Cambridge, 2011).

21. Charles Darwin, *The Voyage of the Beagle*, ed. James Brix (New York, 2000), p. 440.

22. Darwin, 'The ocean throwing its water over the broad reef appears an invinceable enemy, yet we see it resisted and even conquered by means which would have been judged most weak and efficient.' Quoted in Iain McCalman, *Darwin's Armada* (Melbourne, 2009), pp. 40, 79. Another nineteenth-century Pacific voyager recorded similarly: 'Poor old ship! I say again: for six months she has been rolling and pitching about, never for one moment at rest.' Herman Melville, *Typee* [1846], ed. George Woodcock (Harmondsworth, 1972), p. 37.

23. In addition to the works already referenced, important studies include Pieter Geyl, *Orange and Stuart* (London, 1969); Charles Wilson, *Profit and Power: A Study of England and the Dutch Wars* (London, 1957); Charles Wilson, *England's Apprenticeship 1603–1763*, 2nd edn (London, 1986); Jonathan Israel (ed.), *The Anglo-Dutch Moment: Essays on the Glorious Revolution and its World Impact* (Cambridge, 1991); David Ormrod, *The Rise of Commercial Empires: England and the Netherlands in the Age of Mercantilism, 1650–1770* (Cambridge, 2003); Hugh Dunthorne, *Britain and the Dutch Revolt* (Cambridge, 2013); Helmer Helmers, *The Royalist Republic* (Cambridge, 2014); Jonathan Scott, ' "Good Night Amsterdam": Sir George Downing and Anglo-Dutch Statebuilding', *English Historical Review*, 476 (2003).

24. Michael Pye, *The Edge of the World: How the North Sea Made Us Who We Are* (London, 2015), p. 8.

25. Lien Bich Luu, *Immigrants and the Industries of London 1500–1700* (Aldershot, 2005), pp. 27–9.

26. Daniel Defoe, *A Tour Thro' the Whole Island of Britain*, ed. G. D. H. Cole, 2 vols (New York, 1968), vol. II, p. 424.

27. William Camden, *Britain, or a Chorographicall Description of the most flourishing Kingdomes, England, Scotland and Ireland*, trans. Philemon Holland (London, 1610), p. 20.

28. Aylett Sammes, *Britannia Antiqua Illustrata: Or, The Antiquities of Ancient Britain, Derived from the Phoenicians* (London, 1676), p. 26. Concerning the alternative migrational theses of Camden and Sammes see Scott, *When the Waves*, pp. 22–4, 107–11.

29. E. A. Wrigley, R. S. Davies, J. E. Oeppen and R. S. Schofield, *English Population History from Family Reconstitution 1580–1837* (Cambridge, 1997); Van Zanden, *Long Road*, pp. 8, 98–100, 101–44; Adam Fox, *Oral and Literate Culture in Early Modern Britain* (New York, 2000), pp. 18–19.

30. See Peter Stearns, 'Social History and Spatial Scope', *Journal of Social History* 39, 3 (2006), p. 613.

31. Esther Mijers, *'News from the Republick of Letters': Scottish Students, Charles Mackie and the United Provinces, 1650–1750* (Leiden, 2012), Introduction and Chapter 1.

32. Marjorie Rubright, *Doppelganger Dilemmas: Anglo-Dutch Relations in Early Modern Literature and Culture* (Philadelphia, PA, 2014), p. 12.
33. Michael Winship, *Godly Republicanism: Puritans, Pilgrims, and a City on a Hill* (Cambridge, MA, 2012), pp. 5–6.
34. W. M. Elliot Griffis, *The Influence of the Netherlands in the Making of the English Commonwealth and the American Republic*, A Paper read before the Boston Congregational Club, Monday Evening, October 26, 1891 (Boston, MA, 1891), pp. 12–13.
35. Scott, *England's Troubles*, Introduction.
36. J. G. A. Pocock, *The Discovery of Islands: Essays in British History* (Cambridge, 2005). See the discussion in Scott, *England's Troubles*, Introduction.
37. Martin Lewis and Karen Wigen, *The Myth of Continents: A Critique of Metageography* (Los Angeles, CA, 1997); John Gillis, *Islands of the Mind: How the Human Imagination Created the Atlantic World* (Houndmills, 2004); and Philip Steinberg, *The Social Construction of the Ocean* (Cambridge, 2001).
38. Temple, *Observations*, p. 6.
39. William Henry Drayton quoted in Simms, *Three Victories and a Defeat*, p. 605.
40. Scott, *When the Waves*.
41. Greg Dening, *Islands and Beaches: Discourse on a Silent Land: Marquesas, 1774–1880* (Honolulu, 1980), p. 23.
42. R. Bin Wong, *China Transformed: Historical Change and the Limits of European Experience* (Ithaca, NY, 1997); Kenneth Pomeranz, *The Great Divergence: China, Europe and the Making of the Modern World Economy* (Princeton, NJ, 2000).
43. Pomeranz, *Great Divergence*, Ch. 6: 'Abolishing the Land Constraint: The Americas as a New Kind of Periphery'.
44. Broadberry et al., *British Economic Growth*, pp. 384–7; Broadberry and Bishnupriya Gupta, 'The Early Modern Great Divergence: Wages, Prices and Economic Development in Europe and Asia, 1500–1800', Centre for Economic Policy Research Discussion Paper no. 4947, March 2005.
45. Van Zanden, *Long Road*.
46. James Belich, *Replenishing the Earth: The Settler Revolution and the Rise of the Anglo-World, 1783–1939* (Oxford, 2009).
47. Belich, 'Settler utopianism? English Ideologies of Emigration, 1815–1850', in Jonathan Scott and John Morrow (eds), *Liberty, Authority, Formality: Political Ideas and Culture, 1600–1900* (Exeter, 2008).
48. Belich, *Replenishing*, p. 4.
49. De Vries and Van der Woude, *The First Modern Economy*.
50. See Vernon, *Distant Strangers*, Ch. 1.
51. Christopher Bayly, *The Birth of the Modern World 1780–1914* (Oxford, 2004).
52. Donna Tartt, *The Goldfinch* (London, 2013), p. 28.
53. For Theo, survivor of an art gallery bombing, 'The basic fact of existence . . . is catastrophe . . . better never born than born into this . . . sinkhole of hospital beds, coffins, and broken hearts'. Ibid., p. 767.
54. Mary Carruthers, *The Book of Memory: A Study of Memory in Medieval Culture*, 2nd edn (Cambridge, 2008), p. 193.
55. Thomas Sprat, *The History of the Institution, Design, and Progress, of the Royal Society of London. For the Advancement of Experimental Philosophy* (London, 1667), p. 86.
56. Astronomer Royal John Flamsteed quoted in Adrian Johns, *The Nature of the Book: Print and Knowledge in the Making* (Chicago, IL, 1998), p. 501.
57. 'And after all the *Innovation* of which they can be suspected, we find nothing will be indanger'd, but only the *physics* of *Antiquity*.' Sprat, *History of the Royal Society*, p. 328.
58. Ibid., pp. 321–2.
59. Anthony Grafton, *New Worlds, Ancient Texts: The Power of Tradition and the Shock of Discovery* (Cambridge, MA, 1992), Ch. 3.
60. Niccolò Machiavelli, *The Discourses*, ed. Bernard Crick (Harmondsworth, 1985), pp. 122–4; Scott, *Commonwealth Principles*, pp. 212–13.

61. Sprat, *History of the Royal Society*, p. 106.
62. Algernon Sidney, *Discourses Concerning Government*, ed. T. West (Indianapolis, IN, 1990), pp. 461–2. The *Discourses* was written between 1681 and 1683 and first published in 1698.
63. Scott, *Commonwealth Principles*, pp. 184–90.
64. Sidney, *Discourses*, quoted in Scott, *Commonwealth Principles*, pp. 189 and 190.
65. Van Zanden, *Long Road*, p. 292.
66. Ibid.
67. Karel Davids, 'Shifts of Technological Leadership in Early Modern Europe', in Davids and Lucassen (eds), *A Miracle Mirrored*; Gelderblom, *Cities of Commerce*.
68. Hancock, *Citizens of the World*.
69. Paul Slack, *The Invention of Improvement: Information and Material Progress in Seventeenth-Century England* (Oxford, 2014), p. 1.
70. Keith Sinclair, 'Life in the Provinces', in Sinclair (ed.), *Distance Looks Our Way: The Effects of Remoteness on New Zealand* (Auckland, 1961), pp. 37–8.
71. Jo Guldi and David Armitage, *The History Manifesto* (Cambridge, 2014), p. 31.
72. Elena Ferrante, *The Story of the Lost Child* (Melbourne, 2015), p. 337.
73. With thanks to the Pittsburgh office door of Bruce Venarde.
74. John Brewer, *Sinews of Power: War, Money and the English State, 1688–1783* (London, 1989); Charles Tilly (ed.), *The Formation of Nation States in Western Europe* (Princeton, NJ, 1975); Geoffrey Parker, *The Military Revolution: Military Innovation and the Rise of the West*, 2nd edn (Cambridge, 1996).
75. For England see Scott, *England's Troubles*, Parts One and Three; for the Dutch republic Marjolein 't Hart, *The Making of a Bourgeois State: War, Politics and Finance during the Dutch Revolt* (Manchester, 1993), Introduction and Ch. 2; Pepijn Brandon, *War, Capital and the Dutch State (1588–1795)* (Leiden, 2015), Introduction.
76. Steve Hindle, *The State and Social Change in Early Modern England c. 1550–1640* (Basingstoke, 2000); Michael Braddick, *State Formation in Early Modern England c. 1550–1700* (Cambridge, 2000); Mark Goldie, 'The Unacknowledged Republic: Officeholding in Early Modern England', in Tim Harris (ed.), *The Politics of the Excluded c. 1500–1850* (London, 2001). See Scott, reviews of Hindle and Braddick in *English Historical Review* 116, 469 (2001).
77. Van Zanden, *Long Road*, pp. 294–5.
78. Clark, *The Sleepwalkers*, p. xxvii.
79. Ibid., p. 562.
80. The Barrier Reef itself, which is only 18,000 years old, was made possible by the same rising sea levels, which flooded the continental shelf of Eastern Queensland with shallow (and so light) warm water. This process appears to have been observed by local aboriginals, whose songs and dances refer to it.
81. Daniel Statt, *Foreigners and Englishmen: The Controversy over Immigration and Population, 1660–1760* (London, 1995), pp. 25–8.
82. Bethel, *The Present Interest of England, Stated* (London, 1671), p. 33.
83. Weber, *Protestant Ethic*, p. 121.
84. De Vries, *The Industrious Revolution*.
85. Temple, *Observations*, Ch. 3: 'Of their Scituation' [sic].
86. Slack, *The Invention of Improvement*, p. 2.
87. Sprat, *History of the Royal Society*, pp. 422–3.
88. Willem Frijhoff and Marijke Spies, *Dutch Culture in a European Perspective, Volume I: 1650: Hard-Won Unity* (Houndmills, 2004), p. 37.
89. Van Zanden, *Long Road*, p. xxx.
90. Cavert, *The Smoke of London*, Ch. 2: 'Fires: London's Turn to Coal, 1575–1775'.
91. Davids, 'Shifts of Technological Leadership', p. 347.
92. Jan Lucassen, 'Labour and Early Modern Economic Development', in Davids and Lucassen (eds), *A Miracle Mirrored*, pp. 368–74.
93. Quoted by Luu, *Immigrants*, p. 158.
94. Ibid., p. 98.

95. Van Zanden, *Long Road*, p. 99.
96. Broadberry et al., *British Economic Growth*, pp. 210–11.
97. Ibid., p. 211, and see the graph on p. 206.
98. Van Zanden, *Long Road*, p. 98.
99. Scott, *England's Troubles*.
100. Slack, *Improvement*, p. 14.
101. Brandon, *War, Capital*, p. 3.
102. In fact the French Revolution in 1789 was inspired by its English predecessor of 1649, a point made by François Mitterrand when Prime Minister Thatcher visited Paris for the bicentenary in 1989.

PART I ANGLO-DUTCH-AMERICAN EARLY MODERNITY

1. Annie Proulx, *Barkskins* (London, 2016), p. 178. Reprinted by permission of HarperCollins Publishers Ltd © Annie Proulx (2016).
2. Robert Hughes, *Things I Didn't Know: A Memoir* (New York, 2006), p. 358.

2 THE FIRST INDUSTRIAL REVOLUTION

1. C. S. Lewis, *The Lion, the Witch and the Wardrobe* (London, 1989), pp. 16–17, © copyright CS Lewis Pte Ltd 1950, line 5.
2. E. A. Wrigley, *Poverty, Progress and Population* (Cambridge, 2004), p. 36.
3. Ibid., p. 49.
4. Ibid., pp. 24, 41.
5. Peter Laslett, *The World We Have Lost: The World We Have Lost Further Explored*, 4th edn (London, 1995).
6. Belich, 'Settler Utopianism?', in Morrow and Scott (eds), *Liberty, Authority, Formality*.
7. C. S. Lewis, *The Lion, the Witch and the Wardrobe*. The wardrobe, full of soft fur coats, was a conspicuous site of manufacturing. But it led back to something 'hard and rough and even prickly . . . A moment later she found that she was standing in the middle of a wood at night time with snow under her feet and snowflakes falling through the air.' In *The Voyage of the Dawn Treader* and *Perelandra*, Lewis created his own water worlds.
8. Jonathan Israel, *The Dutch Republic: Its Rise, Greatness and Fall, 1477–1806* (Oxford, 1998), p. 113.
9. Early modern Netherlanders often went without fire and light after sunset, for instance in public buildings. By contrast a Dutch official in Brill in 1586 recorded that 'the English nation have a great need for fire and light'. A. T. van Deursen, *Plain Lives in a Golden Age: Popular Culture, Religion and Society in Seventeenth-Century Holland* (Cambridge, 1991), p. 134.
10. Sprat, *The History of the Royal Society*, pp. 70–1.
11. For Enlightenment as a cause of the Industrial Revolution see Joel Mokyr, *The Enlightened Economy: An Economic History of Britain 1700–1850* (New Haven, CT, 2009).
12. During the first century and a half, industrialization appears to have lessened inequality between different parts of the world. Since 1980, however, the most recent phase of financial capitalism has seen a dramatic rise of inequality within all advanced economies. For the suggestion that 'factor markets and market economies always lead to inequality and eventual decline' see Van Bavel, *The Invisible Hand?* (e.g. p. 2).
13. *The Economist* (27 May 2017), Leader, 'Deep Trouble'.
14. J. R. McNeill and Peter Engelke, *The Great Acceleration: An Environmental History of the Anthropocene since 1945* (Cambridge, MA, 2016).
15. Armitage and Guldi, *The History Manifesto*.
16. Though it could be rotated with arable, the practice, called convertible husbandry, was pioneered in Flanders and a backbone of the English agricultural revolution. L. A Clarkson, *The Pre-Industrial Economy in England 1500–1750* (London, 1971), pp. 57–9. The Dutch were the first Europeans to 'break the manure barrier' (De Vries, *The Dutch Rural Economy in*

the Golden Age, Ch. 4). Here as elsewhere – in the use of human waste as agricultural fertilizer – the English followed (Jeremy Black, *London: A History* [Lancaster, 2009], p. 185).

17. James C. Scott, *Against the Grain: A Deep History of the Earliest States* (New Haven, CT, 2017), reviewed by Steve Mithin, 'Why Did We Start Farming?', *London Review of Books* 39, 23 (30 November 2017), pp. 11–12. In Annie Proulx, *Barkskins* (London, 2016), the hunter-gatherer Mi'kMa'ks contemplate the absurdity of agriculture, which imprisons its participants (in terms of diet, labour, physical location and culture) while vandalizing the physical environment.

18. De Vries, *European Urbanisation*, quoted by Wrigley, *Poverty*, p. 23.

19. N. J. G. Pounds, *An Historical Geography of Europe 1500–1840* (Cambridge, 1979).

20. Van Zanden, *Long Road*, pp. 97–8.

21. Israel, *Republic*, pp. 106–8.

22. De Vries and Van der Woude, *First Modern Economy*, p. 195.

23. Ibid.

24. Frijhoff and Spies, *1650: Hard-Won Unity*, p. 53.

25. Van Bavel, *The Invisible Hand?*, pp. 147–8.

26. Jan De Vries, 'The Transition to Capitalism in a Land without Feudalism', in P. Hoppenbrouwers and J. Luiten van Zanden (eds), *Peasants into Farmers? The Transformation of Rural Economy and Society in the Low Countries in Light of the Brenner Debate* (Turnhout, 2001), pp. 76–7.

27. Davids and Lucassen (eds), *A Miracle Mirrored*, pp. 439–40; Frijhoff and Spies, *Hard-Won Unity*, p. 19.

28. Ibid., p. 198.

29. Milja van Tielhof, 'Grain Provision in Holland ca. 1490–1570', in Hoppenbrouwers and Van Zanden (eds), *Peasants into Farmers?*, p. 216.

30. 't Hart, *Bourgeois State*, p. 16.

31. Charles Wilson, *England's Apprenticeship 1603–1763*, 2nd edn (London, 1965), pp. 28–9.

32. Cle Lesger, *The Rise of the Amsterdam Market and Information Exchange: Merchants, Commercial Expansion and Change in the Spatial Economy of the Low Countries c. 1550–1630* (Farnham, 2006).

33. De Vries and Van Der Woude, *First Modern Economy*, p. 355.

34. Ibid., p. 351: declining agricultural prospects in Holland drove increases both in urbanization and in trade.

35. Wrigley, *Poverty*, p. 23.

36. De Vries, *The Industrious Revolution*.

37. Joel Mokyr, 'Introduction' to Laura Cruz and Joel Mokyr (eds), *The Birth of Modern Europe: Culture and Economy, 1400–1800: Essays in Honor of Jan de Vries* (Boston, MA, 2010), p. 4.

38. Fernand Braudel, *Civilization and Capitalism, Volume II: The Wheels of Commerce* (London, 1984), p. 365.

39. Cavert, *Smoke of London*, pp. 11–12.

40. Davids, 'Shifts of Technological Leadership in Early Modern Europe', p. 342; Patrick O'Brien (ed.), *Urban Achievement in Early Modern Europe: Golden Ages in Antwerp, Amsterdam and London* (Cambridge, 2001).

41. Nuala Zahedieh, *The Capital and the Colonies: London and the Atlantic Economy, 1660–1700* (Cambridge, 2010).

42. A. L. Beier and Roger Finlay (eds), *London 1500–1700: The Making of the Metropolis* (Harlow, 1986), pp. 26–7. This was the most important though not the only distinction between the circumstances of London and Paris. London was also a major port, and it was far less dependent for its growth and needs upon the nation's government.

43. N. S. B. Gras, *The Evolution of the English Corn Market from the Twelfth to the Eighteenth Century* (Cambridge, MA, 1915), pp. 76–82, 103–4, 112–14.

44. Gras, *Evolution* notes the stimulus to agricultural improvement furnished by 'the growth of a metropolitan market, with its constant and insatiable appetite . . . and the Dutch example of efficient cultivation' (p. 125).

45. John Evelyn, *Acetaria: A Discourse of Salletts*, quoted in John J. Murray, 'The Cultural Impact of the Flemish Low Countries on Sixteenth- and Seventeeth-Century England', *American Historical Review* 62, 4 (July 1957), p. 161. One sixteenth-century commentator noted the 'use . . . among the poore commons . . . of melons . . . cucumbers, radishes . . . carrots . . . turnips, and all kind of salad herbes' (Peter Ackroyd, *London: The Biography* [London, 2000], p. 313), but by the late seventeenth century they had become fashionable.

46. Lien Bich Luu, p. 34; Ackroyd, *London*, p. 311.

47. Broadberry et al., *British Economic Growth*, p. 396.

48. Algernon Sidney, *Court Maxims*, eds Hans Blom, Eco Haitsma Mulier and Ronald Janse (Cambridge, 1996), pp. 161–2.

49. Thomas Brady quoted in Davids and Lucassen (eds), *A Miracle Mirrored*, p. 348.

50. Pomeranz, *Great Divergence*, Ch. 6.

51. Kenneth Morgan, 'Mercantilism and the British Empire, 1688–1815', in Donald Winch and Patrick O'Brien (eds), *The Political Economy of the British Historical Experience, 1688–1914* (Oxford, 2002), p. 178.

52. Ibid., pp. 189–90.

53. 'Discourse of Western Planting By Richard Hakluyt, 1584', in E. G. R. Taylor (ed.), *The Original Writings & Correspondence of the Two Richard Hakluyts*, 2 vols (London, 1935), vol. 2, p. 235 (and Chs 3–4 in general).

3 A GEOGRAPHY OF INVENTION

1. David Hume, 'Of Civil Liberty', in *Political Essays*, ed. Knud Haakonssen (Cambridge, 1994), p. 54.

2. Emma Rothschild, 'David Hume and the Seagods of the Atlantic', in Susan Manning and Francis D. Cogliano (eds), *The Atlantic Enlightenment* (Aldershot, 2008), p. 82.

3. Pye, *The Edge of the World*; Lesger, *Rise of the Amsterdam Market*.

4. Cavert, *Smoke of London*, pp. 14–15.

5. Peter Burke's comparative social history *Venice and Amsterdam*, 2nd edn (Cambridge, 1994), offers a vantage point for reflection upon this transition.

6. Fernand Braudel, *A History of Civilisations* (New York, 1995); Felipe Fernández-Armesto, *Millennium* (London, 1996); J. R. McNeill and William H. McNeill, *The Human Web: A Bird's-Eye View of World History* (New York, 2003).

7. Gelderblom, *Cities of Commerce*, p. 4.

8. Van Zanden, *Long Road*, p. 293.

9. On Italian, English and American classical republicanism see J. G. A. Pocock, *The Machiavellian Moment: Florentine Political Thought and the Atlantic Republican Tradition* (Princeton, NJ, 1975). A subsequent multi-author account giving Dutch republicanism its place is Martin van Gelderen and Quentin Skinner (eds), *Republicanism: A Shared European Heritage*, 2 vols (Cambridge, 2002). See Scott, *Commonwealth Principles*, Ch. 1.

10. Pinar Emiralioglu, *Geographical Knowledge and Imperial Culture in the Early Modern Ottoman Empire* (London, 2014).

11. J. H. Elliott, *Empires of the Atlantic World: Britain and Spain in America, 1492–1830* (New Haven, CT, 2007), pp. 17, 59.

12. Linda Colley, 'Can History Help?', *London Review of Books* 40, 6 (22 March 2018); James Belich, 'The Black Death and European Expansion', lecture given at the University of Auckland, New Zealand, 21 March 2018.

13. David Wootton, *Invention of Science: A New History of the Scientific Revolution* (New York, 2015), pp. 61–2.

14. Broadberry et al., *British Economic Growth*, pp. 382–3.

15. Geoffrey Parker, *The Army of Flanders and the Spanish Road* (Cambridge, 2004), and *The Grand Strategy of Philip II* (New Haven, CT, 2000).

16. [Daniel Defoe], *An Essay at Removing National Prejudices Against a Union with Scotland* (London, 1706), p. 26; Neil Hanson, *The Confident Hope of a Miracle: The True History of the Spanish Armada* (London, 2003).

17. Lesger, *Amsterdam Market*, pp. 18–23.

18. Israel, *Dutch Republic*, p. 117.

19. De Vries and Van der Woude, *First Modern Economy*, p. 11.

20. Andrew Marvell, *The Character of Holland* (London, 1665), pp. 4, 6, 5.

21. Temple, *Observations*, p. 121.

22. Ibid., pp. 126–7.

23. Ibid., p. 127.

24. Ibid., pp. 129–30, 131, 132.

25. Ibid., p. 132.

26. Ibid., p. 131.

27. Thomas Scott, *The Belgicke Pismire* (London, 1622), pp. 67–8.

28. Alison Games, 'Conclusion: A Dutch Moment in Atlantic Historiography', in Oostindie and Roitman (eds), *Dutch Atlantic Connections*, p. 371, citing Maarten Prak and Jan Luiten van Zanden, *Nederland en het polder-model: Sociaal-economische geschiedenis van Nederland, 1000–2000* (Amsterdam, 2013).

29. Scott, *Belgicke Pismire*, pp. 69–70.

30. Ibid., pp. A2, A4, 69.

31. Simon Schama, *The Embarrassment of Riches: An Interpretation of Dutch Culture in the Golden Age* (New York, 1987), pp. 37–8; Van Deursen, *Plain Lives in a Golden Age*, pp. 12–13.

32. Inhabitants of houses of correction who would not work were reputedly placed in a 'drowning cell' accompanied by rising water and a pump. Schama, *Embarrassment of Riches*, Part One, pp. 17–24.

33. De Vries and Van der Woude, *First Modern Economy*, p. 18.

34. Ibid., p. 10.

35. Ibid., p. 19.

36. Frijhoff and Spies, *1650: Hard-Won Unity*, pp. 172–3.

37. De Vries and Van der Woude, *First Modern Economy*, p. 356.

38. Lesger, *Amsterdam Market*, p. 38.

39. Sir William Petty quoted by Ralph Davis, *The Rise of the English Shipping Industry in the Seventeenth and Eighteenth Centuries* (new edn, St Johns, Newfoundland, 2012), pp. 44, 46.

40. Pye, *Edge of the World*, pp. 237–8.

41. De Vries and Van der Woude, *First Modern Economy*, p. 352.

42. Ibid., p. 353.

43. Ibid., p. 357; Davis, *Shipping*, p. 45.

44. Israel, *Dutch Republic*, p. 111.

45. Ketner, quoted by Lesger, *Amsterdam*, p. 51. In response Lesger discusses Amsterdam's own crucial efforts to accommodate foreigners, but the valid point remains about the invention of a new kind of European trade with the shipping to make it profitable.

46. Israel, *Dutch Republic*, p. 117; Van Deursen, *Plain Lives*, notes that 'the death rate for adult men' who 'drowned at sea and otherwise died in storms' was unusually high in fishing villages (p. 20).

47. [William Monson], 'How to imploy our ffleet against Spain', National Maritime Museum, Greenwich, REC/4, Item 12, ff. 7–8.

48. Ibid., pp. 10, 13.

49. Van Deursen, *Plain Lives*, pp. 14–16.

50. Davids and Lucassen (eds), *A Miracle Mirrored*; Gelderblom, *Cities of Commerce*.

51. Temple, *Observations*, pp. 127–8.

52. Israel, *Dutch Republic*.

53. Maarten Prak, *The Dutch Republic in the Seventeenth Century* (Cambridge, 2005), p. 10.

54. Israel, *Dutch Republic*, pp. 29–30.

55. James Tracy, *A Financial Revolution in the Habsburg Netherlands: Renten and Renteniers in the County of Holland, 1515–1565* (Berkeley, CA, 1985); Brewer, *Sinews of Power*.
56. Temple, *Observations*, pp. 20–1.
57. Ibid., pp. 24–5.
58. Israel, *Dutch Republic*, pp. 145–6.
59. Prak, *Republic*, p. 17.
60. 't Hart, *Bourgeois State*, p. 75.
61. Lesger, *Amsterdam Market*; Prak, *Republic*, p. 18.
62. Israel, *Dutch Republic*, pp. 242, 260.
63. Prak, *Republic*, pp. 27–8.
64. Gelderblom, *Cities of Commerce*, pp. 15–16; Lesger, *Amsterdam Market*, pp. 162–70.
65. Prak, *Republic*, pp. 4–5.
66. Frijhoff and Spies, *1650: Hard-Won Unity*, pp. 19–21.
67. Israel, *Dutch Republic*, p. 320.
68. 't Hart, *Bourgeios State*, p. 23.
69. Israel, *Dutch Republic*, p. 1.
70. Davids and Lucassen (eds), *A Miracle Mirrored*.
71. Ibid., p. 2.
72. Ibid., pp. 439–40.
73. Slack, *Invention*, p. 262.
74. Jonathan Israel quoted by Brandon, *War, Capital*, p. 27.
75. On Dutch stagnation and decline see Van Bavel, *The Invisible Hand?*, pp. 203–6.
76. Ormrod, *Commercial Empires*, p. 49.

4 THE WEST COAST OF THE NORTH SEA

1. William Bradford, *Of Plymouth Plantation*, in Nathaniel and Thomas Philbrick (eds), *The Mayflower Papers: Selected Writings of Colonial New England* (London, 2007), pp. 12–13.
2. Michael Ondaatje, *Warlight* (London, 2018), pp. 140–1.
3. Craig Muldrew, *Food, Energy and the Creation of Industriousness* (Cambridge, 2011), p. 2.
4. Van Tielhof, 'Grain Provision in Holland', pp. 210–11; Gras, *English Corn Market*, pp. 99–103.
5. Broadberry et al., *British Economic Growth*, pp. 119–20.
6. Quoted in Blanning, *The Culture of Power*, pp. 280–1.
7. Wim Klooster, 'Anglo-Dutch Trade in the Seventeenth Century: An Atlantic Partnership?', in Allan MacInnes and Arthur Williamson (eds), *Shaping the Stuart World 1603–1714* (Leiden, 2006), pp. 261–2.
8. [Oldmixon], *The British Empire in America, Containing the History of the Discovery* (London, 1741), pp. 1–27; Andrews, *Trade, Plunder and Settlement*, pp. 49, 334–9.
9. Luu, *Immigrants*, Ch. 1.
10. Dunthorne, *Dutch Revolt*, p. 106.
11. Luu, *Immigrants*, pp. 61–76.
12. Davis, *Shipping*, pp. 1–2.
13. Andrews, *Trade, Plunder and Settlement*, p. 7; J. R. Tanner (ed.), *Samuel Pepys' Naval Minutes* (London, 1926), p. 343.
14. Davis, *Shipping*, pp. 5–8.
15. Ibid., pp. 9–11.
16. Ibid.
17. John C. Appleby, 'War, Politics and Colonization 1558–1625', in Canny (ed.), *The Origins of Empire*, pp. 55–6, 65–7; Kenneth Andrews (ed.), *English Privateering Voyages to the West Indies 1588–1595* (Cambridge, 1959); Andrews, *Trade*, p. 25.
18. Davis, *Shipping*, pp. 9, 32–3.
19. Elliott, *Empires of the Atlantic World*, Ch 2. That 'British America remained in comparison with Spanish America an overwhelmingly rural society' (p. 43) also reflected the differing settlement patterns and population densities of indigenous peoples.

20. Heylyn, *Cosmography in Four Books. Containing the Chorography and History of the Whole World* (London, 1677), p. 4.
21. Sprat, *History of the Royal Society*, p. 41.
22. Phil Withington, *The Politics of Commonwealth: Citizens and Freemen in Early Modern England* (Cambridge, 2005), pp. 5–6.
23. Sir William Petty, *Two Essays in political Arithmetick, Concerning the People, Housing, Hospitals . . . of London and Paris* (London, 1687), p. 12, and Memorandum after p. 21.
24. Slack, *Invention*, p. 9; Cavert, *Smoke*, pp. 11–12. Concerning Peking, this was a possibility of which Petty showed himself aware (*Two Essays*, p. 9).
25. Beier and Finlay in *London*, p. 11, observe that the period of the city's fastest growth (1580–1640) preceded any significant development in the size and nature of the country's political government, which came between 1649 and 1720. See Pounds, *An Historical Geography of Europe 1500–1840*, pp. 222 and 325.
26. Edward Hyde, Earl of Clarendon, quoted by Keith Lindley, *Popular Politics and Religion in Civil War London* (London, 1997), p. 14.
27. Broadberry, *Economic Growth*, p. 211.
28. Muldrew, *Food*, 'Introduction'; Wrigley, *Poverty, Progress and Population*; Emmanuel Le Roi Ladurie, *Peasants of Languedoc* (University of Illinois, 1977).
29. Keith Wrightson, *Earthly Necessities: Economic Lives in Early Modern Britain* (New Haven, CT, 2000).
30. Thomas More, *Utopia*, eds George Logan and Robert Adams (Cambridge, 1989), pp. 18–19.
31. Broadberry et al., *Economic Growth*, pp. 113–14 (and see Table 3.16 on p. 115).
32. Ibid., p. 19.
33. Joan Thirsk (ed.), *The Agrarian History of England and Wales, Volume V, Part II: 1640–1750 Agrarian Change* (Cambridge, 1985), pp. 536–9.
34. Andrew McRae, *God Speed the Plough: The Representation of Agrarian England, 1500–1660* (Cambridge, 1996).
35. Scott, *Commonwealth Principles*, Ch. 3.
36. Holinshed quoted in More, *Utopia*, footnote 17; *Utopia*, pp. 22, 23.
37. Hakluyt, 'Discourse of Western Planting', in *Original Writings*, vol. 2, pp. 233, 234.
38. W. Schenk, *The Concern for Social Justice in the Puritan Revolution* (London, 1948); Scott, *England's Troubles*, Ch. 11.
39. Quoted by Charles Wilson and R. Hooykaas, *The Anglo-Dutch Contribution to the Civilization of Early Modern Society: An Anglo-Netherlands Symposium* (London, 1976), p. 9.
40. [Hakluyt] H. R. the Younger, *Divers Voyages Touching the Discoverie of America and the Islands adjacent unto the same* (London, 1582; facsimile, Ann Arbor, MI, 1996).
41. Ibid., pp. 3–4; William Bourne, 'Hydrographicall discourse to shew the passage unto Cattay five manner of waies, two of them knowen and the other three supposed', in *A Regiment for the Sea: Conteyning most profitable Rules, Mathematicall experiences, and perfect knowledge of Navigation*, 2nd edn (London 1680).
42. Quoted in Karen Ordahl Kupperman, *The Jamestown Project* (Cambridge, MA, 2007), p. 4.
43. Hakluyt, 'Discourse', p. 279.
44. Ibid., p. 211.
45. William J. Smyth, *Map-Making, Landscapes and Memory: A Geography of Colonial and Early Modern Ireland c. 1530–1750* (Notre Dame, IN, 2006), p. 161. In 1569, as Alva recovered the Netherlands, Gilbert took twenty-three Irish castles in six weeks 'and slaughtered all occupants, men, women and children'.
46. Donna Merwick, *The Shame and the Sorrow: Dutch Amerindian Encounters in New Netherland* (Philadelphia, PA, 2006), pp. 115–16.
47. Bradford, *Plymouth Plantation*, p. 4.
48. Merwick, *Shame*, p. 131.
49. Ibid., p. 130.
50. John Dee, *General and Rare Memorials pertaining to the Perfecte Arte of Navigation* (London, 1577), pp. 4–5.

51. Ralegh quoted by Andrews, *Trade*, p. 9; Scott, *When the Waves*, pp. 44–8; Scott, 'Maritime Orientalism'.
52. Evelyn, *Navigation and Commerce*, p. 57. Drake was the first captain to do so, Magellan having perished during the earlier circumnavigation by his crew.
53. Glyndwr Williams, *The Great South Sea: English Voyages and Encounters, 1570–1750* (New Haven, CT, 1997).
54. Andrews, *Trade*, p. 1.
55. Hakluyt, *Principall Navigations*, vol. I, p. 334.
56. Ibid., p. 354.
57. Ibid., p. 356.
58. Wilson, *England's Apprenticeship*, pp. 28–9.
59. Thirsk (ed.), *Agrarian History*, pp. 554–5.
60. Ibid., p. 558.
61. Malcolm Thick, 'Market Gardening in England and Wales', in Thirsk (ed.), *Agrarian History*, pp. 505–6.
62. Scott, *Belgicke Pismire*, pp. 95–6; G. E. Fussell, 'Low Countries' Influence on English Farming', *English Historical Review* 74 (1959).
63. Yarranton, *The Great Improvement of Lands by Clover* (1663), discussed in Wilson, *England's Apprenticeship, 1603–1763*, p. 143.
64. As inspected on many happy field trips with the Downing College historians, 1991–2002, accompanied by my mad English Labrador Jane. Frijhoff and Spies, *Hard-Won Unity*, p. 19.
65. Dunthorne, *Dutch Revolt*, p. 126.
66. Luu, *Immigrants*, p. 71.
67. Ibid., p. 73.
68. Ibid., pp. 32–3.
69. Ibid., pp. 259–60.
70. Ibid., p. 302.
71. Quoted in ibid., p. 1.
72. National Maritime Museum, Greenwich, REC/3 ff. 119–22, 123–7, 129–32, 133–8.
73. K. H. D. Haley, *The British and the Dutch: Political and Cultural Relations through the Ages* (London 1988), pp. 24–5; Dunthorne, *Dutch Revolt*, p. 126.
74. 'These [Dutch] refugees . . . laid the foundation of that commercial and manufacturing supremacy of Great Britain which is today the envy and wonder of the world, and which has changed the character of the islanders from that of shepherds and agriculturists to that of machinists and manufacturers.' Elliot Griffis, *American Republic*, pp. 10–11.
75. Muldrew, *Food*, p. 4.
76. Quote from an anonymous reader of this manuscript for Yale University Press, London.
77. Quoted by Charles Wilson, *Anglo-Dutch Commerce and Finance in the Eighteenth Century* (Cambridge, 1966), p. 4.
78. Sir Josiah Child, *A New Discourse of Trade* (London, 1694), drafted 1669.
79. Davis, *Shipping*, p. 8.
80. Klooster, 'Anglo-Dutch Trade', p. 262.
81. Ibid., p. 3.
82. Dunthorne, *Dutch Revolt*, p. 111.
83. Quoted in Haley, *The British and the Dutch*, p. 60.
84. Ibid., p. 58.
85. Andrews, *Trade*, p. 23.
86. Dunthorne, *Dutch Revolt*, p. 112.
87. Davis, *Shipping*, p. 247.
88. Luu, *Immigrants,* p. 38; Beier and Finlay, *London*, pp. 11–17.
89. Pestana, *English Atlantic*, p. 3.
90. Alison Games, *Migration and the Origins of the English Atlantic World* (Cambridge, MA, 1999), p. 4; on London as migrant destination and way-station see Games, Ch. 1.
91. Perry Miller, *The New England Mind: From Colony to Province* (Cambridge, MA, 1967), p. 6.

5 SEA OF THOUGHT

1. Quoted by Miller, *The New England Mind*, p. 11.
2. Jonathan Fryer (ed.), *George Fox and the Children of Light* (London, 1991), p. 21.
3. Heylyn, *Cosmography*, p. 20.
4. John Dryden, *Essay of Dramatic Poesy*, quoted in Jackson I. Cope and Harold Whitmore Jones (eds), *History of the Royal Society* by Thomas Sprat (St Louis, MO, 1958), Introduction, p. xviii.
5. Wootton, *Invention of Science*, p. 6.
6. For Amsterdam as a world city see Lesger, *Amsterdam Market*, p. 3.
7. Pestana, *English Atlantic*, p. 2: 'By 1660, the English Atlantic was more centralized, more diverse, more divided religiously, and more polarised between those who lacked autonomy and those who had power. Commercial, diverse, inegalitarian, and prickly about its rights, this world was born in the crucible of this revolution.'
8. Review of Peter Marshall, *Heretics and Believers: A History of the English Reformation* (New Haven, CT, 2017), *The Economist* (29 April 2017).
9. James Harrington, 'The Commonwealth of Oceana', in J. G. A. Pocock (ed.), *The Political Works of James Harrington* (Cambridge, 1977), p. 198.
10. Quoted by Games, *Migration*, p. 19.
11. Israel, *The Radical Enlightenment*, p. 141.
12. Van Zanden, *Long Road*, p. 68.
13. Ibid., p. 188.
14. Ibid., pp. 190–7, 190. See also, however, Anthony Grafton, Elizabeth Eisenstein and Adrian Johns, 'AHR Forum: How Revolutionary was the Print Revolution?', *American Historical Review* 107 (2002), pp. 84–128; Keith Thomas, 'The Meaning of Literacy in Early Modern England', in Gerd Baumann (ed.), *The Written Word: Literacy in Transition* (Oxford, 1986), pp. 97–131.
15. Paul Kristeller, 'Humanism', in Charles B. Schmitt, Quentin Skinner and Eckhard Kessler (eds), *The Cambridge History of Renaissance Philosophy* (Cambridge, 1988).
16. Machiavelli, *The Discourses*.
17. Hans Baron, *The Crisis of the Early Italian Renaissance*, 2 vols (Princeton, NJ, 1955).
18. Eric Nelson, 'Greek Nonsense in More's *Utopia*', *Historical Journal* 44, 4 (2001); Scott, *Commonwealth Principles*, pp. 44–9; John Guy, *Thomas More* (London, 2000), pp. 23–9.
19. Mijers, '*News from the Republick of Letters*', p. 5; Richard Tuck, *Philosophy and Government 1572–1651* (Cambridge, 1993); G. Oestreich, *Neostoicism and the Early Modern State* (Cambridge, 1982).
20. John Elliott, *The Old World and the New 1492–1650* (Cambridge, 1992), pp. 10, 51–2; see also Grafton, *New Worlds, Ancient Texts*, esp. Ch. 3.
21. Herodotus, *The Histories*, trans. Aubrey de Selincourt, ed. John Marincola (Harmondsworth, 1972), p. 169. This perspective was not the sole possession of Northern humanists. Grafton, *New Worlds*, p. 55, identifies it in the Italian Peter Martyr in 1516.
22. Jean Bodin, *Six Bookes of a Commonweale*, a facsimile reprint of the English translation of 1606, ed. K. D. McRae (Cambridge, MA, 1962).
23. Edmund Spenser, *The Faerie Queene*, ed. A. C. Hamilton, 2nd edn (Harlow, 2001), Book II, Proem, stanzas 2–3.
24. Quoted in Wootton, *Invention*, p. 39.
25. Sprat, *History of the Royal Society*, p. 39.
26. Ibid., pp. 62–3.
27. Mijers, '*News from the Rebublick of Letters*', pp. 4–5. See also Anthony A. Shelton, 'Cabinets of Transgression: Renaissance Collections and the Incorporation of the New World', in *The Cultures of Collecting*, eds John Elsner and Roger Cardinal (Cambridge, MA, 1994), pp. 177–203.
28. Richard Drayton, *Nature's Government: Science, Imperial Britain and the 'Improvement' of the World* (New Haven, CT, 2000), p. 16.

29. Quoted in ibid.
30. Sugita Genpaku, *Dawn of Western Science in Japan*, trans. Ryozo Matsumoto (Tokyo, 1969), pp. 1–71; Shigeisha Kuriyama, ' "Between Mind and Eye": Japanese Anatomy in the Eighteenth Century', in Charles Leslie and Allan Young (eds), *Paths to Asian Medical Knowledge* (Berkeley, CA, 1992), pp. 21–43.
31. Harrington, *Examination of James Harrington* and *Oceana*, in *Political Works*, pp. 287, 858.
32. Charles Webster, *The Great Instauration: Science, Medicine and Reform, 1626–1660* (London, 1975); Michael Braddick, *God's Fury, England's Fire: A New History of the English Civil Wars* (London, 2008), pp. 156–9; J. C. Davis, *Utopia and the Ideal Society: A Study of English Utopian Writing, 1516–1700* (Cambridge, 1981). See also Chs 6 and 13; Sprat, *History of the Royal Society*, pp. 55–6.
33. Drayton, *Nature's Government*, p. 17.
34. 'Directions for Seamen, bound for far voyages', *Philosophical Transactions*, quoted by Bernard W. Smith, *European Vision and the South Pacific, 1768–1850: A Study in the History of Art and Ideas*, 2nd edn (London, 1989), p. 8.
35. *An Account of Several Late Voyages & Discoveries To the South and North* ... BY Sir JOHN NARBOROUGH, Captain JASMEN TASMAN, Captain JOHN WOOD, and FREDERICK MARTEN of *Hamburgh* (London, 1694, Printed for *Sam. Smith* and *Benj. Walford*, Printers to the *Royal Society*), The Bookseller's Preface, or Introduction p. xxix.
36. Wootton, *Invention of Science*; Johns, *The Nature of the Book*; Mokyr, *Industrial Enlightenment*.
37. R. I. Moore, *The Formation of a Persecuting Society: Authority and Deviance in Western Europe 950–1250*, 2nd edn (Oxford 2007).
38. Haley, *British and the Dutch*, pp. 24–5.
39. Nicholas Tyacke (ed.), *England's Long Reformation, 1500–1800* (London, 1998); Ethan Shagan, *Popular Politics and the English Reformation* (Cambridge, 2002).
40. Temple, *Observations*, p. 166.
41. Speech because early modern reading was not silent. Protestant bibles were read aloud in private homes, churches and sometimes gathered congregations. Other printed material, including news, was shared in public spaces, including piazzas, market places, taverns and coffee houses.
42. Michael Baylor (ed.), *The Radical Reformation* (Cambridge, 1991).
43. Irvin Horst, *The Radical Brethren: Anabaptism and the English Reformation to 1558* (Nieuwkoop, 1972), pp. 30, 36.
44. Patrick Collinson, *Archbishop Grindal 1519–1583: The Struggle for a Reformed Church* (London, 1979).
45. Temple, *Observations*, p. 172.
46. Ibid.
47. Ibid.
48. Mark Greengrass, *Christendom Destroyed, 1517–1648* (New York, 2014), Chs 10–11.
49. Patrick Collinson, *The Elizabethan Puritan Movement* (Oxford, 1990); Peter Lake, 'Calvinism and the English Church, 1570–1635', *Past and Present* 114 (February 1987); Anthony Milton, *Catholic and Reformed* (Cambridge, 1995).
50. Stephen Alford, *The Early Elizabethan Polity: William Cecil and the British Succession Crisis 1558–1569* (Cambridge, 1998).
51. Patrick Collinson, *Richard Bancroft and Elizabethan Anti-Puritanism* (Cambridge, 2013).
52. Mijers, *'News from the Republick of Letters'*, Introduction.
53. Peter Lake, 'Post-Reformation Politics, or on Not Looking for the Long-Term Causes of the English Civil War', in Michael Braddick (ed.), *The Oxford Handbook of the English Revolution* (Oxford, 2015).
54. Jonathan Scott, 'England's Troubles: Exhuming the Popish Plot', in Paul Seaward et al. (eds), *The Politics of Religion in Restoration England* (Oxford, 1991); Catherine Balleriaux, *Reformation Strategies: European Missionaries in the New World, 1550–1700* (London, 2016).

55. *The Popish Plot, taken out of Several Depositions made and sworn before the Parliament* (1678), reprinted in W. Scott (ed.) *Tracts . . . of the Late Lord Somers*, vol. VIII, p. 55.

56. K. L. Sprunger, *Dutch Puritanism: A History of the English and Scottish Churches of the Netherlands in the Sixteenth and Seventeenth Centuries* (Leiden, 1982); John Donoghue, *Fire Under the Ashes: An Atlantic History of the English Revolution* (Chicago, IL, 2013); Michael Winship, *Godly Republicanism: Puritans, Pilgrims, and a City on a Hill* (Cambridge, MA, 2012).

57. Kupperman, *Jamestown*, pp. 90–1.

58. Haley, *British and the Dutch*, p. 69. Robinson was not among them: he died in Leiden in 1625.

59. Winship, *Godly Republicanism*, pp. 112–13.

60. Bradford, *Plymouth Plantation*, pp. 2, 4–5.

61. Ibid., p. 6.

62. Elliot Griffis, *American Republic*, p. 18.

63. Davids, 'The Scholarly Atlantic', pp. 244–5; Mijers, 'News from the Republick of Letters'.

64. Pagden, *Enlightenment*, p. 27.

65. Charles Carlton, *Going to the Wars: The Experience of the British Civil Wars 1638–1651* (London 1992).

66. G. L. V., *British Lightning* (1643), pp. 3–5.

67. Quoted by Brandon, *War, Capital*, p. 3.

68. Scott, *England's Troubles*, Chs 4–6.

69. Quentin Skinner, *The Foundations of Modern Political Thought*, 2 vols (Cambridge, 1978), *vol. I: The Reformation*; James VI and I, *Basilikon Doron. Or His Majesties Instructions to His Dearest Sonne, Henry the Prince*, in *The Workes of the Most High and Mighty Prince, James* (London, 1616); Sir Robert Filmer, *Sir Robert Filmer: Patriarcha and Other Writings*, ed. J. P. Sommerville (Cambridge, 1991).

70. Not all: Portugal in 1640 and Ireland in 1641 remind us otherwise, even if the latter was partly provoked by the Scots.

71. Christopher Goodman, *How Superior Powers ought to be obeyd* (Geneva, 1558; facsimile, Amsterdam, 1972), pp. 28, 140; see also Francis Hotman, *Francogallia*, ed. R. E. Giesey, trans. J. H. M. Salmon (Cambridge, 1972); Martin van Gelderen (ed.), *The Dutch Revolt* (Cambridge, 1993).

72. John Locke, *Two Treatises of Government*, II paras 19, 221; Jonathan Scott, 'The Law of War: Grotius, Sidney, Locke and the Political Theory of Rebellion', *History of Political Thought*, Locke Issue, 1993.

73. Nicholas Tyacke, *Anti-Calvinists: The Rise of English Arminianism, 1590–1640* (Oxford, 1987); Julian Davies, *The Caroline Captivity of the Church* (Oxford, 1992).

74. The quote is from Winship, *Godly Republicanism*, p. 7.

75. Charles I, *Declaration* (1629), in S. R. Gardiner (ed.), *Constitutional Documents of the Puritan Revolution*, p. 95.

76. Dunthorne, *Dutch Revolt*, Chs 1–2.

77. Van Deursen, *Plain Lives*, p. 140.

78. Blanning, *The Culture of Power*, pp. 279–300.

79. Lesger, *Amsterdam*.

80. Quoted in Haley, *British and the Dutch*, p. 33.

81. John Guy, *Tudor England* (London, 1988), p. 270.

82. Patrick Collinson, 'The Elizabethan Exclusion Crisis and the Elizabethan Polity', *Proceedings of the British Academy* 84 (1994).

83. Haley, *British and the Dutch*, p. 39.

84. Stephen Saunders Webb, *The Governors-General: The English Army and the Definition of the Empire 1569–1681* (Chapel Hill, NC, 1979), p. 5.

85. See Temple, *Observations*, pp. 95–6.

86. Quoted in Haley, *British and the Dutch*, p. 45.

87. Scott, *When the Waves*, Chs 3 and 4, pp. 39, 78, 120.

6 THE STORM, 1618–49

1. Sir Thomas Gates, *A true repertory of the wracke, and redemption of Sir Thomas Gates Knight*, published in *Samuel Purchas His Pilgrimes* (1625), vol. 4, bk 9, pp. 6–8.
2. John Rushworth, *Historical Collections . . . beginning the Sixteenth Year of King James, Anno 1618*, 3 vols (London, 1659–82), vol. 1, Preface.
3. Scott, *England's Troubles*, especially Part One.
4. [Marchamont Nedham], *The Case Stated Between England and the United Provinces* (London, 1652), pp. 2–3.
5. Conrad Russell, *Parliaments and English Politics 1621–1629* (Oxford, 1979), p. 83.
6. Richard Bonney, *The European Dynastic States 1494–1660* (Oxford, 1991), p. 354.
7. S. R. Gardiner, *History of England from the Accession of James I*, 10 vols (London, 1895), vol. 1, pp. 103, 293.
8. Edward Hyde, Earl of Clarendon, *The History of the Rebellion: A New Selection*, ed. Paul Seaward (Oxford, 2009), p. 19.
9. Harrington, 'Oceana', in *Works*, p. 198.
10. Jonathan Scott, 'Good News from the Forest Floor', review of Michael Braddick (ed.), *The Oxford Handbook of the English Revolution* (Oxford, 2015), published on H-Albion, January 2016; Scott, *England's Troubles*, Chs 3–4.
11. Van Gelderen, *The Dutch Revolt*, p. x.
12. Hyde, *History of the Rebellion*, vol. 1, p. 5.
13. 't Hart, *Bourgeois Republic*, p. 35.
14. Elliot Griffis, *American Republic*, p. 30.
15. Bernard Bailyn, *The Barbarous Years: The Conflict of Civilizations 1600–1675* (New York, 2013), p. 67.
16. 'Petition of Sir Thomas Dale to the Noble, High and Mighty Lords, the Lords the States General of the United Netherlands', January 1618, quoted by Christian J. Koot, 'Anglo-Dutch Trade in the Chesapeake and the British Caribbean, 1621–1733', in Oostindie and Roitman (eds), *Dutch Atlantic Connections*, p. 76.
17. Klooster, 'Anglo-Dutch Trade', pp. 263–4.
18. Koot, 'Anglo-Dutch Trade', p. 76.
19. Klooster, 'Anglo-Dutch Trade', p. 276.
20. Kenneth Morgan, 'Anglo-Dutch Economic Relations in the Atlantic World, 1688–1783', in Oostindie and Roitman (eds), *Dutch Atlantic Connections*, p. 126.
21. Aza Goudriaan and Fred Van Lieburg (eds), *Revisiting the Synod of Dordt 1618–1619* (Leiden, 2011), pp. xi, 1.
22. Geyl, *Orange and Stuart, 1641–1672*.
23. Quoted in Scott, *England's Troubles*, p. 101.
24. British Library Add MS 4181, 'The Relation of Sr Balthazar Gerbier', ff. 12, 52.
25. Scott, *England's Troubles*, Chs 3–4.
26. Jayne E. E. Boys, *London's News Press and the Thirty Years War* (Woodbridge, 2011), pp. 44, 45.
27. Ibid., Ch. 2 (e.g. p. 34) and Ch. 3 (e.g. p. 74).
28. Ibid., p. 49, summarizing the findings of F. Dahl, *Dutch Corantos*.
29. *Diary of John Rous . . . from 1625 to 1642*, ed. M. A. Everett Green (London, 1856), p. 45; S. L. Adams, 'Foreign Policy and the Parliaments of 1621 and 1624', in K. Sharpe (ed.), *Faction and Parliament* (Oxford, 1978).
30. Democritus Junior, *The Anatomy of Melancholy: What it Is* (Oxford, 1624), pp. 3–4, 14.
31. Micheal Frearson, 'An Aspect of the Production of the Newsbooks of the 1620s', Cambridge seminar paper, 1993.
32. British Library Add MS 4181, ff. 9, 51.
33. [Anon], *Tom Tell-Troath: or a Free Discourse Touching the Manners of the Time*, in Ashton (ed.), *James I*, pp. 218–19.
34. Johann Sommerville, 'James I and the Divine Right of Kings', in Linda Levy Peck (ed.), *The Mental World of the Jacobean Court* (Cambridge, 1991), pp. 65, 68.

35. Rushworth, *Historical Collections*, vol, 1, pp. 40–1.
36. Scott, *Belgicke Pismire*, Preface, p. A3.
37. Ibid., p. 51.
38. Ibid., p. 36.
39. Ibid., pp. 89–90.
40. National Archives, State Papers 16/530/36.
41. Charles I, *Declaration* (1629) in Gardiner (ed.), *Constitutional Documents*, p. 95.
42. S. R. Gardiner (ed.), *Debates in the House of Commons in 1625* (London, 1873), p. 31 (30 June).
43. National Maritime Museum, REC/3, p. 240: 'How a State may the best provide itself for a Warr'.
44. Ibid., p. 241; see also Francis Bacon, 'Of the True Greatness of Kingdoms and Estates', in Abbott (ed.), *Bacon's Essays*, vol. 1, p. 105.
45. Ibid., p. 242. Later John Milton would defend a regicide 'without precedent', as arguing 'the more wisdom, virtue, and magnanimity, that they know themselves able to be a precedent to others'. Milton, *The Tenure of Kings and Magistrates* (1649), in *Complete Prose Works*, p. 237.
46. *To all English Freeholders*, 24 January 1627, quoted in Richard Cust, *The Forced Loan and English Politics 1626–28* (Oxford, 1987), pp. 172–3.
47. Marjolein 't Hart, ' "The Devil or the Dutch": Holland's Impact on the Financial Revolution in England, 1643–1694', *Parliaments, Estates and Representation* 11, 1 (June 1991), pp. 42–6.
48. William J. Ashworth, *The Industrial Revolution: The State, Knowledge and Global Trade* (London, 2017), p. 14.
49. Quoted by John Reeve, *Charles I and the Road to Personal Rule* (Cambridge, 1989), pp. 49–50.
50. Gardiner (ed.), *Commons in 1625*, pp. 114, 78, 31.
51. Scott, *Commonwealth Principles*, Chs 8, 12, and see Ch. 6 below.
52. Quoted in Reeve, *Charles I and the Road to Personal Rule*, pp. 25–6.
53. Gardiner (ed.), *Constitutional Documents*, p. 79.
54. Ibid., p. 95.
55. Charles I, *Proclamation to . . . his Loving Subjects of . . . England* (1639), in Rushworth, *Historical Collections*, vol. 1, p. 830.
56. Davies, *The Caroline Captivity of the Church*; Scott, *England's Troubles*, Ch. 5.
57. Henry May, *The Enlightenment in America* (Oxford, 1976), pp. 44–5.
58. Temple, *Observations*, p. 179.
59. Ole Peter Grell, *Calvinist Exiles in Tudor and Stuart England* (Aldershot, 1996).
60. Wren to Laud in Kenyon (ed.), *The Stuart Constitution 1603–1688*, 2nd edn (Cambridge, 1993), p. 145; Haley, *British and the Dutch*, p. 73.
61. Ormrod, *Commercial Empires*, p. 93.
62. Quoted in Haley, *British and the Dutch*, p. 74.
63. Quoted by Elliott Griffis, *American Republic*, pp. 24–6, 29.
64. Bradford, *Plymouth Plantation*, p. 58.
65. Winthrop, *The Journal of John Winthrop, 1630–49: Abridged Edition*, eds Richard S. Dunn and Laetitia Yeandle (Cambridge, MA, 1996), p. 69.
66. Quoted in Klooster, 'Anglo-Dutch Trade', p. 269. See, however, Pestana, *English Atlantic*, p. 19: 'Competition from other European ports was largely Dutch, but English ships were more important before 1640.'
67. Bradford, *Plymouth Plantation*, p. 78.
68. T. H. Breen, *The Character of the Good Ruler: A Study of Puritan Political Ideas in New England, 1630–1730* (New Haven, CT, 1970), pp. 54–7.
69. Games, *Migration*, p. 21.
70. Dunthorne, *Britain and the Dutch Revolt*, p. 189; Scott, *England's Troubles*, pp. 140–2.
71. Helmers, *Royalist Republic*, Ch. 1.

72. Ibid., pp. 35–6.
73. Richard Baxter, *Reliquiae Baxterianae, or Mr Richard Baxter's Narrative of . . . His Life and Times* (London, 1696), p. 38.
74. Quoted by Dunthorne, *Dutch Revolt*, p. 60.
75. Games, *Migration*, p. 203.
76. Pestana, *English Atlantic*, Ch. 1.
77. *Journal of John Winthrop*, p. 248.
78. Mike Braddick, *The Nerves of State: Taxes and the Financing of the English State, 1558–1714* (Manchester, 1996); D'Maris Coffman, *Excise Taxation and the Origins of Public Debt* (London, 2013).
79. Scott, *When the Waves*, Ch. 4.
80. Braddick, *God's Fury*, Part Three: 'Revolution, 1646–9', Chs 16–21.
81. Scott, *England's Troubles*, Part Two, Chs 10–12.
82. Sidney, *Discourses*, in *Sydney on Government* (London, 1772), p. 11; Scott, *England's Troubles*, Chs 13–14.
83. Glenn Burgess, 'The Impact on Political Thought: Rhetorics for Troubled Times', in John Morrill (ed.), *The Impact of the English Civil War* (London, 1991), p. 67.
84. *Appeale from the degenerate Representative*, in D. M. Wolfe (ed.), *Leveller Manifestos of the Puritan Revolution* (New York, 1967), pp. 160–1.
85. Overton quoted by Dunthorne, *Dutch Revolt*, p. 167.
86. Quoted by Barry Coward, *Oliver Cromwell: A Profile* (London, 1991), p. 42.
87. Dunthorne, *Dutch Revolt*, p. 169.
88. Elliot Griffis, *American Republic*, p. 32.
89. Scott, *England's Troubles*, 'Part II: The English Revolution 1640–1689: Radical Imagination'.
90. Broadberry et al., *British Economic Growth*, p. 396.
91. Prak, *Dutch Republic*, pp. 5–6.
92. Brandon, *War, Capital*, p. 35.

7 THE ANGLO-DUTCH REPUBLIC, 1649–53

1. Quoted in Dunthorne, *Dutch Revolt*, p. 124.
2. John Milton, *A Defence of the English People*, in Milton, *Political Writings*, ed. Martin Dzelzainis (Cambridge, 1991), pp. 88, 155.
3. Hobbes, *Leviathan*, ed. Richard Tuck (Cambridge, 1991), p. 225.
4. 'Certainly observers in the wider Atlantic world understood the radical transformation of their homeland as extreme, shocking, and unprecedented.' Pestana, *English Atlantic*, p. 8.
5. Brian A'Hearn, 'The British Industrial Revolution in a European Mirror', in R. Floud, J. Humphries and P. Johnson (eds), *The Cambridge Economic History of Modern Britain Volume I: 1700–1870* (Cambridge, 2014), p. 12.
6. Ibid., pp. 33, 35–7.
7. Julian Hoppit, 'Political Power and Economic Life, 1650–1870', in Floud et al. (eds), *Cambridge Economic History*, p. 351.
8. Ch. 4 above.
9. Slack, *Invention*, pp. 91, 93.
10. Hoppit, 'Political Power', p. 351.
11. Ashworth, *The Industrial Revolution*, p. 18. Here Ashworth builds upon my own *England's Troubles*, 'Good Night Amsterdam', and *Waves* (Ashworth, Ch. 1, notes 3–4, 10, 16, 23, 35–9).
12. Slack, *Invention*, p. 257.
13. A'Hearn, 'The British Industrial Revolution', p. 36.
14. Temple, *Observations*, pp. 189–90.
15. William Penn, *The Works of William Penn*, 2 vols (London, 1756), vol. 1, pp. 678–9.
16. Slingsby Bethel, *The Interest of Princes and States* (London, 1680), p. 164.

17. Quoted by Roger Downing and Gijs Rommelse, *A Fearful Gentleman: Sir George Downing in The Hague 1658–1672* (Hilversum Verloren, 2011), p. 15. For Bethel and de la Court see Jonathan Scott, *Algernon Sidney and the English Republic 1623–1677* (Cambridge, 1988), Ch. 13: 'The Dutch Connection'.
18. Blair Worden, 'Republicanism, Regicide and Republic: The English Experience', in Martin van Gelderen and Quentin Skinner (eds), *Republicanism: A Shared European Heritage, Volume 1: Republicanism and Constitutionalism in Early Modern Europe* (Cambridge, 2002).
19. Markku Peltonen, 'The Republican Moment of the English Revolution', unpublished paper supplied by the author, February 2017.
20. *A Declaration of the Parliament of England, In Vindication of their Proceedings* (London, 1649), pp. 16–17.
21. Ibid.
22. Quoted in Peltonen, 'Moment', p. 5.
23. Leo Miller, *John Milton and the Oldenburg Safeguard* (New York, 1985), p. 86.
24. *Calendar of State Papers . . . Venice*, vol. XXVIII, 1647–1652 (London, 1927), pp. 325–6.
25. *Mercurius Politicus*, no. 104, 27 May– 3 June 1652, pp. 1,625–39.
26. Frijhoff and Spies, *1650: Hard-Won Unity*, pp. 39, 53; quoted by Brandon, *War, Capital*, p. 42.
27. Ibid., p. 55.
28. Helmers, *Royalist Republic*, Introduction.
29. For English republican writing as moral discourse see Scott, *Commonwealth Principles*.
30. Weber, *Protestant Ethic*, p. 121. Weber's quote is from Sir William Petty, *Political Arithmetic* (London, 1690), in G. A. Aitken (ed.), *Later Stuart Tracts* (London, 1903).
31. National Maritime Museum, REC/3, p. 242.
32. Frijhoff and Spies, *1650: Hard-Won Unity*, p. 21.
33. Burke, *Venice and Amsterdam*, p. 6.
34. Dunthorne, *Dutch Revolt*, p. 204.
35. Quoted by Slack, *Improvement*, p. 95.
36. Scott, *England's Troubles*, Ch. 11: 'Radical Reformation (1): The Power of Love'.
37. Fox, *Journal*, in Fryer (ed.), *George Fox*, p. 22.
38. R.B., *The Poor Man's Friend or a Narrative of what progress many worthy Citizens of London have made in that Godly work of providing for the POOR* (London, 16 March 1649), Epistle.
39. Scott, *England's Troubles*, pp. 266–7. See also Schenk, *The Concern for Social Justice*.
40. *Hartlib Papers*, 2nd edn (Sheffield, HROnline, 2002); Mark Greengrass, Michael Leslie and Tim Raylor (eds), *Samuel Hartlib and Universal Reformation: Studies in Intellectual Communication* (Cambridge, 1994).
41. Temple, *Observations*, pp. 112–13. Frijhoff and Spies, *1650: Hard-Won Unity*, p. 26.
42. Miller, *John Milton and the Oldenburg Safeguard*, p. 37.
43. Ibid., p. 73.
44. British Library Add MS 11602, Gibson 'A Reformation in ye Royall Navy most Humbly Proposed', p. 68.
45. Ibid., pp. 85–6.
46. Sidney, *Discourses*, pp. 278–9.
47. *Armies vindication* (1649), p. 63, quoted by Peltonen, 'Moment', p. 10. This theme is explored in Scott, *When the Waves*, Chs 3–4, and in Ch. 12 below.
48. John Milton, *The Readie and Easie Way*, 2nd edn (London, 1660), pp. 424–5.
49. Ibid., p. 423.
50. '[S]he at once became the most formidable power in the world'. Quoted by Steven Pincus, *Protestantism and Patriotism: Ideologies and the Making of English Foreign Policy 1650–1668* (Cambridge, 1996), p. 2.
51. Michael Oppenheim, *A History of the Royal Navy and of Merchant Shipping in Relation to the Navy* (repr., London, 1961), pp. 303–4.
52. Scott, *England's Troubles*, Part 3; Braddick, *State Formation*.
53. Braddick, *The Nerves of State*.
54. Ashworth, *Industrial Revolution*, p. 17.

55. Oppenheim, *Administration*, p. 347.
56. Henry Roseveare, *The Treasury, 1660–1870: The Foundations of Control* (London, 1973), p. 20. The administration in question was not Cromwellian, but parliamentary and republican.
57. Paul Dickson, *The Financial Revolution in England 1688–1756* (London, 1967), p. 7; see Ch. 10 below.
58. Scott, 'Good Night Amsterdam', p. 354.
59. Ashworth, *Industrial Revolution*, p. 19.
60. Worsley to Samuel Hartlib, 10 August 1649, quoted in Thomas Leng, *Benjamin Worsley (1618–1677): Trade, Interest and the Spirit in Revolutionary England* (Woodbridge, 2008), p. 49.
61. H. Stubbe, *A Further Justification of the Present War Against the United Netherlands* (London, 1673).
62. Mahan, *Sea Power*, p. 53.
63. Bacon, 'Of the True Greatness of Kingdoms and Estates', *Bacon's Essays*, p. 10.
64. Scott, *When the Waves*, esp. Ch. 4.
65. Bernard Capp, 'Naval Operations', in Kenyon and Ohlmeyer (eds), *The Civil Wars: A Military History of England, Scotland and Ireland 1638–1660* (Oxford, 1998), p. 161.
66. Brandon, *War, Capital*, p. 2.
67. Ibid., p. 43.
68. Robert Bliss, *Revolution and Empire: English Politics and the American Colonies in the Seventeenth Century* (Manchester, 1990), pp. 45–61.
69. Koot, 'Anglo-Dutch Trade', pp. 76–80.
70. 'The Act of Navigation is not grounded upon design of keeping strangers ignorant of our coasts . . . but for increasing the English manufacture of shipping. Read the Act.' Samuel Pepys, speaking of 12. Car. II, c.18, in J. Knox Laughton (ed.), *The Naval Miscellany*, vol. 2 (London, 1912), p. 22.
71. Pestana, *English Atlantic*, pp. 86–92.
72. Quoted in Pincus, *Protestantism and Patriotism*, pp. 11–12.
73. Scott, *Commonwealth Principles*, pp. 105, 260, 267–72.
74. Sidney, *Court Maxims*, p. 171. 'The Journal of the Earl of Leicester', in R. W. Blencowe (ed.), *Sidney Papers* (London, 1823), p. 141.
75. Slingsby Bethel, *The World's Mistake in Oliver Cromwell* (London, 1668), p. 3.
76. *The Spectator*, March 2017.
77. Mahan, *Sea Power*, p. 60.
78. Seeley quoted by Pincus, *Protestantism and Patriotism*, p. 2 ('Cromwell's foreign policy' is Pincus' summary); Prak, *Dutch Republic*, pp. 46–7.
79. Brandon, *War, Capital*, p. 50.
80. Israel, *Radical Enlightenment*, p. 22; Scott, *Commonwealth Principles*, pp. 90–8.
81. Ibid., Chs 6–8, 13–14.
82. Jonathan Scott, 'James Harrington's Prescription for Healing and Settling' in Smith and Braddick (eds), *The Experience of Revolution in Seventeenth-Century England* (Cambridge, 2012).
83. Parker, Preface to *The True Portaiture of the Kings of England* (17 August 1650).
84. John Streater, *Observations Historical, Political and Philosophical . . . Upon Aristotle's first Book of Political Government* (1654), no. 1, p. 6.
85. Sidney, *Court Maxims*, pp. 161–2.
86. Scott, *Commonwealth Principles*, pp. 13–14.
87. Ibid., p. 23.
88. Nedham, *The Case Stated Between England*, p. 24.
89. [Pieter de la Court] 'De Witt and other Great Men in Holland', *The True Interest and Political Maxims of the Republic of Holland* (London, 1702). Jonathan Israel, 'Toleration in Seventeenth-Century Dutch and English Thought', in Simon Groenveld and Michael Wintle (eds), *Britain and the Netherlands, Volume XI: Religion, Scholarship and Art* (Zutphen, 1994).

90. Pestana, *English Atlantic*, p. 12.
91. Morgan, 'Anglo-Dutch Economic Relations', p. 136.
92. Frijhoff and Spies, *1650: Hard-Won Unity*, p. 67.
93. Ibid.
94. Scott, 'Classical Republicanism in England and the Netherlands', in Van Gelderen and Skinner, *Republicanism*; Scott, *Commonwealth Principles*; Blair Worden, 'Classical Republicanism and the Puritan Revolution' in V. Pearl, H. Lloyd-Jones and B. Worden (eds), *History and Imagination* (Oxford, 1981).
95. Bibliothèque Nationale, Paris, Fr. MS 23254, 'Lantiniana' (Sidney to Jean-Baptiste Lantin in Paris in 1677), pp. 99–101.
96. Milton, *The Readie and Easie Way*, p. 423.

8 THE REPUBLIC WAS AN EMPIRE, 1649–53

1. Quoted by Brandon, *War, Capital*, p. vi.
2. Andrew Marvell, *The First Anniversary Of the Government under O.C.*, in *The Poems and Letters of Andrew Marvell*, ed. H. M. Margoliouth, 2 vols (Oxford, 1927), vol. 1, pp. 111–12. Marvell was here flattering Cromwell by associating him with a naval achievement which was not his.
3. Slack, *Improvement*, p. 95.
4. *Nineteen Propositions*, in J. P. Kenyon (ed.), *The Stuart Constitution 1603–1688*, 2nd edn (Cambridge, 1993), p. 225.
5. Scott, *Commonwealth Principles*, Chs 4 and 10 in particular.
6. Webb, *Governors-General*, p. 445.
7. Heylyn, *Cosmography*, p. 7.
8. Sidney, *Discourses*, ed. West, p. 209.
9. Greville, *Life of Sir Philip Sidney* (London, 1652), pp. 117–18; Blair Worden, *The Sound of Virtue: Philip Sidney's Arcadia and Elizabethan Politics* (New Haven, CT, 1996), Ch. 3.
10. Thucydides, *History of the Peloponnesian War*, pp. 147–8, 149–50.
11. Smith, *A Discourse of the Commonweal*, p. 25; Hiram Morgan, 'The Colonial Venture of Sir Thomas Smith in Ulster, 1571–1575', *Historical Journal* 28 (1985).
12. Marchamont Nedham, *The Case of the Commonwealth of England Stated*, ed. P. A. Knachel (Charlottesville, VA, 1969).
13. Scott, *England's Troubles*, Ch 13; Scott, *Commonwealth Principles*, Ch 10.
14. Slack, *Improvement*, p. 97.
15. Ibid., p. 98.
16. Milton, *Second Defence of the English People*, pp. 668, 670.
17. Thomas Burton, *Diary of Thomas Burton*, ed. J. T. Rutt, 4 vols (London, 1828), vol. 4, pp. 179, 183, 188, 190.
18. Prak, *Dutch Republic*, p. 47.
19. *Calendar of State Papers and Manuscripts relating to English Affairs . . . in the archives . . . of Venice* (London, 1927), vol. 28, p. 239.
20. Pestana, *English Atlantic*, p. 87.
21. Robert Brenner, *Merchants and Revolution: Commercial Change, Political Conflict, and London's Overseas Traders, 1550–1653* (Princeton, NJ, 1993), p. 580.
22. Morgan, 'Anglo-Dutch Economic Relations', pp. 122–3.
23. Oppenheim, *Administration*, p. 303.
24. Mahan, *Sea Power*, p. 60.
25. Oppenheim, *Administration*, p. 19.
26. Brenner, *Merchants*, p. 580.
27. Roger Hainsworth and Christine Churches, *The Anglo-Dutch Naval Wars, 1652–1674* (Stroud, 1998), p. 22.
28. Brenner, *Merchants*, pp. 578–9.

29. *Calendar of State Papers . . . in the archives . . . of Venice*, vol. 28. pp. 187–8.
30. Robert Bliss, *Revolution and Empire: English Politics and the American Colonies*, pp. 45–61.
31. Brenner, *Merchants*, pp. 580, 592.
32. Council and Assembly of Barbados, *A Declaration Set forth* (The Hague, 1651), quoted by Koot, 'Anglo-Dutch Trade', p. 85.
33. 'The humble Remonstrance of John Bland of London' quoted by Koot, ibid., p. 86.
34. Davis, *Shipping*, pp. 11–12; Prak, *Dutch Republic*, p. 47.
35. Klooster, 'Anglo-Dutch Trade', p. 276.
36. Hainsworth, *Naval Wars*, pp. 14–15.
37. Quoted in Leng, *Worsley*, p. 67.
38. Hainsworth, *Naval Wars*, p. 15.
39. Morgan, 'Anglo-Dutch Economic Relations', pp. 121–2.
40. Mahan, *Sea Power*, pp. 61–2.
41. Jones, *Anglo-Dutch Wars*, pp. 107–9.
42. Leo Miller, *John Milton's Writings in the Anglo-Dutch Negotiations, 1651–1654* (Pittsburgh, NJ, n.d), p. 173.
43. Israel, *Dutch Republic*, p. 714.
44. Jonathan Israel, 'England, the Dutch Republic, and Europe in the Seventeenth Century', *Historical Journal* 40, 4 (1997), pp. 1,117–21.
45. Jones, *Anglo-Dutch Wars*, pp. 18,107; Pincus, *Protestantism and Patriotism*, pp. 35, 75.
46. Prak, *Republic*, pp. 46–8.
47. Quoted by Brandon, *War, Capital*, p. 51.
48. Quoted in Pincus, *Protestantism and Patriotism*, p. 44.
49. Davis, *Shipping*, pp. 292–3.
50. Pincus, *Protestantism and Patriotism*, p. 14.
51. Dunthorne, *Dutch Republic*, p. 122 and see pp. 128–9.
52. Jones, *Anglo-Dutch Wars*.
53. [Marchamont Nedham], *The Case Stated Between England and the United Provinces*, p. 13.
54. Ibid., p. 14.
55. *Calendar of State Papers Venice*, p. 237.
56. Ibid., p. 242.
57. Gibson, 'Heads of a Discourse between an English and Dutch Sea Captain', British Library Add MS 11602, ff. 90–1.
58. Hainsworth *Naval Wars*, p. 20.
59. *Diary of Thomas Burton*, vol. 3, pp. 111–12.
60. Brandon, *War, Capital*, pp. 84–6, 136.
61. Ibid., pp. 87, 89.
62. Ibid., p. 86.
63. Davis, *Shipping*, p. 12.
64. Ibid., pp. 17–18.
65. Gibson, 'Observations Upon Islands in Generall and England in particular relating to safety and strength at Sea', NMM REC/6' Item 17, ff. 273–4.
66. 't Hart', *Bourgeois State*, p. 59.
67. Jonathan Israel, 'The Emerging Empire: The Continental Perspective, 1650-1713', in Canny (ed.), *The Oxford History of the British Empire*, p. 423; Armitage, *Ideological Origins*, Chs 4–5.
68. On this see most recently Priya Satia, *Empire of Guns: The Violent Making of the Industrial Revolution* (New York, 2018), Introduction and Chs 1–4.
69. Patrick O'Brien, 'Trade, Economy, State and Empire', in P. J. Marshall (ed.), *The Oxford History of the British Empire, Volume II: The Eighteenth Century* (Oxford, 1998), p. 64; Ashworth, *Industrial Revolution*.
70. O'Brien, *Trade*, p. 54.
71. Brandon, *War, Capital*, p. 50.
72. [Nedham], *The Case Stated*, pp. 23, 29.

73. Ibid., p. 29.
74. Ibid., p. 53.

9 THE EMPIRE WAS UNIQUE

1. Kent Archives Office, De Lisle MS U1475 Z1/9, loose pages, fifth item, fols 2–3.
2. Willem Usselincx quoted by Benjamin Schmidt, 'The Dutch Atlantic', in Greene and Morgan (eds), *Atlantic History*, p. 171.
3. Wim Klooster, *The Dutch in the Americas, 1600–1800* (Providence, RI, 1997), p. 42.
4. Benjamin Schmidt, *Innocence Abroad: The Dutch Imagination in the New World, 1570–1670* (Cambridge, 2001), Preface.
5. Hakluyt, 'Discourse', p. 212.
6. Andrew Hadfield, *Literature, Politics and National Identity: Reformation to Renaissance* (Cambridge, 1994), pp. 91–104.
7. Merwick, *Shame*, pp. 118, 126, 137.
8. Bradford, *Plymouth Plantation*, p. 83.
9. 'To inflict maximum suffering with total destruction seems to have been the order of the day ... The terms of the peace to which the Indians submitted virtually put an end to the Pequots as a distinct tribe.' Douglas Leach, *The Northern Colonial Frontier* (New York, 1966), p. 37.
10. The accounts both of fruitful abundance and of slaughter are from John Underhill, *News from America* (1638), discussed by Merwick, *Shame*, pp. 126–9.
11. Bradford, *Plymouth Plantation*, pp. 84–5. Winthrop without emotion summarized the fatalities as 'two chief sachems, and one hundred and fifty fighting men, and about one hundred and fifty old men, women, and children, with the loss of two English (whereof but one was) killed by the enemy', *Journal*, pp. 122–3.
12. Sebastian Barry's novel *Days Without End* (2017) features a similar massacre of Sioux in mid-nineteenth-century Wyoming, provoking the emigré Irish soldier Thomas McNulty to remember the Cromwellian conquest of Ireland.
13. Quoted by Leach, *Frontier*, p. 37.
14. Peter Mancall, 'Native Americans and Europeans in English America, 1500–1700', in Canny (ed.), *Origins of the British Empire*.
15. Brandon, *War, Capital*, p. 30.
16. Van Bavel, *The Invisible Hand?*, pp. 191–2, 199.
17. Lucassen, 'Labour and Early Modern Economic Development', in Davids and Lucassen (eds), *A Miracle Mirrored*, p. 369.
18. Thus about the collection *Dutch Atlantic Connections* Alison Games commented: 'The absence of attention to religion in the Dutch world ... is striking, in light of the attention paid by scholars to religion, and especially toleration, in the Dutch Republic.' ('Conclusion', p. 370). This omission appears to be revealing rather than accidental.
19. Mike Dash, *Batavia's Graveyard: The True Story of the Mad Heretic Who Led History's Bloodiest Mutiny* (New York, 2002).
20. William Eisler, *The Furthest Shore: Images of Terra Australis from the Middle Ages to Captain Cook* (Cambridge, 1995), pp. 70–1.
21. Quoted in Peter Timms, *In Search of Hobart* (Sydney, 2009), p. viii.
22. 'Journal or Description by me, Abel Jans Tasman, of a Voyage Made from the City of Batavia ... December Anno 1642 ... For the Discovery of the Unknown South Land', in John Beaglehole (ed.), *Abel Janszoon Tasman & The Discovery of New Zealand* (Wellington, 1942), pp. 45, 49–52, 53; see also Donald Denoon et al. (eds), *The Cambridge History of the Pacific Islanders* (Cambridge, 1997), pp. 127–8 and Ch. 4.
23. Maori had arrived in New Zealand from Eastern Polynesia fewer than three hundred years previously, making this the last substantial temperate climate territory to acquire human inhabitants. Scott, 'Epilogue: Wave after Wave', in Frances Steel (ed.), *New Zealand and the Sea: Historical Perspectives* (Wellington, 2018), pp. 312–13.

24. Charles Boxer, *The Dutch Seaborne Empire, 1600–1800* (London, 1965), p. 79.
25. Ibid., p. 86.
26. Van Deursen, *Plain Lives*, p. 23.
27. Pepijn Brandon observes that the Dutch Golden Age 'was never "golden" for those who sailed its ships, fought its wars, worked the plantations of the East and the West as enslaved labourers, or harvested the nutmeg that made fortunes for the VOC'. *War, Capital*, p. 7, note 23.
28. John McNeill, 'The American Demographic Catastrophe', lecture given at the University of Auckland to History 103 Global History, 3 March 2016.
29. Vincent Brown, *The Reaper's Garden: Death and Power in the World of Atlantic Slavery* (Cambridge, MA, 2008), p. 33.
30. 'Throughout the eighteenth century, the death rate for the British in Jamaica exceeded 10 percent a year', ibid., p. 13.
31. Merwick, *Shame*, p. 106.
32. Klooster, *Dutch in the Americas*, p. 23.
33. Klooster, 'Anglo-Dutch Trade', pp. 266–8, 273.
34. Schmidt, 'The Dutch Atlantic', in Greene and Morgan (eds), *Atlantic History*, p. 174.
35. Klooster, *Dutch in the Americas*, p. 28.
36. Bailyn, *The Barbarous Years*, pp. 192–4; Lucassen, 'Labour and Early Modern Economic Development', in Davids and Lucassen (eds), *A Miracle Mirrored*, pp. 368–74.
37. Bailyn, *The Barbarous Years*, p. 196.
38. Quoted in ibid., p. 260.
39. Games, 'Conclusion', p. 362.
40. Games, *Migration*, pp. 206–16 ('A Hybrid World').
41. Quoted in Bailyn, *Barbarous Years*, p. 256.
42. Mahan, *Sea Power*, p. 57.
43. Ibid., p. 55.
44. Joyce Goodfriend, Benjamin Schmidt and Annette Stott (eds), *Going Dutch: The Dutch Presence in America, 1609–2009* (Leiden, 2008), Introduction, p. 2.
45. Russell Shorto, *The Island at the Centre of the World: The Untold Story of Dutch Manhattan and the Founding of New York* (London, 2004), pp. 2–3.
46. Kevin Baker, 'They Took Manhattan', *The New York Times* (24 April 2004).
47. Donna Merwick, *Stuyvesant Bound: An Essay on Loss Across Time* (Philadelphia, PA, 2013), p. xiii.
48. Quoted in Bailyn, *Barbarous Years*, p. 19. Bailyn discusses the impact of the transfer of this mentality west across the Atlantic.
49. Canny, *Making Ireland British*.
50. Bailyn, *Barbarous Years*, p. 119.
51. Ibid.
52. Alison MacDiarmid, 'Humans and Marine Ecosystems: Insights from Large, Remote, Late-Settled Islands', in Steel (ed.), *New Zealand and the Sea*, p. 147.
53. Sinclair, 'Life in the Provinces', in Sinclair (ed.), *Distance Looks Our Way*, p. 28.
54. Peter Gilderdale, 'Taming the Migratory Divide', in Steel (ed.), *New Zealand and the Sea*, p. 4 (read in draft).
55. Scott, *Vox Populi*, no page number.
56. On all of which see Trevor Burnard, 'The British Atlantic', in Jack P. Greene and Philip D. Morgan (eds), *Atlantic History: A Critical Appraisal* (Oxford, 2009), p. 117.
57. Kupperman, *Jamestown*.
58. Ibid., p. 83.
59. Games, *Migration*, p. 16.
60. Robert Hughes, *The Fatal Shore: The Epic of Australia's Founding* (New York, 1986), Chs 5–6.
61. Bailyn, *Barbarous Years*, p. 79.
62. Koot, 'Anglo-Dutch Trade', pp. 76–7.

63. Ibid., p. 74.

64. Bailyn, 'Preface' to David Armitage and Michael Braddick (eds), *The British Atlantic World, 1500–1800* (Houndmills, 2009), p. xvi.

65. Downing to Winthrop, 26 August 1645, in *Winthrop Papers*, vol. 6, 1650–1654, ed. Malcolm Freiburg (Boston, MA, 1992), pp. 42–4.

66. Games, 'Conclusion: A Dutch Moment in Atlantic Historiography', pp. 357–8, discussing Russell R. Menard, *Sweet Negotiations: Sugar, Slavery, and Plantation Agriculture in Early Barbados* (Carlottesville, VA, 2006); Klooster, 'Anglo-Dutch Trade', pp. 270–3; Brown, *Reaper's Garden*, p. 14.

67. Klooster, 'Anglo-Dutch Trade', p. 274.

68. Alfred W. Crosby, *Ecological Imperialism: The Biological Expansion of Europe, 900–1900*, 2nd edn (Cambridge, 2004); J. R. McNeill, *Mosquito Empires: Ecology and War in the Greater Caribbean, 1620–1914* (Cambridge, 2010).

69. See Richard Grove, *Green Imperialism: Colonial Expansion, Tropical Island Edens and the Growth of Environmentalism, 1600–1860* (Cambridge, 1995), and Drayton, *Nature's Government*.

70. Brown, *Reaper's Garden*, pp. 15–17.

71. Bailyn, 'Preface' to Armitage and Braddick (eds), *British Atlantic*, pp. xvi–xvii.

72. Trevor Burnard, 'The British Atlantic', in Greene and Morgan (eds), *Atlantic History*, p. 117.

73. Ibid.

74. Israel, 'The Emerging Empire'.

75. Frank Fox, *Great Ships: The Battlefleet of King Charles II* (Greenwich, 1980), pp. 55–7.

76. J. D. Davies, *Gentlemen and Tarpaulins: The Officers and Men of the Restoration Navy* (Oxford, 1991), p. 15.

77. Pepys found Gibson in particular 'mighty understanding and acquainted with all things in the Navy': *Diary IX*, p. 16.

78. Downing and Rommelse, *Fearful Gentleman*, pp. 84, 110.

79. Quoted by Koot, 'Anglo-Dutch Trade', p. 87.

80. Hilary Beckles, 'The "Hub of Empire": The Caribbean and Britain in the Seventeenth Century', in Nicholas Canny (ed.), *The Oxford History of the British Empire, Volume 1: The Origins of Empire* (Oxford, 1998), p. 236.

81. John Ogilby, *America: Being the Latest, and Most Accurate Description of the New World* (London, 1671), pp. 185, 212.

82. John Narborough, 'A Journal kept by Captain John Narborough', in *An Account of Several Late Voyages to the South and North*, pp. 10–11; J. C. Beaglehole (ed.), *The Journals of Captain James Cook on His Voyages of Discovery: The Voyage of the Endeavour 1768–1771* (Cambridge, 1955), pp. cclxxxii–cclxxxiii, 11.

83. [Daniel Defoe], *A General History of Discoveries and Improvements in Useful Arts* (London, 1725–6), pp. 287–98.

84. Narborough, 'A Journal', pp. 10–11, 30, 36. A manuscript with colour ink sketches is in the British Library, Sloane MS 3833.

85. Awnsham and John Churchill, 'An Introductory Discourse, Containing, The whole History of Navigation from its Original to this time', in *A Collection of Voyages and Travels, Some Now Printed from Original Manuscripts*, 6 vols (London, 1732), vol. 1, p. lxiv.

86. J. C. Beaglehole (ed.), *The Voyage of the Resolution and Adventure 1772–1775* (Cambridge, 1961), pp. 88–9.

87. K. G. Davies, 'Joint-Stock Investment in the Later Seventeenth Century', *Economic History Review*, 4, 3 (1952).

88. Bliss, *Revolution and Empire*, p. 174; Beckles, 'The "Hub of Empire" ', p. 236; Scott, 'Good Night Amsterdam', pp. 351–2; Games, *Web of Empire*, pp. 290–2.

89. Charles Wilson, *Profit and Power: A Study of England and the Dutch Wars* (London, 1957), p. 102.

90. David Ormrod, 'Cultural Production and Import Substitution: The Fine and Decorative Arts in London, 1660–1730', in O'Brien (ed.), *Urban Achievement*, p. 228.

91. De Vries, *The Industrious Revolution*, Chs 2–4.
92. Ormrod, 'Cultural Production', p. 212.
93. Nuala Zahedieh, 'Overseas Trade and Empire', in Floud et al. (eds), *Cambridge Economic History*, p. 418.

10 ISLE OF PINES

1. Sidney, *Discourses* in *Sydney on Government*, p. 209.
2. *The Declaration of Breda* in Kenyon (ed), *Stuart Constitution*, p. 332.
3. Temple, *Observations*, p. 182.
4. Sir William Petty, *Political Arithmetic* (1690), in Aitken (ed.), *Later Stuart Tracts*, p. 21.
5. Quoted in John Spurr, *The Restoration Church of England, 1646–89* (New Haven, CT, 1991), p. 47.
6. Bodleian Library, Clarendon MS 105, f. 18, Downing to Clarendon, 2 September 1661.
7. Henry Roseveare, 'Prejudice and Policy: Sir George Downing as Parliamentary Entrepreneur', in Peter Mathias (ed.), *Enterprise and History: Essays in Honour of Charles Wilson* (Cambridge, 1986), p. 141.
8. Steven Pincus, *1688: The First Modern Revolution* (New Haven, CT, 2009), p. 55.
9. Bethel, *The World's Mistake* (1668); *The Interest of England, Stated* (1671); *The Interest of Princes and States* (1680).
10. Statt, *Foreigners and Englishmen*, pp. 66–7, 81–3, and Chs 2 and 3 in general.
11. Ibid., pp. 31–2 and Ch. 4.
12. [Penn], *England's Present Interest Discover'd With Honour to the Prince and Safety to the People* (1675), pp. 12–13.
13. See also the satirical ballad *The Quakers Farewel to England, or* Their Voyage to *New Jersey*, scituate on the Continent of *Virginia*, and bordering upon *New England* (London, 1675).
14. Elliott Griffis, *American Republic*, p. 38.
15. Gabriel Thomas, *An Historical and Geographical Account of Pensilvania* (1698), in Albert Cook Myers (ed.), *Narratives of Early Pennsylvania West New Jersey and Delaware 1630–1707* (New York, 1912), pp. 317–19.
16. Ibid., pp. 315–16.
17. Graunt and Petty, and Pepys, quoted by Michael Mckeon, *Politics and Poetry in Restoration England* (Cambridge, MA, 1975), p. 101.
18. Philip Curtin, *The Atlantic Slave Trade: A Census* (Madison, WI, 1969), pp. 119n, 216.
19. Scott, *England's Troubles*, Part Three.
20. Sidney, *Court Maxims*, pp. 161–2.
21. British Library, Egerton MS 2538, Downing to Nicholas, 2 May 1662, f. 61.
22. Quoted in Pincus, *Protestantism and Patriotism*, p. 292.
23. Scott, 'Good Night Amsterdam'.
24. Bodleian Library, Oxford, MS Clarendon, vol. 104, f. 8 (30 August 1661).
25. Brandon, *War, Capital*, p. 93.
26. Su Fang Ng, 'Dutch Wars, Global Trade, and the Heroic Poem: Dryden's *Annus mirabilis* (1666) and Amin's *Sya'ir perang Mengkasar* (1670)', *Modern Philology* 109, 3 (February 2012).
27. Mckeon, *Politics and Poetry*, p. 111.
28. Downing and Rommelse, *Fearful Gentleman*, pp. 131–2.
29. Ibid., pp. 135–7.
30. Merwick, *Stuyvesant Bound*, pp. 104–6.
31. Quoted by Shorto, *Island at the Centre of the World*, pp. 343–4.
32. Morgan, 'Anglo-Dutch Economic Relations', p. 126.
33. Ibid., pp. 129–31.
34. Games, *Migration*, p. 190.
35. Brandon, *War, Capital*, p. 111.
36. Prak, *Dutch Republic*, p. 49.

37. Mahan, *Sea Power*, p. 101.
38. Quoted in Davies, *Gentlemen and Tarpaulins*, p. 33.
39. Scott, 'Good Night Amsterdam'.
40. C. D. Chandaman, *The English Public Revenue 1660–1688* (Oxford, 1975), pp. 278, 279. 't Hart, ' "The Devil or the Dutch" ', p. 47, also emphasizes the enduring importance of Downing's Dutch-inspired reorganization of the Treasury.
41. Tracy, *Financial Revolution in the Habsburg Netherlands*.
42. Hyde, *Life of Clarendon*, vol. 11, pp. 195–6.
43. Ashworth, *Industrial Revolution*, pp. 19–20.
44. Dickson, *Financial Revolution*, p. 9.
45. Brewer, *Sinews of Power*, p. 133.
46. Both quoted in Schama, *Embarrassment of Riches*, p. 263.
47. Downing and Rommelse, *Fearful Gentleman*, p. 140.
48. Quoted in Pincus, *Protestantism and Patriotism*, p. 346.
49. Mahan, *Sea Power*, p. 131.
50. Downing and Rommelse, *Fearful Gentleman*, p. 147.
51. Mahan, *Sea Power*, p. 132.
52. Downing and Rommelse, *Fearful Gentleman*, p. 147. See the reproduction of Ludolf Bakhuizen, *The Royal Charles Carried into Dutch Waters* (National Maritime Museum) on the jacket of Scott, *Commonwealth Principles*.
53. Samuel Pepys, *The Diary of Samuel Pepys 1660–1669*, eds R. C. Latham and W. Mathews, 11 vols (London, 1971–83), *vol. VIII: 1667*, pp. 268–9.
54. Quoted in Pincus, *Protestantism and Patriotism*, pp. 417–18.
55. Fox, *Great Ships*, pp. 92–4.
56. Pepys Library, Magdalene College, Cambridge MS 2888. 'The political grounds and maxims of the Republic of Holland and West Friesland', translation by Toby Bonnell of *Aanwysing der heilsam politike Gronden en Maximen van de Republicke van Holland en West-Vriesland* (Leiden and Rotterdam, 1669).
57. Haley, *British and the Dutch*, p. 9.
58. Richard Ollard, *Pepys: A Biography* (London, 1974), p. 167; British Library, Add MS 11684, ff. 31–3: 'The Dutch Action at Chatham Examined'. Gibson's authorship is not certain. The document is signed 'JM'. But it is among Gibson's papers, apparently in his hand, and certainly in his tone. Both the existence of the manuscript and some indeterminacy regarding authorship are presumably explained by Gibson's (and Pepys') liability for investigation.
59. Ibid., p. 32a.
60. Ibid., p. 32b.
61. Ibid., p. 31a.
62. Ibid., p. 31b.
63. Ibid., p. 33b.
64. Ibid., pp. 32b–33a.
65. Sir William Monson, *The Naval Tracts of Sir William Monson*, ed. M. Oppenheim, 5 vols (London, 1902–14), vol. 5, pp. 12 and 5–15.
66. Marvell, *The Poems and Letters of Andrew Marvell*, vol. 1, pp. 154, 158–9.
67. Ibid., p. 163.
68. O. Nicastro (ed.), *Henry Neville e L'isola di Pines* (Pisa, 1998), pp. 67, 69, 81–9.
69. Combined with a late average age of marriage, the temporary infertility accompanying breast-feeding (lactational amenorrhea) was the leading seventeenth-century English means of birth control. Average duration of breast-feeding was 12–19 months. Wrigley, Davies and Schofield, *English Population History*, pp. 446, 465, 478.
70. Gaby Mahlberg, 'Republicanism as Anti-Patriarchalism in Henry Neville's *The Isle of Pines* (1668)', in Morrow and Scott (eds), *Liberty, Authority, Formality: Political Ideas and Culture, 1600–1900* (Exeter, 2008).
71. Nicastro (ed.), *L'isola di Pines*, p. 73.
72. Ibid., p. 105.

73. Ibid., p. 119.
74. Ibid., pp. 109, 111.
75. Quoted in Elliott, *Empires*, p. 18.
76. Marvell, *Poems and Letters*, p. 142.
77. NMM, REC/6 Item 24; 'Sir H Shere's [sic] proposal to King James for preserving the Naval Royal in Port from any Insult', 4 May 1688, pp. 343–4, 353.
78. *Diary of Pepys, VIII: 1667*, pp. 268–9.
79. Pepys, *Samuel Pepys and the Second Dutch War: Pepys' Navy White Book and Brooke House Papers*, ed. Robert Latham (London, NRS, 1996), pp. 225–6.
80. Prak, *Dutch Republic*, p. 50.
81. *His Majesties Gracious Speech to both Houses of Parliament Jan 7 1674* [O.S.], p. 6; M. Mignet, *Negociations Relative à La Succession D'Espagne Sous Louis XIV*, vol. 3 (Paris, 1842), pp. 190 and 187–97.
82. John Miller, *James II* (London, 1991), p. 60.
83. Mignet, *Negociations*, p. 102.
84. J. S. Clarke, *The Life of James the Second*, 2 vols (London, 1816), vol. 1, p. 422; see also James MacPherson (ed.), *Original Papers; Containing the Secret History of Great Britain*, 2 vols (London, 1775), vol. 1, pp. 48, 50.
85. Ronald Hutton, 'The Religion of Charles II', in Malcolm Smuts (ed.), *The Stuart Court and Europe* (Cambridge, 1996), p. 234.
86. On the king's campaign for a 'stricter alliance' see A. Bryant (ed.), *The Letters, Speeches and Declarations of King Charles II* (London, 1935), pp. 142, 150, 163, 165, 181–3, 223–4; and R. Norrington (ed.), *My Dearest Minette: The Letters between Charles II and . . . Henrietta, Duchesse d'Orleans* (London, 1996), pp. 156–82, 210–11. Leopold von Ranke, *History of England Principally in the Seventeenth Century*, 6 vols (Oxford, 1873), vol. 3, p. 495, emphasizes that the religious project was driven not by James but 'the King himself'.
87. Mignet, *Negociations*, vol. 3, pp. 7–8, 100–6, 115–24, 128, 132, 187–97.
88. Paris, Ministère des Affaires Etrangères, Archives Diplomatiques, Correspondence Politique Angleterre, vol. 95, pp. 235–6; also pp. 241, 247–8, 258–9.
89. Ibid., p. 229. For the shared perception of a continued English republican danger see Colbert to 'Sire' [the king], 19 August 1669, pp. 57–8.
90. Dale Hoak and Mordechai Feingold (eds), *The World of William and Mary: Anglo-Dutch Perspectives on the Revolution of 1688–89* (Stanford, CA, 1996), pp. 6–7.
91. Miller, *Charles II*, p. 194. Mignet, *Negociations*, pp. 7–8, sets this antipathy in wider contexts.
92. Scott, *England's Troubles*, pp. 172–6; for an alternative explanation see Hutton, 'The Making of the Secret Treaty of Dover', *Historical Journal* 29, 2 (1986).
93. Scott, *England's Troubles*, pp. 62–5.
94. Francis Gregory, *David's Returne From His Banishment* (Oxford, 1660), pp. 11, 14.
95. Miller, *Charles II*, pp. 219–20.
96. Magdalene College, Cambridge, Pepys Library MS 2142, ff. 2–3.

11 THE REVOLUTION COMPLETED, 1672–1702

1. PRO SP8/1/Part 2, fols 224–5 quoted in Pincus, *1688*, p. 228.
2. Miller, *Charles II*, p. 244. Thus the French themselves doubted 'the sincerity of the English alliance, when . . . the people and the nobles were murmuring against it, and Charles II was perhaps alone in his kingdom in wishing it?' The French historian Troude, paraphrasing M. D'Estrees, quoted by Mahan, *Sea Power*, p. 155. It is impossible not to remember Donald Trump talking to Sergei Kislyak in early 2017 ('I was under great pressure because of Russia. That's now taken off!').
3. Scott, *England's Troubles*, pp. 29–30.
4. Prak, *Dutch Republic*, pp. 51–2.
5. Schama, *Embarrassment of Riches*, p. 277.

6. Prak, *Dutch Republic*, p. 51.
7. Temple, *Observations*, p. 242.
8. Mahan, *Sea Power*, p. 154.
9. Prak, *Dutch Republic*, p. 52.
10. K. H. D. Haley, *The First Earl of Shaftesbury* (Oxford, 1968), p. 330; *William of Orange and the English Opposition 1672–4* (1953).
11. Quoted in Charles-Edouard Levillain, 'The Intellectual Origins of the Anglo-Dutch Alliance, 1667–1677', accessed online, p. 10.
12. *A Speech Made by a True Protestant English Gentleman To Incourage the City of London to Petition for the Sitting of the Parliament* [London, 1680], p. 2.
13. Scott, *Restoration Crisis*, Ch. 6, 'European Politics'; Scott, 'Unfinished Family Business. Algernon Sidney's arguments with Sir William Temple, Henry Hammond, Henry Sidney, Charles II and the Public Executioner', *Seventeenth Century*, 31, 4 (2016), pp. 391–410.
14. *The Humble Address of the Commons in Parliament Assembled, Presented to His Majesty, Monday 28th day of November 1680* (London, 1680), p. 76. There is much overlap with [Andrew Marvell] *An Account of the Growth of Popery and Arbitrary Government* (Amsterdam, 1677; repr. 1971).
15. *Humble Address*, pp. 77–82.
16. J. J. Jusserand, *Recueil des Instructions Donnees Aux Ambassadeurs et Ministres de France*, vol. XXV: *Angleterre* (Paris, 1929), p. 271.
17. Grant Tapsell, *The Personal Rule of Charles II, 1681–85: Politics and Religion in an Age of Absolutism* (London, 2007).
18. Israel, 'The Dutch Role', in Israel (ed.), *The Anglo-Dutch Moment*, p. 106.
19. John Evelyn, *Memoirs*, ed. W. Bray, 2 vols (London, 1818), vol. 1, pp. 614–15.
20. A. Grey, *Debates of the House of Commons 1667–1694*, 10 vols (London, 1763), vol. 9, p. 97.
21. Quoted in Israel and Parker, 'Of Providence and Protestant Winds', in Israel (ed.), *The Anglo-Dutch Moment*, pp. 335–6.
22. Quoted in Jardine, *Going Dutch*, p. 16.
23. Israel, 'The Dutch Role in the Glorious Revolution', in Israel (ed.), *The Anglo-Dutch Moment*, pp. 119–20; Prak, *Dutch Republic*, pp. 56–7.
24. Van Bavel, *The Invisible Hand?*, p. 214; Prak, *Dutch Republic*, p. 57.
25. William II, *The Declaration of His Highness . . . for restoring the laws and liberties of England, Scotland, and Ireland* (1688), in Rodert Beddard (ed.), *A Kingdom Without a King* (Oxford, 1988), p. 125.
26. John Childs, *The British Army of William III 1689–1702* (Manchester, 1987), pp. 4–5.
27. *The Debate at Large between the Lords and Commons . . . Anno 1688 . . . Relating to the Word ABDICATED*, 2nd edn (London, 1705), p. 13.
28. Grey, *Debates*, vol. 9, pp. 30, 33.
29. Linda Colley, *Britons: Forging the Nation 1707–1787* (New Haven, CT, 1992).
30. Quoted in Tony Claydon, *William III and the Godly Revolution* (Cambridge, 1996), p. 141.
31. Bodleian Library, Oxford, Sheres 'Third Chapter . . . of Naval War' (no page nos).
32. Scott, *England's Troubles*, Ch. 21.
33. Quoted in Brewer, *Sinews of Power*, p. 142.
34. Geoffrey Holmes, *The Making of a Great Power: Late Stuart and Early Georgian Britain, 1660–1722* (Harlow, 1993), pp. 245–6.
35. Robert Molesworth, *An Account of Denmark, As It Was in the Year 1692* (London, 1698), Preface.
36. Frijhoff and Spies, *1650: Hard-Won Unity*, p. 21.
37. O'Brien, 'Trade, Economy, State and Empire', p. 70.
38. Quoted in Blanning, *The Culture of Power*, p. 309.
39. Ibid., p. 307 (and see pp. 3, 10).
40. Brewer, *Sinews of Power*, p. 133.
41. 't Hart, 'Devil or the Dutch', p. 52.

42. Alistair Birchall, ' "A Bank settled on a good Fund": The Million Bank and Joint-Stock Securities during the English Financial Revolution', unpublished MA thesis, University of Auckland, 2017, p. 2.
43. Morgan, 'Anglo-Dutch Economic Relations', p. 124.
44. Daniel Defoe, *An Essay Upon Projects* (London, 1697), p. 1.
45. Blanning, *The Culture of Power*, p. 270.
46. Quoted in Hoppit, 'Political Power', p. 355. Hoppit's analysis of this legislation is on pp. 355–7.
47. Temple, *Observations*, pp. 75–6.
48. Morgan, 'Anglo-Dutch Economic Relations', p. 123.
49. Braudel, *Civilisation and Capitalism, Volume III: The Perspective of the World*, p. 365.
50. Statt, *Foreigners*, pp. 29–30.
51. Ibid., pp. 30–1.
52. Ormrod, *Commercial Empires*, pp. 92–3.
53. Robert Wodrow quoted in Black, *London*, p. 160.
54. Morgan, 'Anglo-Dutch Economic Relations', p. 123.
55. Ormrod, *Commercial Empires*, pp. 92–3.
56. Quoted in Statt, *Foreigners*, p. 119.
57. Claydon, *William III*, pp. 122–4.
58. Quoted in Black, *London*, p. 190.
59. James Miller, 1731, quoted in Blanning, *The Culture of Power*, p. 272.
60. Brandon, *War, Capital*, pp. 20–1.
61. Andrew Fletcher, *A Discourse concerning the Affairs of Spain: written in the month of July, 1698*, in *Political Works*, ed. J. Robertson (Cambridge, 1997), p. 90.
62. Ibid., p. 115.
63. Fletcher, *A Discourse*, p. 114.
64. Robertson, *History of the Reign of the Emperor Charles V*, quoted in J. G. A. Pocock, *Barbarism and Religion, Volume II: Narratives of Civil Government* (Cambridge, 1999), p. 296.
65. Dunthorne, *Dutch Republic*, p. 172. The words belong to Dunthorne rather than Voltaire.

12 A MARITIME MONARCHY

1. Bodleian Library, Oxford, Rawl MS D 147, 'Navall Essays written by Sir Hen Shere Whilst a Prisonr in ye Gatehouse Anno 1691', p. 67.
2. National Maritime Museum REC/1 Item 56: 'A Discourse on the Necessity of Maintaining Freedom of the Seas', f. 11.
3. Drake blamed Doughty for 'these mutinies and discords that are growne amongst us'. Quoted in Williams, *The Great South Sea*, p. 23.
4. National Maritime Museum REC/1 'A Discourse', ff. 9, 11.
5. Scott, *When the Waves*, Chs 3–6; Norbert Elias, *The Genesis of the Naval Profession* (Dublin, 2007).
6. See Henry Savile, *A Rough Draught of a New Modell at Sea*, in *The Works of George Savile, Marquis of Halifax*, ed. Mark Brown, 3 vols (Oxford, 1989), vol. 1, pp. 297–8; Henry Sheres, 'A Discourse touching ye decay of our Naval Discipline' [1694], National Maritime Museum REC/4, Item 4.
7. Sheres, 'A Discourse touching ye decay', pp. 12–13, 22–3.
8. In Ming and Qing China also, 'gentry, military and merchant families' were 'successfully consolidated' by participation, via the highly competitive civil service examination, in the bureaucratic government of the empire. Benjamin Elman, 'Classical Reasoning in Late Imperial Chinese Civil Examination Essays', *Renwen Xuebao (Journal of Humanities East/ West)* 20 (1999), p. 364.
9. Slack, *Improvement*, pp. 259–60.
10. Mahan, *Sea Power*, pp. 54–5.

11. Quoted in Blanning, *The Culture of Power*, p. 303. Defoe claimed that far 'from being inconsistent with a gentleman . . . trade in England makes gentlemen, and has peopled this nation with gentlemen'. Quoted in Hancock, *Citizens of the World*, p. 281.
12. Sprat, *History of the Royal Society*, p. 408.
13. Quoted in Brandon, *War, Capital*, p. 12.
14. Sprat, *History of the Royal Society*, p. 86.
15. Evelyn, *Navigation and Commerce, Their Original and Progress*, p. 3.
16. Ibid., pp. 33, 35.
17. Ibid., p. 36.
18. Mckeon, *Politics and Poetry*, p. 70 and note 12.
19. [Defoe] *A General History of Discoveries and Improvements*, pp. 102–7.
20. *A Collection of Voyages and Travels . . . Now first Published in English. In Six Volumes. With a General PREFACE, giving an Account of the Progress of NAVIGATION, from its first Beginning* (London, 1732), *Introductory Discourse*, p. xxxiv.
21. Niels Steensgaard, 'The Growth and Composition of the Long-Distance Trade of England and the Dutch Republic before 1750', in James Tracy (ed.), *The Rise of Merchant Empires: Long Distance Trade in the Early Modern World* (Cambridge, 1990).
22. John Pollexfen, 1697, quoted by De Vries, *Industrious Revolution*, p. 134.
23. Paul Langford, *A Polite and Commercial People: The New Oxford History of England, 1727–1783* (Oxford, 1989), pp. 166–7.
24. Steensgard, 'Growth and Composition', p. 129.
25. Morgan, 'Mercantilism and the British Empire', p. 176.
26. Jane T. Merritt, *The Trouble With Tea: The Politics of Consumption in the Eighteenth-Century Global Economy* (Baltimore, MD, 2017), Ch. 2: 'The English Commercial Empire Expands'.
27. Ibid., pp. 299–300.
28. Langford, *A Polite and Commercial People*, pp. 164–5.
29. Quoted in Holmes, *Great Power*, p. 305.
30. Quoted in De Vries, *Industrious Revolution*, p. 132.
31. Langford, *A Polite and Commercial People*, pp. 391–2 (and see maps).
32. Hoppit, 'Political Power', pp. 356–7.
33. De Vries, *Industrious Revolution*, Ch. 4; Neil McKendrick, John Brewer and J. H. Plumb (eds), *Birth of a Consumer Society* (Bloomington, IN, 1982).
34. Dominique Margairaz, 'City and Country: Home, Possessions, and Diet, Western Europe 1600–1800', in Frank Trentmann (ed.), *The Oxford Handbook of the History of Consumption* (Oxford, 2012), p. 192.
35. Ibid., p. 201.
36. Hancock, *Citizens of the World*, pp. 86–7.
37. Defoe, *Tour*, p. 6.
38. Ibid., pp. 349–50.
39. Hancock, *Citizens of the World*, p. 86.
40. *Annus Mirabilis*, 163–64, quoted in Mckeon, *Politics and Poetry*, p. 71 (and p. 68).
41. Addison quoted in Hancock, *Citizens of the World*, p. 85.
42. Defoe, *Tour*, p. 168.
43. Dickson, *The Financial Revolution*, pp. 304–7; Peter Spufford, 'Access to Credit and Capital in the Commercial Centres of Europe', in Davids and Lucassen (eds), *A Miracle Mirrored* (Cambridge, 1995), p 328; Wilson, *Anglo-Dutch Commerce and Finance*; Murray, 'Cultural Impact'.
44. Ann Carlos, Jennifer Key and Jill Dupree, 'Learning and the Creation of Stock-Market Institutions', *Journal of Economic History* 58, 2 (1998).
45. John Houghton, *A Collection for Improvement of Husbandry and Trade* (1694). I am grateful to Alistair Birchall for this reference.
46. Black, *London*, p. 200.
47. Van Bavel, *The Invisible Hand?*, pp. 198–9.
48. Murrin, 'Great Inversion', p. 383.
49. Morgan, 'Mercantilism and the British Empire', pp. 171–2.

50. This hypothesis will be researched in this author's next study, *London's Eye, 1660–1780: Inside the Mind of the First World City*.
51. Sprat, *History of the Royal Society*, pp. 87–8.
52. Quoted in George H. Cunningham, *London* (London, 1927), p. vii.
53. Sir William Petty, *Observations* (London, 1687), p. 2.
54. Petty, *Two Essays . . . Concerning . . . London and Paris*, p. 7; Petty, *Observations*, p. 4.
55. Petty, *Two Essays*, pp. 8–11.
56. Sir William Petty, *Five Essays in Political Arithmetick* (London, 1687), pp. 40–5.
57. Petty, *Observations*, p. 2. Petty's estimate of Rome's population was 119,000 and of London's 695,718.
58. Petty, *Five Essays*, p. 20.
59. Bob Clarke, *From Grub Street to Fleet Street: An Illustrated History of English Newspapers to 1899* (Aldershot, 2004), Chs 2–4; Hancock, *Citizens*, p. 33; Black, *London*, p. 200.
60. *An Account of Several Late Voyages & Discoveries To the South and North . . .* BY Sir JOHN NARBOROUGH, Captain JASMEN TASMAN, Captain JOHN WOOD, and FREDERICK MARTEN of *Hamburgh*, The Bookseller's Preface, or Introduction, p. v.
61. Ibid., pp. xiii–xiv.
62. Ibid., pp. xvii–xviii.
63. I hadn't understood this until it was explained to me in a tutorial at the University of Auckland by a student from Fiji.
64. '*The History of the* ANSWERS RETURN'D BY Sir PHILIBERTO VERNATTI Resident in *Batavia . . .* To certain Inquiries sent thither by Order of the *Royal Society*, and recommended by Sir *ROBERT MORAT*', in Sprat, *History*, pp. 158–72. Oysters, crabs, Durian fruit, ambergris and coconut trees are foci of interest. See also in the same volume, pp. 307–11: 'The History of the Generation and Ordering of GREENOYSTERS Commonly called Colchester-Oysters'.
65. Ibid., pp. vi–vii, x–xi.
66. *Voyage of the Endeavour*, p. 299 and note 3 (see also p. 274). *The Endeavour Journal of Banks*, vol. 2, pp. 1–2 and note 1. The copy of *Several Late Voyages* (1694) published electronically by Early English Books Online from the British Library carries Banks' signature. Banks donated his books to the library.
67. Carrington, Introduction, p. xxv.
68. Beaglehole (ed.), *The Voyage of the Endeavour*, p. cclxxxii.
69. Ibid., pp. 117, 156–7. Banks agreed that while Tupia was 'skilld in the mysteries of their religion . . . what makes him more than any thing else desireable is his experience in the navigation of these people and knowledge of the Islands in these seas; he has told us the names of above 70.' *The Endeavour Journal of Joseph Banks 1768–1771*, ed. J. C. Beaglehole, 2 vols (Sydney, 1962), vol. 1, p. 312.
70. Atholl Anderson, 'Finding Tonganui: East Polynesian Seafaring and Migration to New Zealand', in Steel (ed.), *New Zealand and the Sea*.
71. Quoted by Anne Salmond, *The Trial of the Cannibal Dog: The Remarkable Story of Captain Cook's Encounters in the South Seas* (New Haven, CT, 2003), p. 149.
72. Beaglehole (ed.), *The Endeavour Journal of Banks*, vol. 1, pp. 471, 472.
73. Quoted in Simon Schaffer, 'Visions of Empire: Afterword', in David Miller and Peter Reill (eds), *Visions of Empire: Voyages, Botany, and Representations of Nature* (Cambridge, 1996), p. 338.
74. Beaglehole (ed.), *The Endeavour Journal of Banks*, vol. 2, pp. 38–40.
75. Beaglehole (ed.), *Voyage of the Endeavour*, pp. 290–1 (March 1770). This authority was Tupia. See *Voyage of the Endeavour*, pp. 176, 244; *Endeavour Journal of Banks*, vol. 1, pp. 403–5; vol. 2, p. 30.
76. Cook had been instructed to 'observe with accuracy the Situation of such Islands as you may discover . . . without Suffering yourself however to be thereby diverted from the Object which you are always to have in View, the Discovery of the Southern Continent'. *Voyage of the Endeavour*, p. cclxxxiii.
77. Ibid., pp. 387, 392–3.

78. E. G. R. Taylor, *The Haven-Finding Art: A History of Navigation from Odysseus to Captain Cook* (New York, 1957), plate XXIV; Beaglehole (ed.), *Resolution and Adventure*, pp. 327–8.
79. Quoted in Smith, *European Vision and the South Pacific*, p. 61.
80. The Tongan archipelago (discovered by Tasman in 1643) elicited praise comparable to Tahiti (Beaglehole, ed., *Resolution and Adventure*, pp. 260–5). As late as January 1775 South Georgia in the South Atlantic was mistaken for 'part of a great Continent' (ibid., p. 625).
81. Hughes, *The Fatal Shore*, p. 145.

13 ARCHIPELAGIC STATE FORMATION, 1578–1783

1. [Defoe], *A General History of Discoveries and Improvements*, pp. 285–6.
2. Slack, *Improvement*, pp. 10–11.
3. Ibid., p. 12.
4. A model reconstruction of this Atlantic economy in its global context is David Hancock, *Citizens of the World: London Merchants and the Integration of the British Atlantic Community*.
5. Quoted in Gordon Wood, *The Creation of the American Republic 1776–1787* (Williamsburg, VA, 1969), p. 8.
6. Bernard Bailyn, *The Ideological Origins of the American Revolution* (Cambridge, MA, 1971), pp. 34–5, 40, 45, 132; Peter Karsten, *Patriot Heroes in England and America* (Madison, WI, 1978), pp. 62, 70, 72; Caroline Robbins, 'Discourses Concerning Government: Handbook of Revolution', *William and Mary Quarterly* 3rd series, 4 (1947). By far the predominant political texts held by eighteenth-century American libraries, public and private were *Cato's Letters*, Locke's *Two Treatises* and Sidney's *Discourses Concerning Government*. H. Trevor Colbourn, *The Lamp of Experience* (Chapel Hill, NC, 1965), pp. 199–232.
7. Wood, *Creation*, p. 45 (quote from John Adams).
8. Webb, *Governors-General*, p. 441.
9. Pestana, *English Atlantic*, Ch. 3.
10. Eric Nelson, *The Royalist Revolution: Monarchy and the American Founding* (Cambridge, MA, 2014) p. 3.
11. On which see my *England's Troubles*, p. 496.
12. A position reiterated in J. G. A. Pocock, 'From *The Ancient Constitution* to *Barbarism and Religion*: The *Machiavellian Moment*, the History of Political Thought and the History of Historiography', *History of European Ideas* 43, 2 (2017), p. 143.
13. Ibid.; Jonathan Scott, 'Classical Republicanism in England and the Netherlands', in Martin van Gelderen and Quentin Skinner (eds), *Republicanism: A Shared European Heritage, Volume 1: Republicanism and Constitutionalism in Early Modern Europe* (Cambridge, 2002); Scott, 'James Harrington's Prescription'.
14. Sidney, *Discourses*, ed. West, pp. 49, 143–4.
15. Scott, 'What were Commonwealth Principles?'; Scott, *Commonwealth Principles*.
16. *Declaration of Independence* (1776).
17. *Declaration of the Rights of Man and of the Citizen* (1789).
18. Scott, *Algernon Sidney and the English Republic*, p. 5; Rachel Hammersley, 'Camille Desmoulins's *Le Vieux Cordelier*: A Link between English and French Republicanism', *History of European Ideas* 27 (2001); Rachel Hammersley, *The English Republican Tradition and Eighteenth-Century France: Between the Ancients and the Moderns* (Manchester, 2010); Keith Michael Baker, 'Transformations of Classical Republicanism in Eighteenth-Century France', *Journal of Modern History* 73 (March 2001).
19. May, *Enlightenment in America*, p. 155 (and pp. 153–6).
20. Quoted in Wood, *American Republic*, p. 128.
21. Ibid., p. 92 (Adams again).
22. Brandon, *War, Capital*, p. 29.
23. Ibid., p. 30.
24. Armitage, *Ideological Origins*, p. 173.
25. Slack, *Improvement*, p. 259.

26. Quoted in ibid.
27. Temple, *Observations*, p. 78.
28. Ibid., p. 227.
29. D. M. Wolfe (ed.), *Leveller Manifestoes of the Puritan Revolution* (New York, 1967); A. S. P. Woodhouse (ed.), *Puritanism and Liberty: Being the Army Debates (1647–1649) from the Clarke Manuscripts with Supplementary Documents* (London, 1951).
30. Brian Levack, *The Formation of the British State: England, Scotland and the Union* (Oxford, 1987), p. 50.
31. Ibid., pp. 48–51, 67.
32. Brandon, *War, Capital*, p. 58.
33. David Hayton, 'Constitutional Experiments and Political Expediency, 1689–1725', in Ellis and Barber (eds), *Conquest and Union: Fashioning a British State, 1485–1725* (London, 1995).
34. Christopher Bayly, *Imperial Meridian: The British Empire and the World, 1780–1830* (London, 1989), pp. 77–99; Holmes, *Great Power*, pp. 222–4.
35. Defoe, *A Tour Thro the Whole Island*, vol. II, p. 541.
36. Constitutional Society of Birmingham, October 1774, quoted in H. T. Dickinson, *Liberty and Property: Political Ideology in Eighteenth-Century Britain* (New York, 1977), p. 206.
37. Ibid., p. 140.
38. Charles de Secondat, baron de Montesquieu, *The Spirit of the Laws*, eds Anne Cohler, Basia Carolyn Miller and Harold Samuel Stone (Cambridge, 1989), p. 156.
39. Hume, *Political Essays*, ed. Haakonssen, pp. 1, 85–6.
40. [Jonathan Boucher], *A Letter From a Virginian to the Members of the Congress to be held at Philadelphia* (Boston, MA, 1774), p. 43.
41. Quoted in Johns, *Nature of the Book*, p. 68.
42. William Lee quoted by P. J. Marshall, 'A Nation Defined by Empire, 1755–1776', in Marshall, *A Free though Conquering People* (Oxford, 1998), p. 222.
43. Quoted in Pauline Maier, *From Resistance to Revolution* (New York, 1972), p. 246.
44. Holmes, *Great Power*, p. 315.
45. *An Account of Divers Proceedings*, quoted in Scott, *England's Troubles*, p. 165.
46. *An Essay at Removing National Prejudices Against a Union with Scotland* (London, 1706), pp. 17, 3.
47. Ibid., p. 26.
48. Wood, *American Republic*, p. 369.
49. Hainsworth, *Naval Wars*, p. 10
50. Ezra Stiles quoted by Wood, *American Republic*, p. 355.
51. Ibid., pp. 356–7.
52. Brendan Simms, 'Why we Need a British Europe, not a European Britain', *New Statesman* (9 July 2015).
53. Quotes in Wood, *American Republic*, p. 561.
54. Ibid., pp. 519, 521.
55. Quoted by Nelson, *Royalist Revolution*, p. 1.
56. John M. Murrin, 'The Great Inversion, or Court versus Country: A Comparison of the Revolution Settlements in England (1688–1721) and America (1776–1816)', in J. G. A. Pocock (ed.), *Three British Revolutions: 1641, 1688, 1776* (Princeton, NJ, 1980), pp. 407–8.
57. David Armitage, *The Declaration of Independence: A Global History* (Cambridge, MA, 2007), p. 104.
58. Ibid., pp. 17, 19–21, 106.
59. Edmund Burke, quoted in ibid., p. 87.
60. Armitage, *Declaration*, pp. 91–2.
61. Quoted in ibid., p. 47.
62. Ibid., pp. 42–4.
63. 't Hart, *Bourgeois State*, p. 26.
64. Brandon, *War, Capital*, p. 46.

65. Temple, *Account of the United Provinces*, p. 50.
66. Frijhoff and Spies, *1650: Hard-Won Unity*, pp. 77–8.
67. E. H. Kossmann and A. F. Mellink (eds), *Texts concerning the Revolt of the Netherlands* (Cambridge, 1974), 'Introduction', p. 37.
68. Ibid., p. 32.
69. *Treaty of the Union*, in ibid., p. 166.
70. Dunthorne, *Dutch Revolt*, pp. 200–1.
71. Quoted by Armitage, *Declaration*, pp. 47, 50 (and see p. 66).
72. Quoted by Elliot Griffis, *American Republic*, p. 24; see also Goodfriend, Schmidt and Stott (eds), *Going Dutch*, Introduction, p. 3.

14 ANGLO-DUTCH-AMERICAN ENLIGHTENMENT

1. Sidney, *Discourses*, ed. West, pp. 357–8.
2. Thomas Paine, *Rights of Man, Being an Answer to Mr Burke's Attack on the French Revolution – Part I*, in *Political Writings of Thomas Paine*, 2 vols (Middletown, NJ, 1839), vol. 2, p. 48.
3. Slack, *Improvement*, p. 5.
4. Edward Said, *Orientalism* (New York, 1979); Scott, 'Maritime Orientalism, or the Political Theory of Water', *History of Political Thought*, vol. 1, 2015. This article argues that orientalism was ancient, deriving from cultural and rhetorical strategies deployed by Athens to distinguish itself from Persia (and Sparta).
5. More, *Utopia*; Michel de Montaigne, 'Of Cannibals', in Montaigne, *The Complete Works: Essays, Travel Journal, Letters*, trans. Donald Frame (Stanford, CA, 2003), pp. 182–93.
6. Wootton, *Invention*, p. 6; Anthony Pagden, *The Enlightenment: And Why it Still Matters* (Oxford, 2015), Ch. 1.
7. Hazard, *The European Mind 1680–1715* (Harmondsworth, 1964), p. 24.
8. Ibid., p. 44.
9. Most influentially Ernst Cassirer, *The Philosophy of the Enlightenment* (Princeton, NJ, 1951); Peter Gay, *The Enlightenment: An Interpretation*, 2 vols (London, 1967–70).
10. Susan Manning and Francis D. Cogliano (eds), *The Atlantic Enlightenment* (Aldershot, 2008); May, *Enlightenment in America*, pp. 105–6.
11. Roy Porter, *The Creation of the Modern World: The Untold Story of the British Enlightenment* (New York, 2000).
12. Jonathan Israel, *Radical Enlightenment: Philosophy and the Making of Modernity 1650–1750* (Oxford, 2001).
13. Slack, *Invention*, p. 8.
14. Hazard, *European Mind*, p. 93.
15. Ibid., p. 96.
16. Fox, *Oral and Literate Culture in Early Modern Britain*, p. 14.
17. Israel, *Dutch Republic*, pp. 2–4, 5.
18. Ibid., p. 5.
19. Israel, *Radical Enlightenment*, p. vi.
20. Mark Kishlansky, *A Monarchy Transformed: Britain 1603–1714* (London, 1996), pp. 1, 2–3.
21. Ibid., p. 4.
22. John Skelton, 'The Image of Ipocrisie', 1533. 'Belgians invented the Game of Cricket', *Television New Zealand News*, Wednesday 4 March 2009 (online resource).
23. Ormrod, 'Cultural production . . . in London', in O'Brien (ed.), *Urban Achievement*, pp. 215–18 and note 19.
24. Majolein 't Hart, 'The Glorious city: Monumentalism and Public Space in Seventeenth-Century Amsterdam', in O' Brien (ed.), *Urban Achievement*, p. 139.
25. Cornelis Schoneveld, *Sea-Changes: Studies in Three Centuries of Anglo-Dutch Cultural Transmission* (Amsterdam, 1996), p. 198.
26. Scott, *When the Waves*, p. 24; Rubright, *Doppelganger Dilemmas*, pp. 87–8 and Ch. 2.
27. Rubright, *Doppelganger Dilemmas*, p. 5.

28. Frijhoff and Spies, *1650: Hard-Won Unity*, p. 263.
29. Johns, *Nature of the Book*, p. 72.
30. Ibid., pp. 169–71, 447–8.
31. Milton, *Joannis Miltoni Angli pro Populo Anglicano Defensio* (London, 1651); Vossius quoted by H. Scherpbier, *Milton in Holland: A Study in the Literary Relations of England and Holland before 1730* (Amsterdam, 1969), p. 6; John Aubrey wrote: 'the only inducement of severall foreigners that came over into England, was chiefly to see Oliver Protector, and Mr John Milton . . . He was much more admired abrode then at home.' John Aubrey, *Aubrey's Brief Lives*, ed. Oliver Lawson Dick (London, 1958), p. 202.
32. Frihoff and Spies, *1650: Hard-Won Unity*, pp. 288–90; Scott, 'Classical Republicanism in Seventeenth-Century England and the Netherlands', in Skinner and Van Gelderen (eds), *Republicanism*, vol. 1.
33. Johns, *Nature of the Book*, pp. 516–19; Joel Mokyr, 'An Age of Progress', in Floud et al. (eds), *Cambridge Economic History*.
34. Jardine, *Going Dutch*, Chs 10–11.
35. Johns, *Nature of the Book*, p. 523.
36. Davids, 'The Scholarly Atlantic'. See above, Introduction, note 4.
37. Levine, *Between the Ancients and the Moderns*, pp. ix, 29.
38. Sprat, *History of the Royal Society*, p. 64.
39. Ibid., p. 64.
40. Ibid., p. 76.
41. W. J. Cameron, *New Light Upon Aphra Behn* (Auckland, 1961), p. 73.
42. Scott, *Commonwealth Principles*, pp. 122–4. See Scott, 'The Law of War: Grotius, Sidney, Locke and the Political Theory of Rebellion', *History of Political Thought*, Locke Issue, 1993.
43. Scott, 'Unfinished Family Business'.
44. *Court Maxim*, pp. 101, 104–5.
45. Ibid., pp. 101–2.
46. Sidney, *Discourses* in *Sydney on Government*, pp. 187–8. See Jonathan Scott, *Algernon Sidney and the Restoration Crisis, 1677–1683* (Cambridge, 1991), pp. 239–40, 260–3.
47. Richard Ashcraft, *Revolutionary Politics and John Locke's Two Treatises of Government* (Princeton, NJ, 1986), p. 536; Scott, *English Republic*, pp. 219–21.
48. Scott, *Commonwealth Principles*, pp. 122–4; Scott, 'The Law of War: Grotius, Sidney, Locke and the Political Theory of Rebellion'.
49. John Marshall, *John Locke, Toleration and Early Enlightenment Culture* (Cambridge, 2006), pp. 470–86.
50. Maurice Cranston, *John Locke* (New York, 1979), p. 295.
51. Laslett (ed.), *Locke's Two Treatises of Government*, pp. 314–15, 319.
52. Scott, *English Republic*, p. 219 and Ch. 13.
53. James Tully, *A Discourse on Property* (London, 1980). These understandings of liberty, resistance and property were interdependent. It was because people belonged to their Maker that invasion of their lives, liberties and estates was an assault upon the Law of Nature.
54. Quoted by Statt, *Foreigners*, p. 45.
55. Ibid., p. 48.
56. Quoted by ibid., p. 46.
57. Temple, *Observations*, p. 192.
58. Ibid., p. 187.
59. Ibid., p. 188.
60. Charles Davenant, *An Essay upon the Ways and Means of Supplying the War* (London, 1695), p. 74, uses almost identical language. In a country with 'few inhabitants . . . [there is] nothing but sloth and poverty; but when great numbers are confined to a narrow compass of ground, necessity puts them upon invention, frugality and industry.'
61. Statt, *Foreigners*, p. 89.
62. Quoted by Scott Sowerby, 'Pantomime History', a review of Steve Pincus, *1688: The First Modern Revolution* (2009), in *Parliamentary History*, vol. 30, pt 2 (2011), pp. 242–3.

63. Gary De Krey, *London and the Restoration, 1659–83* (Cambridge, 2005).
64. Ashworth, *Industrial Revolution*, p. 8; Black, *London*, pp. 149–50, 156.
65. Statt, *Foreigners*, Chs 5–6 and p. 121.
66. Ibid., Ch. 7 and p. 191.
67. A'Hearn, 'British Industrial Revolution in a European Mirror', p. 39.
68. Anne J. Kershen, *Strangers, Aliens and Asians: Huguenots, Jews and Bangladeshis in Spitalfields 1660–2000* (Abingdon, 2005), p. 168.
69. Ibid.
70. Fijhoff and Spies, *1650: Hard-Won Unity*, p. 141.
71. Quoted in Blanning, *The Culture of Power*, p. 310.
72. Scott, *Commonwealth Principles*, Chs 6 and 14.
73. Hume, 'Essay Twenty-Seven: Idea of a Perfect Commonwealth', in *Political Essays*.
74. Scott, *Commonwealth Principles*, pp. 82–4, 135–8; Hammersley, 'Camille Desmoulins's *Le Vieux Cordelier*'.
75. *Mercurius Politicus*, no. 52 (29 May–5 June 1651), p. 831; Sidney, *Discourses*, ed. West, pp. 357–8.
76. Paine, *Rights of Man*, in *Works*, p. 48.
77. William Falconer, *Remarks on the influence of climate, situation, nature of country . . . on the disposition and temper* (London, 1781), pp. 170–1.
78. Ibid., p. 172.
79. Scott, *When the Waves*, Chs 2, 8; Scott, 'Maritime Orientalism'.
80. Falconer, *Remarks*, pp. 172–3.
81. Dunbar, *Essays on the History of Mankind in Rude and Cultivated Ages*, reprint of 1781 edition, ed. James Dunbar (Bristol, 1995), p. 271.
82. Ibid., pp. 261–2.
83. Ibid., p. 287.
84. Quoted by Hugh Trevor-Roper, 'Introduction', in Edward Gibbon, *Decline and Fall of the Roman Empire*, 3 vols (New York, 1993), vol. 1, p. lxxxix.
85. Quoted by Adam Sisman, *Hugh Trevor-Roper: The Biography* (London, 2010), p. 400. The last judgement recalls to mind the scene in *Dr Strangelove* where Peter Sellers, desperately trying to extract a coin from a vending machine, explains that he is trying to save the world only to be told that, on the contrary, he is vandalizing the property of the Coca-Cola Corporation.
86. Dunbar, *Essays on the History*, p. 280.
87. Ibid., p. 281.
88. Ibid., p. 284.

15 AN EMPIRE OF CUSTOMERS

1. Adam Smith, *An Inquiry into the Nature and Causes of the Wealth of Nations*, eds R. H. Campbell and A. S. Skinner, 2 vols (Indianapolis, IN, 1981), vol. 2, p. 661 (Book IV, Ch. viii, para. 53).
2. Sven Beckert, 'The Wages of War Capitalism', Ch. 3 of *Empire of Cotton* (New York, 2014); Satia, *Empire of Guns*.
3. Ashworth, *Industrial Revolution*, p. 4.
4. Robert S. DuPlessis, *The Material Atlantic: Clothing, Commerce, and Colonization in the Atlantic World, 1650–1800* (Cambridge, 2016), p. 17.
5. Ibid., p. 178.
6. Satia, *Empire of Guns*, p. 125.
7. Hancock, *Citizens of the World*, pp. 217–19; Ashworth, *Industrial Revolution*, p. 3.
8. Langford, *A Polite and Commercial People*, pp. 168–9.
9. Zahedieh, 'Overseas Trade', p. 412.
10. On London's Atlantic trade see Zahedieh, *The Capital and the Colonies*; on Bristol, Kenneth Morgan, *Bristol and the Atlantic Trade in the Eighteenth Century* (Cambridge, 1993).

11. Richard Brown, *Society and Economy in Modern Britain, 1700–1850* (London, 1991), p. 169.
12. DuPlessis, *Material Atlantic*, p. 4.
13. Ibid., pp. 7–8.
14. Proulx, *Barkskins*, p. 13. This book is a tremendous historical as well as literary achievement.
15. Fred Anderson, *The War that Made America* (New York, 2005).
16. Quoted by Burnard, 'The British Atlantic', in Greene and Morgan (eds), *Atlantic History*, p. 113.
17. Anderson, *War*, p. 12.
18. Morgan, 'Mercantilism', p. 169.
19. Smith, *Wealth of Nations*, quoted by Jack Greene (ed.), *Exclusionary Empire: English Liberty Overseas, 1600–1900* (Cambridge, 2010), 'Introduction: Empire and Liberty', p. 11.
20. De Vries, *Industrious Revolution*; Merritt, *Trouble with Tea*, Ch. 3, 'The Rise of a Tea-fac'd Generation' (on the rise, and social and geographical spread, of American consumer demand).
21. Jack P. Greene, 'The Revolution Revisited', in *Interpreting Early America: Historiographical Essays* (Charlottesville, VA, 1996), p. 506.
22. Van Bavel, *The Invisible Hand?*, pp. 219–20.
23. Burnard, 'The British Atlantic', pp. 119–20.
24. Greene, *Interpreting Early America*, pp. 105–12, 120–5.
25. Quoted in DuPlessis, *Material Atlantic*, p. 222.
26. Ibid., p. 197.
27. Greene, *Exclusionary Empire*, p. 6.
28. Smith, *Wealth of Nations*, vol. 2, p. 585. For the classical republican understanding of liberty, which has been detected in eighteenth-century America by Robbins, Bailyn and Pocock, see Scott, *Commonwealth Principles*, Ch. 1.
29. Malcolm Gaskill, *Between Two Worlds: How the English Became Americans* (Oxford, 2014); on a later, comparable case see James Belich, *Paradise Reforged: A History of the New Zealanders from the 1880s to the Year 2000* (Auckland, 2001).
30. John Smail, *Merchants, Markets and Manufacture: The English Wool Textile Industry in the Eighteenth Century* (Basingstoke, 1999), p. 3. In 1772–4 textiles constituted half of British exports to the Empire as a whole and 53.4 per cent of those to America and Africa. Woollens were the dominant sector. Price, 'The Imperial Economy', p. 87.
31. Smail, *Merchants*, p. ix.
32. Ibid., pp. 5–6.
33. Ibid., pp. 7–9.
34. Ibid., pp. 9, 151.
35. Ibid., p. 151.
36. Hancock, *Citizens of the World*, p. 37.
37. Zahedieh, 'Overseas Trade', p. 412.
38. De Vries, *The Industrious Revolution*, p. 6.
39. Beckert, *Empire of Cotton*, pp. 73–4.
40. Ibid., p. 76.
41. Jacob M. Price, 'The Imperial Economy', in Marshall (ed.), *Oxford History of the British Empire, Volume II*, p. 99.
42. Oliver Dickerson, *The Navigation Acts and the American Revolution* (Philadelphia, PA, 1951), pp. 279–80.
43. Langford, *A Polite and Commercial People*, p. 373.
44. Pitt, quoted by Dickinson, *Writings*, I, viii–ix.
45. Merritt, *Trouble With Tea*, Ch. 4, 'Politicizing American Consumption'.
46. Langford, *A Polite and Commercial People*, p. 539.
47. Quoted by Dickerson, *Navigation Acts*, pp. 281–2.
48. Ibid., pp. 282–3.
49. Morgan, 'Mercantilism and the British Empire', p. 170.

50. Burke, 'Speech on Conciliation with America', March 1775, selected in Iain Hampsher-Monk, *The Political Philosophy of Edmund Burke* (Harlow, 1987), p. 115.
51. Langford, *A Polite and Commerial People*, p. 557.
52. Brown, *Society and Economy*, p. 164.
53. Smith, *Wealth of Nations*, vol. 2, p. 661.
54. Ibid.
55. Quoted by Sven Beckert, *Empire of Cotton*, p. 76.
56. Ashworth, *Industrial Revolution*, p. 4.
57. Simms, *Three Victories and a Defeat*, pp. 663, 681.

16 CULTURES OF INVENTION

1. *Reasons for Giving Encouragement to the Sea-Faring People of Great Britain* (London, 1737), p. 32.
2. Wrigley, *Poverty, Progress*, p. 36.
3. Ibid., p. 62.
4. Grove, *Green Imperialism*; Drayton, *Nature's Government*; and see Ch. 5 above.
5. Slack, *Invention*, pp. 98–9; H. R. Trevor-Roper, 'Three Foreigners: The Philosophers of the Puritan Revolution', in Trevor-Roper, *Religion, the Reformation and Social Change* (London, 1967). On this classic essay see Mark Greengrass, 'Three Foreigners: The Philosophers of the Puritan Revolution', in Blair Worden (ed.), *Hugh Trevor-Roper: The Historian* (London, 2016).
6. Claudio Magris, *Danube: A Sentimental Journey from the Source to the Black Sea* (Harvill, 2001; first published 1986).
7. Lesger, *Amsterdam Market*, p. 139.
8. 't Hart, 'The Glorious City', in O'Brien (ed.), *Urban Achievement*, p. 131.
9. Frijoff and Spies, *1650: Hard-Won Unity*, pp. 19–20.
10. Ibid., p. 21.
11. [Monson] 'On the fishery', National Maritime Museum, Greenwich, REC/4, Item 14, p. 1.
12. Klooster, *Dutch in the Americas*, p. 3.
13. Israel, *Dutch Republic*, p. 15.
14. Frijhoff and Spies, *1650: Hard-Won Unity*, p. 156.
15. National Maritime Museum, REC 4, Item 14, f. 10.
16. De Vries and Van Der Woude, *First Modern Economy*, p. 357.
17. British Library, Harleian MSS, III, 99, quoted in HMC *Report of the MSS of the Rt Hon Viscount De L'Isle Vol V Sidney Papers, 1611–1626*, 'Introduction', p. vi.
18. Temple, *Observations*, p. 129.
19. Ibid.
20. Ibid., p. 125.
21. National Maritime Museum, REC 6: Richard Gibson, Item 17: 'Observations Upon Islands in General and England in particular', f. 273.
22. Ibid.
23. Davis, *Shipping*, p. 14.
24. Ibid., p. 18.
25. Dryden, *Annus Mirabilis: The Year of Wonders, 1666*, stanza 1.
26. 'A Memorial of Sir *Walter Raleigh* to Q. *Elizabeth* Touching the Port of *Dover*', in Sir Walter Raleigh, *A Discourse of Seaports; Principally of the Port and Haven of Dover* (London, 1700), p. 2.
27. Slack, *Invention*, p. 257.
28. Ibid.
29. Israel, 'The Emerging Empire'.
30. *Reasons for Giving Encouragement To The Sea-Faring People of Great Britain*, p. 32.
31. Mahan, *Sea Power*, p. 95.

32. See Chs 3, 4 and 11. This is emphasized much more strongly by Slack, *Invention*.
33. Sprat, *History of the Royal Society*, pp. 406–7.
34. Ibid., p. 113.
35. Rubright, *Doppelganger Dilemmas*, p. 164.
36. 't Hart, 'The Glorious City', in O'Brien (ed.), *Urban Achievement*, p. 131.
37. Slack, *Invention*, p. 95.
38. Quoted by Jardine, *Going Dutch*, p. 316.
39. Braudel, *The Perspective of the World*, p. 365.
40. Quoted by Joseph Levine, *Between the Ancients and the Moderns*, p. 15.
41. Ibid., p. 178; William Maitland, *The History of London from its Foundation to the Present Time*, 2 vols (London, 1756), vol. 1, p. 446.
42. Anon., *Orvietan: or a Counter-Poison Against the Infectious Ayr of London*, quoted by Cavert, *Smoke*, p. 3.
43. Quoted in Robert O. Bucholz and Joseph P. Ward, *London: A Social and Cultural History, 1550–1750* (Cambridge, 2012), p. 330. On the new fire-prevention requirements see Maitland, *History of London*, p. 450. For seventeenth-century fire engines see Ackroyd, *London*, p. 220.
44. Maitland, *History of London*, vol. 1, pp. 437–8.
45. Muldrew, *Food, Energy and the Creation of Industriousness*; E. A. Wrigley, *Energy and the English Industrial Revolution* (Cambridge, 2010); Jonathan Sawday, *Engines of the Imagination: Renaissance Culture and the Rise of the Machine* (New York, 2007).
46. Luu, *Immigrants*, p. 35.
47. Jean-Pierre Grosley, 1765, quoted in Cavert, *Smoke*, p. xv.
48. O'Brien, 'Trade, Economy, State and Empire', p. 59.
49. Ormrod, *Rise of Commercial Empires*, pp. 346, 347.
50. Wrigley, *Poverty, Progress*, p. 33.
51. Ibid., pp. 19, 44–5.
52. The words are de Vries and van der Woude quoted by Wrigley, *Poverty, Progress*, p. 27; ibid., p. 37.
53. Hancock, *Citizens of the World*, p. 32.
54. Mokyr, *Enlightened Economy*, p. 165.
55. Ibid.
56. O'Brien, 'Trade, Economy, State, and Empire', pp. 58–9.
57. Mokyr, *Enlightened Economy*, p. 160.
58. A'Hearn, 'The Industrial Revolution in a European Mirror', pp. 30–1.
59. Ashworth, *Industrial Revolution*, p. 9.
60. Zahedieh, 'Overseas Trade', p. 414.
61. A'Hearn, 'The Industrial Revolution in a European Mirror', p. 31.
62. Ormrod, *Commercial Empires*, p. 349.
63. James Horn, 'British Diaspora', in Marshall, *Oxford History of the British Empire, Volume II*, pp. 29–31. During the seventeenth century 70 per cent of migrants were English; during the eighteenth century 70 per cent were Scots and Irish.

CONCLUSION: 1649: REVOLUTIONARY TURNPIKE

1. Quoted in Jardine, *Going Dutch*, pp. 319–20.
2. Johan Soderberg, Ulf Jonssen and Christer Persson, *A Stagnating Metropolis: The economy and Demography of Stockholm, 1750–1850* (Cambridge, 1991), p. 10.
3. Slack, *Invention*, p. 258.
4. Scott, *England's Troubles*, Part Three; Scott, *Commonwealth Principles*, Introduction.
5. Christopher Hill, 'A Bourgeois Revolution?', in Pocock (ed.), *Three British Revolutions*, p. 120.
6. Ibid., pp. 115–16; see also pp. 117–18.
7. Ibid., p. 117.
8. Scott, *When the Waves*, Introduction and Chapter One.

9. Ibid., p. 117.
10. Van Bavel, *The Invisible Hand?*, pp. 222–3.
11. Davis, *Shipping*, p. 377.
12. Ibid., p. 388.
13. *Chaos: or, a Discourse Wherein is presented to the view of the Magistrate . . . a Frame of Government by way of a Republique* (18 July 1659) sought to address the social and economic ills of the realm partly by tackling this problem.
14. Bucholz and Ward, *London*, pp. 365–6.
15. Soderberg et al., *Stagnating Metropolis*, p. 10.
16. Charles Dibdin, *The Musical Tour* (Sheffield, 1788), pp. 15, 83, 194, quoted in Langford, *A Polite and Commercial People*, p. 674 (error: 'arts of the north').
17. According to a 2017 survey by the Migration Observatory. 'After Brexit, England will have to rethink its identity', *Guardian* (8 January 2018).
18. Quoted by Vernon, *Distant Strangers*, p. xiv.
19. This is not what I learned growing up in 1960s and 1970s New Zealand. As late as 1985, at a high-table dinner at Magdalene College, Cambridge, I explained to the assembled company that by comparison with other European empires Britain had left its ex-colonies in good time and good order. 'That's an interesting argument,' came one response: 'there is only one problem.' 'What is that, Eamon?' 'You are making it to an Irishman.'
20. John le Carré, *A Legacy of Spies* (London, 2017), p. 262. This conversation takes place in Freiburg.
21. Writing in 1781 James Dunbar recorded his astonishment that Cook 'with a company of 118 men, performed a voyage of three years and eighteen days, throughout all the climates from 52 degrees north to 71 degrees south latitude, with the loss of a single man only by disease, a proportion so moderate, that the bills of mortality, in no climate or condition of society, can furnish such another example'. Dunbar, *Essays on the History of Mankind*, p. 376. On proximity versus distance, and movement, see Richard White, 'What is Spatial History?', *Stanford University Spatial History Lab*, 1 February 2010, pp. 2–3.

BIBLIOGRAPHY

PRIMARY SOURCES

I. ARCHIVAL

Bibliothèque Nationale, Paris
Fr. MS 23254, 'Lantiniana'. Notes by Jean-Baptiste Lantin of a conversation with Algernon Sidney over dinner at the Hotel D'Antragues in Paris, 1677.

Bodleian Library, Oxford
Clarendon MS 104, f.8 Downing to Clarendon, 30 August 1661.
Clarendon MS 105 f.18 Downing to Clarendon, 2 September 1661.
Rawl MS D 147, 'Navall Essays written by Sir Hen Shere Whilst a Prisonr in ye Gate-House Anno 1691'.

British Library, London
Add MS 4181: 'The Relation of Sr Balthazar Gerbier'.
Add MS 11602: Gibson, 'A Reformation in ye Royall Navy most Humbly Proposed'.
Add MS 11602: Gibson, 'Heads of a Discourse between an English and Dutch Sea Captain'.
Add MS 11684: 'The Dutch Action at Chatham Examined'.
Egerton MS 2538: Downing to Nicholas, 2 May 1662.
Sloane MS 3833: Journal of Narborough's voyage to Chile, 1669–71.

Kent Archives Office, Maidstone
De Lisle MS U1475 Z1/9, loose pages, fifth item, fols 2–3.

Ministère des Affaires Etrangères, Paris
Archives Diplomatique, Correspondence Politique Angleterre, vol. 95.

National Archives, Kew, London
State Papers 16/530/36.

National Maritime Museum, Greenwich, London
REC/1 Item 56: 'A Discourse on the Necessity of Maintaining Freedom of the Seas'.
REC/3 ff. 119–22; 123–7; 129–32; 133–8.
REC/3 f. 240: 'How a State may the best provide itself for a Warr'.
REC/4 Item 4: Henry Sheres, 'A Discourse touching ye Decay of our Naval Discipline' [1694].
REC/4 Item 12: [William Monson], 'How to imploy our ffleet against Spain'.
REC/4 Item 14: [Monson], 'On the fishery'.
REC/6 Item 17: [Gibson], 'Observations Upon Islands in Generall and England in particular relating to safety and strength at Sea'.

BIBLIOGRAPHY

REC/6 Item 24: 'Sir H Shere's [sic] proposal to King James for preserving the Naval Royal in Port from any Insult', 4 May 1688.

Pepys Library, Magdalene College, Cambridge
MS 2142, ff. 2–3.
MS 2888, 'The political grounds and maxims of the Republic of Holland and West Friesland', translation by Toby Bonnell of *Aanwysing der heilsam politike Gronden en Maximen van de Republicke van Holland en West-Vriesland* (Leiden and Rotterdam, 1669).

2. PRINTED PRIMARY

An Account of Several Late Voyages & Discoveries To the South and North . . . BY Sir JOHN NARBOROUGH, Captain JASMEN TASMAN, Captain JOHN WOOD, and FREDERICK MARTEN of *Hamburgh* (London, 1694, Printed for *Sam. Smith* and *Benj. Walford*, Printers to the *Royal Society*), 'The Bookseller's Preface'.

[Anon.], *The Quakers Farewel to England, or* Their Voyage to *New Jersey*, scituate on the Continent of *Virginia*, and bordering upon *New England* (London, 1675).

[Anon.], *Tom Tell-Troath: or a Free Discourse Touching the Manners of the Time*, in Robert Ashton (ed.), *James I by His Contemporaries* (London, 1969).

Aubrey, John, *Aubrey's Brief Lives*, ed. Oliver Lawson Dick (London, 1958).

Bacon, Sir Francis, 'Of the True Greatness of Kingdoms and Estates', in E. A. Abbott (ed.), *Bacon's Essays*, 2 vols (London, 1889), vol. 1.

Banks, Joseph, *The Endeavour Journal of Joseph Banks 1768–1771*, ed. J. C. Beaglehole, 2 vols (Cambridge, 1968).

Baxter, Richard, *Reliquiae Baxterianae, or Mr Richard Baxter's Narrative of . . . His Life and Times* (London, 1696).

Baylor, Michael (ed.), *The Radical Reformation* (Cambridge, 1991).

Bethel, Slingsby, *The Interest of Princes and States* (London, 1680).

Bethel, Slingsby, *The Present Interest of England, Stated* (London, 1671).

Bethel, Slingsby, *The World's Mistake in Oliver Cromwell* (London, 1668).

Bodin, Jean, *Six Bookes of a Commonweale*, a facsimile reprint of the English translation of 1606, ed. K. D. McRae (Cambridge, MA, 1962).

[Boucher, Jonathan], *A Letter From a Virginian to the Members of the Congress to be held at Philadelphia* (Boston, MA, 1774).

Bourne, William, 'Hydrographicall discourse to shew the passage unto Cattay five manner of waies, two of them knowen and the other three supposed', in *A Regiment for the Sea: Conteyning most profitable Rules, Mathematicall experiences, and perfect knowledge of Navigation*, 2nd edn (London 1680).

Bradford, William, *Of Plymouth Plantation*, in Nathaniel and Thomas Philbrick (eds), *The Mayflower Papers: Selected Writings of Colonial New England* (London, 2007).

Bryant, A. (ed.), *The Letters, Speeches and Declarations of King Charles II* (London, 1935).

Burke, Edmund, 'Speech on Conciliation with America', March 1775, selected in Iain Hampsher-Monk, *The Political Philosophy of Edmund Burke* (Harlow, 1987).

[Burton, Robert], Democritus Junior, *The Anatomy of Melancholy: What it Is* (Oxford, 1624).

Burton, Thomas, *Diary of Thomas Burton*, ed. J. T. Rutt, 4 vols (London, 1828), vol. 4.

Calendar of State Papers . . . relating to the English affairs existing in the archives . . . of Venice, vol. XXVIII, 1647–1652 (London, 1927).

Camden, William, *Britain, or a Chorographicall Description of the most flourishing Kingdomes, England, Scotland and Ireland*, trans. Philemon Holland (London, 1610).

Chaos: or, a Discourse Wherein is presented to the view of the Magistrate . . . a Frame of Government by way of a Republique (18 July 1659).

Charles I, *Declaration* (1629) in S. R. Gardiner (ed.), *The Constitutional Documents of the Puritan Revolution 1625–1660* (Oxford, 1979).

Charles I, *Proclamation to . . . his Loving Subjects of . . . England* (1639), in Rushworth, *Historical Collections*, vol. 1.

Charles II, *His Majesties Gracious Speech to both Houses of Parliament Jan 7 1674* [O.S.].

Charles II, *The Declaration of Breda*, in Kenyon (ed.), *Stuart Constitution*.

Child, Sir Josiah, *A New Discourse of Trade* (London, 1694).

Churchill, Awnsham and John, 'An Introductory Discourse, Containing, The whole History of Navigation from its Original to this time', in *A Collection of Voyages and Travels . . . Now first Published in English. In Six Volumes. With a General PREFACE, giving an Account of the Progress of NAVIGATION, from its first Beginning*, 6 vols (London, 1732), vol. 1.

Cook, James, in J. C. Beaglehole (ed.), *The Journals of Captain James Cook on His Voyages of Discovery: The Voyage of the Endeavour 1768–1771* (Cambridge, 1955).

Cook, James, in J. C. Beaglehole (ed.), *The Voyage of the Resolution and Adventure 1772–1775* (Cambridge, 1961).

Darwin, Charles, *The Voyage of the Beagle*, ed. James Brix (New York, 2000).

Davenant, Charles, *An Essay upon the Ways and Means of Supplying the War* (London, 1695).

The Debate at Large between the Lords and Commons . . . Anno 1688 . . . Relating to the Word ABDICATED, 2nd edn (London, 1705).

Declaration of [American] Independence (1776).

Declaration of the Rights of Man and of the Citizen (1789).

A Declaration of the Parliament of England, In Vindication of their Proceedings (London, 1649).

Dee, John, *General and Rare Memorials pertaining to the Perfecte Arte of Navigation* (London, 1577).

[Defoe, Daniel], *A General History of Discoveries and Improvements in Useful Arts* (London, 1725–6).

[Defoe, Daniel], *An Essay at Removing National Prejudices Against a Union with Scotland* (London, 1706).

Defoe, Daniel, *An Essay Upon Projects* (London, 1697).

Defoe, Daniel, *A Tour Thro' the Whole Island of Britain*, ed. G. D. H. Cole, 2 vols (New York, 1968).

[de la Court, Pieter,] 'De Witt and other Great Men in Holland', *The True Interest and Political Maxims of the Republic of Holland* (London, 1702).

Downing, George, to Winthrop, 26 August 1645, in *Winthrop Papers*, vol. 6: 1650–1654, ed. Malcolm Freiburg (Boston, MA, 1992).

Dryden, John, *Annus Mirabilis: The Year of Wonders, 1666* (London, 1667).

Dryden, John, *Essay of Dramatic Poesy*, quoted in Jackson I. Cope and Harold Whitmore Jones (eds), *History of the Royal Society* by Thomas Sprat (St Louis, MO, 1958), Introduction, p. xviii.

Dunbar, James, *Essays on the History of Mankind in Rude and Cultivated Ages*, reprint of 1781 edition, ed. James Dunbar (Bristol, 1995).

Elliot Griffis, W. M., *The Influence of the Netherlands in the Making of the English Commonwealth and the American Republic*, A Paper read before the Boston Congregational Club, Monday Evening, Oct 26, 1891 (Boston, 1891).

Evelyn, John, *Memoirs*, ed. W. Bray, 2 vols (London 1818), vol. 1.

Evelyn, John, *Navigation and Commerce, Their Original and Progress* (London, 1674).

Falconer, William, *Remarks on the influence of climate, situation, nature of country . . . on the disposition and temper* (London, 1781).

Filmer, Sir Robert, *Sir Robert Filmer: Patriarcha and Other Writings*, ed. J. P. Sommerville (Cambridge, 1991).

Fletcher, Andrew, *A Discourse concerning the Affairs of Spain: written in the month of July, 1698*, in *Political Works*, ed. J. Robertson (Cambridge, 1997).

Fox, George, in Jonathan Fryer (ed.), *George Fox and the Children of Light* (London, 1991).

Gardiner, S. R. (ed.), *Debates in the House of Commons in 1625* (London, 1873).

Gates, Sir Thomas, *A true repertory of the wracke, and redemption of Sir Thomas Gates Knight*, published in Purchas, *Hakluytus Posthumus or Samuel Purchas His Pilgrimes*, 4 vols (London, 1625), vol. 4.

Genpaku, Sugita, *Dawn of Western Science in Japan*, trans. Ryozo Matsumoto (Tokyo, 1969), pp. 1–71.

G. L. V., *British Lightning* (London,1643).

Goodman, Christopher, *How Superior Powers ought to be obeyd of their Subjects and Wherin they may lawfully by God's Worde be disobeyed and resisted* (Geneva, 1558; facsimile, Amsterdam, 1972).

Gregory, Francis, *David's Returne From His Banishment* (Oxford, 1660).

Greville, Fulke, Lord, *Life of Sir Philip Sidney* (London, 1652).

Grey, A., *Debates of the House of Commons 1667–1694*, 10 vols (London, 1763), vol. 9.

Hakluyt, Richard, *The Principall Navigations, Voiages and Discoveries of the English Nation*, 2 vols (London, 1589).

Hakluyt, Richard the Younger, 'Discourse of Western Planting By Richard Hakluyt, 1584', in E. G. R. Taylor (ed.), *The Original Writings & Correspondence Of The Two Richard Hakluyts*, 2 vols (London, 1935).

[Hakluyt] H. R. the Younger, *Divers Voyages Touching the Discoverie of America and the Islands adjacent unto the same* (London, 1582; facsimile, Ann Arbor, MI, 1996).

Harrington, James, 'The Commonwealth of Oceana', in J. G. A. Pocock (ed.), *The Political Works of James Harrington* (Cambridge, 1977).

The Hartlib Papers, 2nd edn (Sheffield, HROnline, 2002).

Herodotus, *The Histories*, trans. Aubrey de Selincourt, ed. John Marincola (Harmondsworth, 1972).

Heylyn, Peter, *Cosmography in Four Books. Containing the Chorography and History of the Whole World* (London, 1677).

Historical Manuscripts Commission, *Report of the MSS of the Rt Hon Viscount De L'Isle, Volume V: Sidney Papers, 1611–1626*, 'Introduction', eds William Shaw and G. Dyfnaltt Owen (London, 1962).

'*The History of the* ANSWERS RETURN'D BY Sir PHILIBERTO VERNATTI Resident in *Batavia* . . . To certain Inquiries sent thither by Order of the *Royal Society*, and recommended by Sir *ROBERT MORAT*', in Sprat, *History of the Royal Society*, pp. 158–72.

Hobbes, Thomas, *Leviathan*, ed. Richard Tuck (Cambridge, 1991).

Hotman, Francois, *Francogallia*, ed. R. E. Giesey, trans. J. H. M. Salmon (Cambridge, 1972).

The Humble Address of the Commons in Parliament Assembled, Presented to His Majesty, Monday 28th day of November 1680 (London, 1680).

Hume, David, 'Of Civil Liberty', in *Political Essays*.

Hume, David, 'Idea of a Perfect Commonwealth', in *Political Essays*.

Hume, David, *Political Essays*, ed. Knud Haakonssen (Cambridge, 1994).

Hyde, Edward, Earl of Clarendon, *History of the Rebellion and Civil Wars in England*, ed. W. D. Macray, 6 vols (Oxford, 1888).

Hyde, Edward, Earl of Clarendon, *The Continuation of the Life of Edward Earl of Clarendon*, vol. II (Oxford, 1760).

Hyde, Edward, Earl of Clarendon, *The History of the Rebellion: A New Selection*, ed. Paul Seaward (Oxford, 2009).

James VI and I, *Basilikon Doron. Or His Majesties Instructions to His Dearest Sonne, Henry the Prince*, in *The Workes of the Most High and Mighty Prince, James* (London, 1616).

Jusserand, J. J., *Recueil des Instructions Donnees Aux Ambassadeurs et Ministres de France*, vol. XXV: *Angleterre* (Paris, 1929).

Kenyon, J. P. (ed.), *The Stuart Constitution 1603–1688*, 2nd edn (Cambridge, 1993).

Knox Laughton, J. (ed.), *The Naval Miscellany*, vol. 2 (London, 1912).

Kossmann, E. H., and A. F. Mellink (eds), *Texts concerning the Revolt of the Netherlands* (Cambridge, 1974).

Locke, John, *Two Treatises of Government*, in Peter Laslett (ed.), *Locke's Two Treatises of Government*, 2nd edn (Cambridge 1967).

Machiavelli, Niccolò, *The Discourses*, ed. B. Crick (Harmondsworth, 1985).

MacPherson, James (ed.), *Original Papers; Containing the Secret History of Great Britain*, 2 vols (London, 1775), vol. 1.

Maitland, William, *The History of London From its Foundation to the Present Time*, 2 vols (London, 1756).

[Marvell, Andrew] *An Account of the Growth of Popery and Arbitrary Government* (Amsterdam 1677; repr. 1971).

Marvell, Andrew, *The Character of Holland* (London, 1665).

Marvell, Andrew, *The Character of Holland* (London, 1672).

Marvell, Andrew, *The First Anniversary Of the Government under O.C.*, in *The Poems and Letters of Andrew Marvell*, ed. Margoliouth, vol. 1.

Marvell, Andrew, *The Poems and Letters of Andrew Marvell*, ed. H. M. Margoliouth, 2 vols (Oxford, 1927), vol. 1.

Marvell, Andrew, *The Poems of Andrew Marvell*, ed. Nigel Smith, rev. edn (Harlow, 2007).

Mercurius Politicus, no. 52, 29 May–5 June 1651; no. 104, 27 May–3 June 1652.

Mignet, M., *Negociations Relative à La Succession D'Espagne Sous Louis XIV*, vol. 3 (Paris, 1842).

Miller, Leo, *John Milton's Writings in the Anglo-Dutch Negotiations, 1651–1654* (Pittsburgh, PA, n.d).

Milton, *Joannis Miltoni Angli pro Populo Anglicano Defensio* (London, 1651).

Milton, John, *Second Defence of the English People* (London, 1654), in *Complete Prose Works*, vol. 4.

Milton, John, *The Readie and Easie Way*, 2nd edn (London, 1660).

Milton, John, *The Tenure of Kings and Magistrates*, in *Complete Prose Works*, gen. ed. D. M. Wolfe, 8 vols (New Haven, CT, 1953–82), vol. 3.

Molesworth, Robert, *An Account of Denmark, As It Was in the Year 1692* (London, 1698).

Monson, Sir William, *The Naval Tracts of Sir William Monson*, ed. M. Oppenheim, 5 vols (London, 1902–14), vol. 5.

Montaigne, Michel de, 'Of Cannibals', in Montaigne, *The Complete Works: Essays, Travel Journal, Letters*, trans. Donald Frame (Stanford, CA, 2003).

Montesquieu, Charles de Secondat, baron de, *The Spirit of the Laws*, eds Anne Cohler, Basia Carolyn Miller and Harold Samuel Stone (Cambridge, 1989).

More, Thomas, *Utopia*, eds George Logan and Robert Adams (Cambridge, 1989).

Narborough, John, 'A Journal kept by Captain John Narborough', in *An Account of Several Late Voyages to the South and North*.

Nedham, Marchamont, *The Case of the Commonwealth of England Stated*, ed. P. A. Knachel (Charlottesville, VA, 1969).

[Nedham, Marchamont], *The Case Stated Between England and the United Provinces* (London, 1652).

Neville, Henry, *The Isle of Pines*, in O. Nicastro (ed.), *Henry Neville e L'isola di Pines* (Pisa, 1998).

Norrington, R. (ed.), *My Dearest Minette: The Letters between Charles II and . . . Henrietta, Duchesse d'Orleans* (London, 1996).

Ogilby, John, *America: Being the Latest, and Most Accurate Description of the New World* (London, 1671).

[Oldmixon, John], *The British Empire in America, Containing the History of the Discovery* (London, 1741).

[Overton, Richard], *An Appeale from the Degenerate Representative*, in D. M. Wolfe (ed.), *Leveller Manifestos of the Puritan Revolution* (New York, 1967).

Paine, Thomas, *Rights of Man, Being an Answer to Mr Burke's Attack on the French Revolution – Part I*, in *Political Writings of Thomas Paine*, 2 vols (Middletown, NJ, 1839), vol. 2.

Parker, Henry, Preface to *The True Portraiture of the Kings of England* (17 August 1650).

[Penn, William], *England's Present Interest Discover'd With Honour to the Prince and Safety to the People* (1675).

Penn, William, *The Works of William Penn*, 2 vols (London, 1756), vol. 1.

Pepys, Samuel, *The Diary of Samuel Pepys 1660–1669*, eds R. C. Latham and W. Mathews, 11 vols (London, 1971–83).

Pepys, Samuel, *Samuel Pepys and the Second Dutch War: Pepys' Navy White Book and Brooke House Papers*, ed. Robert Latham (London, 1996).

Pepys, Samuel, *Samuel Pepys' Naval Minutes*, ed. J. R. Tanner (London, 1926).

Petty, Sir William, *Five Essays in Political Arithmetick* (London, 1687).

Petty, Sir William, *Observations upon the Cities of London and Rome* (London, 1687).

Petty, Sir William, *Political Arithmetic* (London, 1690), in G. A. Aitken (ed.), *Later Stuart Tracts* (London, 1903).

Petty, Sir William, *Two Essays in political Arithmetick, Concerning the People, Housing, Hospitals . . . of London and Paris* (London, 1687).

The Popish Plot, taken out of Several Depositions made and sworn before the Parliament (1678), reprinted in W. Scott (ed.), *Tracts . . . of the Late Lord Somers*, 13 vols (London, 1808–15), vol. 8.

Ralegh, Sir Walter, 'A Memorial of Sir *Walter Raleigh* to Q. *Elizabeth* Touching the Port of *Dover*', in Sir Walter Raleigh, *A Discourse of Seaports; Principally of the Port and Haven of Dover* (London, 1700).

R. B., *The Poor Man's Friend or a Narrative of what progress many worthy Citizens of London have made in that Godly work of providing for the POOR* (London, 16 March 1649).

Reasons for Giving Encouragement to the Sea-Faring People of Great Britain (London, 1737).

Rous, John, *Diary of John Rous . . . from 1625 to 1642*, ed. M. A. Everett Green (London, 1856).

Rushworth, John, *Historical Collections . . . beginning the Sixteenth Year of King James, Anno 1618*, 3 vols (London, 1659–82), vol. 1.

Sammes, Aylett, *Britannia Antiqua Illustrata: Or, The Antiquities of Ancient Britain, Derived from the Phoenicians* (London, 1976).

Savile, George, *A Rough Draught of a New Modell at Sea* in *The Works of George Savile, Marquis of Halifax*, ed. Mark Brown, 3 vols (Oxford, 1989), vol. 1.

Scott, Thomas, *The Belgicke Pismire* (London, 1622).

Sidney, Algernon, *Court Maxims*, eds Hans Blom, Eco Haitsma Mulier and Ronald Janse (Cambridge, 1996).

Sidney, Algernon, *Discourses Concerning Government*, ed. T. West (Indianapolis, IN, 1990).

Sidney, Algernon, *Discourses Concerning Government* in *Sydney on Government: the Works of Algernon Sydney*, ed. J Robertson (London, 1772).

Sidney, Robert, 2nd Earl of Leicester, 'The Journal of the Earl of Leicester', in R. W. Blencowe (ed.), *Sydney Papers* (London, 1823).

Skelton, John, 'The Image of Ipocrisie', 1533. 'Belgians invented the Game of Cricket', *Television New Zealand News*, Wednesday 4 March 2009 (online resource).

Smith, Sir Thomas, *A Discourse of the Commonweal of This Realm of England*, ed. Mary Dewar (Charlottesville, VA, 1969).

A Speech Made by a True Protestant English Gentleman To Incourage the City of London to Petition for the Sitting of the Parliament [London, 1680].

Spenser, Edmund, *The Faerie Queene*, ed. A. C. Hamilton, 2nd edn (Harlow, 2001).

Sprat, Thomas, *The History of the Institution, Design, and Progress, of the Royal Society of London. For the Advancement of Experimental Philosophy* (London, 1667).

Streater, John, *Observations Historical, Political and Philosophical . . . Upon Aristotle's first Book of Political Government* (1654), no. 1.

Stubbe, H., *A Further Justification of the Present War Against the United Netherlands* (London, 1673).

Tasman, Abel, 'Journal or Description by me, Abel Jans Tasman, of a Voyage Made from the City of Batavia . . . December Anno 1642 . . . For the Discovery of the Unknown South Land', in John Beaglehole (ed.), *Abel Janszoon Tasman & The Discovery of New Zealand* (Wellington, 1942).

Temple, Sir William, *Observations Upon the United Provinces of the Netherlands* (London, 1673).

Thomas, Gabriel, *An Historical and Geographical Account of Pensilvania* (1698), in Albert Cook Myers (ed.), *Narratives of Early Pennsylvania West New Jersey and Delaware 1630–1707* (New York, 1912).

BIBLIOGRAPHY

Thucydides, *History of the Peloponnesian War*, ed. M. I. Finley, trans. Rex Warner (Harmondsworth, 1975).

Van Gelderen, Martin (ed.), *The Dutch Revolt* (Cambridge, 1993).

Weber, Max, *The Protestant Ethic & the Spirit of Capitalism: New Introduction and Translation by Stephen Kalberg* (Los Angeles, CA, 2002).

William III, *The Declaration of His Highness . . . for restoring the laws and liberties of England, Scotland, and Ireland* (1688), in Robert Beddard (ed.), *A Kingdom Without a King* (Oxford, 1988).

Winstanley, Gerrard, et al., *The True Levellers' Standard Advanced, or, The State of Community opened, and presented to the Sons of Men* (1649), in Christopher Hill (ed.), *Winstanley: The Law of Freedom and Other Writings* (Harmondsworth, 1973).

Winstanley, Gerrard, in G. H. Sabine (ed.), *The Works, with an Appendix of Documents Relating to the Digger Movement* (Ithaca, NY, 1951).

Winthrop, John, *The Journal of John Winthrop, 1630–49: Abridged Edition*, eds Richard S. Dunn and Laetitia Yeandle (Cambridge, MA, 1996).

Wolfe, D. M. (ed.), *Leveller Manifestoes of the Puritan Revolution* (New York, 1967).

Woodhouse, A. S. P. (ed.), *Puritanism and Liberty: Being the Army Debates (1647–1649) from the Clarke Manuscripts with Supplementary Documents* (London, 1951).

SECONDARY SOURCES

Ackroyd, Peter, *London: The Biography* (London, 2000).

Adams, S. L., 'Foreign Policy and the Parliaments of 1621 and 1624', in K. Sharpe (ed.), *Faction and Parliament* (Oxford, 1978).

A'Hearn, Brian, 'The British Industrial Revolution in a European Mirror', in R. Floud, J. Humphries and P. Johnson (eds), *The Cambridge Economic History of Modern Britain, Volume I: 1700–1870* (Cambridge, 2014).

Alford, Stephen, *The Early Elizabethan Polity: William Cecil and the British Succession Crisis 1558–1569* (Cambridge, 1998).

Anderson, Atholl, 'Finding Tonganui: East Polynesian Seafaring and Migration to New Zealand', in Steel (ed.), *New Zealand and the Sea*.

Anderson, Fred, *The War that Made America* (New York, 2005).

Andrews, Kenneth R., *Trade, Plunder and Settlement: Maritime Enterprise and the Genesis of the British Empire, 1480–1630* (Cambridge, 1984).

Andrews, Kenneth R. (ed.), *English Privateering Voyages to the West Indies 1588–1595* (Cambridge, 1959).

Appleby, John C., 'War, Politics and Colonization 1558–1625', in Canny (ed.), *The Origins of Empire*.

Armitage, David, *The Declaration of Independence: A Global History* (Cambridge, MA, 2007).

Armitage, David, *The Ideological Origins of the British Empire* (Cambridge, 2000).

Ashcraft, Richard, *Revolutionary Politics and John Locke's Two Treatises of Government* (Princeton, NJ, 1986).

Ashworth, William J., *The Industrial Revolution: The State, Knowledge and Global Trade* (London, 2017).

Bailyn, Bernard, 'Preface' to David Armitage and Michael Braddick (eds), *The British Atlantic World, 1500–1800*, 2nd edn (Houndmills, 2009).

Bailyn, Bernard, *The Barbarous Years: The Conflict of Civilizations 1600–1675* (New York, 2013).

Bailyn, Bernard, *The Ideological Origins of the American Revolution* (Cambridge, MA, 1971).

Baker, Keith Michael, 'Transformations of Classical Republicanism in Eighteenth-Century France', *Journal of Modern History* 73 (March 2001).

Baker, Kevin, 'They Took Manhattan', *The New York Times* (24 April 2004).

Balleriaux, Catherine, *Reformation Strategies: European Missionaries in the New World, 1550–1700* (London, 2016).

Baron, Hans, *The Crisis of the Early Italian Renaissance*, 2 vols (Princeton, NJ, 1955).

Bayly, Christopher, *Imperial Meridian: The British Empire and the World, 1780–1830* (London, 1989).

Bayly, Christopher, *The Birth of the Modern World 1780–1914: Global Contrasts and Comparisons* (Oxford, 2004).

Beckert, Steve, 'The Wages of War Capitalism', Ch. 3 of *Empire of Cotton* (New York, 2014).

Beckles, Hilary, 'The "Hub of Empire": The Caribbean and Britain in the Seventeenth Century', in N. Canny (ed.), *The Oxford History of the British Empire, Volume 1: The Origins of Empire* (Oxford, 1998).

Beier, A. L. and Roger Finlay (eds), *London 1500–1700: The Making of the Metropolis* (Harlow, 1986).

Belich, James, *Paradise Reforged: A History of the New Zealanders from the 1880s to the Year 2000* (Auckland, 2001).

Belich, James, *Replenishing the Earth: The Settler Revolution and the Rise of the Anglo-World, 1783–1939* (Oxford, 2009).

Belich, James, 'Settler Utopianism? English Ideologies of Emigration, 1815–1880', in J. Morrow and J. Scott (eds), *Liberty, Authority, Formality: Political Ideas and Culture, 1600–1900* (Exeter, 2008).

Bin Wong, R., *China Transformed: Historical Change and the Limits of European Experience* (Ithaca, NY, 1997).

Black, Jeremy, *London: A History* (Lancaster, 2009).

Blanning, T. C. W., *The Culture of Power and the Power of Culture: Old Regime Europe 1660–1789* (Oxford, 2002).

Bliss, Robert, *Revolution and Empire: English Politics and the American Colonies in the Seventeenth Century* (Manchester, 1990).

Bonney, Richard, *The European Dynastic States 1494–1660* (Oxford, 1991).

Botton, Alain de, *The Art of Travel* (London, 2003).

Boxer, Charles, *The Dutch Seaborne Empire, 1600–1800* (London, 1965).

Boys, Jayne E. E., *London's News Press and the Thirty Years War* (Woodbridge, 2011).

Braddick, Michael, *God's Fury, England's Fire: A New History of the English Civil Wars* (London, 2008).

Braddick, Michael, *State Formation in Early Modern England c.1550–1700* (Cambridge, 2000).

Braddick, Michael, *The Nerves of State: Taxes and the Financing of the English State, 1558–1714* (Manchester, 1996).

Brandon, Pepijn, *War, Capital and the Dutch State (1588–1795)* (Leiden, 2015).

Braudel, Fernand, *A History of Civilisations* (New York, 1995).

Braudel, Fernand, *Civilization and Capitalism, Volume III: The Perspective of the World*, trans. Sian Reynolds (London, 1984).

Breen, T. H., *The Character of the Good Ruler: A Study of Puritan Political Ideas in New England, 1630–1730* (New Haven, CT, 1970).

Brenner, Robert, *Merchants and Revolution: Commercial Change, Political Conflict, and London's Overseas Traders, 1550–1653* (Princeton, NJ, 2003).

Brewer, John, *Sinews of Power: War, Money and the English State, 1688–1783* (London, 1989).

Broadberry, Stephen and Gupta, Bishnupriya, 'The Early Modern Great Divergence: Wages, Prices and Economic Development in Europe and Asia, 1500–1800', Centre for Economic Policy Research Discussion Paper no. 4947 (March 2005).

Broadberry, Stephen, Bruce M. S. Campbell, Alexander Klein, Mark Overton and Bas van Leeuwen, *British Economic Growth 1270–1870* (Cambridge, 2015).

Brown, Richard, *Society and Economy in Modern Britain, 1700–1850* (London, 1991).

Brown, Vincent, *The Reaper's Garden: Death and Power in the World of Atlantic Slavery* (Cambridge, MA, 2008).

Bucholz, Robert O. and Joseph P. Ward, *London: A Social and Cultural History, 1550–1750* (Cambridge, 2012).

Burgess, Glenn, 'The Impact on Political Thought: Rhetorics for Troubled Times', in John Morrill (ed.), *The Impact of the English Civil War* (London, 1991).

Burke, Peter, *Venice and Amsterdam*, 2nd edn (Cambridge, 1994).

Burnard, Trevor, 'The British Atlantic', in Jack P. Greene and Philip D. Morgan (eds), *Atlantic History: A Critical Appraisal* (Oxford, 2009).

Burton, Jessie, *The Miniaturist* (London, 2014).

Cameron, W. J., *New Light Upon Aphra Behn* (Auckland, 1961).

Canny, Nicholas, 'Atlantic History and Global History', in Jack P. Greene and Philip D. Morgan (eds), *Atlantic History: A Critical Appraisal* (Oxford, 2009).

Canny, Nicholas, *Making Ireland British, 1580–1650* (Oxford, 2001).

Capp, Bernard, 'Naval Operations', in Kenyon and Ohlmeyer (eds), *The Civil Wars: A Military History of England, Scotland and Ireland 1638–1660* (Oxford, 1998).

Carlos, Ann, Jennifer Key and Jill Dupree, 'Learning and the Creation of Stock-Market Institutions', *Journal of Economic History* 58, 2 (1998).

Carlton, Charles, *Going to the Wars: The Experience of the British Civil Wars 1638–1651* (London 1992).

Cassirer, Ernst, *The Philosophy of the Enlightenment* (Princeton, NJ, 1951).

Cavert, William M., *The Smoke of London: Energy and Environment in the Early Modern City* (Cambridge, 2016).

Chandaman, C. D., *The English Public Revenue 1660–1688* (Oxford, 1975).

Childs, John, *The British Army of William III 1689–1702* (Manchester, 1987).

Clark, Christopher, *The Sleepwalkers: How Europe Went to War in 1914* (London, 2012).

Clarke, Bob, *From Grub Street to Fleet Street: An Illustrated History of English Newspapers to 1899* (Aldershot, 2004).

Clarke, J. S., *The Life of James the Second*, 2 vols (London, 1816), vol. 1.

Clarkson, L. A., *The Pre-Industrial Economy in England 1500–1750* (London, 1971).

Claydon, Tony, *William III and the Godly Revolution* (Cambridge, 1996).

Coffman, D'Maris, *Excise Taxation and the Origins of Public Debt* (London, 2013).

Cogswell, Thomas, *The Blessed Revolution: English Politics and the Coming of War* (Cambridge, 1989).

Colley, Linda, *Britons: Forging the Nation 1707–1787* (New Haven, CT, 1992).

Colley, Linda, 'Can History Help?', *London Review of Books* 40, 6 (22 March 2018).

Collinson, Patrick, *Archbishop Grindal 1519–1583: The Struggle for a Reformed Church* (London, 1979).

Collinson, Patrick, *Richard Bancroft and Elizabethan Anti-Puritanism* (Cambridge, 2013).

Collinson, Patrick, 'The Elizabethan Exclusion Crisis and the Elizabethan Polity', *Proceedings of the British Academy* 84 (1994).

Collinson, Patrick, *The Elizabethan Puritan Movement* (Oxford, 1990).

Collinson, Patrick, *The History of a History Man: Or, the Twentieth Century Viewed from a Safe Distance* (Woodbridge, 2011).

Coulbourn, H. Trevor, *The Lamp of Experience* (Chapel Hill, NC, 1965).

Coward, Barry, *Oliver Cromwell: A Profile* (London, 1991).

Cranston, Maurice, *John Locke* (New York, 1979).

Crosby, Alfred W., *Ecological Imperialism: The Biological Expansion of Europe, 900–1900*, 2nd edn (Cambridge, 2004).

Cunningham, George H., *London* (London, 1927).

Curtin, Philip, *The Atlantic Slave Trade: A Census* (Madison, WI, 1969).

Cust, Richard, *The Forced Loan and English Politics 1626–28* (Oxford, 1987).

Dash, Mike, *Batavia's Graveyard: The True Story of the Mad Heretic Who Led History's Bloodiest Mutiny* (New York, 2002).

Davids, Karel, 'Shifts of Technological Leadership in Early Modern Europe', in Davids and Lucassen (eds), *A Miracle Mirrored*.

Davids, Karel, 'The Scholarly Atlantic: Circuits of Knowledge between Britain, the Dutch Republic and the Americas in the Eighteenth Century', in Gert Oostindie and Jessica V.

Roitman (eds), *Dutch Atlantic Connections, 1680–1800: Linking Empires, Bridging Borders* (Leiden and Boston, MA, 2014).

Davids, Karel and Jan Lucassen (eds), *A Miracle Mirrored: The Dutch Republic in European Perspective* (Cambridge, 1995).

Davies, J. D., *Gentlemen and Tarpaulins: The Officers and Men of the Restoration Navy* (Oxford, 1991).

Davies, Julian, *The Caroline Captivity of the Church* (Oxford, 1992).

Davies, K. G., 'Joint-Stock Investment in the Later Seventeenth Century', *Economic History Review*, 4, 3 (1952).

Davis, J. C., *Utopia and the Ideal Society: A Study of English Utopian Writing, 1516–1700* (Cambridge, 1981).

Davis, Ralph, *The Rise of the English Shipping Industry in the Seventeenth and Eighteenth Centuries* (new edn, St Johns, Newfoundland, 2012).

De Krey, Gary, *London and the Restoration, 1659–83* (Cambridge, 2005).

Dening, Greg, *Islands and Beaches: Discourse on a Silent Land: Marquesas, 1774–1880* (Honolulu, 1980).

Denoon, Donald et al. (eds), *The Cambridge History of the Pacific Islanders* (Cambridge, 1997).

De Vries, Jan, *The Dutch Rural Economy in the Golden Age* (New Haven, CT, 1974).

De Vries, Jan, *The Industrious Revolution: Consumer Behaviour and the Household Economy, 1650 to the Present* (Cambridge, 2008).

De Vries, Jan, 'The Transition to Capitalism in a Land without Feudalism', in Hoppenbrouwers and Van Zanden (eds), *Peasants into Farmers?*

De Vries, Jan and Ad van der Woude, *The First Modern Economy: Success, Failure, and the Perseverance of the Dutch Economy, 1500–1815* (Cambridge, 1997).

Dickerson, Oliver, *The Navigation Acts and the American Revolution* (Philadelphia, PA, 1951).

Dickinson, H. T., *Liberty and Property: Political Ideology in Eighteenth-Century Britain* (New York, 1977).

Dickson, Paul, *The Financial Revolution in England 1688–1756* (London, 1967).

Donoghue, John, *Fire Under the Ashes: An Atlantic History of the English Revolution* (Chicago, IL, 2013).

Downing, Roger and Gijs Rommelse, *A Fearful Gentleman: Sir George Downing in The Hague 1658–1672* (Hilversum, 2011).

Drayton, Richard, *Nature's Government: Science, Imperial Britain and the 'Improvement' of the World* (New Haven, CT, 2000).

Dunthorne, Hugh, *Britain and the Dutch Revolt* (Cambridge, 2013).

DuPlessis, Robert S., *The Material Atlantic: Clothing, Commerce, and Colonization in the Atlantic World, 1650–1800* (Cambridge, 2016).

Dzelzainis, Martin, (ed.), *John Milton: Political Writings* (Cambridge, 1991).

Economist, The (27 May 2017), Leader, 'Deep Trouble'.

Eisler, William, *The Furthest Shore: Images of Terra Australis from the Middle Ages to Captain Cook* (Cambridge, 1995).

Elias, Norbert, *The Genesis of the Naval Profession* (Dublin, 2007).

Elliott, J. H., *Empires of the Atlantic World: Britain and Spain in America, 1492–1830* (New Haven, 2007).

Elliott, John, *The Old World and the New 1492–1650* (Cambridge, 1992).

Elman, Benjamin, 'Classical Reasoning in Late Imperial Chinese Civil Examination Essays', *Renwen Xuebao (Journal of Humanities East/West)* 20 (1999).

Emiralioglu, Pinar, *Geographical Knowledge and Imperial Culture in the Early Modern Ottoman Empire* (London, 2014).

Feingold, Mordechai and Dale Hoak (eds), *The World of William and Mary: Anglo-Dutch Perspectives on the Revolution of 1688–89* (Stanford, CA, 1996).

Fernández-Armesto, Felipe, *Millennium* (London, 1996).

Ferrante, Elena, *The Story of the Lost Child* (Melbourne, 2015).

Fox, Adam, *Oral and Literate Culture in Early Modern Britain, 1500–1700* (New York, 2000).

Fox, Frank, *Great Ships: The Battlefleet of King Charles II* (Greenwich, 1980).

Frijhoff, Willem and Marijke Spies, *Dutch Culture in a European Perspective, Volume I: 1650: Hard-Won Unity* (Houndmills, 2004).

Fussell, G. E., 'Low Countries' Influence on English Farming', *English Historical Review* 74 (1959).

Games, Alison, 'Conclusion: A Dutch Moment in Atlantic Historiography', in Oostindie and Roitman (eds), *Dutch Atlantic Connections*.

Games, Alison, *Migration and the Origins of the English Atlantic World* (Cambridge, MA, 1999).

Games, Alison, *Web of Empire: English Cosmopolitans in an Age of Empire* (London, 2008).

Gardiner, S. R., *History of England from the Accession of James I*, 10 vols (London, 1895), vol. 1.

Gaskill, Malcolm, *Between Two Worlds: How the English Became Americans* (Oxford, 2014).

Gay, Peter, *The Enlightenment: An Interpretation*, 2 vols (London, 1967–70).

Gelderblom, Oscar, *Cities of Commerce: The Institutional Foundations of International Trade in the Low Countries, 1250–1650* (Princeton, NJ, 2013).

Geyl, Pieter, *Orange and Stuart, 1641–1672* (London, 2001).

Gilderdale, Peter, 'Taming the Migratory Divide', in Steel (ed.), *New Zealand and the Sea*.

Gillis, John, *Islands of the Mind: How the Human Imagination Created the Atlantic World* (Houndmills, 2004).

Goldie, Mark, 'The Unacknowledged Republic: Officeholding in Early Modern England', in Tim Harris (ed.), *The Politics of the Excluded c. 1500–1850* (London, 2001).

Goodfriend, Joyce, Benjamin Schmidt and Annette Stott (eds), *Going Dutch: The Dutch Presence in America, 1609–2009* (Leiden, 2008).

Goudriaan, Aza and Fred Van Lieburg (eds), *Revisiting the Synod of Dordt 1618–1619* (Leiden, 2011).

Grafton, Anthony, *New Worlds, Ancient Texts: The Power of Tradition and the Shock of Discovery* (Cambridge, MA, 1992).

Grafton, Anthony, Elizabeth Eisenstein and Adrian Johns, 'AHR Forum: How Revolutionary was the Print Revolution?', *American Historical Review* 107 (2002), pp. 84–128.

Gras, N. S. B., *The Evolution of the English Corn Market from the Twelfth to the Eighteenth Century* (Cambridge, MA, 1915).

Greene, Jack P., 'The Revolution Revisited', *Interpreting Early America: Historiographical Essays* (Charlottesville, VA, 1996).

Greene, Jack P. (ed.), *Exclusionary Empire: English Liberty Overseas, 1600–1900* (Cambridge, 2010).

Greene, Jack P. and Philip D. Morgan (eds), *Atlantic History: A Critical Appraisal* (Oxford, 2009).

Greengrass, Mark, *Christendom Destroyed, 1517–1648* (New York, 2014).

Greengrass, Mark, Michael Leslie and Tim Raylor (eds), *Samuel Hartlib and Universal Reformation: Studies in Intellectual Communication* (Cambridge, 1994).

Greengrass, Mark, 'Three Foreigners: The Philosophers of the Puritan Revolution', in Blair Worden (ed.), *Hugh Trevor-Roper: The Historian* (London, 2016).

Grell, Ole Peter, *Calvinist Exiles in Tudor and Stuart England* (Aldershot, 1996).

Grove, Richard, *Green Imperialism: Colonial Expansion, Tropical Island Edens and the Growth of Environmentalism, 1600–1860* (Cambridge, 1995).

Guldi, Jo and David Armitage, *The History Manifesto* (Cambridge, 2014).

Guy, John, *Thomas More* (London, 2000).

Guy, John, *Tudor England* (London, 1988).

Hadfield, Andrew, *Literature, Politics and National Identity: Reformation to Renaissance* (Cambridge, 1994).

Hainsworth, Roger and Christine Churches, *The Anglo-Dutch Naval Wars, 1652–1674* (Stroud, 1998).

Haley, K. H. D., *The British and the Dutch: Political and Cultural Relations through the Ages* (London, 1988).

Haley, K. H. D., *The First Earl of Shaftesbury* (Oxford, 1968).

Haley, K. H. D., *William of Orange and the English Opposition 1672–4* (1953).

BIBLIOGRAPHY

Hammersley, Rachel, 'Camille Desmoulins's *Le Vieux Cordelier*: A Link between English and French Republicanism', *History of European Ideas* 27 (2001).

Hammersley, Rachel, *The English Republican Tradition and Eighteenth-Century France: Between the Ancients and the Moderns* (Manchester, 2010).

Hancock, David, *Citizens of the World: London Merchants and the Integration of the British Atlantic Community, 1735–1785* (Cambridge, 1995).

Hayton, David 'Constitutional Experiments and Political Expediency, 1689–1725', in Ellis and Barber (eds), *Conquest and Union: Fashioning a British State, 1485–1725* (London, 1995).

Hazard, Paul, *The European Mind 1680–1715* (Harmondsworth, 1964).

Helmers, Helmer, *The Royalist Republic* (Cambridge, 2014).

Hill, Christopher, 'A Bourgeois Revolution?', in J. G. A. Pocock (ed.), *Three British Revolutions: 1641, 1688, 1776* (Princeton, NJ, 1980).

Hindle, Steve, *The State and Social Change in Early Modern England c. 1550–1640* (Basingstoke, 2000).

Holmes, Geoffrey, *The Making of a Great Power: Late Stuart and Early Georgian Britain, 1660–1722* (Harlow, 1993).

Hoppenbrouwers, P. and J. Luiten van Zanden (eds), *Peasants into Farmers? The Transformation of Rural Economy and Society in the Low Countries in Light of the Brenner Debate* (Turnhout, 2001).

Hoppit, Julian, 'Political Power and Economic Life, 1650–1870', in Floud et al. (eds), *Cambridge Economic History*.

Horst, Irvin, *The Radical Brethren: Anabaptism and the English Reformation to 1558* (Nieuwkoop, 1972).

Hughes, Robert, *The Fatal Shore: The Epic of Australia's Founding* (New York, 1986).

Hughes, Robert, *Things I Didn't Know: A Memoir* (New York, 2006).

Hutton, Ronald, 'The Making of the Secret Treaty of Dover', *Historical Journal* 29, 2 (1986).

Hutton, Ronald, 'The Religion of Charles II', in Malcolm Smuts (ed.), *The Stuart Court and Europe* (Cambridge, 1996).

Israel, Jonathan, 'England, the Dutch Republic, and Europe in the Seventeenth Century', *Historical Journal* 40, 4 (1997).

Israel, Jonathan, *Radical Enlightenment: Philosophy and the Making of Modernity 1650–1750* (Oxford, 2001).

Israel, Jonathan, *The Dutch Republic: Its Rise, Greatness and Fall, 1477–1806* (Oxford, 1998).

Israel, Jonathan, 'The Dutch Role in the Glorious Revolution', in Israel (ed.), *The Anglo-Dutch Moment*.

Israel, Jonathan, 'The Emerging Empire: The Continental Perspective, 1650–1713', in Canny (ed.), *The Oxford History of the British Empire*.

Israel, Jonathan, 'Toleration in Seventeenth-Century Dutch and English Thought', in Simon Groenveld and Michael Wintle (eds), *Britain and the Netherlands, Volume XI: Religion, Scholarship and Art* (Zutphen, 1994).

Israel, Jonathan (ed.), *The Anglo-Dutch Moment: Essays on the Glorious Revolution and its World Impact* (Cambridge, 1991).

Israel, Jonathan and Geoffrey Parker, 'Of Providence and Protestant Winds', in Israel (ed.), *The Anglo-Dutch Moment*.

Jardine, Lisa, *Going Dutch: How England Plundered Holland's Glory* (New York, 2008).

Johns, Adrian, *The Nature of the Book: Print and Knowledge in the Making* (Chicago, IL, 1998).

Jones, J. R., *The Anglo-Dutch Wars of the Seventeenth Century* (London, 1996).

Jones, Ryan Tucker, *Empire of Extinction: Russians and the North Pacific's Strange Beasts of the Sea, 1741–1867* (Oxford, 2014).

Karsten, Peter, *Patriot-Heroes in England and America* (Madison, WI, 1978).

Kershen, Anne J., *Strangers, Aliens and Asians: Huguenots, Jews and Bangladeshis in Spitalfields 1660–2000* (Abingdon, 2005).

Kishlansky, Mark, *A Monarchy Transformed: Britain 1603–1714* (London, 1996).

Klooster, Wim, 'Anglo-Dutch Trade in the Seventeenth Century: An Atlantic Partnership?', in Allan MacInnes and Arthur Williamson (eds), *Shaping the Stuart World 1603–1714* (Leiden, 2006).

Klooster, Wim, *The Dutch in the Americas, 1600–1800* (Providence, RI, 1997).

Koot, Christian J., 'Anglo-Dutch Trade in the Chesapeake and the British Caribbean, 1621–1733', in Oostindie and Roitman (eds), *Dutch Atlantic Connections*.

Kristeller, Paul, 'Humanism', in Charles B. Schmitt, Quentin Skinner and Eckhard Kessler (eds), *The Cambridge History of Renaissance Philosophy* (Cambridge, 1988).

Kupperman, Karen Ordahl, *The Jamestown Project* (Cambridge, MA, 2007).

Kuriyama, Shigeisha, ' "Between Mind and Eye": Japanese Anatomy in the Eighteenth Century', in Charles Leslie and Allan Young (eds), *Paths to Asian Medical Knowledge* (Berkeley, CA, 1992), pp. 21–43.

Lake, Peter, 'Calvinism and the English Church, 1570–1635', *Past and Present* 114 (February 1987).

Lake, Peter, 'Post-Reformation Politics, or on Not Looking for the Long-Term Causes of the English Civil War', in Michael Braddick (ed.), *The Oxford Handbook of the English Revolution* (Oxford, 2015).

Langford, Paul, *A Polite and Commercial People: The New Oxford History of England, 1727–1783* (Oxford, 1989).

Laslett, Peter, *The World We Have Lost: The World We Have Lost Further Explored*, 4th edn (London, 1995).

Leach, Douglas, *The Northern Colonial Frontier* (New York, 1966).

Le Carré, John, *A Legacy of Spies* (London, 2017).

Leng, Thomas, *Benjamin Worsley (1618–1677): Trade, Interest and the Spirit in Revolutionary England* (Woodbridge, 2008).

Le Roi Ladurie, Emmanuel, *Peasants of Languedoc* (University of Illinois, 1977).

Lesger, Cle, *The Rise of the Amsterdam Market and Information Exchange: Merchants, Commercial Expansion and Change in the Spatial Economy of the Low Countries c. 1550–1630* (Ashgate, 2006).

Levack, Brian, *The Formation of the British State: England, Scotland and the Union* (Oxford, 1987).

Levillain, Charles-Edouard, 'The Intellectual Origins of the Anglo-Dutch Alliance, 1667–1677', accessed online.

Levine, Joseph M., *Between the Ancients and the Moderns: Baroque Culture in Restoration England* (New Haven, CT, 1999).

Lewis, C. S., *The Lion, the Witch and the Wardrobe* (London, 1998).

Lewis, Martin and Karen Wigen, *The Myth of Continents: A Critique of Metageography* (Los Angeles, CA, 1997).

Lindley, Keith, *Popular Politics and Religion in Civil War London* (London, 1997).

Lucassen, Jan, 'Labour and Early Modern Economic Development', in Davids and Lucassen (eds), *A Miracle Mirrored*.

Luu, Lien Bich, *Immigrants and the Industries of London 1500–1700* (Aldershot, 2005).

McCalman, Iain, *Darwin's Armada* (Melbourne, 2009).

MacDiarmid, Alison, 'Humans and Marine Ecosystems: Insights from Large, Remote, Late-Settled Islands', in Steel (ed.), *New Zealand and the Sea*.

McKendrick, Neil, John Brewer and J. H. Plumb (eds), *Birth of a Consumer Society* (Bloomington, IN, 1982).

Mckeon, Michael, *Politics and Poetry in Restoration England* (Cambridge, MA, 1975).

McNeill, J. R., *Mosquito Empires: Ecology and War in the Greater Caribbean, 1620–1914* (Cambridge, 2010).

McNeill, J. R. and Peter Engelke, *The Great Acceleration: An Environmental History of the Anthropocene since 1945* (Cambridge, MA, 2016).

McNeill, J. R. and William H. McNeill, *The Human Web: A Bird's-Eye View of World History* (New York, 2003).

McRae, Andrew, *God Speed the Plough: The Representation of Agrarian England, 1500–1660* (Cambridge, 1996).

Magris, Claudio, *Danube: A Sentimental Journey from the Source to the Black Sea* (Harvill, 2001; first published 1986).

Mahan, Alfred Thayer, *The Influence of Sea Power Upon History 1660–1783*, 12th edn (Boston, MA, 1918).

Mahlberg, Gaby, 'Republicanism as Anti-Patriarchalism in Henry Neville's *The Isle of Pines* (1668)', in Morrow and Scott (eds), *Liberty, Authority, Formality: Political Ideas and Culture, 1600–1900* (Exeter, 2008).

Maier, Pauline, *From Resistance to Revolution* (New York, 1972).

Mancall, Peter, 'Native Americans and Europeans in English America, 1500–1700', in Canny (ed.), *Origins of the British Empire*.

Manning, Susan and Francis D. Cogliano (eds), *The Atlantic Enlightenment* (Aldershot, 2008).

Margairaz, Dominique, 'City and Country: Home, Possessions, and Diet, Western Europe 1600–1800', in Frank Trentmann (ed.), *The Oxford Handbook of the History of Consumption* (Oxford, 2012).

Marshall, John, *John Locke, Toleration and Early Enlightenment Culture* (Cambridge, 2006).

Marshall, P. J., 'A Nation Defined by Empire, 1755–1776', in Marshall, *A Free though Conquering People* (Oxford, 1998).

May, Henry, *The Enlightenment in America* (Oxford, 1976).

Merritt, Jane T., *The Trouble with Tea: The Politics of Consumption in the Eighteenth-Century Global Economy* (Baltimore, MD, 2017).

Merwick, Donna, *Stuyvesant Bound: An Essay on Loss Across Time* (Philadelphia, PA, 2013).

Merwick, Donna, *The Shame and the Sorrow: Dutch Amerindian Encounters in New Netherland* (Philadelphia, PA, 2006).

Mijers, Esther, *'News from the Republick of Letters': Scottish Students, Charles Mackie and the United Provinces, 1650–1750* (Leiden, 2012).

Miller, John, *James II* (London, 1991).

Miller, Leo, *John Milton and the Oldenburg Safeguard* (New York, 1985).

Miller, Perry, *The New England Mind: From Colony to Province* (Cambridge, MA, 1967).

Milton, Anthony, *Catholic and Reformed* (Cambridge, 1995).

Mithin, Steve, 'Why Did We Start Farming?', review of James C. Scott, *Against the Grain: A Deep History of the Earliest States* (New Haven, CT, 2017), *London Review of Books* 39, 23 (30 November 2017), pp. 11–12.

Mokyr, Joel, 'An Age of Progress', in Floud et al. (eds), *Cambridge Economic History*.

Mokyr, Joel, 'Introduction' to Laura Cruz and Joel Mokyr (eds), *The Birth of Modern Europe: Culture and Economy, 1400–1800: Essays in Honor of Jan de Vries* (Boston, MA, 2010).

Mokyr, Joel, *The Enlightened Economy: An Economic History of Britain 1700–1850* (New Haven, CT, 2009).

Moore, R. I., *The Formation of a Persecuting Society: Authority and Deviance in Western Europe 950–1250*, 2nd edn (Oxford 2007).

Morgan, Hiram, 'The Colonial Venture of Sir Thomas Smith in Ulster, 1571–1575', *Historical Journal* 28 (1985).

Morgan, Kenneth, 'Anglo-Dutch Economic Relations in the Atlantic World, 1688–1783', in Oostindie and Roitman (eds), *Dutch Atlantic Connections*.

Morgan, Kenneth, *Bristol and the Atlantic Trade in the Eighteenth Century* (Cambridge, 1993).

Morgan, Kenneth, 'Mercantilism and the British Empire, 1688–1815', in Donald Winch and Patrick O'Brien (eds), *The Political Economy of the British Historical Experience, 1688–1914* (Oxford, 2002).

Muldrew, Craig, *Food, Energy and the Creation of Industriousness* (Cambridge, 2011).

Murray, John J., 'The Cultural Impact of the Flemish Low Countries on Sixteenth- and Seventeeth-Century England', *American Historical Review* 62, 4 (July 1957).

Murrin, John M., 'The Great Inversion, or Court versus Country: A Comparison of the Revolution Settlements in England (1688–1721) and America (1776–1816)', in J. G. A. Pocock (ed.), *Three British Revolutions: 1641, 1688, 1776* (Princeton, NJ, 1980).

Nelson, Eric, 'Greek Nonsense in More's *Utopia*', *Historical Journal* 44, 4 (2001).

Nelson, Eric, *The Royalist Revolution: Monarchy and the American Founding* (Cambridge, MA, 2014).

Ng, Su Fang, 'Dutch Wars, Global Trade, and the Heroic Poem: Dryden's *Annus mirabilis* (1666) and Amin's *Sya'ir perang Mengkasar* (1670)', *Modern Philology* 109, 3 (February 2012).

O'Brien, Patrick, 'Trade, Economy, State and Empire', in P. J. Marshall (ed.), *The Oxford History of the British Empire, Volume I: The Eighteenth Century* (Oxford, 1998).

O'Brien, Patrick (ed.), *Urban Achievement in Early Modern Europe: Golden Ages in Antwerp, Amsterdam and London* (Cambridge, 2001).

Oestreich, G., *Neostoicism and the Early Modern State* (Cambridge, 1982).

Ollard, Richard, *Pepys: A Biography* (London, 1974).

Ondaatje, Michael, *Warlight* (London, 2018).

Oppenheim, Michael, *A History of the Royal Navy and of Merchant Shipping in Relation to the Navy* (repr., London, 1961).

Ormrod, David, 'Cultural Production and Import Substitution: The Fine and Decorative Arts in London, 1660–1730', in O'Brien (ed.), *Urban Achievement*.

Ormrod, David, *The Rise of Commercial Empires: England and the Netherlands in the Age of Mercantilism, 1650–1770* (Cambridge, 2003).

Pagden, Anthony, *The Enlightenment: And Why it Still Matters* (Oxford, 2015).

Parker, Geoffrey, *The Army of Flanders and the Spanish Road* (Cambridge, 2004).

Parker, Geoffrey, *The Grand Strategy of Philip II* (New Haven, CT, 2000).

Parker, Geoffrey, *The Military Revolution: Military Innovation and the Rise of the West*, 2nd edn (Cambridge, 1996).

Pestana, Carla Gardina, *The English Atlantic in an Age of Revolution 1640–1661* (Cambridge, MA, 2004).

Pincus, Steven, *Protestantism and Patriotism: Ideologies and the Making of English Foreign Policy 1650–1668* (Cambridge, 1996).

Pincus, Steven, *1688: The First Modern Revolution* (New Haven, CT, 2009).

Pocock, J. G. A., *Barbarism and Religion, Volume II: Narratives of Civil Government* (Cambridge, 1999).

Pocock, J. G. A., 'From *The Ancient Constitution* to *Barbarism and Religion*: The Machiavellian Moment, the History of Political Thought and the History of Historiography', *History of European Ideas* 43, 2 (2017).

Pocock, J. G. A., *The Discovery of Islands: Essays in British History* (Cambridge, 2005).

Pocock, J. G. A., *The Machiavellian Moment: Florentine Political Thought and the Atlantic Republican Tradition* (Princeton, NJ, 1975).

Pomeranz, Kenneth, *The Great Divergence: China, Europe and the Making of the Modern World Economy* (Princeton, NJ, 2000).

Porter, Roy, *The Creation of the Modern World: The Untold Story of the British Enlightenment* (New York, 2000).

Pounds, N. J. G., *An Historical Geography of Europe 1500–1840* (Cambridge, 1979).

Prak, Maarten, *The Dutch Republic in the Seventeenth Century* (Cambridge, 2005).

Price, Jacob M., 'The Imperial Economy', in Marshall (ed.), *Oxford History of the British Empire, Volume II*.

Proulx, Annie, *Barkskins* (London, 2016).

Pye, Michael, *The Edge of the World: How the North Sea Made Us Who We Are* (London, 2015).

Ranke, Leopold Von, *History of England Principally in the Seventeenth Century*, 6 vols (Oxford, 1873), vol. 3.

Reeve, John, *Charles I and the Road to Personal Rule* (Cambridge, 1989).

Robbins, Caroline, '*Discourses Concerning Government*: Handbook of Revolution', *William and Mary Quarterly* 3rd series, 4 (1947).

Roseveare, Henry, 'Prejudice and Policy: Sir George Downing as Parliamentary Entrepreneur' in Peter Mathias (ed.), *Enterprise and History: Essays in Honour of Charles Wilson* (Cambridge, 1986).

Roseveare, Henry, *The Treasury, 1660–1870: The Foundations of Control* (London, 1973).

Rothschild, Emma, 'David Hume and the Seagods of the Atlantic', in Manning and Cogliano (eds), *The Atlantic Enlightenment* (Aldershot, 2008).

Rubright, Marjorie, *Doppelganger Dilemmas: Anglo-Dutch Relations in Early Modern Literature and Culture* (Philadelphia, PA, 2014).

Russell, Conrad, *Parliaments and English Politics 1621–1629* (Oxford, 1979).

Said, Edward W., *Orientalism* (New York, 1979).

Salmond, Anne, *The Trial of the Cannibal Dog: The Remarkable Story of Captain Cook's Encounters in the South Seas* (New Haven, CT, 2003).

Satia, Priya, *Empire of Guns: The Violent Making of the Industrial Revolution* (New York, 2018).

Sawday, Jonathan, *Engines of the Imagination: Renaissance Culture and the Rise of the Machine* (New York, 2007).

Schaffer, Simon, 'Visions of Empire: Afterword', in David Miller and Peter Reill (eds), *Visions of Empire: Voyages, Botany, and Representations of Nature* (Cambridge, 1996).

Schama, Simon, *The Embarrassment of Riches: An Interpretation of Dutch Culture in the Golden Age* (New York, 1987).

Schenk, W., *The Concern for Social Justice in the Puritan Revolution* (London, 1948).

Scherpbier, H., *Milton in Holland: A Study in the Literary Relations of England and Holland before 1730* (Amsterdam, 1969).

Schmidt, Benjamin, *Innocence Abroad: The Dutch Imagination in the New World, 1570–1670* (Cambridge, 2001).

Schmidt, Benjamin, 'The Dutch Atlantic', in Greene and Morgan (eds), *Atlantic History: An Appraisal* (Oxford, 2009).

Schoneveld, Cornelis, *Sea-Changes: Studies in Three Centuries of Anglo-Dutch Cultural Transmission* (Amsterdam, 1996).

Scott, Jonathan, *Algernon Sidney and the English Republic, 1623–1677* (Cambridge, 1988).

Scott, Jonathan, *Algernon Sidney and the Restoration Crisis, 1677–1683* (Cambridge, 1991).

Scott, Jonathan, 'Classical Republicanism in England and the Netherlands', in Martin van Gelderen and Quentin Skinner (eds), *Republicanism: A Shared European Heritage, Volume 1: Republicanism and Constitutionalism in Early Modern Europe* (Cambridge, 2002).

Scott, Jonathan, *Commonwealth Principles: Republican Writing of the English Revolution* (Cambridge, 2004).

Scott, Jonathan, 'England's Troubles: Exhuming the Popish Plot', in Paul Seaward et al. (eds), *The Politics of Religion in Restoration England* (Oxford, 1991).

Scott, Jonathan, *England's Troubles: Seventeenth-Century English Political Instability in European Context* (Cambridge, 2000).

Scott, Jonathan, 'Good News from the Forest Floor', review of Michael Braddick (ed.), *The Oxford Handbook of the English Revolution* (Oxford, 2015), published on H-Albion, January 2016.

Scott, Jonathan, 'Good Night Amsterdam: Sir George Downing and Anglo-Dutch Statebuilding', *English Historical Review*, 476 (2003).

Scott, Jonathan, 'James Harrington's Prescription for Healing and Settling', in Smith and Braddick (eds), *The Experience of Revolution in Seventeenth-Century England* (Cambridge, 2012).

Scott, Jonathan, 'The Law of War: Grotius, Sidney, Locke and the Political Theory of Rebellion', *History of Political Thought*, Locke Issue, 1993.

Scott, Jonathan, 'Maritime Orientalism, or, the Political Theory of Water', *History of Political Thought* 1 (2014).

Scott, Jonathan, review of Hindle and Braddick in *English Historical Review* 116, 469 (2001).

Scott, Jonathan, 'Unfinished Family Business: Algernon Sidney's Arguments with Sir William Temple, Henry Hammond, Henry Sidney, Charles II and the Public Executioner', *Seventeenth Century* 31, 4 (2016), pp. 391–410.

Scott, Jonathan, 'Wave after Wave', Epilogue to F. Steel (ed.), *New Zealand and the Sea* (Wellington, 2018).

Scott, Jonathan, 'What the Dutch Taught Us: The Late Emergence of the Modern British State', *Times Literary Supplement* (16 March 2001).

Scott, Jonathan, 'What were Commonwealth Principles?', *Historical Journal* 1 (2004).

Scott, Jonathan, *When the Waves Ruled Britannia: Geography and Political Identities, 1500–1800* (Cambridge, 2011).

Shagan, Ethan, *Popular Politics and the English Reformation* (Cambridge, 2002).

Shelton, Anthony A., 'Cabinets of Transgression: Renaissance Collections and the Incorporation of the New World', in *The Cultures of Collecting*, eds John Elsner and Roger Cardinal (Cambridge, MA, 1994), pp. 177–203.

Shorto, Russell, *The Island at the Centre of the World: The Untold Story of Dutch Manhattan and the Founding of New York* (London, 2004).

Simms, Brendan, *Three Victories and a Defeat: The Rise and Fall of the First British Empire, 1714–1783* (London, 2007).

Simms, Brendan, 'Why we Need a British Europe, not a European Britain', *New Statesman* (9 July 2015).

Sinclair, Ian, 'The Last London', *London Review of Books* 39, 7 (30 March 2017).

Sinclair, Keith, 'Life in the Provinces', in Sinclair (ed.), *Distance Looks Our Way: The Effects of Remoteness on New Zealand* (Auckland, 1961).

Sisman, Adam, *Hugh Trevor-Roper: The Biography* (London, 2010).

Skinner, Quentin, *The Foundations of Modern Political Thought*, 2 vols (Cambridge, 1978).

Slack, Paul, *The Invention of Improvement: Information and Material Progress in Seventeenth-Century England* (Oxford, 2014).

Smail, John, *Merchants, Markets and Manufacture: The English Wool Textile Industry in the Eighteenth Century* (Basingstoke, 1999).

Smith, Bernard William, *European Vision and the South Pacific, 1768–1850: A Study in the History of Art and Ideas*, 2nd edn (Oxford, 1989).

Smyth, William J., *Map-Making, Landscapes and Memory: A Geography of Colonial and Early Modern Ireland c. 1530–1750* (Notre Dame, IN, 2006).

Soderberg, Johan, Ulf Jonssen and Christer Persson, *A Stagnating Metropolis: The Economy and Demography of Stockholm, 1750–1850* (Cambridge, 1991).

Sommerville, Johann, 'James I and the Divine Right of Kings', in Linda Levy Peck (ed.), *The Mental World of the Jacobean Court* (Cambridge, 1991).

Sowerby, Scott, 'Pantomime History', a review of Steve Pincus, *1688: The First Modern Revolution* (2009), in *Parliamentary History* 30, pt 2 (2011).

Sprunger, K. L., *Dutch Puritanism: A History of the English and Scottish Churches of the Netherlands in the Sixteenth and Seventeenth Centuries* (Leiden, 1982).

Spufford, Peter, 'Access to Credit and Capital in the Commercial Centres of Europe', in Karel Davids and Jan Lucassen (eds), *A Miracle Mirrored: The Dutch Republic in European Perspective* (Cambridge, 1995).

Spurr, John, *The Restoration Church of England, 1646–89* (New Haven, CT, 1991).

Statt, Daniel, *Foreigners and Englishmen: The Controversy over Immigration and Population, 1660–1760* (London, 1995).

Stearns, Peter, 'Social History and Spatial Scope', *Journal of Social History* 39, 3 (2006).

Steel, Frances (ed.), *New Zealand and the Sea: Historical Perspectives* (Wellington, 2018).

Steensgaard, Niels, 'The Growth and Composition of the Long-Distance Trade of England and the Dutch Republic before 1750', in James Tracy (ed.), *The Rise of Merchant Empires: Long Distance Trade in the Early Modern World* (Cambridge, 1990).

Steinberg, Philip, *The Social Construction of the Ocean* (Cambridge, 2001).

Tapsell, Grant, *The Personal Rule of Charles II, 1681–85: Politics and Religion in an Age of Absolutism* (London, 2007).

Tartt, Donna, *The Goldfinch* (London, 2013).

't Hart, Marjolein C., " 'The Devil or the Dutch": Holland's Impact on the Financial Revolution in England, 1643–1694', *Parliaments, Estates and Representation* 11, 1 (June 1991).

't Hart, Marjolein C., 'The Glorious City: Monumentalism and Public Space in Seventeenth-Century Amsterdam', in O'Brien (ed.), *Urban Achievement.*

BIBLIOGRAPHY

't Hart, Marjolein C., *The Making of a Bourgeois State: War, Politics and Finance during the Dutch Revolt* (Manchester, 1993).

Taylor, E. G. R., *The Haven-Finding Art: A History of Navigation from Odysseus to Captain Cook* (New York, 1957).

Thick, Malcolm, 'Market Gardening in England and Wales', in Thirsk (ed.), *Agrarian History.*

Thirsk, Joan (ed.), *The Agrarian History of England and Wales, Volume V, Part II: 1640–1750 Agrarian Change* (Cambridge, 1985).

Thomas, Keith, 'The Meaning of Literacy in Early Modern England', in Gerd Baumann (ed.), *The Written Word: Literacy in Transition* (Oxford, 1986), pp. 97–131.

Tilly, Charles (ed.), *The Formation of Nation States in Western Europe* (Princeton, NJ, 1975).

Timms, Peter, *In Search of Hobart* (Sydney, 2009).

Tombs, Robert, *The English and Their History* (London, 2015).

Tracy, James, *A Financial Revolution in the Habsburg Netherlands: Renten and Renteniers in the County of Holland, 1515–1565* (Berkeley, CA, 1985).

Trevor-Roper, H. R., 'Introduction', Edward Gibbon, *Decline and Fall of the Roman Empire*, 3 vols (New York, 1993), vol. 1.

Trevor-Roper, H. R., 'Three Foreigners: The Philosophers of the Puritan Revolution', in Trevor-Roper, *Religion, the Reformation and Social Change* (London, 1967).

Tuck, Richard, *Philosophy and Government 1572–1651* (Cambridge, 1993).

Tully, James, *A Discourse on Property* (London, 1980).

Tyacke, Nicholas, *Anti-Calvinists: The Rise of English Arminianism, 1590–1640* (Oxford, 1987).

Tyacke, Nicholas (ed.), *England's Long Reformation, 1500–1800* (London, 1998).

Van Bavel, Bas, *The Invisible Hand? How Market Economies have Emerged and Declined since AD 500* (Oxford, 2016).

Van Deursen, A. T., *Plain Lives in a Golden Age: Popular Culture, Religion and Society in Seventeenth-Century Holland* (Cambridge, 1991).

Van Gelderen, Martin and Quentin Skinner (eds), *Republicanism: A Shared European Heritage*, 2 vols (Cambridge, 2002).

Van Tielhof, Milja, 'Grain Provision in Holland ca. 1490–1570', in Hoppenbrouwers and Van Zanden (eds), *Peasants into Farmers?*

Van Zanden, Jan Luiten, *The Long Road to the Industrial Revolution: The European Economy in a Global Perspective, 1000–1800* (Leiden, 2009).

Vernon, James, *Distant Strangers: How Britain Became Modern* (Berkeley, CA, 2014).

Webb, Stephen Saunders, *The Governors-General: The English Army and the Definition of the Empire 1569–1681* (Chapel Hill, NC, 1979).

Webster, Charles, *The Great Instauration: Science, Medicine and Reform, 1626–1660* (London, 1975).

White, Richard, 'What is Spatial History?', *Stanford University Spatial History Lab* 1 (February 2010).

Williams, Glyndwr, *The Great South Sea: English Voyages and Encounters, 1570–1750* (New Haven, CT, 1997).

Wilson, Charles, *Anglo-Dutch Commerce and Finance in the Eighteenth Century* (Cambridge, 1966).

Wilson, Charles, *England's Apprenticeship 1603–1763*, 2nd edn (London, 1986).

Wilson, Charles, *Profit and Power: A Study of England and the Dutch Wars* (London, 1957).

Wilson, Charles and R. Hooykaas, *The Anglo-Dutch Contribution to the Civilization of Early Modern Society: An Anglo-Netherlands Symposium* (London, 1976).

Winship, Michael, *Godly Republicanism: Puritans, Pilgrims, and a City on a Hill* (Cambridge, MA, 2012).

Withington, Phil, *The Politics of Commonwealth: Citizens and Freemen in Early Modern England* (Cambridge, 2005).

Wood, Gordon, *The Creation of the American Republic 1776–1787* (Williamsburg, VA, 1969).

Wootton, David, *Invention of Science: A New History of the Scientific Revolution* (New York, 2015).

Worden, Blair, 'Classical Republicanism and the Puritan Revolution' in V. Pearl, H. Lloyd-Jones and B. Worden (eds), *History and Imagination* (Oxford, 1981).

Worden, Blair, 'Republicanism, Regicide and Republic: The English Experience', in Martin van Gelderen and Quentin Skinner (eds), *Republicanism: A Shared European Heritage, Volume 1: Republicanism and Constitutionalism in Early Modern Europe* (Cambridge, 2002).

Worden, Blair, *The Sound of Virtue: Philip Sidney's* Arcadia *and Elizabethan Politics* (New Haven, CT, 1996).

Wrightson, Keith, *Earthly Necessities: Economic Lives in Early Modern Britain* (New Haven, CT, 2000).

Wrigley, E. A., *Energy and the English Industrial Revolution* (Cambridge, 2010).

Wrigley, E. A., *Poverty, Progress and Population* (Cambridge, 2004).

Wrigley, E. A., R. S. Davies, J. E. Oeppen and R. S. Schofield, *English Population History from Family Reconstitution 1580–1837* (Cambridge, 1997).

Zahedieh, Nuala, 'Overseas Trade and Empire', in Floud et al. (eds), *Cambridge Economic History*.

Zahedieh, Nuala, *The Capital and the Colonies: London and the Atlantic Economy, 1660–1700* (Cambridge, 2010).

UNPUBLISHED SECONDARY MATERIAL

Belich, 'The Black Death and European Expansion', lecture given at the University of Auckland, 21 March 2018.

Birchall, Alistair, ' "A Bank settled on a good Fund": The Million Bank and Joint-Stock Securities during the English Financial Revolution', unpublished MA thesis, University of Auckland, 2017.

Frearson, Michael, 'An Aspect of the Production of the Newsbooks of the 1620s', Cambridge seminar paper, 1993.

McNeill, John, 'The American Demographic Catastrophe', lecture given at the University of Auckland, 3 March 2016.

Peltonen, Markku, 'The Republican Moment of the English Revolution', unpublished paper kindly supplied by the author, February 2017.

INDEX

INDEX

population 47
printing and architecture 76
stagnation 301
supranational importance of 39
Town Hall 137
unique global roles 225
wages 255
Anabaptists 88, 109
Anatomy Lesson of Dr Tulp, The (Rembrandt van Rijn) 85
Andes 171
Anglicans *see* Church of England
Anglo-Dutch wars 96, 147
  first 128, 133, 150–4, 290, 303
  second 130, 175, 179–81, 199, 256, 290, 303
  third 180, 195–6, 218, 303
Anglo-Scots Agreement Committee of Both Kingdoms 130
Angola 162–3
Anjou, Duke of 248
Antarctic 231, 232
Anthropocene era 31
Anti-Gallican Association 208
Antigua 168
Antwerp
  Amsterdam and 54, 74
  development of 6, 47
  fall of 37
  finishing of broadcloth 63
  location and description 49
  London's links to 7
  new English industry from 75, 76
  Nieuwe Beurs 291
  overland exports 62
  resources and markets 284
  Spanish sack of 37, 57, 58
  supranational importance of 39
  urbanization and 34
  value of exported goods 52
Appalachians 271
architecture 76
Aristotle 236, 238, 255
Arlington, Lord 191
Armada (Dutch) 199
Armada (Spanish) 48, 95, 98, 199
armies 105
Arminianism 101, 108, 109
Armitage, David 247
Arundel, Lord 191
Ashley Cooper, Anthony 170
Asia 159
Assembly of Commoners 201
Athens

cultural relativism and 84
cultural superiority 265
Leiden sees itself as 137
model for English Republic 142
a product of liberty 264
Sicilian grain supply 284
Thucydides on 6
victory of Salamis 72
Atlantic
  diasporas and the birth of capitalism 4, 48
  England and 42
  Europe and 47
  Hakluyt's accounts 69, 70
  largest naval operation 198
  London and 39
  middle passage 162
  Pacific and 225
  slave trade 162, 269
  trading systems 276
'Atlantic Archipelago' 9–10
Augustus, Emperor 219
Australia 160, 167, 231–2, 264
Austria 91
Aylmer, John 63
Aztecs 46

Bacon, Sir Francis
  Dutch philosophy and 255
  experimental science 86
  Hartlib circle and 122
  Heylyn quotes 79–80
  on navies 132
Baker, Kenneth 308
Balkans 46
Baltic
  agricultural revolution and 12
  Breton salt and wine 286
  decline of 301
  demand for grain grows 54
  domination of Hanse 55
  English merchants in 64
  *fluitschip*s 54
  importance of grain trade 6, 36, 37, 39, 41, 52, 284
  regional changes and 4
  shipping 76
Bancroft, Archbishop Richard 89, 93
Bank of Amsterdam 205, 247
Bank of England 204–6, 224, 247, 254
Bank of Scotland 254
Bank of the United States 247
Banks, Joseph 228, 230, 231, 232
Banqueting House (Whitehall) 115
Barbados 111, 146, 163, 168

370